*Praise for* Death and the Virgin

'kidmore writes brilliantly and his research is impeccable'
*Sunday Times*

'Solves one of the greatest Tudor mysteries . . . and is set to become
classic'  Andrew Roberts, *Daily Telegraph*

'A riveting exemplar of the degree to which it is, and is not, possible
to solve a historical mystery'  *Guardian*

'The death of Amy Robsart in September 1560 remains one of the
fascinating unsolved mysteries of Tudor history . . . Chris Skidmore
deftly takes us through the whole scene and in doing so considers
a completely new possibility which changed my mind'
Antonia Fraser, *Mail on Sunday*

'Chris Skidmore has found new documents to make a breakthrough
n the mystery of who murdered the wife of Robert Dudley, the
scandalously intimate friend of Elizabeth I. His close reading of the
material and his dramatic deductions are compulsory reading for
vone interested in this fascination and tragic story of the little
r own wife of the man who hoped to marry the Queen of England'
Philippa Gregory

'The brilliance of *Death and the Virgin* is that Skidmore has done
is homework . . . The result is as gripping as an Agatha Christie
thriller'  *Daily Express*

'Skidmore paints wonderful, intimate scenes of Elizabeth and
Dudley . . . there are also some wonderful period facts'
*Literary Review*

'The books of Skidmore . . . should be required reading for everyone
who gets their history from television'  *History Today*

Chris Skidmore was born in Bristol in 1981. His first book, *Edward VI: The Lost King of England*, was published in 2007. He previously taught at Bristol University and is a Fellow of the Royal Historical Society. In 2010 he was elected as Member of Parliament for Kingswood.

*By Chris Skidmore*

Edward VI: The Lost King of England
Death and the Virgin: Elizabeth, Dudley and the
Mysterious Fate of Amy Robsart

# DEATH AND THE VIRGIN

*Elizabeth, Dudley and the
Mysterious Fate of Amy Robsart*

## CHRIS SKIDMORE

PHOENIX

A PHOENIX PAPERBACK

First published in Great Britain in 2010
by Weidenfeld & Nicolson
This paperback edition published in 2011
by Phoenix,
an imprint of Orion Books Ltd,
Orion House, 5 Upper St Martin's Lane,
London WC2H 9EA

An Hachette UK company

1 3 5 7 9 10 8 6 4 2

ISBN: 978-0-7538-2701-7

Typeset by Input Data Services Ltd,
Bridgwater, Somerset

Printed and bound in the UK by CPI Mackays, Chatham ME5 8TD

To my mother, Elaine

# ⤞ Contents ⤜

*List of Illustrations*   ix
*Acknowledgements*   xi
*A Note on Money*   xiii

Prologue   1
Introduction   5


## PART ONE: *Beginnings*

1. Rites of passage   11
2. A meeting   15
3. Carnal marriages   18
4. My father's heart   22
5. Shameful slanders   26
6. God will revenge   33

7. These beasts do well behold   37
8. Common conditions   41
9. Anatomies of hearts   47
10. Not being altogether in quiet   50
11. Rehabilitation   55
12. Men dismayed   62


## PART TWO: *God sent us our Elizabeth*

13. A passing   67
14. Marvellous in our eyes   70
15. Master of the Horse   76
16. My Ladye   82
17. Young folks, heretics and traitors   85

18. The court   89
19. Becoming queen   95
20. Coronation   99
21. God send our mistress a husband   105


## PART THREE: *A great resort of wooers*

22. Many great difficulties   115
23. God hath increased you with honour   125
24. A visit   133
25. She is well worth the trouble   136
26. A journey   145
27. Te stante virebo   149
28. Veracious news   162

29. Cumnor Place   169
30. No reputation in the world   174
31. Let the malicious report what they list   180
32. A deep dungeon of sorrow   186
33. With as much speed as you can   192
34. I dare not write that I might speak   196

## PART FOUR: *Either chance or villainy*

35. My wife is dead  203
36. Well-chosen men  208
37. It doth plainly appear  213
38. So pitifully slain?  216
39. An evil toy in her mind  219
40. The coroner's report  230


## PART FIVE: *He is infamed by the death of his wife*

41. Forget me not  237
42. My ears glow to hear  243
43. All the resort is to him  245
44. Neither touching his honesty nor her honour  250
45. If her Majesty so foully forget herself  255
46. A proposal  263
47. Many things handled of marriage  268
48. Death possessed every part of me  275
49. The inward, suspicious mind  280
50. Sparks of dissention  287


## PART SIX: *We all be flesh and blood*

51. The murder of his sister  299
52. Rather yet never had wife than lose them  307
53. I may fall many ways  313
54. No man can tell  319
55. Your old patient  328
56. Leicester's Commonwealth  335
57. The scar remains  342
58. The journal  352
59. The queen's man  367


Finis  373

*Appendices*  377
*List of Abbreviations*  390
*Notes*  392
*Bibliography*  408
*Index*  420

# ⤞ Illustrations ⤝

## PLATE SECTION

Queen Elizabeth I, by Federico Zuccaro, *c.* 1557–1609, black and red chalk (The Trustees of the British Museum)

Robert Dudley, Earl of Leicester, by Federico Zuccaro, *c.* 1557–1609, black and red chalk (The Trustees of the British Museum)

Elizabeth I's Procession Arriving at Nonsuch Palace, by Joris Hoefnagel, Flemish engraving (Private Collection/Bridgeman Art Library)

William Cecil, 1st Baron Burghley, by or after Arnold van Brounckhorst, oil on panel, *c.* 1560s (National Portrait Gallery, London)

Elizabeth I, unknown artist, oil on panel, *c.* 1559 (National Portrait Gallery, London)

The Queen in her Litter, from 'The Progresses of Queen Elizabeth 1', ink on paper (Private Collection/Bridgeman Art Library)

Robert Dudley, Earl of Leicester, *c.* 1560s, oil on panel (Yale Center for British Art, Paul Mellon Collection/Bridgeman Art Library)

Amy Dudley, by Lavinia Teerlinc, miniature (Yale Center for British Art, Paul Mellon Collection/Bridgeman Art Library)

Cumnor Place (courtesy of Edward Impey)

Staircase at Cumnor Place (The Trustees of the British Museum)

Eighteenth-century drawing of Cumnor Place, by Samuel Lysons, *Magna Britannia*, 1806

Photograph of the coroner's report of into Amy Dudley's death (National Archives, Kew)

Queen Elizabeth receives Dutch ambassadors, gouache on card, Neue Galerie, Kassel, Germany (Museumslandschaft Hessen Kassel/Bridgeman Art Library)

Lettice Knollys, Countess of Leicester, *c.* 1585, attributed to George Gower (Longleat House, Wiltshire/Bridgeman Art Library)

Portrait of Queen Elizabeth I, by Steven van der Meulen (Sotheby's Picture Library)

La Volta, Penshurst Place (courtesy of Viscount de l'Isle)

# TEXT ILLUSTRATIONS

p. 51    Amy's letter, British Library, Harleian MS 4712, fo. 275

p. 193   Amy's final letter, Longleat House, Wiltshire, Dudley Papers, vol. IV, fo. 7r

p. 236   Dudley's letter to Cecil, Hatfield House, Cecil Papers, vol. 153, fo. 47r

p. 242   Cecil's memorandum, Hatfield House, Cecil Papers, vol. 155, fo. 28r

p. 388   Page from The Journal, British Library, Additional MS 48023, fo. 353v

# Acknowledgements

This book has taken far longer to write than I had expected, during which time I have accumulated a large number of debts. Foremost, I am extremely grateful to Alan Samson at Weidenfeld & Nicolson for his patience and commitment, and to the excellent editing skills of Bea Hemming, who has tirelessly guided this book through many versions. Penny Gardiner has also been a great critical friend, whose advice and ideas have been greatly appreciated.

I am also indebted to the remarkable generosity of several scholars, without whom the book would likely have remained unwritten. It was my former supervisor Dr Steven Gunn who first directed me to Amy Robsart's coroner's report, while Dr Paul Cavill gave up his time to transcribe and translate the document. Dr Edward Impey has been extremely generous in providing me with copies of his thesis and drawings of Cumnor Place, while Gary Hill has been an enormous inspiration from the start of my research, showing me around the ruins of Cumnor Place and directing me to the archaeological investigations into the site of Amy's tomb. I have greatly appreciated our conversations, and I look forward to the publication of his painstaking research on Amy, which will no doubt supplant my own. I am also extremely grateful for the expert medical advice given to me by Dr Ian Leslie and Professor Seth Love in discussing the nature of Amy's injuries.

During my research, several archivists and libraries have made my work far easier than I imagined it would be. I would like to thank the staff of the National Archives and the British Library; Alison Day, the archivist at Berkshire Record Office, for providing me with copies of relevant wills; Jose Maria Burrieza Mateos at the Archivo General at Simancas for supplying me with copies from the archives there; Kate Harris at Longleat for sending photos of relevant documents, including Amy's last letter; Robin Harcourt-Williams and Vicki Perry at Hatfield House for also providing copies of William Cecil's papers; the staff at the Pepys Library, Magdalene College, Cambridge, for allowing me to transcribe Robert Dudley's letters there. I would also like to thank the kind generosity of the Marquess of Bath for permission to use Robert Dudley's private papers at Longleat; the Marquess of Salisbury for access and permission to quote from William Cecil's private papers at Hatfield House; Magdalene College, Cambridge, for permitting me to reprint Robert Dudley's letters; the trustees of the British Library for permission to reprint several manuscript pages in their collection; and the National Archives for allowing me to publish Amy's coroner's report.

Finally, there are friends whom I would like to thank: Robin Ganguly and Fred Bosanquet put up with me while I was writing this book, as did Charlotte Leslie who also provided me with ideas and advice – more than she probably realises. Michael Gove was extremely generous in allowing me a sabbatical from work to write the book. I would like to thank them all for their patience and understanding. My agent, Jonathan Pegg, has also been – as ever – a great source of encouragement and advice. Most of all, once again, I would like to thank my parents for their support, without which I would have struggled to complete this book. I could not have asked for more, especially from my mother, Elaine, and it is to her that I dedicate this book.

Chris Skidmore
Bitton, November 2009

# ⤜ A Note on Money ⤛

In 1560, £1 (li) had the purchasing power of £209 in today's money. There were twelve shillings (s) in every £1, making them worth £17.40 today. A penny (d) was worth a twelfth of a shilling and its current value is around £1.45. This measure is based on the retail price index, designed to calculate the cost of everyday items such as food, drink and other basic necessities.

When attempting to give a relative value to salaries and large monetary transactions, an income of £50 in 1560 would be the equivalent of just over £140,000 in today's money.

These estimates are based on the calculations of Professors Lawrence H. Officer and Samuel H. Williamson, from their website *measuringworth.com.*

# → Prologue ←

As the summer of 1560 drew to a close, the queen's progress returned to Windsor Castle. Throughout the usual sultry months of July and August, when the oppressive heat and stench made life in London unbearable, Elizabeth and her court made their annual journey through the Home Counties, stopping off on their winding route at royal hunting lodges and stately homes. Here the nobility reluctantly bore the cost of hosting the queen and a train which included not merely the queen's gentle-women but hundreds of attendants and servants, gentlemen and nobles, cooks and royal halberdiers, with nearly two and a half thousand pack-horses carrying luggage, beds and provisions, packed away in four hundred carts trundling along their daily journey of around ten miles. The sight had onlookers at the roadsides staring in amazement.

This year, however, it had rained most of the summer; contemporaries agreed that the weather had been 'foul' – 'it is warmer in the kitchen than in the hall', one nobleman joked.[1] The ground had become so sodden that another considered how people from 'the highest to the lowest' would find only 'soft ways' ahead, while he dreaded 'howsoever they find their lodging and fare'.[2] As the royal travelling circus snaked south, it passed through Richmond, Sutton, Farnham, then down to Portsmouth, where the Royal Fleet had assembled in anticipation of the queen's arrival. It then continued to Southampton, Winchester and Basing, completing its journey in Windsor at the beginning of September. The progress was a time of endless banquets and hunting. Everyone enjoyed the recreation – everyone, that is, except one.

Sir William Cecil, the queen's chief adviser and Secretary of State, had been in despair for months. It was his duty to conduct the business of state, yet for weeks Elizabeth had been neglecting her official role, postponing decisions and preferring instead to spend her days hunting stags in her royal parks and her nights dancing the galliard at banquets and revels. Cecil began to speak openly to his friends of retiring per-manently from public life.

It was almost two years since Elizabeth had become queen. She was a few days short of her twenty-seventh birthday, yet, despite having received marriage offers from princes across Europe, she had stubbornly remained single, maintaining to all who would listen that she had no wish to take a husband. Her insistence had not prevented rumours from claiming otherwise. For months, feverish speculation had burned surrounding her relationship with her Master of the Horse, a gentleman named Robert Dudley, who had been placed in charge of her stable. His role, however, encompassed far more than that. Dudley's lodgings had been moved next to the queen's, and there was talk amongst the ambassadors that they were never out of each other's company.

Aged 28, Dudley was nearly six feet tall and had a strong, athletic build; his striking dark features earned him the nickname 'the gypsy' and made him an instant attraction at court. The Venetian ambassador described him as 'a very handsome young man (*giovane bellissimo*)', while Elizabeth's first biographer William Camden opined that he was 'a man of flourishing age, and comely feature of body and lims'.[3] Elizabeth, who 'always took personage in the way of affection', was privately smitten. Later, she would admit that 'she was no angel, and did not deny she had some affection for Lord Robert for the many good qualities he possessed'.[4]

The pair's growing closeness scandalised the court, for Robert Dudley was a married man. But there was little sign of his wife at court. With no permanent residence to call her own, his wife, Amy, stayed with family friends while her husband remained constantly at the queen's side; it was hardly a satisfactory arrangement, but not an unusual one for the age. Nevertheless, the fact that a married man should be seen to court the queen, winning Elizabeth's undivided attention – and the lavish grants that came with it – and at the same time distracting her from the important business of finding her own husband and producing a treasured heir, was enough to earn Dudley the hatred of the nobility. One ambassador even remarked that 'it is a marvel that he has not been slain long ere this, for whenever they behold him they wish he might be hanged'. There had been talk of an assassination attempt against him, and the greatest peer of the realm, the Duke of Norfolk, had personally reproached Dudley over his dalliances with Elizabeth, warning him that he would not die in his bed if he continued in his ways.

Dudley paid little attention. That summer, after entertaining the queen to a banquet at his lodgings in Kew at the beginning of her progress, he was by her side whenever she returned from the hunt. On Elizabeth's birthday, 7 September, he boasted to the Earl of Sussex how she had become 'a great huntress and doth follow it daily from morning till night'. The horses she rode, 'she spareth not to tire as fast as they can go'.

Cecil had grown weary of their games. Little more than a week earlier he wrote in despair to his friend and confidant Sir Nicholas Throckmorton, the English ambassador in Paris: 'I dare not write that I might speak. God send her Majesty understanding what shall be her surety. And so full of melancholy, I wish you were free from it ... God send me hence with words to pray and sue for her Majesty with all the power of mind and body ... I beseech you either return my letter or keep it safe for me. For letters may be misinterpreted and I do not mean to so deserve.'

In the corridors of Windsor Castle in early September Cecil managed to snatch a brief conversation with the Spanish ambassador, Don Alvaro de la Quadra, Bishop of Aquila, who had recently rejoined the court (as, unable to meet the exorbitant costs of the journey, he had been absent from its travels for over a month). De la Quadra sensed quickly that something was not right. Unable to conduct his duties without Elizabeth's attention, Cecil told the Spanish ambassador of how he had begun to consider retirement, telling him, 'It was a bad sailor who on seeing a great storm coming did not seek a harbour while he could'. There was little else that could be done. Cecil felt Dudley's influence to be so widespread that he 'had made himself lord of all affairs and of the queen's person, to the extreme injury of all the kingdom', and he was sure that Dudley intended to marry the queen. As for himself he rarely saw her, for Dudley had 'led her to spend all day hunting with much danger to her life and health'. Once more he repeated his desire to retire to his private house, though, he joked, the Tower seemed a more likely option.

'For the love of God warn the queen of these dangers and persuade her not to ruin her affairs as she has done and to watch out for herself and her kingdom,' he begged the ambassador, resolving that Dudley 'would be better in paradise than here'. He then ended their conversation with a revelation that amazed de la Quadra.

'They intended,' Cecil whispered, 'to kill the wife of Robert and now published that she was ill, although she was not but on the contrary was very well and protected herself carefully from being poisoned. God would never permit that so great an evil nor could a good result come of an evil business.'

'I was certain that he spoke truly and was not deceiving me,' the startled de la Quadra wrote to his master, the Spanish king, Philip II. He might have recalled the words that he himself had written ten months before, in November 1559, stating how he had received reports from 'a certain person who is accustomed to give me veracious news', that Dudley 'has sent to poison his wife'. At that time he believed that Elizabeth was merely putting off her suitors and delaying the question of her marriage, 'until this wicked deed of killing his wife is consummated'. For the moment, the ambassador chose not to draw any conclusions.

On Sunday 8 September, 1560, the sun rose across Cumnor Place a few minutes before 5 o'clock in the morning. It was here that Amy, Dudley's wife, was staying with her household. The medieval manor house in Berkshire was owned by George Owen, one of the royal physicians who had treated Henry VIII, but had been rented by Sir Anthony Forster, a friend and a member of Dudley's household, whose hospitality Amy was enjoying. She had not seen her husband for nearly a year.

Amy awoke early that morning. Her servants were the first to notice that she was in a strange mood. Agitated, she was determined to be alone. Nearby, at the town of Abingdon four miles away, the Fair of Our Lady was taking place, and Amy instructed her entire household to attend. One of her gentlewomen, an elderly widow named Mrs Odingsells, refused. She confronted Amy and told her that 'it was no day for gentlewomen to go in' – Sundays were usually reserved for the attendance of common people at the fair. It would be best if they attended the following day: 'the morrow was much better,' she remarked, 'and then she would go.'

Hearing this, Amy grew 'very angry', replying that she 'might choose and go at her pleasure'. She insisted that the rest of her household should leave for the day. When asked who would keep her company, Amy answered that Mrs Owen, the sister of George Owen, would join her for dinner.

According to a later report, once the household had departed, two gentlewomen – perhaps Mrs Odingsells and Mrs Owen – were playing cards when they heard a crash.

'Down for a shilling,' one of them joked.

'Up for another,' the other replied, and they continued their game.

# Introduction

This is the story of a death. It was a death that scandalised Tudor England. In September 1560, Amy Robsart, the wife of Robert Dudley, Queen Elizabeth's favourite courtier, was found dead. Her body was discovered at the foot of a staircase, reported to be just eight steps high. Her neck appeared to be broken, yet, according to reports, her headdress remained intact upon her head and there was no other mark upon her body.

How had Amy died? Was her death an accident, a simple fall down a staircase? At the time, few believed this was the case. The scandal surrounding Amy's death was instantaneous; people were quick to draw their own conclusions. 'Here in these parts seemeth ... to be a grievous and dangerous suspicion and muttering on the death of her', one preacher observed days after Amy's death.

From the start, Robert Dudley was an obvious suspect. The motive was clear: his wife's death now gave him the freedom and opportunity to marry Elizabeth, with whom he had been seen cavorting at court. For the foreign ambassadors stationed at court, reporting every juicy scrap of gossip to their royal masters on the Continent, proving Dudley's guilt seemed to be a mere formality. Just six months before Amy's death, he had boasted that his situation would soon be a very different one: 'if he live another year, he will be in a very different position from now,' the Spanish ambassador had heard him say: 'They say that he thinks of divorcing his wife.'

Amy, on the other hand, was nowhere to be seen. Rumours had circulated long before, in November 1559, to the effect that Dudley was attempting to have his wife poisoned. 'Although he is married to a beautiful wife he is not living with her,' the Imperial ambassador Bruener commented at the time; 'I have been told by many persons, [he] is trying to do away with her by poison.' The Spanish ambassador de la Quadra believed that both Dudley and Elizabeth had arranged a pact whereby they would marry after Amy had died. 'Lord Robert has sent to poison his wife', he had been told; 'Certainly all the Queen has done with us ... and will do with the rest in the matter of her marriage is only keeping Lord Robert's enemies and the country engaged with words until this wicked deed of killing his wife is consummated.'

Across the courts of Europe, rumours began to spread that Dudley, known plainly as 'the queen's horse keeper', had murdered his wife in order to marry Elizabeth. English ambassadors reporting back from abroad did their best to impress upon the queen the precarious nature of her situation. If she was foolish enough to marry Dudley now, they argued, it would prove her undoing – she could wake up to find herself plain mistress Elizabeth.

For the English ambassador in Paris, Sir Nicholas Throckmorton, it was too much to bear. 'I wish I were either dead, or that I were hence,' he wrote to a friend, 'that I might not hear the dishonorable and naughty reports that are here made of ye Queen's Majesty my gracious sovereign lady' that made 'every hair of my head' stand on end 'and my ears glow to hear'. 'I am almost at my wits end and know not what to say: one laugheth at us, another threateneth, another revileth her Majesty and some let not to say what religion is this that a subject shall kill his wife, and ye Prince not only bear withal but marry with him.'

Many were convinced of Dudley's guilt, but could he really have wanted his wife dead, and in such suspicious circumstances? It would have surely been the last thing that he could have wished for. The news seems to have genuinely shocked him; he admitted to being 'much perplexed' upon hearing it. Dudley understood full well that the mystery behind his wife's demise had thrown his own reputation, and with it his chance to marry the queen, into jeopardy. 'Considering what the malicious world will bruit,' he wrote, panicked and stunned on first hearing the news, 'I can take no rest ... I have no way to purge myself of the malicious talk that I know the wicked world will use.' Amy's death had left him isolated and confused; he was, in his own words, 'as it were in a dream, and too far, too far from the place I am bound to be'.

Determined to clear his name and salvage his reputation before it was too late, Dudley immediately sent his trusted servant Thomas Blount to Cumnor to investigate. His reports back opened up new lines of enquiry. According to the testimony of her maid, Mrs Picto, Amy had been spotted praying on her knees to God, pleading that her 'desperation' might end. It was enough to convince Blount that she had an 'evil toy' in her mind. Why, after all, had Amy insisted that she wished to be alone on the day of her death, growing angry at those who attempted to refuse her wishes? Had she planned to take her own life? 'My Lord,' he wrote back to Dudley, 'it is most strange that this chance should fall upon you.

It passeth the judgment of any man to say how it is; but truly the tales I do hear of her maketh me think that she had a strange mind in her.' What that mind was, Blount would only divulge to Dudley in person, 'as I will tell you at my coming'.

Rumours had also been rife about the state of Amy's health, where it had been reported early on in Elizabeth's reign that she was suffering from a 'malady' to one of her breasts. Could Amy have had underlying health problems that might have contributed to her death, an illness that was perhaps the cause of her desperation that she prayed to be delivered from?

In the end, the jury of the coroner's investigation into Amy's death returned a verdict of accidental death. Elizabeth herself may have been satisfied that the verdict was enough to acquit her favourite, but that did not prevent Dudley's many enemies believing otherwise. Intending to smear the reputation of the queen's favourite, suspicions and rumours of murder abounded. A year after Amy's death, the Earl of Arundel was already raking over the inquest, searching for any incriminating evidence that he could find to bring down his enemy. The mystery of Amy's death continued to linger throughout the course of Elizabeth's reign and would cast a long shadow over her favourite. 'He is infamed by his wife's death,' wrote William Cecil seven years after the event.

The death of Amy Robsart remains one of the great mysteries of English history. It is a mystery that has fascinated generations of historians and writers. Was her death a simple accident or was she murdered? If she was, who killed her? In the centuries after her death, Amy's fate spawned numerous ballads and speculative accounts of her final moments, including Sir Walter Scott's famous novel *Kenilworth*, a hopelessly anachronistic depiction of Amy's life in which she was cruelly treated by her husband, shunned by the queen and forced to live in exile from her court. The popular success of *Kenilworth* saw Victorians flocking to glimpse a sight of the ruined building at Cumnor. Even Victor Hugo was inspired to write a play about Amy's life and death, while romantic artists depicted scenes in which Amy's body lies at the foot of a stairwell, two sinister faces emerging from the shadows.

Yet exactly what happened on 8 September 1560 has never been fully explained. Despite extensive scrutiny in which new evidence has emerged piece by piece, the causes of Amy's death remain unsolved. But this does not mean that there is no case to investigate. This book intends to reveal more than we have ever known of this episode before. Historical documents have been revisited, clues retraced, many by going back to the original manuscripts in the National Archives, the British Library, the Dudley Papers at Longleat House, William Cecil's papers at Hatfield House and the Spanish Archives at Simincas to uncover clues that have previously gone unnoticed.

In the course of researching Amy's death, new documents have also come to light. Most notably, for the first time the original coroner's report that investigated her death, which had been presumed lost for centuries, has been discovered in the National Archives. The report of this inquest provides new information not only about exactly how Amy died, including more details of the precise physical injuries to Amy's body that caused her death, but also reveals for the first time the names of the jurors and of the coroner who investigated Amy's death.

Original letters from Amy, Dudley, William Cecil and other prominent courtiers are printed in full, while I have made use of the extensive research into Cumnor Place conducted by Dr Edward Impey, allowing a full reconstruction of the stairs down which Amy is supposed to have fallen. Fresh accusations about who might have been responsible for Amy's death and the complex circumstances leading up to it are fully explored.

Many questions continue to be asked about the mysterious death of Amy Robsart. I hope that this book is able to answer some of them. For the historian, the truth is neither impossible nor improbable: it can only be, quite simply, whatever remains.

# PART ONE

->-<-

## Beginnings

# I

# Rites of passage

Time was precious. The rebels had already defeated an expeditionary party of the king's forces sent to crush them. They had taken Norwich, where, under the direction of their leader, a local tanner named Robert Kett, they had demanded that all 'bond men be made free'. It was reported that some 16,000 rebels had now set up camp on Mousehold Heath, just outside the city. Beneath a great oak they called the 'Tree of Reformation' local gentlemen had been rounded up by Kett and his followers, then put on trial and sentenced to imprisonment, even death.

It was August 1549. The boy king Edward VI had succeeded his father Henry VIII only two years previously. As Edward was too young to govern, his uncle, Edward Seymour, Duke of Somerset, had stepped into the vacuum of power. A man of Protestant leanings who championed religious reform, Somerset had promised a new regime and a 'milder climate' in which men might have freedom to speak their minds without fear of execution. But his leniency had backfired. It was an age of rising prices and high inflation; religious changes during the Reformation had seen the very fabric of medieval Catholicism torn down as saints' images were smashed, and altars and centuries-old shrines were destroyed; unrest and disturbance followed. Somerset had been slow to sense it – and now the country was in open rebellion. In Cornwall, Catholic rebels calling for the abolition of the new church service in English were besieging Exeter, while in York, Essex, Oxfordshire, Suffolk and Norfolk, in what became known as the 'commotion time', revolts erupted, driven by religious reformers who demanded an end to the unpopular enclosures of common land by the nobility.

At court, men were horrified at what seemed to be a breakdown in the social order. The common people, one of Edward's advisers lamented, had 'become a king'; 'Alas! That ever this day should be seen in this time!' The situation was growing out of control. There were fears that the capital might be under threat, and in the atmosphere of instability, rumours that the young king was dead were only dispelled when Edward showed himself in the streets on horseback. The rebellion needed to be crushed, fast. In desperation, Somerset appointed John Dudley, Earl of Warwick, to defeat the rebels. Travelling up from London with a force of 5,000 men, Warwick was determined to end the rebellion by whatever means necessary.

Both Edward Seymour and John Dudley, better known by their landed titles as simply Somerset and Warwick, had been leading courtiers in the last decade of Henry's reign, but there was now a sense of remarkable transfer in their fortunes. Somerset, the elder brother of Henry's third wife Jane Seymour, had come to be regarded as the more senior, and as uncle of the new king Edward VI, was the natural choice as Protector, the de facto king of the realm. Warwick's background was rather more chequered. His father was Edmund Dudley, a brilliant lawyer who had risen to become one of Henry VII's ministers, and who was deeply unpopular with the nobility as a result of his punitive system of fines and threats. Intending to begin his reign afresh, the young Henry VIII had Edmund executed for treason.

Edmund's son worked hard to restore the family name; his military reputation on land and at sea earned him the king's respect, and by 1542 he had been elevated to the peerage as Viscount Lisle. Both John Dudley and Edward Seymour were proud men, jealous of their reputations. Upon Edward VI's accession to the throne both were given instant promotions, Seymour becoming the Duke of Somerset and the King's Protector, while Dudley was raised to Earl of Warwick and Lord High Chamberlain of England. Almost immediately after Edward's succession, it had become clear they were to be rivals. 'Although they both belong to the same sect they are nevertheless widely different in character,' the Imperial ambassador observed. Warwick, he believed, 'being of high courage will not willingly submit to his colleague. He is, moreover, in higher favour both with the people and with the nobles.'[1] Yet behind his charming and charismatic exterior, Warwick was a ruthless operator. 'He had such a head,' one courtier later recalled, 'that he seldom went about anything but he conceived first three or four purposes beforehand.'

As he marched out of the capital, Warwick understood the burden placed upon him. He had taken two of his sons, Ambrose and Robert, with him on the campaign. Warwick had thirteen children in total, eight sons and five daughters, though two of his sons and three of the daughters died before the age of ten.[2] Henry, the eldest son and heir to the family, had been killed during the Siege of Boulogne, Henry VIII's last military campaign, in 1544. When John Dudley had been elevated to the title of Earl of Warwick in 1547, the title of Viscount Lisle passed to his next eldest surviving son, John. Ambrose and Robert were the second and third surviving sons, and while they might not be expected to inherit the family title and the obligations that went with it, Warwick was a devoted father to all his children ('a few children, which God has sent me,' he later confessed, 'also helps to pluck me on my knees').[3]

Born in June 1532, Robert had only just turned 17. He had spent much of his youth at the royal court, having been brought up in the household of the young Prince Edward as one of the 'young lords attendant' who shared his lessons and acted as companions and playmates to their royal friend. It was a position usually reserved for the sons of the ancient nobility, but Warwick's rapid rise through the ranks at court ensured that his sons would receive some of the best education in all of Europe. When not at their studies, the young lords developed their military skills under expert tuition. They learned how to fight with swords and pikes, and practise the novel art of defence, or 'fencing', of which John Dudley had become a strong patron, with the first English school set up at his London residence, Ely Place. He was keen for his sons to be ready to emulate his own success on the battlefield, and to gain the military training and experience requisite for a young nobleman seeking glory and honour in armed combat. The Norfolk rebellion would prove the perfect opportunity to practise what they had learned, a rite of passage that would allow them to witness first hand the experience of the battlefield.

With a mixture of trepidation and excitement, Robert and Ambrose marched with their father into the West Midlands, where they watched 6,000 foot soldiers and 1,500 horsemen amass outside Warwick Castle. Despite his young age and inexperience, Robert himself had been placed in charge of a company of foot soldiers. Tall, with a strong athletic physique and dark good looks, he was already showing signs of the features that would later mark out his attraction at court. Riding in his armour in front of his troops, he was no doubt eager to prove his valour on the battlefield against the rebels.

There was perhaps another reason why Warwick had decided to take his sons with him into combat. The defeat of the expeditionary force led by the Marquis of Northampton had badly shaken the government, especially the news of the death of Lord Sheffield, clubbed to death by some of Kett's men after falling from his horse. Whereas Northampton had failed to pacify the rebels and had been forced to flee, Warwick was determined to show the necessary courage to succeed. His army was already five times the size of Northampton's, and was soon to be joined by over a thousand troops raised from Lincolnshire. The presence of his sons helped convince his officers and men that their commander had the confidence to defeat the rebels.

Before the royal army reached its destination, it had travelled through Cambridge and on to Newmarket. As it neared where the rebellion was taking place, on the night of 22 August its troops came to rest in the fields outside the town of Wymondham, the home town of Robert Kett. It was here that, as his men bedded down in tents for the evening, Warwick, his sons and their officers lodged in the medieval manor of Stanfield Hall, the home of Sir John Robsart and his wife.

# A meeting

Sir John Robsart was a powerful local gentleman, who had been a Justice of the Peace since 1532. Knighted upon Edward's coronation, he was the appointed Sheriff of Norfolk and Suffolk from 1547 to 1548. He was also a substantial landowner, owning three manors in the north-west of Norfolk with enough land to graze 3,000 sheep.

Although Sir John owned the manor of Syderstone, the manor house there lay in ruins and had long been uninhabitable. After marrying Elizabeth Appleyard in 1530, he moved into her house, Stanfield Hall. Elizabeth was the daughter of John Scott of Camberwell and had previously been married to Roger Appleyard, an influential member of the landed gentry. His premature death had left Elizabeth a widow, and the heir to his sizeable estate. It was just what Sir John had been looking for: not only was Elizabeth the member of a distinguished Norfolk family like his own; she brought with her a landed estate and house suitable for his means, a great improvement on his ruined manor house at Syderstone.

Sir John quickly became the adoptive father to Elizabeth's four children by her previous marriage: John, Philip, Anna and Frances. Sir John already had an illegitimate son, Arthur, though naturally he wanted his own heir to inherit his estate. A daughter, Amy, was born to the couple two years later. Any disappointment that the child was not a male quickly evaporated, and Sir John proudly entered her name in his missal:

*Amea Robsart generosa filia Johno Robsart Armiger nata fuit in vii die Junij*
*in Anno Dom Angelismo cccccxxxii*
*Amy Robsart beloved daughter of John Robsart Knight was born on the 7th*
*day of June in the Blessed Year of Our Lord 1532.*

If this missal is correct, Amy was almost identical in age to Robert Dudley, who later revealed his own birthday to be on 24 June of the same year.[1]

As a result of his marriage, Sir John Robsart became well entrenched in the Norfolk gentry. He soon married his stepchildren off to other respectable local families: the Bigots, the Huggins and the Sheltons.

Frances had recently been betrothed to William, the eldest son of Sir John Flowerdew of Hethersett, a lawyer and landowner who was also steward of Robsart's Norfolk estates. Sir John's wife brought new, now less welcome, connections: her previous husband's sister, Alice Appleyard, was married to the leader of the rebellion, Robert Kett. For more than a decade the Flowerdews and the Ketts had been in conflict over Sir John Flowerdew's decision to enclose some nearby common land, erecting hedges around it. Kett's decision to become involved with the rebellion was influenced by Flowerdew's offer of 3s 4d to an angry mob to pull down Kett's own hedges. When Kett agreed instead to pull them down himself, he offered to lead them into open rebellion against the 'power of great men' and 'importunate lords'. Sir John Robsart found himself caught in the middle of the conflict between his sister-in-law's husband and his stepdaughter's future father-in-law. Potentially more serious consequences were no doubt pressing upon his mind too: among the gentry that had been captured by the rebels and taken up to Mousehold Heath were his own stepsons, John and Philip Appleyard.

Yet Sir John was determined to stand on the side of the king and the law, against the rebels – no matter what family connections persisted. He was a committed Protestant, and a firm believer in royal supremacy as the natural order of things. When Sir John came to draw up his will in October 1535, he referred to his sovereign Henry VIII as being 'within his realme supreame hede of the church immediately under God'.[2] When the preacher Thomas Beacon dedicated his work *The Fortresse of the Faithful* to him in 1550, he did so in honour of the 'godly affection and christian zeal which both you and . . . your wife have borne toward the pure religion of God these many years'. It is likely that Amy was brought up to share her father's religious views, which happened to chime strongly with Robert Dudley's own religious outlook as a committed reformer. 'I never altered my mind or thought from my youth touching my religion,' he later admitted, 'I was ever from my cradle brought up in it'.[3]

It could have been here at Stanfield Hall on their way to meet Kett's rebels that Robert first set eyes upon Sir John's only daughter, Amy, who had recently turned 17. There is a possibility that Amy and Robert had met before: Sir John Robsart had enjoyed favour with the Howards, the dukes of Norfolk, before the Third Duke's downfall and imprisonment in 1546, alongside his son, Henry Howard, Earl of Surrey. It has been suggested that Amy may have ended up as a maid or a companion to the Howard children in their house at Kenninghall, and may even have attended the family on their travels to London after the Duchess of Richmond had gained guardianship of the children in 1548. Amy's surviving letters, written in a fine calligraphic hand, attest to the fact that she must have had a good formal education, perhaps the kind received in a noble household. If this was indeed the case, Amy just might have already met or seen Robert at official functions at court, though the evidence is too slim to know for certain.

What is certain is that Warwick's sudden arrival at Stanfield Hall must have been the most memorable occasion of Amy's life to date. A sea of thousands of men – some estimates put the size of the royal army at over ten thousand – were camped out in the fields adjoining the back garden of her home, while the guest list for dinner that night was far from what a country gentleman like her father was accustomed to: one earl, one marquis and three lords sat around the table in the Great Hall, not to mention the two young sons of the earl. Still, there would have been little occasion for merriment, with the visitors deep in serious discussion about the best tactics for dealing with the growing rebellion. It was later said that while on their journey to Norwich, Warwick and his officers did not once take off their armour, 'remaining still in a readiness, if the enemies should have made any sudden invasion against them'.[4]

Amy might not have spoken to her future husband that night, but she would have noticed him. Clad in a full suit of armour, with his dark hair and features, Robert, the youngest of the earl's sons, would have stood out from his elder brother Ambrose and the rest of the noblemen arguing tactics around the dinner table.

By dawn, however, he was gone, having departed with his company to make the final journey towards Norwich.

# Carnal marriages

On the battlefield the rebels barely stood a chance. When routed by Warwick's army, many simply fled, including Kett, who was discovered hiding in a nearby barn. His was one of the many executions that followed; hanged in chains off the wall of Norwich Castle, his body was left dangling there until the flesh fell away from the rotten corpse.

Although the rebellions were all eventually put down, Somerset's reputation had been irreparably damaged and he never recovered his authority. Amidst rumours of a plot to have him arrested, he fled to Windsor Castle, taking Edward with him. For a week it seemed that the nation would descend into civil war, with the nobility on one side and Somerset on the other. Armed conflict was narrowly avoided when Somerset was tricked into giving himself up, but both sides had come too close to civil war for the situation to continue.

Somerset was arrested and stripped of his position; in his place, Warwick soon became the leading figurehead as Lord President of the Council. He skilfully outmanoeuvred his enemies, defeating a Catholic faction who wished to make Edward's sister Princess Mary regent, by drawing himself close to the king and embracing his reformed religion. One reason for Warwick's success was that he had refused to have Somerset executed, knowing that the young King Edward was unwilling for his uncle to die. The following spring, Somerset was released from the Tower, and as part of his reconciliation with Warwick, it was agreed that Somerset's daughter Anne would marry Warwick's eldest surviving son, John Dudley, Lord Lisle. Their marriage was celebrated at the royal palace of Sheen on 3 June 1550, in a weekend of festivities attended by the king. Theirs was not the only marriage that had been arranged, for the next day Robert Dudley married Amy Robsart.

Compared to the lavish festivities that had accompanied his brother John's ceremony, Robert and Amy's wedding was a quiet affair. Taking place in front of the same audience, it must have been something of an anticlimax for those who had attended the sumptuous banquet of the night before and were perhaps now feeling somewhat the worse for wear.

The young king recalled in his diary that there had been a 'fair dinner made and dancing' at the former ceremony; afterwards, from a bower of woven branches, Edward watched two teams of six gentlemen take part in a joust. There was no such splendour for Robert and his new bride. The ceremony was once again attended by the king, though the only mention Edward made in his diary refers to the bizarre festivities that had been hastily organised in place of a tournament, in which 'there certain gentlemen that did strive who should first take away a goose's head, which was hanged alive on two cross posts.'[1]

The contrast between John's and Robert's marriages could not have been greater. John had married the daughter of a duke; Robert, the daughter of a Norfolk squire. Of course, Robert was Warwick's third surviving son – he could not have expected to compete with his elder brother in the marriage stakes – but compared to his other brothers and sisters, he had fared badly. His brother Ambrose married the daughter of the Attorney General, William Whorwood, and even his younger brother Henry was betrothed to Margaret, the daughter of Henry VIII's Lord Chancellor, Thomas Audley. His sister Mary would later become the wife of Henry Sidney, one of Edward's gentlemen of the Privy Chamber. There was little doubting that Robert, the son of an earl who had become the most powerful man in the kingdom, had married a woman who was several degrees beneath him in the social hierarchy.

It points to one conclusion: Robert married Amy for love. A crucial piece of evidence exists to support this. Years later, musing on Robert and Amy's marriage, Cecil wrote the telling words in a memorandum: '*Nuptii carnales a laetitia incipiunt et in luctu terminantur*' – 'carnal marriages begin in joy and end in weeping'.[2] With the knowledge of events later to unfold, these words have been frequently mistranslated to imply that Robert and Amy's marriage was an unhappy one, with the force of the '*a*' being taken to mean 'without', yet this is both incorrect and presses the case too far. Evidence from Amy's own letters several years into their marriage, with her being 'not altogether quiet' upon Dudley's 'sudden departing', suggest otherwise. As do Cecil's words '*nuptii carnales*', which suggest that Robert and Amy had a healthy sex life. Certainly when Robert was placed in the Tower three years later, Amy and other wives were 'to have access unto their husbands, and there to tarry with them so long and at such times, as by him shall be thought meet'.

Cecil, who despite his relative youth would shortly be appointed Principal Secretary to the Privy Council under Warwick's government, most likely attended Robert and Amy's wedding at Sheen, where he would have had the opportunity of meeting the young couple. It must have been their youth that first struck Cecil. Both were still 17, though Amy's eighteenth birthday was just four days away. The couple were remarkably young to be getting married. In Tudor England, the average age for a first marriage was 27 for men and 25 for women. In particular, it was widely believed that young men were unsuited to settling down so soon: 'until a man grow into the age of twenty-four years', wrote one author, 'he is wild, without judgment and not of sufficient experience to govern himself'.

Amid the muted wedding celebrations, it is almost possible to imagine the young couple, anxious on beginning their new life together. Through surviving portraits and descriptions Robert's features are well known to us. According to the historian William Camden, he was 'a man of tall personage, a manly countenance, somewhat brown of visage, strongly featured, and thereto comely proportioned in all lineaments of body'. His facial features were 'of sweet aspect, but high-foreheaded, which was of no discommendation'. His large pupils, piercing in gaze, appear almost black in portraits of him. Later he would grow a reddish moustache and forked beard, but probably for the moment we should imagine him as an unshaven youth, yet to reach his full maturity. He had a large, strong-bridged aquiline nose, matched with an angular jutting chin. But it was his athletic physique, honed through regular exercise – Dudley was a keen horse rider, tennis player and jouster who had a celebrated reputation on the tiltyard – that drew the attention of onlookers, combined with a lofty stance, his shoulders raised back and his head held high, a pose barely short of arrogance.

With Amy it is a different story. No picture of her is known to have survived, though according to the Imperial ambassador Caspar Bruener, writing in 1559, she was 'a very beautiful wife'. We can also get a sense of the clothes that Amy wore from her tailor's bills, which include payments for scarlet petticoats, loose gowns of russet taffeta or damask, 'laced all thick overthwart the garde', a 'round kirtell' of black velvet, white satin sleeves and a bodice of crimson velvet.

Yet there is a possibility that a portrait miniature painted by the Flemish artist Lavinia Teerlinc, and traditionally dated to around 1550, might be of Amy. The sitter, whose identity has long remained a mystery, wears a black bodice, squared across the shoulders. She has a nose slightly too large for her face, her pursed lips seem too small, while her pale features redden around the cheeks. Her light auburn hair is parted in the middle, beneath a headdress of white and black, fringed with gold. Her eyebrows are faint, almost wispy; her eyes are pale blue. Rather than stare directly at the viewer, she looks outwards, as if in contemplation. Significantly, set against a background of azure blue, typical of a Teerlinc miniature, there is a Latin inscription 'An[n]o XVIII' denoting the sitter's age: 18 – Amy's age just days after her marriage.

In particular, attention has focused upon the intricate oval brooch worn by the sitter. A black classical face is centred in the middle of the brooch, typical of the kind of jewellery worn by many ladies at court during the period. What makes its design so unusual, however, is the foliage on either side of the brooch; to the right is a spray of yellow flowers, identified as gillyflowers, and to the left are acorns and oak leaves. The gillyflower was also a well-known symbol representing marriage, betrothal and fidelity, yet it is difficult to understand why the lady in the portrait would wish to be pictured with acorns and oak leaves pinned to her breast, unless the device was part of some wider symbolism privately understood by the sitter. There is good reason to suggest that this might indeed be the case. The acorn and the oak was a symbol taken up by Amy's husband Robert when he was later imprisoned in the Tower. There, into the sandstone wall of his cell, as a pun on his own name, similar to the Latin for an oak tree, *robur*, he carved acorns and oak leaves. The combination of this symbol, together with the gillyflowers symbolising marriage, is highly suggestive. Was the miniature painted to mark the occasion of a wedding? If so, the face that stares out at us might just be the only surviving likeness of Amy.[3]

# ⊁ 4 ⊰

## My father's heart

Robert and Amy may have married for love; but, in the sixteenth century, marriage could rarely be a matter of love alone. Considerations of wealth and politics were simply too great for that. It was particularly common among landowning families for fathers to decide who their children might marry, especially when the family inheritance was at stake. Robert and Amy would have had little choice but to dutifully obey their parents' wishes, as countless other sons and daughters of nobles and gentlemen had done for generations before them. When Sir Walter Mildmay, Chancellor of the Exchequer under Henry VIII, insisted that his son Anthony marry the fourteen-year-old girl he had chosen for him, Anthony initially resisted, demanding to know more about the world before he settled down, but he soon relented and gave in to his father's demands.

For women the choice was perhaps more stark. Entirely dependent on their parents, few ever thought to disobey their commands; Amy would have been no exception. When Joan Hayward was chosen as the wife of the heir of Longleat, John Thynne, she was told that she could meet the young man, her future husband, if she wished, but it was still expected that she marry him, whether she liked him or not. In response, Joan's answer was typical of the age: 'I do put my trust in God and in my good father that God will put into my father's heart to choose me such a one as God will direct my heart not to dislike.'[1] Certainly for Sir John Robsart, his daughter Amy's marriage to the son of an earl must have been beyond his wildest expectations; he had everything to gain and nothing to lose.

Could Robert's marriage to Amy have been an arranged one? The fact that it came so soon after his elder brother John's arranged marriage to Somerset's daughter, certainly suggests that Warwick had meticulously planned his sons' wedding arrangements in advance. It may have been that Robert's union with Amy was part of a series of alliances that Warwick had been making at that time, strengthening his own base of political support. Sir John Robsart was a key ally of his in Norfolk, and through his marriage to Elizabeth Appleyard had established a strong series of connections amongst the Norfolk gentry, built upon intermarriage, that might prove politically valuable to the earl, who was especially keen to avoid any repeat of Kett's rebellion the previous year. Amy also had the benefit of being Sir John Robsart's only legitimate heir, and would therefore inherit his Norfolk manors. She may not have been able to compete with the rich heiresses Robert's brothers John and Ambrose had wed, but she might provide Robert with enough land to establish himself as a wealthy country gentleman. Few could have predicted that Robert's aspirations would one day reach far higher.

The clearest sign that Robert and Amy's marriage would need to address more temporal concerns appears in the marriage contract drawn up by Warwick and Sir John Robsart, a fortnight before the wedding, on 20 May 1550. The details had obviously been pored over by both fathers for some time, each seeking the best deal for his child. For Sir John, the problem also lay with how his wife Elizabeth might receive an income after his death. Reluctant for his entire estate to pass to his daughter and her husband immediately after his death, he managed to ensure that a clause was added to the marriage contract stating that Amy and Robert would only inherit the Robsart estate of the manors of Syderstone, Newton and Great Bircham in north-west Norfolk after both he and his wife were dead. For Warwick, while sympathetic to Sir John's obvious concerns, this was insufficient. He needed to ensure that the young couple would have enough to get by on. In return for a down payment or dowry of £200, it was agreed that Sir John was to pay Robert an annual allowance of £20. To complement this, Warwick added another £50, provided from the rents of some land of his in Leicestershire. Since the couple were unlikely to inherit Amy's family estate in the near future, Warwick also provided them with the lands of the priory of Coxford, close to her parents' estate, in the hope that one day they would be amalgamated.[2]

What about the soon-to-be married couple? There is little evidence of their participation in any of the finer details of the contract, which would have been ironed out between the two fathers. Only a final clause in the contract, coming almost as an afterthought, indicates that there were two other parties in the arrangement; the marriage, both Sir John and Warwick agreed, should only take place 'if the said Robert and Amye will thereunto condescend and agree'. At this stage, one suspects, they were hardly likely not to.[3]

Through his son's marriage to Amy, it was clear that Warwick intended to establish Robert as the most influential landholder in north-west Norfolk. Possibly he considered that his son might one day be able to supplant the dormant power of the Howard family in the county, whose downfall in the final months of the reign of Henry VIII had left Norfolk without a resident magnate – a dangerous vacuum of power and authority that needed to be filled, as Kett's rebellion had sorely proved.

In the years that followed Robert was introduced gradually into local county administration, first becoming joint Steward and Constable of the castle and manor of Castle Rising in December 1550, together with his new father-in-law. The following year, in autumn 1551, he was appointed an elected knight of the shire and went on to share the Lord Lieutenancy of the county with his father-in-law in 1552. He soon ingratiated himself with the local gentlemen; the preacher John Aylmer later wrote how 'your Lordship's name is in Norfolk of some authority and your person well beloved.'[4] In February 1553, Warwick granted Dudley the manor of Hemsby near Great Yarmouth, 'so his son might be able to keep a good house in Norfolk', and in July he received a grant of Saxlingham Manor near Holt.[5]

As a son of the most important nobleman in the land, Robert Dudley knew that his real future lay at court. It was here that he and Amy spent most of their time, lodging at his parents' home at Ely Place in Holborn. In August 1551 Dudley was made a gentleman of the Privy Chamber, giving him privileged access to the young King Edward. The appointment was also a sign of his father's increasing control of the king's person. Two months later Warwick moved against Somerset, who was arrested suddenly at court and executed the following spring for his role in a putative and somewhat suspect assassination attempt against his rival.

Around the same time Warwick also awarded himself a dukedom, becoming the Duke of Northumberland. It was the highest rank a nobleman could achieve. The significance of Warwick's elevation should not be underestimated. Henry VIII only created two dukedoms during his reign, including one to his illegitimate son Henry Fitzroy, while Elizabeth I never created any dukes: Warwick's elevation was the first outside the royal family since the Wars of the Roses.

As his father's star continued to rise, Dudley's career also prospered. A skilled horseman, he now took a regular part in the royal jousts, tilts and barriers, commonly termed 'triumphs'. In December 1551 he ran six courses at the tilt as part of the Christmas festivities, reappearing on Twelfth Night and once more eleven days later, when his team was defeated by his brothers John and Ambrose, who won by '4 taints'.*

Dudley's activities at court extended beyond mere entertaining. Where there were lucrative positions on offer, he filled them. He was appointed to the office of Master of the Buckhounds in September 1552, a role which entailed organising the king's hunting parties, breeding the royal hounds and ensuring that there was a steady supply of deer in the parks and chases. It also brought Dudley the not insignificant salary of £33 6s 8d per annum.[6] In February 1553, he was given the honorary position of chief carver.

With higher office came the prospect of material reward. At the end of December 1552, Dudley was appointed keeper of Somerset Place, the magnificent newly built palace on the banks of the Thames, the finest renaissance building in London, designed by Warwick's rival the Duke of Somerset before he was executed. For the rest of Edward's reign Dudley and his wife lived in these splendid surroundings, undoubtedly the most sumptuous private residence in the capital. It was also during this period that Elizabeth agreed to exchange her London residence at Durham Place for Somerset Place. Although she never visited while Robert Dudley was living there, the fact that he had been chosen to be the keeper of the princess's official home would bring the pair even closer.

* Broken lances

# Shameful slanders

The story of Elizabeth's enigmatic bond with her favourite Robert Dudley is an enduring one. For the thirty years from the beginning of Elizabeth's reign until the day of Dudley's death they were barely out of each other's sight. Their relationship has intrigued generations of historians as much as it baffled her contemporaries. At the time, people blamed astronomy for the 'most strait conjunction of their minds'; that the 'hidden consent of the stars at the hour of their birth' – rumoured to be on the same day[1] – explained their unique attraction, 'a man cannot easily say'.[2]

By the early 1550s, Dudley and Elizabeth had already known each other for some time. Dudley later told the French ambassador that 'they had first become friends before she was eight years old', which would place their first meeting between 1540 and 1541.[3] It would have been during this period that Robert Dudley was placed in the household of Edward, Prince of Wales, the future Edward VI, probably in 1544.

The 'young lords attendant upon the Prince' were mostly sons of the nobility, boys slightly older than him who were destined to form the next generation of the nobility. Very much the forerunner of the boarding school, the boys were taught in lessons by Edward's tutors Richard Cox, John Cheke and Roger Ascham, while William Buckley initially remained in overall charge as the Master of the Henchmen.[4] Buckley also acted as the boys' maths tutor. He was a captivating and engaging teacher who believed in making learning a pleasure; one of his works, *Arithmetica Memorativa*, comprised of Latin verses designed to teach the rules of arithmetic so that they might more easily be committed to memory.[5] Most the tutors had been schooled at Cambridge, the academic power-house of the Reformation. They were all of a humanist persuasion, and helped shape the young minds of the future generation of men who would one day act as the advisers to Elizabeth.

Though by no means a scholar himself, John Dudley was determined that his children were well educated in the classics, and a surviving list of books owned by his eldest son, John, attests to the deep culture of knowledge and learning that their father had ensured his sons were steeped in. Walter Haddon later admitted to Robert Dudley that 'you have certainly inherited a love of scholarship, for your father, although he acknowledged himself uneducated, was yet most devoted to learning ... although he received no formal education, he valued highly one able to make a modest display of academic ability'.[6] It is more likely, however, that the influence of Robert's mother, Jane Dudley, was equally responsible for his education; as a girl she had been brought up at court with Mary Tudor and her friend Catherine Parr, where she had studied under the Spanish humanist Juan Luis Vives. Vives' work, *The Education of a Christian Woman*, helped to inspire a generation of young women to take up learning which ultimately they passed on to their children.

Elizabeth was also to benefit from this flourishing of new learning at court. As a young girl she did not have a tutor of her own, having to make do with the occasional lesson from Richard Cox when he was not preoccupied with Edward's studies. Henry VIII's marriage to Catherine Parr in July 1543 changed this. Catherine was determined to ensure that all of Henry's children were well-educated, and soon Elizabeth was given her own private tutor, William Grindal, another Cambridge scholar who was accounted 'the best Grecian one of them', fluent in both Latin and ancient Greek. Grindal was succeeded in 1548 by Roger Ascham, while Elizabeth also began to take French lessons with Edward's French tutor, Jean Belmain. Soon Elizabeth would be fluent in Latin, equally comfortable speaking or writing the language; French and Italian became 'like English' to her.

It has often been speculated that Elizabeth and Robert might have shared lessons together; though they certainly shared the same tutors, there is little evidence to support this affectionate theory. Besides, though his brothers John and Ambrose had both taken to the liberal arts, Robert had shown an early disdain for the classics and favoured mathematics. This was much to Roger Ascham's disapproval, who later reminded him that in trading his learning of Cicero's works for the study of mathematics, navigation and astrology – one of Dudley's great passions – 'you did yourself injury in changing Tully's wisdom with Euclid's pricks and lines'.[7]

Contemporary scholars were divided about the benefits of a mathematical education, which some believed 'withdraw the mind from the practical concerns of life and render it less fit to face concrete and mundane realities'. Yet Dudley's early education in the sciences would inspire him to become a patron of the golden age of Elizabethan maritime – and indeed global – expansion. One of the most important works on navigation published in the sixteenth century, William Cunningham's *The Cosmographical Glass*, which appeared in the first year of Elizabeth's reign, was actually dedicated to Dudley, thanking him for 'your Lordship's encouragement of me to knowledge, both in words and most liberal rewards'.[8] Dudley's interest in geography, cartography and astronomy, which he retained throughout his life, may have been inspired by the famous scientist Dr John Dee, who had stayed in his father's household when Robert was a boy. It is possible that Dee acted as Dudley's science teacher; if so, it was yet another passion that Dudley and Elizabeth, who was on good terms with Dee, seemed to share. Later, during her reign, they visited Dee's house at Mortlake together, to 'see some of the properties of that glass [supposedly given to Dee by angels] to her Majesty's great contentment and delight'.[9]

Elizabeth, like Dudley, was a middle child who, although she was a princess, was not considered to be of any real importance. The daughter of Henry VIII by his second marriage to Anne Boleyn, she was third in line to the throne after her younger brother Edward VI and her elder sister Mary. As a result, few expected her ever to become queen. Many even doubted her legitimacy as an heir to the throne, since her father had passed an act of attainder against her mother, which effectively annulled their marriage, stripped Elizabeth of her legitimacy and briefly removed her from the succession altogether.

Yet Elizabeth's status as princess meant that she could never live entirely in the shadows. From an early age, it was assumed that she would be married off at the earliest dynastic opportunity. When Elizabeth was barely sixteen months old, Henry VIII had opened negotiations with Francis I to marry her to the French king's third son, the Duke of Angoulême.[10] Other possible marriages were mooted during her father's and brother's reigns, with sons of the Earl of Arran, the King of Denmark, the Duke of Ferrara, the Duke of Guise, John Frederick of Saxony and the son of the Duke of Florence.[11] Elizabeth remembered them all, recalling that:

> In the king my brother's time, there was offered me a very honourable
> marriage or two, and Ambassadors sent to treat with me touching the
> same, where upon I made my humble suit unto his highness ... that it

would like the same to give me leave, with his graces favour, to remain in the estate I was, which of all others best liked and pleased me ... I am even at this present of the same mind, and so intend to continue ... I so well like this estate, as I persuade unto myself there is not any kind of life comparable unto it.[12]

This was how Elizabeth, mindful of her status as the Virgin Queen, would later prefer to remember the past. The truth was altogether different.

It was during her brother Edward's reign that, as a precocious teenager, Elizabeth went to live with her stepmother, the former queen Catherine Parr. Barely weeks after Henry VIII's death, Catherine had begun a secret relationship with Sir Thomas Seymour, the then Lord Admiral and younger brother of Edward's Protector, the Duke of Somerset. Athletic and well built, with a russet beard and piercing blue eyes, Sir Thomas bore more than a passing resemblance to Elizabeth's own father, Henry VIII. Soon Catherine and Sir Thomas were married, causing scandal at court, since it followed so soon after Henry's death. Then came the news that, at the age of 36, Catherine was expecting Seymour's child.

While Catherine was pregnant, Sir Thomas began to turn his attentions elsewhere: to Elizabeth. At first his playful behaviour seemed innocent enough, tickling the princess in her bed with Catherine even joining in. On one occasion, Elizabeth's gentlewoman, Catherine Ashley, discovered the princess with her gown cut up 'into a hundred pieces'. Elizabeth explained: Seymour had done it, and 'the queen [Catherine Parr] held her while my lord did so dress it'.[13] What Catherine was playing at is hard to imagine, though perhaps she felt that if she joined in the fun and kept a careful watch over the pair, her errant husband's activities with the teenage Elizabeth would at least be able to be monitored and controlled.

Catherine's hopes were swiftly dashed. Soon Sir Thomas began to visit Elizabeth in her bedchamber early in the morning, 'in his nightgown, barelegged in his slippers'. If Elizabeth was awake, he would bid her good morning, patting her on the back, 'or on the buttocks familiarly'. When the princess was still sleeping, he would pull open the curtains of the bed and jump in, 'as though he would come at her'.[14]

At first Elizabeth avoided Seymour's advances, but the young girl fast became curious, flattered by the attention that the most attractive man at court was paying her. She struggled to hide her affection, blushing at any mention of his name. Privately, she could not stop talking about him, and Ashley recalled how 'she hath spoken to me of him many times'.[15] Catherine began to grow suspicious. On one occasion, she caught Elizabeth with Seymour, 'where they were all alone, he having her in his arms'. Catherine was enraged. 'Of this was much displeasure', Catherine Ashley later recalled.[16] Elizabeth would have to go. As Catherine's pregnancy reached its final stages, Elizabeth was sent away, but not before her stepmother gave her some words of advice, warning her of the damage that might be done to her reputation by her conduct. Elizabeth, ashamed, 'answered little'.

After a difficult pregnancy, Catherine gave birth to a baby girl. But within days Catherine succumbed to puerperal fever and died. For Elizabeth, it would serve as another painful reminder of the sacrifices that marriage and love might bring.

Seymour did not allow his wife's death to deter him. He was once again free to marry, and was overheard saying that he 'would wear black for one year, and would then know where to have a wife'.[17] Soon he was in contact with Elizabeth's servant Thomas Parry, asking 'whether her great buttocks were grown any less or no?'[18] Elizabeth, too, was being urged to consider the opportunities to be had. Yet the princess remained cautious. When Ashley pressed her to write a letter of condolence to Seymour, she refused, 'lest she be thought to woo him'.[19]

Elizabeth was not Seymour's only project. For months he had been grooming the king, supplying Edward with pocket money in the hope that the boy would be bribed into signing a parliamentary bill agreeing that Seymour might become his governor, a position he had long coveted. When this failed, Seymour looked to new enterprises to secure the power his brother enjoyed. Attempting to win over the support of members of the nobility, including Lady Jane Grey's father, Henry, Marquis of Dorset, he planned nothing less than a full-scale civil war. One suspects that Seymour never quite recovered his sanity after his wife's death: he later admitted that he had been 'so amazed' that he had 'small regard either to myself or my doings'. In an extraordinary scheme that echoed his brother Somerset's flight to Windsor, he resolved that he would kidnap Edward and take him to Holt Castle. It was only the barking of the king's dog at midnight as Seymour broke into Edward's bedchamber, pistol in hand, that scuppered his plans. Tried and found guilty, he was executed in March 1549, his execution warrant signed by the shaky, almost illegible, hand of his own brother.

In his final hours Seymour had attempted to write to Elizabeth secretly, hiding the letter in the soles of his velvet shoes. The letter was discovered and never delivered. Later, Elizabeth reflected wistfully that his life could have been spared; 'if his brother [Somerset] had been suffered to speak with him, he had never suffered'. Hearing of his execution, she merely remarked that 'this day died a man of much wit, and very little judgment'.[20]

Worse, perhaps, was to come. The investigations into Seymour's actions had uncovered the tales of his behaviour with the princess. Elizabeth, who 'wept all night, and lowred all the next day', was enraged when she discovered that Catherine Ashley was to be removed from her household. She wrote to Somerset that 'There goeth rumours abroad, which be greatly both against my Honour, and Honesty'. Gossips had said that she was 'with child by my Lord Admiral', and that she had been placed in the Tower. 'My Lord,' Elizabeth protested, 'these are shameful slanders.' She wished to come to court to protest her innocence, 'that I may show myself there as I am', and urged him to issue a proclamation against any such rumours.[21]

Somerset ignored her pleas and the investigations were ordered to continue. Elizabeth was aghast. At least she could count on the confidentiality of her household, she believed. 'They all sing one song,' the frustrated examiner wrote back to Somerset, 'and so I think they would not do, unless they had set the note before.' The questioning intensified. Under pressure and suffering from the harsh conditions of his imprisonment, her servant Thomas Parry was the first to crumble. When Elizabeth found out, she condemned him as a 'false wretch, and said he had promised he would never confess it to death'.[22]

Confess what exactly? It seems that after Catherine's death, Elizabeth had remained in contact with Seymour, using Thomas Parry as a go-between in a pretence of conducting a suit for a property in London. 'They used me but for an instrument,' Parry admitted, 'to serve their purposes to be brought to pass, and to have entered further.'[23] So what was the exact nature of Elizabeth and Sir Thomas Seymour's relationship? The evidence suggests that the princess was keen to keep in contact with Sir Thomas, perhaps to see where matters might lead, possibly even towards marriage. There can be little doubt that her early association with him was a formative episode in the mind of the young princess. Impressionable, vulnerable, it was her first encounter with a man, and she had found it thrilling.

No evidence has come to light that Elizabeth ever embarked upon a full sexual relationship with Sir Thomas. As will be seen, there is little to suggest that Elizabeth ever gave up her virginity, let alone at the young age of thirteen to a man three times her age.

Elizabeth nevertheless had had a taste of what it was to love. Passion had overcome her; her illicit meetings with Seymour behind Catherine's back were foolish, but she could not resist. Now that had been taken away from her. The escapade was but an unfortunate memory; but once again it was a memory, like her mother's death upon the block, that forged in her own mind the dangerously close bond between love and marriage and death and destruction.

## ➤➤ 6 ◄◄

# God will revenge

As the Seymours' fortunes faded, so the Dudleys rose to power, a rise which also witnessed a marked turnaround in Elizabeth's prospects. She was immediately given her own palace at Hatfield, with her own surveyor to keep her lands and affairs in check. His name was William Cecil. It was the start of a long and affectionate friendship that spanned nearly fifty years.

When she visited court, Elizabeth was treated with full regal dignity, and in January 1551 was 'most honourably received by the Council ... to show the people how much glory belongs to her who has embraced the new religion and is become a very great lady.'[1] Restored to her position as the king's favourite sister (Mary was in disgrace for allowing Catholics to come to hear mass in her household), Elizabeth was finally granted her full yearly allowance of £3,000 due to her under her father's will. For the first time she was able to live the life of a princess, and the next two years were some of the happiest of her life.

But for Elizabeth and for Dudley and his wife Amy, living comfortably as one of the most influential couples at court, life was about to undergo a dramatic change.

The Twelfth Night festivities of 1553 were cut short when the king began to feel unwell. What started with a strained cough soon developed into something far more serious. At 15, Edward was on the brink of manhood, ready to assume the mantle of his kingship. During the previous summer he had regularly taken part in hunting expeditions and training exercises, and had even made his first royal progress out of the capital, going as far as Portsmouth on horseback. Now bedridden, his cough grew worse: 'the matter he ejects from his mouth is sometimes coloured by a greenish yellow and black, sometime pink, like the colour of blood.'[2] In April, Edward was moved to Greenwich in order to 'take the air'. It seemed to help. His sister Mary wrote to him, congratulating him on his recovery from his 'rhume cough', but she was premature.[3] Edward was in fact dying.

This much he knew, perhaps: in his own hand he had drawn up a will, his 'devise' as he termed it, setting out his wish for the succession after his death. Its contents were breathtaking. Edward was determined to turn the entire Tudor succession envisaged by his father on its head. Both his sisters, Mary and Elizabeth, were to be written out entirely. Instead, he nominated the male heirs of his cousin Frances Grey or her daughter Jane to inherit the throne. The only problem with this was that there were no male heirs. Frances was 36 and had not given birth for nine years; her daughter Jane, who had only just turned 16, was unmarried.

In the hope that this might change, Jane and her sisters were hastily married, Jane to Robert Dudley's younger brother, Guildford. A new Parliament was summoned for September to ratify the king's new will. But it soon became apparent to all that these plans were optimistic. For Edward, time was running out: 'the sputum which he brings up is livid, black, fetid and full of carbon,' wrote one doctor. 'It smells beyond measure.' The young boy, now too weak to leave his bed, was 'racked by violent coughing' and remained 'tormented by constant sleeplessness'.[4]

An heir would have to be found, fast. The king, an ardent Protestant, still refused to allow Mary, a Catholic, to inherit his throne; more curiously, he also rejected Elizabeth from the succession. 'It was the fate of my other sister,' the dying king told his council, 'to have Anne Boleyn for a mother', who had been 'more inclined to couple with a number of courtiers rather than reverencing her husband'; having been 'cast off by my father', he believed that Elizabeth was nothing but a 'bastard and sprung from an illegitimate bed'.[5] There was no one else but his cousin Jane. With a few strokes of the pen, the king altered his 'devise': Jane was now Edward's sole heir.

When Edward finally died on 6 July 1553, Warwick, now Duke of Northumberland, moved fast to seize the Tower. The number of guards was doubled and a watch placed on all the ports. Four days later, Jane was proclaimed queen in front of a thousand silent Londoners, their faces 'sorrowful and averted'.[6] Only one man stood out, shouting that Mary was their rightful queen. For that offence his ears were severed 'at the root' the next morning.

It would be crucial for the success of the new regime that Mary was captured. The princess was currently residing near Cambridge, at Sawston

Hall, yet Northumberland was unsettled: Mary had been summoned to court, but he had yet to hear any response back from her. Northumberland's first thought was to call upon his son Robert. His growing influence in Norfolk might help counter any support that Mary might attempt to gather. Having been ordered to bring Mary back to the capital, Dudley rode through the night along the highway towards Cambridge, arriving at Sawston Hall as the dawn broke across the fields.

He was too late. Tipped off secretly that her brother was near death, Mary had fled, some two days before Edward died, heading towards the Duke of Norfolk's estate at Framlingham Castle. In his rage, Dudley ordered that Sawston Hall be ransacked and burnt. It was a costly mistake, earning his father 'the deepest hatred in the surrounding countryside'. As the local gentry began to hear what had taken place at the Hall, they flocked to Mary's side.

There was little choice left but to face Mary and her growing army in combat. In London, few were prepared to volunteer, and Northumberland was forced to lead the army himself, trusting his Council to look after their new Queen Jane. A few days later, he marched out of the capital, leaving Jane in the Tower with the rest of the Council. It was their treachery he feared most. 'If ye mean deceit, though not forthwith yet hereafter,' he told them on his departure, 'God will revenge the same.'[7] Northumberland's march out of London was reminiscent of a time four years earlier, when he had been cheered by the people as he rode along its streets ready to defeat Kett's rebels. This time, however, the streets were eerily silent. 'The people press to meet us,' he said nervously to a colleague, 'but not one sayeth God speed us.'[8]

Northumberland reached Cambridge on 14 July. His troops had already begun to desert him. Meanwhile men flocked to Mary's side at Framlingham, including the earls of Sussex, Bath and Oxford: power was ebbing swiftly away from Jane as Mary gathered her forces ready to face the battlefield. Four days later the Council in London had joined them and proclaimed Mary queen at Cheapside, amid scenes of jubilant rejoicing, 'what with shouting and crying of the people, and ringing of the bells'.[9] Hearing the news while he was still stationed at Cambridge, Northumberland rushed to follow, but the following day he was arrested and taken back to the capital a prisoner bound for the Tower.

So, too, was Robert. After he had failed to capture Mary and made the rash mistake of sacking Sawston Hall, he had ridden on into Norfolk where he had managed to assemble tenants and friends, not without some success. He had travelled to King's Lynn, where he had proclaimed Jane queen at the marketplace there with the support of the mayor and three hundred townsmen. Unfortunately, he had done so on the same day that the people in the capital were proclaiming Mary queen.

When news reached Norfolk of Mary's proclamation in London, Robert was arrested and taken to Mary's residence at Framlingham Castle, where he threw himself prostrate at the new queen's feet and begged for pardon. On 26 July 1553 he was taken to the Tower, where the cells were already overcrowded with the latest political prisoners, including his father, brothers, and the former queen, Jane Grey. At first, Robert was sent with his brother Guildford to the Bell Tower, before being placed in the Beauchamp Tower along with his other brothers, Ambrose, Henry and John.

# These beasts do well behold

On the morning of 22 August, Northumberland was executed upon the scaffold. The trial had been hastily arranged, the verdict was perhaps inevitable. After his sentence had been passed, the duke had begged for forgiveness, specifically requesting that Mary 'be gracious to my children, which may hereafter do her Grace good service, considering that they went by my commandment who am their father, and not of their own free wills.'[1] Once again, efforts to restore the Dudley name had begun; chief among those working on Robert's behalf was his mother, Jane, Duchess of Northumberland, who, after realising that her husband's execution was inevitable, was desperate to save her sons.

Before Northumberland faced death that summer morning, Robert and his brothers would be dealt one final humiliation: they were forced to witness their father take mass and receive the sacrament with the full Roman rite. 'Truly, I profess here before you all that I have received the sacrament according to the true Catholic faith,' Northumberland said after the ceremony, turning to his sons, 'the plague that is upon the realm and upon us now is that we have erred from the faith these sixteen years.'[2] Did Northumberland really believe his own words? He repeated as much on the scaffold; perhaps he thought it was a price worth paying if it meant that his sons would be saved. From their cell windows, the Dudley brothers would not have been able to witness their father's final moments. But they would have been able to view the return of his dismembered body, wheeled along in a wooden cart on its way to the chapel of St Peter ad Vincula, to be laid to rest alongside the remains of his old foe, the Duke of Somerset.

Now began perhaps the most difficult period of Robert Dudley's life. For eighteen months he remained imprisoned, not knowing whether his life would end there. His rank ensured that his stay was at least comfortable. At a time when prisoners were expected to pay for their incarceration, those with wealth were able to avoid the familiar terrors and squalor of the Tower. Receiving a stipend (£2 3s 4d a week) for their 'diet' and two servants each (13s 4d a week), they could purchase whatever food they liked and were allowed furniture, books, even pets. For exercise, they were allowed to walk on the flat lead roofs connecting the Beauchamp and Bell Towers. Robert may even have been able to visit the Tower menagerie that included a tiger, a lynx, a wolf, an eagle, porcupines and an old lion named Edward VI. He certainly seems to have developed an affection for the porcupines there, with his household accounts referring to the purchase of apples, bought 'at sundry times for the porpontyes'.[3]

To while away the hours of endless boredom during the winter nights, the Dudley brothers carved an elaborate memorial into the wall of their cell, featuring the family heraldic emblem of a bear alongside a ragged staff. It can clearly be seen there today. Beneath it they carved the verse:

> You that these beasts do well behold and see
> May deem with ease wherefore here made they be,
> With borders eke wherin there may be found
> Four brothers' names, who list to search the ground.

Within the border, Robert carved his own particular symbol into the wall: the oak spray that also featured in Lavinia Teerlinc's miniature, possibly commissioned to celebrate his marriage to Amy.

Not all freedoms were denied the brothers, for they were also granted permission to see their wives. A letter from the Privy Council to the Lieutenant of the Tower is more explicit: he was 'to permit these ladies following to have access unto their husbands, and there to tarry with them so long and at such times, as by him shall be thought meet; that is to say, the Lord Ambrose's wife, the Lord Robert's wife.'[4] It is the first mention we have of Amy since her marriage to Robert in June 1550. More than three years had passed since then; she was now a grown woman of 21. There is no evidence as to Amy's whereabouts during that period, though it is fair to suspect that she had been living with her husband in Somerset Place, observing his rise to power and perhaps occasionally attending court, right up until Edward VI's death.

It is striking, however, that there is no sign of any children born to the couple. In an age when infant mortality was high, this seems even more extraordinary. Since more than one in eight children died in their first year and only three-quarters of children survived past the age of ten, the role of most Tudor women was to give birth as often as possible. Robert Dudley had experienced the necessity of having a large family to counter what was considered inevitable; his own mother Jane Dudley had borne thirteen children, eight of whom had survived. The Privy Council letter implies that Robert and Amy were still believed to have a normal married life (or at least it gave them the freedom to continue doing so); the couple were hardly estranged at this time. The demands of court life might have meant that Robert would have spent precious little time with his wife, but this was often the case with courtiers, and did not prevent them fathering children; it had not stopped his father, after all.

The couple's childless marriage seemed unusual to others too. Cecil later took it as evidence of Dudley's unsuitability as a husband. Whereas other men had 'been blessed with multitudes of children', when assessing Robert's marriage to Amy, Cecil wrote simply *nuptiae steriles* – meaning 'sterile marriages' – to which he added the explanation: 'himself married, and no children'.

Mary's accession must have thrown Amy's married life into confusion. Previously she had been living a comfortable life married to the son of the most important man in the country. Now her father-in-law was dead, condemned to a traitor's death. At that moment she had last seen her husband Robert when he had departed for Norfolk in pursuit of Mary; now he was a prisoner in the Tower, likely awaiting the same fate as his father. Then there was her own security to consider. It was unlikely that Queen Mary would allow the wife of a man who had taken up arms against her to continue residing at Somerset House, one of her own royal residences. Amy found herself not only without a husband, but also without a home.

Fortunately, both Amy's parents were still alive. It was her mother's family who must have come to the rescue. Before she had married her first husband, Roger Appleyard, Amy's mother Elizabeth had lived in Camberwell with her family. Her father, John Scott, was an important member of the Inner Temple in London who had become the third Baron of the Exchequer in 1528. John died in 1532, though the family still owned a town house in Camberwell which Amy would later visit. While Robert remained in the Tower, Amy most likely stayed there, visiting her husband when occasion might demand, waiting anxiously to hear what his fate might be.

Though he had been imprisoned since his arrest in July, Robert Dudley was the last member of his family to be formally charged. Unlike his father and his brothers, he had not proclaimed Jane queen in the capital. His treasons had taken place in Norfolk, where it had taken some time to gather the evidence against him. A commission eventually held at Norwich found him guilty of possessing King's Lynn 'in warlike manner', where he had 'traitrously published and proclaimed to be Queen of this realm of England one Jane Dudley'. On 22 January 1554, having been conveyed through London on foot from the Tower, Robert was taken to the Guildhall, where a formal sentence of execution for treason was passed.[5]

# Common conditions

At court, events were moving fast, as the new queen planned the nation's restoration to the Catholic faith – much to Elizabeth's consternation. Elizabeth had returned to court on her sister's triumph; they rode into London together as a symbol of unity, and Elizabeth carried Mary's train at her coronation. Though their views may have differed on religion, Elizabeth believed implicitly in her sister's divine right to rule: unlike Jane, she recognised that her own place in the succession was dependent on her duty to obey.

But as the new regime began to return to papal obedience, privately the princess struggled to conform. She avoided going to mass until she was forced to in September 1553. The same month Thomas Cranmer, the former Archbishop of Canterbury, was arrested and placed in the Tower. Uncertainty and fear now reigned in the thoughts of most Protestants; Elizabeth was no exception. She asked to return to her estates for Christmas, rather than remain at court. Other Protestants had already fled the realm in exile, including Lady Catherine Knollys, the daughter of Anne Boleyn's sister, Mary. Elizabeth wrote to her cousin, wishing her farewell: 'think this pilgrimage rather a proof of your friends, than a leaving of your country.' She ended the letter not with her usual, ornate calligraphic signature, but instead with the Italian words, 'Cor Rotto' – Broken Heart.[1]

Elizabeth posed a significant problem for Mary. She was the obvious figurehead around which religious discontent might form. Mary also never forgot their bitter family history that had nearly destroyed her: Elizabeth would always remain the daughter of the woman who stole her father and ripped her family apart. Hiding her private emotions, she told the Spanish ambassador of the time, Simon Renard, that Elizabeth would become, like her mother, a woman 'who had caused great trouble in the Kingdom'.[2]

Although Elizabeth remained officially a bastard from the time when Henry had passed an Act of Parliament declaring Mary, as his daughter from his marriage to Catherine of Aragon, to be his legitimate heir,

Henry VIII's final will had at least guaranteed Elizabeth's rights as successor to the throne. Whatever the legitimacy of her status, Elizabeth remained a risk: better she be placed in the Tower, Renard had argued. Mary's Privy Council disagreed, pointing out that any such rebellious behaviour would be tempered by her choosing a husband who might not only take her hand in marriage, but, even better, take her out of the country altogether. Several names came to mind: Emmanuel Philibert, the Duke of Savoy, the Marquis of Baden and the Spanish Duke of Segorbe's son were all considered, though favourite among Mary's councillors was Edward Courtenay, the great-grandson of Edward IV and the last of the Yorkist line. Courtenay had languished in the Tower since he was twelve years old. On her accession, Mary released him from his imprisonment and granted him the title of the Earl of Devon. A Catholic from birth, it was thought that he might keep Elizabeth 'in the religion she now professed'. No one thought to consult Elizabeth on the matter. The idea was quickly dropped, however, when Mary's cousin, Emperor Charles V, expressed his opposition to the plans.

Mary also had her own marriage to consider. Upon becoming queen, she faced a dilemma. She had at once become God's divinely appointed monarch, the most powerful person in the realm. Yet, as a mortal woman, she would be expected to allow her husband to rule over her. It was a problem that reflected acutely Elizabeth's own predicament years later. Yet Mary chose to marry; for her husband, she picked the most powerful man in Christendom – Philip of Spain, the Emperor Charles V's son. It was an odd match. Philip (Felipe in Spanish) was 27; tall and athletic, he was in the prime of his life. Mary was eleven years older, and by now was short-sighted with few remaining teeth. According to one of Philip's ambassadors, she was 'not beautiful, small, flabby rather than fat'. But dynastic consideration always overrode the niceties of physical attraction, let alone love. Philip would take Mary as his bride; his duty to the Spanish nation and the Hapsburg dynasty demanded nothing less.

Mary's decision to return to Rome and marry a foreigner caused simmering discontent. In the middle of a freezing cold winter, Philip's cousin Count Egmont, who had arrived to complete the marriage negotiations, was pelted with snowballs as he rode through the capital. Robert Dudley's sentencing in fact took place on the eve of what was to become the largest rebellion of Mary's reign. Headed by Thomas Wyatt, the son of the poet who was reputed to be Anne Boleyn's lover, the rebels raised 3,000 men and marched on London. Wyatt's bizarre plan was to have Elizabeth and Courtenay married and both placed on the throne. When the Duke of Norfolk failed to stop the rebels at Rochester, the capital came under direct attack. Without the support of London's citizens, the rebellion fell apart, but not before Wyatt had reached Whitehall. For a while, the outcome hung in the balance. 'We shall all be destroyed this night,' cried one of Mary's ladies-in-waiting as an armed guard was assembled outside the queen's presence chamber.[3]

The rebellion proved even more serious than it first seemed. It had been planned for months, and had been supposed to take place on Palm Sunday. But gossip and rumour had seen the news leak out prematurely. The rebels, disorganised as they were, decided to strike before details of the plot were fully uncovered. One of the conspirators was none other than Lady Jane Grey's father, Henry, Duke of Suffolk. He fled northwards towards his home in Leicestershire, attempting to rally the people with the battle cry 'Resistance to the Spaniard!' It was met with little enthusiasm, for the marriage contract between Mary and Philip had by now been agreed, in which Philip would remain the queen's subordinate, accepting the limits placed upon him by her Council. This did not stop Suffolk issuing a proclamation against the royal marriage, highlighting the risk of foreign domination that it might bring. When Mary discovered Suffolk's involvement in the rebellion, she knew instantly what needed to be done. As the rebels drew closer to the capital and streetfighting broke out along Charing Cross, she signed the death warrants of both Jane and Guildford Dudley. Given the uncertainty of her present situation, they were, she considered, simply too dangerous to keep alive.

On the morning of 12 February, Robert Dudley embraced his brother Guildford for the last time. Taking place upon Tower Hill, his execution was out of sight from the brothers' cell, though they would have had a clear view of their sister-in-law's final moments as she mounted the scaffold outside the White Tower. There Jane prayed, handing to the Lieutenant of the Tower a small prayer book as a gift. On its flyleaf she had written an inscription: 'the day of death is better than the day of our birth'; she had signed her name 'Jane Dudley'.

In the end, the rebellion petered out; Wyatt's men were too exhausted to continue the fight. Perhaps news of the executions had finally broken their morale. They surrendered and were rounded up. For Robert Dudley, the spectre of the gallows loomed once more.

That spring, a lengthy list of prisoners arrested after the failed rebellion joined the Dudley brothers in the Tower. One of them was Elizabeth.

Evidence soon emerged that Thomas Wyatt had written to Elizabeth and Courtenay, informing them of his plans and stating that he wished to place them on the throne. These letters, however, had been intercepted, as had a letter from the French ambassador suggesting that Elizabeth knew of the plot. On the same day that Jane was executed, Elizabeth was summoned to London. The princess pleaded that she was ill with a headache which she 'had never felt the like'. For Elizabeth, the Tower brought its own separate terrors: it was here that her mother had met her death upon the block. Now her cousin Jane was dead; Elizabeth feared that she would be next.

Elizabeth's biographer, William Camden, believed that the strange and enduring bond that would later form between Elizabeth and Robert Dudley had been forged under the 'common conditions of Imprisonment under Queen Mary'. Ever since, there has been romantic speculation that they may have met in these shared confines, smuggled messages to one another, caught the occasional glimpse of each other through barred windows as one or the other passed in the courtyard below. This is unlikely. Though Elizabeth had been placed in the upper chamber of the Bell Tower, barely a few yards from Dudley's cell, she was also under the strictest security, being guarded by five armed attendants at all times. Even a 4-year-old boy, one of the sons of the wardens, who had the temerity to present the royal prisoner with a small bouquet of flowers, was warned that he would be whipped if he ever approached her again.

Besides, Elizabeth spent only two months at the Tower, between mid-March and mid-May. During this time, her fate hung in the balance. Many, including the Spanish ambassador and Stephen Gardiner, the Archbishop of Winchester and Mary's chancellor, agreed that she should die along with Courtenay. 'It seems to me that she ought not to spare [either], for while they are alive there will always be plots to raise them to the throne and it would be just to punish them, as it is publicly known that they are guilty and so deserve death.'[4]

Upon examination, Elizabeth denied everything. She had heard nothing about Wyatt's uprising, she claimed. She declared her full allegiance to her sister Mary, just as she affirmed that she would always remain a loyal Catholic. It was not the truth, but it was enough to secure her her freedom. On 19 May she was freed from the Tower.

Five months after Elizabeth's release, Robert Dudley was also freed. Freedom, however, came at a human cost. By October, it was clear that the eldest of the brothers, John, weakened by a prolonged illness, was dying. Out of compassion, Mary granted the release of the three brothers on 18 October 1554.[5] Three days later, John was dead.

A few months after their release, the Dudley brothers were pardoned.[6] On the same day, their mother Jane, Duchess of Northumberland, died. The pardon of her three surviving sons was the fulfilment of her dying wish. She had fought tirelessly to save them, first from the scaffold and then to secure their rehabilitation at court. In her will, written in her own hand, she thanked those who had helped her to make 'so many friends about the King's Majesty'; to those who had 'did her Sons Good' she beseeched them 'for God's sake to continue to be Good Lords to her Sons'.[7]

The duchess's hopes came true. That winter, both Robert and Ambrose were back at court, taking part in a tournament in which they headed the list of defenders against the Spanish lords who had accompanied Philip overseas.[8] Yet suspicion surrounding the Dudleys remained, and in the summer of 1555 they were ordered to leave London during Mary's confinement. But by late 1555, Dudley had joined Philip's own entourage on the Continent, and was given the trusted task of delivering both the king's diplomatic and personal letters, including one personal letter to Mary herself. Their attainders remained in place, however, meaning that the three surviving Dudley sons were unable to inherit the property decreed to them by their mother in her will, including the manor of Hales Owen in Worcestershire, left to the eldest surviving brother, Ambrose. In an act of somewhat unusual generosity, Mary waived her right to confiscate Hales Owen for the Crown, and allowed Ambrose to inherit the manor, in spite of his attainder.[9] Still, there was nothing for Robert. Sir John Robsart, Amy's father, had died in June 1554. Dudley and his wife might have expected to gain something from Sir John's estate, yet under the terms of the marriage settlement, the Robsart estate – the Norfolk manors of Syderstone, Bircham Newton and Great Bircham, and the Suffolk manor of Bulkham – would descend to Dudley and Amy only after the deaths of both Sir John and his wife Elizabeth.

With neither lands to his name nor a home to reside in after the confiscation of his estate by the Crown, Dudley was destitute, until his elder brother Ambrose came to his rescue. In November 1555, it was agreed between the brothers that Robert, having been 'left with nothing to live by and having most need of friendly and brotherly love', could inherit Hales Owen in return for settling his mother's debts and payments to Lord Ambrose of £800 and to his uncle, Sir Andrew Dudley, of £300.[10] One of the attorneys involved in the transaction was a former leading household officer of his father's, Thomas Blount of Kidderminster, who became chief steward of the manor. Assiduous and hardworking, he would remain a faithful and trusted servant to Dudley.[11]

Obtaining Hales Owen proved to be a turning point for Dudley. The value of the land would provide enough capital for future loans and mortgages, and even though Dudley never lived there, let alone made any visit to the manor, he was proud to style himself 'Lord Dudley of Halesowen'.[12] Yet he continued to struggle. Even with a piece of land to call his own, meeting the simple debts of his deceased mother proved a problem. In December 1556 Dudley had to enter into a bond of £20 with Thomas Borrowe, a London gentleman, just in order to pay off one of her outstanding apothecary's bills of £5.[13]

## ➤ 9 ◀

# Anatomies of hearts

Philip II of Spain arrived on the shores at Southampton in July 1554. Five days later he and Mary were married. Whereas Mary soon fell in love with her attractive husband and everything that he stood for, Philip was in no doubt as to the purpose of their union. An heir that would unite the realms of England and Spain would become one of the most powerful princes in Christendom. That, after all, was the point of a royal marriage. But at 39, time was running out for the queen. 'If God is pleased to grant her a safe delivery,' the Spanish ambassador told the Emperor Charles V, 'things will take a turn for the better. If not, I forsee disturbance and a change for the worse on so great a scale that the pen can hardly set it down.'[1]

Mary soon became pregnant. For months the court prepared for the birth. A cradle 'very sumptuously and gorgeously trimmed' sat in the queen's bedchamber, and letters in French were sent to ambassadors abroad, ready to immediately announce the event. To counter for that one uncertainty – the sex of the child – a short space was left after the word *fil* in the unfortunate event that '*fille*' might have to be inserted instead. On 30 April it was announced that Mary had given birth. In celebration, bells were rung and bonfires lit. But the announcement was false: there was no child. Nor would there ever be one.

Mary had all the symptoms of being pregnant. She had ceased to menstruate and her abdomen and breasts had become swollen, but these were more likely to have been the signs of the ovarian dropsy which had affected her her whole adult life. In her desperation, Mary and her doctors had chosen to believe in the illusion of pregnancy rather than face reality.

She continued to cling to the hope that she might still become pregnant. Mary's grandmother Isabella had, after all, given birth to her mother Catherine when she was 34. Philip, however, had grown impatient with his ageing wife. He could wait no longer, he told her. Other countries in the empire needed his attention and he would have to leave England by August. Mary was distraught. Spending hours in silence, sitting on cushions on the floor with her knees drawn up beneath her chin, she stared blankly into the distance. She had failed as a woman, she must have thought; she had failed as a queen. Now she was about to lose the man she loved.

After she had been released from the Tower, Elizabeth had been sent to Oxfordshire, to the home of Sir Henry Bedingfield in Woodstock. She remained essentially a prisoner. One day, watching Bedingfield unlock six pairs of gates before locking them once again behind her, she told him that he was nothing more than a common gaoler. He denied it; he was merely doing his duty, he said. But Elizabeth was a prisoner none-theless. On the window pane in her chamber, with a diamond she scratched the words:

> Much suspected, by me
>> Nothing proved can be,
>>> Quoth Elizabeth, Prisoner.

Elizabeth eventually returned to her house at Hatfield. Sequestered under house arrest, she witnessed for herself the fall-out from her sister's decision to choose a foreign king as her husband. There was other news to be faced, too. Mary and her ministers had embarked upon a policy of persecution of English Protestants. As the burnings intensified, including those of Thomas Cranmer and her brother Edward's favourite preacher, Hugh Latimer, Mary's regime grew increasingly unpopular. Those who had perished in the flames were held as martyrs to their cause. For her part, Mary earned the epithet of 'bloody Mary'.

Elizabeth now faced a new, entirely different threat. Since Mary's false pregnancy, attention turned to the question of who would inherit her throne. 'As there is no hope of fruit from the English marriage,' one ambassador wrote, 'discussions are going on everywhere about the consort to be given to Elizabeth, who is and will continue to be lawful heir unless the king and queen have issue.'[2] The princess remained a magnet for discontent and sedition. In August 1556, an impostor named Cleobury, pretending to be Courtenay, proclaimed Elizabeth queen and her 'beloved bedfellow' king. Mindful of Jane's treatment, Elizabeth wrote hastily to her sister, expressing her devout loyalty and sorrow that her name had once more been used in a plot of which she had no knowledge. If surgeons could make 'anatomies of hearts', she said, she wished that the queen could see fully into hers, 'like as I have been your faithful subject from the beginning of your reign, so shall no wicked person cause me to change to the end of my life'.[3]

Philip also seems to have done everything in his power to restore relations between his wife and her sister. When Courtenay died in suspicious circumstances in exile in Padua in September 1556, the way was opened up for Elizabeth to marry a foreigner as her husband of choice. Philip had exactly the candidate in mind; he was determined that, as part of a foreign alliance that he wished to enter into, the princess should marry his cousin Emmanuel Philibert, Prince of Piedmont and the Duke of Savoy.[4] In an attempt to please her husband, Mary invited Elizabeth to court and beseeched her to marry Philibert, although she insisted that any marriage would have to be passed before Parliament (something Philip was deeply unhappy about, knowing that most Englishmen opposed any attempt to marry the heiress to the throne to a foreigner).[5]

The suit failed to materialise, however, as Elizabeth refused; but this did not prevent further interest in her hand in marriage among the courts of Europe and beyond. The princess was, after all, as Francis Walsingham aptly termed it, 'the best marriage in her parish'. In November 1557, King Gustavus of Sweden sent an envoy in an attempt to marry his son Eric to Elizabeth, presenting his suit directly to Elizabeth rather than the queen. Mary was furious at such an affront, and only calmed down when she had heard that her sister had rejected his suit since she 'had never heard of his Majesty before this time'. Nevertheless, Mary remained suspicious, and decided to send Sir Thomas Pope to Hatfield to understand Elizabeth's intentions better. Elizabeth stuck to her word. When Pope suggested to her that he 'thought few or none would believe but that her Grace would be right well content to marry so there were some honourable marriage offered her', she replied: 'Upon my truth and fidelity, and as God be merciful unto me, I am not at this time minded otherwise than I have declared unto you; no, though I were offered the greatest prince in all Europe.' When it came to Eric of Sweden's suit for marriage, she hoped that, though she had 'so well liked the message and the messenger ... from henceforth I never hear of one nor the other'.[6] The hope was to be in vain.

# Not being altogether in quiet

Mr Flowerdew,

I understand by Gryse that you put him in remembrance of that you spake to me of, concerning the going of certain sheep at Siderstern; and although I forgot to move my lord thereof before his departing, he being sore troubled with weighty affairs, and I not being altogether in quiet for his sudden departing, yet, notwithstanding, knowing your accustomed friendship towards my lord and me, I neither may nor can deny you that request, in my lord's absence, of mine own authority, yea and [if] it were a greater matter, as if any good occasion may serve you to try me; desiring you further that you will make sale of the wool so soon as is possible, although you sell it for VI s. the stone, or as you would sell for yourself; for my lord so justly required me, at his departing, to see those poor men satisfied, as though it had been a matter depending on life; wherefore I force not to sustain a little loss thereby to satisfy my lord's desire, and so to send that money to Gryse's house to London, by Bridewell, to whom my lord hath given order for the payment thereof. And thus I end, always troubling you, wishing that occasion may serve me to requite you, until that time I must pay you with thanks; and so to God I leave you.

From Mr Hyde's, this vii of August,
Yours assured, during life,

Amye Duddley.[1]

Until now Amy has been a silent figure in our story, a name with no voice. For the first time, through her own words, she begins to come to life.

On first reading, the subject of Amy's letter is admittedly quite plain. It is addressed to a 'Mr Flowerdew', no doubt John Flowerdew, the steward of Dudley's estates in Norfolk, and probably a relation of Amy's through marriage, concerning the sale of wool from the sheep at Syderstone. It seems that there were servants and shepherds there who needed paying; Amy had spoken previously with Flowerdew about the situation,

in standing I understand by this y[a]t you put
hym in remembrance of y[a]t you spake to me of
consernyng the doyng of sertayne thing[es] at syfforne
althow I forgat to move my lorde therof before
his departyng he beyng sore trubled w[i]th waighty
affaires & I not beyng all together in quiet for
his soden departyng yet not w[i]th standyng knowing
your accostomed fryndshype towardes my lorde
& me ~~................~~ I nether may nor
can deny you y[e] requeste in my lordes absence
of myne owne autoryte y[e] & it war a gretar
matter as if any good occasyon may serve you so
trye me desyryng you furder y[a]t you will make
salle of y[e] wolle so sone as yt possible althow
you sell yt for vid the stone or as you wolde
sell for your self for my lorde so ernestly
required me at his departyng to se those por
men satysfyed as thow yt had bene a matter
dependyng upon lyff wherfore I force not to
sustayne a little loss therby to satysfye my
lordes desyre & so to send yt mony to
grysses hows to london by tryd will be
whom my lorde hathe geven order for
the payment therof & thus I ende att this
tyme desyryng you w[i]shyng y[e] occasyon may
I must pray you w[i]th all y[e] tymes
I leve you from m[y] hayden this xij of
August

Amy Dudley

                    your assured duryng
                    lyff Amy Duddley

and had promised to mention it to her husband. Dudley, however, had been forced to depart suddenly, and Amy had forgotten to speak with him. Having now been informed by 'Gryce', probably William Grice of Great Yarmouth, who had been acting as Dudley's attorney since March 1556, that Flowerdew had been pressing for an answer, in order to settle the debts, Amy urged Flowerdew to sell wool from sheep at Syderstone at whatever price, even if it is at a loss, so that the men might be paid.

These are the basic details of its contents. Yet the letter provides us with much more information than this. Firstly, it reveals that Amy was given some control of the running of the estate; she was able to make decisions 'of mine own authority' in her husband's absence. She was also in touch with the estate managers concerning matters of payment; Amy writes how John Flowerdew had already 'spake' with her about the sheep at Syderstone. Her business sense is perhaps to be wondered at, and might suggest an inexperience in these matters – her generous orders to Flowerdew to sell the wool at whatever price 'as you would sell for yourself' to ensure that the 'poor men' were paid as soon as possible are certainly in contrast to her husband, who later instructed Flowerdew to make improvements to the sheep-pens there, and to remove 'such servants or shepherds as be unmeet to have charge there, even in such sort as any way I would or should do myself'.

Nevertheless, it was unusual for a wife to have much influence over the financial running of an estate. Once marriages had been made, the wife was subordinate to her husband's rule. 'The wife is so much in the power of her husband,' wrote Sir Thomas Smith, 'that her goods by marriage are straight made her husband's, and she loseth all her administration which she had of them.'[2] Thomas Cranmer's *Homily on Marriage* insisted that 'the woman is a weak creature not endued with like strength and constancy of mind; therefore ... they be the more prone to all weak affections and dispositions of mind, more than men be'.[3] Women were to obey their husbands' command because 'the husband hath the preeminence and is master and ruler of his wife', another marriage guide counselled.[4]

Amy's letter reveals that she was in fact no exception. The conventional sense and tone of her language illustrates that she considered herself a traditional wife, bound to obey her husband's wishes. She describes her husband Robert as her 'lord' from whom she would take orders; indeed she had written to Flowerdew principally 'to satisfy my lord's desire'. When Dudley 'justly required' her to arrange for several debts to be paid, we get a sense of the urgency with which he treated his wife; his orders were, Amy recalled, 'as though it had been a matter depending upon life'. Amy was ever the part of the obedient wife, even if it meant that she might 'sustain a little loss'.

Leaving aside Amy's duty-bound obedience to her husband or her 'lord', one can almost get a sense of her personality from her letter; Dudley's sudden departure had clearly left her somewhat disturbed, as Amy mentions, 'not being altogether in quiet for his sudden departing', while there is something almost pathetic in Amy's apologetic tone in her letter to Flowerdew, 'thus I end, always troubling you'. Her signature too seems faint and scratched compared to the text of the letter, and her black pen marks, scrawling through parts of the letter where she had changed her mind about what she had written, indicate a certain hesitation and care in choosing her words. Amy's neat calligraphic handwriting suggests that she had been well-educated, though one can perhaps detect her Norfolk accent in the phonetic spelling of her words, such as 'undarstand', 'fryndshyppe' or 'trobelyng'.

Traditionally, historians have suggested that Amy's letter was written in 1559, after Elizabeth's accession. Eager to read Amy's vexed comments that she was not 'altogether in quiet' for Dudley's 'sudden departing' as evidence that she had been abandoned by her husband, they have been tempted to place the particular date of Amy's letter, 7 August, in that year – when Dudley was at the Earl of Arundel's home at Nonsuch Palace in Surrey with the court, and where Elizabeth was the guest of honour at a lavish banquet.

These were not, however, the 'weighty affairs' that Dudley had been 'sore troubled with'. The letter was in fact written two years earlier, in the summer of 1557, and refers not to Dudley's departure for court, but his departure across the Channel: for in August 1557 he went to fight the the French on behalf of Philip II of Spain, in the force led by the Earl of Pembroke at the siege of St Quentin. Dudley's departure to France for an indefinite period of time would also indicate why Amy had been tasked with dealing with estate matters normally reserved for her husband, who could have easily handled the business himself if he had merely departed from Hyde's to London. It further explains Dudley's desire to see his debts and any outstanding wages paid, 'as though it had been a matter depending on life'. Indeed, Dudley and Amy both knew that he might not come back alive.

# Rehabilitation

Since his pardon, Robert Dudley had worked hard to regain favour at court. He had done so principally through the queen's new husband, Philip of Spain, with whom he had ingratiated himself, becoming a member of his gentlemen pensioners, tasked with carrying out royal duties. Dudley seems to have made many friends among his Spanish counterparts, whose portraits still hung on the walls of his castle at Kenilworth many years later.[1] Spanish friends included the Duke of Medinaceli, the Principal Gentleman of the Bedchamber, and Don Diego de Mendoza, men who had worked with Dudley's mother Jane to secure her sons' release. She remembered them with gratitude in her will as those who 'did [her] Sons Good', beseeching them 'for God's sake to continue [to be] Good Lords to my sons in their needs'.[2]

As his career progressed, there was less time for Dudley to visit his wife. For a large part of 1556, Dudley seems to have been abroad, having travelled to Calais to inspect its fortifications, as part of a team led by the Earl of Pembroke. He is next heard of in March 1557, 'having been beyond the sea with King Philip', bringing news to Queen Mary that her beloved husband was once more to return, on what would prove to be his final visit to England.[3]

Amy and Robert had been married for some time now. They had recently celebrated their seventh wedding anniversary. Although they remained childless, they were still both young at 25 – the age when most couples would be considering marriage – and there was every chance that children might yet be forthcoming. We know little of Amy's life during this period, though contemporary accounts of the activities of women from her background suggest that she would have spent most of her time at leisure. 'Although the women there are entirely in the power of their husbands except for their lives,' wrote Emanuel van Meteren, a Netherlander visiting England,

> yet they are not kept so strictly as they are in Spain or elsewhere. Nor
> are they shut up, but they have the free management of the house or

housekeeping ... They go to market to buy what they like best to eat. They are well dressed, fond of taking it easy, and commonly leave the care of household matters and drudgery to their servants. They sit before their doors, decked out in fine clothes, in order to see and be seen by the passers-by ... All the rest of their time they employ in walking and riding, in playing at cards or otherwise, in visiting their friends and keeping company, conversing with their equals (whom they term 'gossips') and their neighbours, and making merry with them at childbirths, christenings, church-ings, and funerals; and all this with the permission and knowledge of their husbands, as such is the custom ... This is why England is called 'The Paradise of Married Women'.[4]

There is little to suggest that Amy's life would have been any different. Certainly if later payments made by Dudley to his wife that survive in his household accounts are able to reveal anything, it suggests that Amy spent much of her time amusing herself with the latest fashions, buying jewellery, ribbon, silks, shoes and other personal items such as a looking glass, and visiting relations in London.

Amy's letter to Flowerdew gives us an important clue as to her where-abouts during this period, for it is signed 'from Mr Hyde's'. Since the mid-nineteenth century, historians have mistaken 'Mr Hyde' as being William Hyde the younger, of South Denchworth, Berkshire. As Dench-worth was only a few miles away from Cumnor Place, where Amy would eventually come to reside at some point during early 1560, it seemed only natural that she had travelled the short distance from William Hyde's house. When a Berkshire antiquary discovered that a Mrs Odingsell, one of Amy's companions at Cumnor, was the sister of William Hyde of Denchworth, it became generally accepted as fact that Amy had been staying at Denchworth.[5]

Except that she had not. We now know that Amy had been residing at the home of William Hyde of Throcking, an isolated hamlet in the north-east of Hertfordshire. There is more than enough evidence to prove this. Dudley's accounts reveal that when he journeyed up to visit Amy in 1559, he stopped off at Waltham, Ware, and finally at Buntingford, the usual stopping-off points for a journey into Hert-fordshire, but none of these towns is anywhere near Denchworth. A later manuscript confirms this. Stating that Dudley 'left her first at Hydes house in Hertfordshire', it becomes clear that this is the William Hyde in question. It is perhaps no surprise that twenty years later, when William Hyde of Throcking came to make his will, he named Dudley, 'my singular good lord', as its overseer. He even named one of his daughters, somewhat unusually for a girl, Dudley.[6]

Midway between London and the Robsart estate in Norfolk, Throcking was a convenient base for Amy to stay. It was set in just over 1,000 acres of arable and grass-land, with very little surrounding woodland, and it seems that she resided there periodically for at least two years, between 1557 and mid-1559. There were only eight inhabitants living in Throcking in the fifteenth century, and the population does not seem to have grown much during the sixteenth century. The Hyde family had owned the manor since 1395. William Hyde had been Lord of the Manor since 1553, when he had inherited it from his grandfather George Hyde.[7] According to George's will, drawn up in 1549, there was a mansion house at Throcking until it was probably demolished in the late seventeenth century. It must have been here that Amy stayed; according to the authors of the Victoria County History of Hertford, 'the foundations of the old house may still be traced in a meadow called the Pightle, which lies to the south of the church. There are the remains of an old brick wall, and a deep depression in the ground appears to denote the position of the cellars. Near by is a moat, which probably ran round the house.' The house must have been fairly impressive, and sat next to the small thirteenth-century Holy Trinity Church, to which Amy would have easily been able to walk to attend services; indeed 'traces of a path which led from the house to the south porch of the church are also to be found'.[8] The church had been extensively rebuilt in the fifteenth century; more recently its wall paintings, including a crucifixion scene featuring three painted red crosses between four and six feet high and contained within circles, had been whitewashed over, a sign that the Reformation had reached the village.[9]

While Amy resided at Hyde's 'mansion house' at Throcking, Dudley spent most of his time at court. He lived either at his uncle Sir Andrew Dudley's home in Tothill Street, Westminster, or in the grand mansion of Christchurch by St Bartholomew the Grand, which belonged to Margaret, the wife of his recently deceased brother, Lord Henry Dudley, and the daughter of Henry VIII's former chancellor, Thomas Audley. The second location seems more likely: it was to Christchurch that he had books delivered in 1557, and later, in 1559, he arranged for some of his belongings to be removed from there.[10] Amy may have also stayed there from time to time, for the couple were certainly together when they both signed a legal document for the sale of some land in March 1558.[11]

The location of Hyde's house in Throcking, so close to Elizabeth's residence at Hatfield does, however, raise some interesting questions about Dudley's relationship with Elizabeth during this period. No direct evidence survives of any contact that they might have had with each other though the seventeenth-century historian Gregorio Leti tells a story of how Dudley sent Elizabeth a gift of £200, delivered by a lady to the princess at Hatfield, together with a note of devotion and assurance, which pledged that he 'would willingly lose his life if that would be of any service to her or procure her liberty'.[12]

Leti, who was in the custom of creating his own tales when it suited him, has frequently been dismissed by historians who have found no other evidence of Dudley's generosity. This is unfair. In 1561, the scholar and diplomat Hubert Languet recalled that Elizabeth told him that she was more attached to Dudley than anyone else, since 'when she was deserted by everybody in the reign of her sister not only did he never lessen in any degree his kindness and humble attention to her, but he even sold his possessions that he might assist her with money, and therefore she thought it just that she should make some return for his good faith and constancy.'[13] And a year later, Elizabeth's jeweller John Dymock, upon travelling to the Swedish court, recalled a meeting that he had with the Swedish King Eric:

> The king asked me what the cause was that my L Robert is so much in favour, whereunto I said, because I understood that he had served her majesty in time that she was but Lady Elizabeth, in her trouble he did sell away (as I had heard say) a good piece of his land to aid her, which was the cause and divers supposed that she did so much favour him now.[14]

Elizabeth was certainly in financial difficulty during this period; the Venetian ambassador, writing in May 1557, observed that Elizabeth, starved of an allowance by Mary, was constantly in debt and could barely afford to keep herself in the dignity that her office demanded. 'It seems strange and vexatious to everybody that being the daughter of a king she should be treated and acknowledged so sparingly,' he observed.[15] If Dudley had made an offer of money and support, it would certainly have been a welcome one.

It scarcely seems conceivable, however, that Dudley would have been able to afford to send Elizabeth such as vast sum as £200. Dudley also had existing obligations: he owed his brother Ambrose £800, Henry £300 and he was committed to paying his sister Catherine a stipend of 50 marks a year, as set out in his late mother's will. But in the spring of 1557 there was a stroke of good fortune; his mother-in-law Lady Elizabeth died, leaving the couple in full possession of her family estate at Syderstone.[16]

There were instant gains to be made from the quick sale of parts of the estate. On 30 May Dudley sold the manor of Bulkham in Suffolk to Robert Armiger of Hollesley for £500. The estate sale included '16 messuages (dwellings), 16 tofts, 16 cottages, 400 acres of land, 100 acres of meadow, 100 acres of pasture, 40 acres of wood, 400 acres of broom and heath, 40 acres of alder grove, 100 acres of marsh' together with 40s worth of rents.[17]

The death of Amy's mother saw a dramatic transformation in Dudley's finances. But it was still not enough to fund his increasingly expensive lifestyle. In the spring of 1557, Dudley took out mortgages on parts of Hales Owen in order to pay off his earlier debts, and to fund new, as yet unspecified, projects. In May 1557, he also borrowed heavily from London merchants, to the sum of £740.[18] By July, Dudley was forced to mortgage the whole of Hales Owen to Anthony Forster in return for loans totalling £1,928 6s 8d.

Forster then allowed Dudley to lease the manor off him. A gentleman with a reputation for honesty, Forster was a close associate and friend of the Dudley family, and would later become one of Dudley's 'men of business', acting as his auditor and eventually comptroller. He was also well connected; his wife was the daughter of the brother of Lord Williams of Thame, and he would go on to become MP for Abingdon from 1566 to 1572. According to the Latin inscription on his tomb, 'he knew how to strike the . . . lyre, rejoiced to settle young plants in the earth and with remarkable skill to build noble houses'. It seems certain that Forster was entering into the transaction out of goodwill; he had no personal interest in the lands in Norfolk, as he lived in Berkshire. Indeed, he had recently secured a lease on Cumnor Place, the medieval manor house 5 miles outside Oxford that he would later offer as a place for Dudley's wife Amy to stay.[19]

Dudley's financial activities were not confined merely to repaying his debts. He was keen to make his name and earn honour on the battlefield, and the planned campaign to St Quentin in France seemed the perfect opportunity. The remortgaging of Hales Owen and the money raised appears to have funded his own company of men for the campaign, with his coat and conduct money paid from Hales Owen.[20] Yet Dudley's hopes of leading his own troops into battle were quickly cut short. Having paid for the equipment of forty men, only five turned up for the muster, and Dudley was forced instead to accept an appointment as Master of the Ordnance to the Earl of Pembroke, the leader of the expeditionary force.[21] The position was an unusually high rank for someone of Dudley's relative youth. His brothers Ambrose and Henry travelled with him, as part of a force totalling some 6,000 men.

The fighting was some of the fiercest ever seen by English troops. 'For my part,' wrote the Earl of Bedford, 'I have not seen the like in all my life.'[22] It was during the siege of the town of St Quentin that, before Robert Dudley's 'own eyes', his brother Lord Henry was killed on 27 September 1557. According to *Holinshed's Chronicle*, Henry had paused to adjust his horse and was killed outright by a cannon shot. Henry's sacrifice was enough to convince Mary of the Dudley brothers' dedication. During the Parliament of 1558 she granted one more display of royal generosity and reversed their attainders.[23] This restored the full rights of inheritance to Northumberland's surviving sons and allowed them to inherit their mother's property.

On Dudley's return to England, the final inheritance of the Robsart estate following his mother-in-law's death that winter prompted him seriously to address his finances. This was no doubt behind his decision to sell Hales Owen, first to his associates Thomas Blount and George Tuckey in March 1558 for £3,000 – a fictitious sale, designed to raise the necessary capital to repay Anthony Forster while seeming to go through the formal procedures.[24] The property was eventually sold later in October to John Lyttleton, a distant relative of Dudley's whose lands bordered the Hales Owen estate, for £2,000.[25]

Dudley's financial position was now comfortable, yet he and his wife still had no house to live in. The manor house at Syderstone was a ruin, as it had been when Sir John Robsart inherited it. Instead, he had chosen to live at Stanfield Hall, the house that his wife Elizabeth had inherited from her first marriage to Nicholas Appleyard. On Elizabeth's death, this passed to her son and Amy's half-brother, John Appleyard.

Dudley now faced the same problem, owning significant amounts of land in Norfolk, yet without a family home that he might consider his own. 'I must, if to dwell in that country, take some house other than mine own,' he wrote to John Flowerdew, 'for it were wanteth all such chief commodities as a house requireth, which is, pasture, wood, water & c.' By July 1558, he was looking to purchase the manor of Flitcham, nearby to the Robsart estate, making arrangements with John Flowerdew to survey the property and land. It seems that Dudley still hoped to establish himself as a great Norfolk landowner, with a family estate and wife settled firmly in the county, instead of the less than ideal peripatetic nature of his and Amy's current lifestyle. He could hardly have realised how, in less than six months' time, his life would undergo a sudden change.

# 12

# Men dismayed

When Mary Tudor rode into London in August 1553, making her first entry as queen, the streets were 'so full of people shouting and crying "Jesus save her Grace", with weeping tears for joy ... the like was never seen before'.[1] By 1558, those days were long in the memory. Now even the stones seemed to turn against her. When a mysterious voice was heard behind a wall in the capital, it praised Princess Elizabeth as the country's future queen. Over 10,000 people gathered outside, only to be dispersed when members of the Council turned up to restore order. Behind the wall a young woman was eventually discovered, and, forced to confess her crime, she was set upon the pillory several months later as an example for all to view.

The number of men and women punished by Mary's Council for speaking 'horrible lies and seditious words against the Queen's majesty' had risen sharply. Yet such punishments had little effect. There were persistent rumours that Edward VI had not really died, that he would rise up and one day claim the throne from his detested sister. In an attempt to quash them, Mary sent letters to all her justices across the realm with orders to 'use all the best means and ways ye can, in the diligent examining and searching out, from Man to Man, the Authors and Publishers of these vain Prophesies, and untrue Bruits, the very foundation of all Rebellions'. The fires at Smithfield blazed more fiercely than before as the burnings of Protestant martyrs continued, but they could not prevent the spread of that particular heresy. Philip and his Spanish colleagues were alarmed at the severity of the policy; one Spanish cleric even preached a sermon at court, urging the queen to cease the persecution. But Mary refused. It was not that she was a cruel or vindictive person – all the evidence as to her character points to the contrary – but Mary viewed herself as the saviour of men's souls. By punishing the heretics, she believed, she was saving them and her people from eternal damnation. Few others saw it that way.

Mary's problems extended overseas too. Despite routing the French at the siege of St Quentin, Philip disbanded his army for the winter soon afterwards. The French reoccupied the territory, and continued to press forward. On 7 January 1558, Calais was lost. It had been in English hands for over two hundred years, and its strategic and economic importance could not be overestimated. The English soldiers who had fought abroad were devastated. 'They went to the wars hanging down their looks,' Sir Thomas Smith recalled. 'They came from thence as men dismayed and forlorn.'[2] The defeat led to fresh animosity between the English and the Spanish, who were blamed for not coming to the aid of the stricken port. The chronicler Holinshed, writing twenty years later, recalled Mary's aggrieved words when she discovered the news: 'When I am dead and opened, you will find Calais lying in my heart.'

After Philip's departure, Mary fell into a depression. She knew she was dying; at 42, she was seriously ill, probably with ovarian cancer. Attention had already turned to the woman people expected to become their new queen: Elizabeth. 'There is not a heretic or traitor in all the kingdom,' the Spanish ambassador Feria wrote to Mary's husband Philip in Spain, 'who has not joyfully raised himself from the grave to come to her [Elizabeth's] side.' Feria considered the whole situation a disaster. 'Four years ago your Majesty could have disposed of Madam Elizabeth by marrying her off to someone of your own choosing. Now she will marry whomsoever she desires and your Majesty has no power to influence her decision ... Madam Elizabeth already sees herself as the next Queen ... It is impossible to persuade her otherwise than that the kingdom will not consent to anything else, and would take up arms on her behalf.'

Along with his letter, Feria also included a list of the men whom he considered would rise to prominence under the new regime, now that it seemed inevitable. They included William Cecil, almost certain to be appointed Secretary of State, the Earl of Bedford, Sir Nicholas Throckmorton and John Harington, a former servant of Sir Thomas Seymour. Among them, there was another, more familiar name: Lord Robert Dudley.

# PART TWO

>-<

God sent us our Elizabeth

# 13

# A passing

There was nothing remarkable about the queen's death. As the November morning dawned across the parks of St James's Palace, it began as every day in her life had done, with Mary hearing mass. '*Misere nobis, Misere nobis, Dona nobis pacem,*' she responded frailly from her bed, to the priest who conducted the Latin ceremony. He took the sacrament in his hands, but Mary's thoughts were elsewhere and she seemed 'to meditate something with herself' as she drifted in and out of sleep. Suddenly, at the Elevation of the Host, the climax of the ceremony, she re-awoke. 'She adored it with her voice and countenance,' remembered one of her gentlewomen, and 'presently closed her eyes and rendered her blessed soul to God'. As Mary lapsed finally into unconsciousness, no one noticed her passing. Those present at her bedside 'thought her better, and that she would fain sleep'. The attendant doctor knew otherwise, recognising that she had 'made her passage'. He alone had witnessed the fleeting change from life into death, and the imperceptible transition from the reign of one queen to another.

For weeks Mary had lain dying in her bed, too weak even to read what was to be the last letter from her absent husband, King Philip II. Responding with a mere smile, all she could do was send a ring, as a pledge of her loyalty and love.[1] Those nearby observed her 'much sighing' and believed that she was dying as a result of 'thought and sorrow' rather than any disease. Seeing her gentlewomen sobbing as her condition deteriorated, Mary had attempted to offer them comfort, telling them 'what good dreams she had, seeing many little children like angels playing before her, singing pleasing notes, giving her more than earthly comfort'. Whatever happened, she told them, they should know that God would 'in mercy turn all to the best'. Those who were prepared to listen to the queen's words were few, for only the queen's most loyal servants remained in attendance. Once she had taken to her bed, all assumed that she would never leave it.

For many, there was already a new queen to worship – Elizabeth. Courtiers flocked from Mary's court to pay their respects to the woman they knew would be their future queen. The crowds on the road to Elizabeth's residence at Hatfield grew, 'constantly increasing with great frequency'.[2] Of those travelling to Hatfield to pay their respects to the queen-in-waiting, one was the Spanish ambassador, Feria. 'It appears to me that she is a woman of extreme vanity,' he wrote to Philip after a bruising encounter with the young princess, when she told him that she owed nothing of her good fortune, as the ambassador had claimed, to his supposed assistance. 'She seems greatly to admire her father's system of government. I fear that in religion she will not go right, as she seems inclined to favour men who are supposed to be heretics, and they tell me the ladies who are about her are all so. She appears highly indignant at the things that have been done against her during her sister's reign.' Observing how Elizabeth 'seems to me incomparably more feared than her sister and gives her orders and has her way as absolutely as her father did,' Feria was certain of one thing: 'She is determined to be governed by no one.'

The ambassador could have had no idea of just how far Elizabeth intended to depart from the policies of her sister's reign. Elizabeth knew secretly that under her own regime, Mary's attempts to return to Rome and restore the Catholic faith to parishes across the land would be short-lived. Like her brother Edward, Elizabeth had been brought up and educated amongst reformers, not least her own mother, who strongly favoured the Gospel over the Established Church. And though Elizabeth's own religious tastes remained far more conservative than the radical Calvinism of the later years of her brother's reign, there was little chance that she was going to tolerate the supremacy of the pope in any form.

Mary had understood this. As she lay dying, she had sent two gentlemen to her sister 'to let her know that as it had pleased the Lord God to end her days', she now acknowledged and accepted that 'she as her sister should become Queen, and prayed her to maintain the kingdom and the Catholic religion, in words replete with much affection'. Elizabeth was spirited in her reply. She insisted that she would be free to choose her own councillors. And as for religion, she is said to have stated, 'I promise this much, that I will not change it, provided only that it can be proved by the word of God, which shall be the only foundation and rule of my religion.' Elizabeth would have her way regardless. Meanwhile, Mary stuck rigidly to her detested policy of persecution of Protestants that had made her so unpopular.

By June, it had been noted that there were 'now burning in Smithfield seven at one fire'. On 11 November, the final Protestant martyrs were burned. After their names, the register ends: 'Six days after these were burned to death God sent us our Elizabeth.'

# Marvellous in our eyes

Aware that Mary's final days approached, Elizabeth had asked to be brought news of the queen's passing as soon as it occurred. But she needed definite proof that her sister was dead. To announce her accession prematurely could be taken for treason, after all. When the final moment came, therefore, she asked Sir Nicholas Throckmorton to bring her the coronation ring, slipped from the finger of her sister's dead hand. On the morning of 17 November 1558, as soon as the queen's body was cold, Throckmorton sneaked into Mary's chamber. With the ring safely in his possession, he rode furiously down the road from St James's Palace to Hatfield to greet the new queen.

When he arrived, however, Throckmorton found that he had been overtaken by several members of the Privy Council and 'my news was stale'. It was they who approached Elizabeth as she walked in the park, stopping her to tell her the news as she stood beneath a leafless oak tree. Elizabeth knelt on the grass, and turning her eyes towards the sky exclaimed: '*A domino factum est et mirabile in oculis nostris*'. The words were from Psalm 118, verse 23 – 'This is the Lord's doing: and it is marvellous in our eyes.' Those listening would have immediately understood Elizabeth's meaning, for the previous verse reads: 'The same stone which the builders refused: is become the head-stone in the corner.' Elizabeth, twice disinherited, imprisoned, must have relished every word.

This, at least, was the story told by Robert Naunton in his *Fragmenta Regalia*, written seventy years after the event. There is no other evidence that Elizabeth spoke these words, as Naunton suggested, 'after a good time of respiration'. Elizabeth had waited too long for hesitation. There does exist in the State Papers, however, a speech headed 'Words spoken by the Queen to the lords at her accession'. Despite being traditionally placed at the scene of her first Council meeting three days later, it is more likely that Elizabeth delivered these words to the assembled Council and noblemen at Hatfield on the day she discovered she had become Queen of England. The law of nature moved her 'to sorrow for my sister', she told them. 'The burden that is fallen upon me maketh me amazed.'

But she was determined to serve her new office from 'the bottom of my heart'. It was here that she made a vital distinction: she had 'one body naturally considered', but through God she had also taken on 'a body politic to govern'. She urged them to support both her separate bodies, private and public, so that she might 'make a good account to almighty God and leave some comfort to our posterity in earth'.[1]

The distinction that Elizabeth drew between her 'body natural' and her 'body politic' was one that would affect her for the rest of her life. Her body was indeed that of a woman, with private thoughts and feelings; but it was also that of a queen, upon which rested the hopes and fears of the realm for their monarch. She had been ordained by God to serve, as she later put it, as his 'handmaid', for it was her duty to protect 'her people', and as mentioned, 'leave some comfort to our posterity'. But what of her own posterity? Already the tension in Elizabeth's speech was explicit. Would she allow her natural body, Elizabeth the woman, to succumb to the wishes and demands of her duties as Elizabeth the queen? For now, that was a question no one cared to answer.

While Elizabeth accustomed herself to her accession, news of Mary's death was not yet public knowledge. There were signs that change had come. Back in the capital, the dead queen's royal court was slowly dissolving. The court of the day was, after all, only made up of those whom the reigning monarch chose to appoint to run the royal household, including the attendants of the queen's private apartments, the Presence Chamber where the queen received official visitors, and her private quarters, the Privy Chamber.

It was late in the morning of 17 November 1558 when the Lord Chancellor announced to Parliament news of Mary's death and Elizabeth's accession, which was greeted with a cry of 'God save Queen Elizabeth!' from the assembled Lords and Commons. By mid-afternoon the news of the new queen's accession had reached the outside world. 'All the churches in London did ring, and at night did make bonfires and set tables in the street, and did eat and drink and make merry for the new Queen Elizabeth.'[2] People celebrated the passing of the old queen as much as the accession of the new, as the contrast was already being drawn between Elizabeth and her sister. At a dinner held in York that night, the speaker had the honour of announcing to the audience that 'Queen Elizabeth our most gracious sovereign is come to her just inheritance & kingdom thus to reign over us'. Unlike Mary, the daughter of the Spanish Catherine of Aragon, Elizabeth was 'a prince of no mingled blood of Spaniard or stranger, but born mere English here amongst us and therefore most natural to us'.[3]

That same evening, Elizabeth dined with some of Mary's councillors. Many of them must have known that their positions would not be tenable for long. The new regime had yet to be shaped, and one of the first actions Elizabeth took as queen was a cull of Mary's Council, which had grown to an unwieldly thirty-nine members. Elizabeth reduced this number to nineteen, of whom only ten had seen service under Mary.

Elizabeth had her own team of advisers whom she now wished to promote. One man stood out from the rest. Already at the centre of Elizabeth's affairs, William Cecil had helped plan the smooth transition of power from one queen to the next. Now he was to be given the most important role in government, that of Secretary of State. Cecil had been secretary to the Privy Council during Edward VI's reign, where his evident talents for administration and political dealing had flourished. Cecil's return to power and the political arena he had once haunted was recognised by his friend John Allen, who wrote to the Secretary in December, congratulating him on his return to 'your old room'.[4]

Yet Cecil's appointment was more than just a return to a past administration. The new queen trusted Cecil implicitly, 'above all others'. She had appointed him surveyor of her estates in 1550; in the meantime a close personal bond had grown between the pair. At his appointment, she told him: 'This judgment I have of you: that you will not be corrupted with any manner of gift, and that you will be faithful to the state, and that without respect of my private will, you will give me that counsel that you think best, and if you shall know anything necessary to be declared to me of secrecy, you shall show it to myself only.'[5] It was a pact that, though tested at times, was never broken. Elizabeth later nicknamed him 'Sir Spirit' and came increasingly to depend on his judgment. As the queen's closest adviser, the exact role of the Secretary was hard to define, for it was all-encompassing. The Spanish ambassador was more accurate than he realised when in December that year he described Cecil as 'the man who does everything'. Staying up into the early hours with Elizabeth, Cecil pored over every detail of government policy. And as the mass of his surviving private papers attest, nothing escaped his grasp.

He became Elizabeth's mouthpiece; at times their separate voices are indistinguishable, as Cecil crafted the thoughts and polished the words of the queen's proclamations, letters and speeches. Frequently she would instruct him to draft her missives for her, as when, several years later, she wrote:

> In such a manner of labyrinth am I placed by the answer that I am to give to the queen of Scotland that I do not know in what way I will be able to satisfy her, since I will not have given her any answer for all this time, nor do I know what I now should say. Therefore let there be found something good that I will be able to put into ... written instructions and show me your opinion in this matter.[6]

At times, Elizabeth's anxiety proved trying to all who encountered her trenchant indecision making. She could rarely read a letter through just once, nor make a decision without reviewing it, often having changed her mind several times beforehand. 'It maketh me weary of my life,' admitted Sir Thomas Smith, one of William Cecil's friends, 'the time passing almost irrecuperable, the advantage lost, the charges continuing, nothing resolved ... day by day, and hour by hour, deferred until anon, none, and tomorrow'. 'For matters of state I will write as soon as I can,' Cecil lamented on a separate occasion, admitting that the queen's vacillations were tiresome at best. 'Sometimes so, sometimes no, and at all times, uncertain and ready to stays and revocations ... this irresolution doth weary and kill her ministers, destroy her actions, and overcome all good designs and counsels.'[7] Elsewhere, he could be less than diplomatic: 'The lack of a resolute answer from her Majesty driveth [me] to the wall.'[8] It was often best if decisions could be kept away from the queen, something Cecil considered part of his job. Once, after a messenger had revealed too much information to Elizabeth, Cecil rebuked him, telling him that he 'wished I had not told the Queen's Majesty a matter of such weight, being too much he said for a woman's knowledge.'[9]

There were other facets of the Queen's personality that needed equal tact. One particular talent that the Secretary perfected was how to deal with Elizabeth's volatile moods. 'When she smiles', one observer later recalled, 'it was a pure sunshine, that everyone did choose to bask in, if they could; but anon came a storm from a sudden gathering of clouds, and the thunder fell in wondrous manner on all alike.'[10] In order to combat this, future Secretaries of State were advised to

Have, in a little paper, note of such things as you are to propound to her Majesty and divide it into titles of public and private suits ... Learn before your access her Majesty's disposition by some of the Privy Chamber, with whom you must keep credit, for that will stand you in much stead ... When her Highness is angry or not well disposed, trouble her not with any matter which you desire to have done, unless extreme necessity urge it. When her Highness signet [papers] it shall be good to entertain her with some relation or speech whereat she may take some pleasure ... avoid opinion of being new-fangled and a bringer-in of new customs.[11]

Cecil was a master of political control, whose hands were on every lever of the machinery of government. He was the most talented man of his generation, and he knew it. And beneath his emotionless façade was a ruthless streak that ensured he got his way. Only occasionally do we catch a glimpse of this cold determination, such as when he wrote furiously to the Lord Chancellor, Sir Nicholas Bacon: 'I pray you, my lord, forget not other men's vocations and degrees. I am, though unworthy, her Majesty's Secretary ... I am no clerk to write your resolutions, nor letters for you or the Council. There be clerks for that purpose. Yet have I, for service ... forborne wife, children, kin, friends, house; yea all mine own to serve, which I know not that any other hath done in this time.'[12]

As a commoner from a humble background, Cecil was careful to behave respectfully among the nobility – the traditional counsellors and advisers to the monarch. He recognised that to outreach himself could only lead to his downfall, as it had done for Henry VIII's Secretary, Thomas Cromwell. Instead, a combination of sheer hard work and humility salved any dented pride the nobility might have felt at his exalted position and favour with the queen.[13] Later, Cecil would advise his son Robert how to ride out the roughest storms of Tudor politics:

Be sure to keep some great man thy friend; but trouble him not for trifles. Present him with many yet small gifts and of little charge. And if thou hast cause to bestow any great gratuity, let it be some such thing as may daily be in his sight. Otherwise in this ambitious age thou shalt remain as a hop without a pole living in obscurity, and be made a football for every insulting companion.

Towards thy superiors be humble yet generous; with thy equals familiar, yet respective; towards thy inferiors show much humility with some familiarity – as to bow thy body, stretch forth thy hand and uncover thy head, and such like compliments. The first prepares the way to advancement; the second makes thee known as a man well bred; the third gains a good report which once gotten is easily kept.[14]

Immediately after his appointment, Cecil set to work, drawing up lists of actions that would need to be taken. There was much to be done. In the wake of Mary's death, the country's stock was disastrously low. Not only had Calais been lost, the Crown was almost £300,000 in debt and still losing huge sums of money. Morale was even lower. 'I should not have seen England weaker in strength, men, money and riches,' Sir Thomas Smith wrote of the state of England under Mary. 'As much affectionate as you note me to be to my country and my countrymen, I assure you I was then ashamed of both.'[15] The final years of Mary's reign had witnessed 'nothing but fining, heading, hanging, quartering and burning ... A few priests, men in white rochets, ruled all'. The clerk of the Council, Armagil Waad, accurately summed up the nation's woes in a lengthy paper he had prepared, aptly titled 'The Distresses of the Commonwealth'. The problems were endless: 'The Queen poor, the realm exhausted, the nobility poor and decayed. Want of good captains and soldiers. The people out of order. Justice not executed. All things dear. Excess in meat, drink and apparel. Divisions among ourselves.'[16]

These were just some of the issues facing Elizabeth's new Council as it met for the first time beneath the oak beams of Hatfield Hall. There were also more personal decisions to be resolved. The queen would need to decide whom she would appoint to her royal household, positions currently filled by Mary's acolytes. She had her own favourites: 'the old flock of Hatfield' who had proved their loyalty, remaining with her during her most difficult and dangerous times as princess, including Catherine Ashley as chief gentlewoman of her Privy Chamber, and her close adviser Thomas Parry as Treasurer of the Household.[17] An agenda was drawn up, or rather a series of jottings in Cecil's scrawled hand listing the intended changes. Among them, one simply referred to 'the stable'. Opposite, Cecil wrote, 'Lord Robert Dudley'.[18]

# Master of the Horse

Robert Dudley's appointment as Master of the Queen's Stables, or Master of the Horse, could be seen as a restoration to a position previously held by the Dudley family. During Edward VI's reign, his elder brother John had held the office, while the royal stables had been little affected by the intervening years under Mary, with most of its servants remaining in place.[1] The position was the third in the rank of major Household offices, after the Lord Steward and Lord Chamberlain. It was a relatively new post, created in the fourteenth century as a deputy to the Royal Constable, and until the middle of the sixteenth century the office was usually held by a knight, since it came fifth in the hierarchy of officers. Henry VIII usually appointed his companions at the tilt or the hunting chase, men such as Sir Thomas Knyvet, Sir Henry Guildford, Sir Nicholas Carew and Sir Anthony Browne, since it was usual for the Master of the Horse to be combined with a related office. It did not even figure in Henry VIII's Act of Precedence in 1539, setting out the roles of the nobility at court. Dudley's tenure of the office would change all that.

Ostensibly, Dudley's official role was to attend to the royal stables located in the Royal Mews at Charing Cross which provided for the queen and her vast entourage, taking care to purchase horses and see that they were well looked after. The stables employed a large number of staff, whose wages in 1554 totalled £1,132 10s 2½d. There were other royal stables scattered across the country, along with several studs (termed 'races'), of which the largest was Tutbury Castle in Staffordshire. A surviving account details the care that was involved in treating and dressing the wounded animals. Various entries included 'dressing the bay jennet with the great cod, for the hurt in one of his hips', 'dressing Bay Prince of his sore eye', for 'Bay Star, dressed under the belly', 'dressing Gray Jennet on the shoulder'; other payments included 'for malt and other medicines, for brimstone, for venerick'.[2] With his excellent equestrian skills and passion for outdoor sports, the job suited Dudley perfectly. Like Henry VIII, he took a keen interest in the new Italian art of riding, and was concerned to improve the stock of the royal horses through better breeding methods. The office brought him a salary of 100 marks a year, his own suite of rooms at court where he was attended by his stable officials and servants, and his own personal allowance of four horses, worth £400 a year, complete with full sets of riding equipment.[3]

But the role entailed far more than this. Dudley would be responsible for planning the queen's progresses during the summer months, accompanying her whenever she rode. The office brought a certain prestige: the Master of the Horse was allowed his own special cart to carry his equipment and personal goods whenever the court went on progress; when Elizabeth rode out of the capital, it was the Master's duty to ride immediately behind her almost as if he were her consort; and when the queen needed to mount or dismount her horse, it was her Master of the Horse who was on hand to help her.[4]

There can be little doubt that Elizabeth was responsible for Dudley's appointment. On 17 November, Cecil had proposed that Dudley might (perhaps conveniently) be sent overseas as an envoy to Philip of Spain, together with Sir Peter Carew, who incidentally was Sir Nicholas Throckmorton's choice of candidate for the office of Master of the Horse.[5] The following day, however, the appointment was overruled and Lord Cobham was chosen as envoy instead.[6]

Dudley was to stay just where Elizabeth wanted him – constantly by her side. Like Cecil, Robert was one of the few men who had remained loyal to her during her sister's reign. He was a man she could trust: she had known him for fifteen years, since her childhood at least; he may well have assisted her financially in her time of need, in spite of his own precarious financial situation. 'She is quite certain that he would sacrifice his life for hers', the Spanish ambassador later reported of a conversation he had with the queen, 'and that if one of them had to die, he would willingly be the one.'[7]

Elizabeth herself later confessed that she had shown Dudley favour 'because of his excellent disposition and his many merits'. It was an attraction that was hard to pin down: Elizabeth admitted that although his brother Ambrose shared his 'grace and good looks', for instance, 'his manner was rather rough and he was not so gentle as Lord Robert'.[8] Dudley seemed the perfect embodiment of what it was to be a man. 'Nature has implanted so many graces' in him, she wrote, 'that if she wished to marry she would prefer him to all the princes in the world'.[9] Even Cecil would admit that 'on account of his eminent endowments of mind and body' Dudley was 'so dear to the Queen'.[10]

As a friend of his once remarked, Dudley could claim to 'know the Queen and her nature better than any man'.[11] He had an innate understanding of her character, he knew how to keep her entertained and, perhaps most importantly, he knew how to make her laugh. Elizabeth avoided seriousness and solemnity wherever possible and was fond of 'merry tales'. English ambassadors serving overseas were always advised to include among their dispatches 'one half paper of court news and accidents' to keep the queen entertained. This aspect of her personality was quickly noticed by foreigners who sought to play it to their own advantage; when Elizabeth's cousin Mary Stuart sent her ambassador to the queen in 1564, he was ordered 'to leave matters of gravity and cast in merry purposes, she being well informed of that Queen's natural character'.[12]

Through a mixture of his charm, wit and flattery, Dudley was able to bring out a lighter side in Elizabeth at times when the burdens of state became tedious or depressing. To the frustration of those around them, they frequently shared private jokes, teased each other, or laughed together at some amusement that few others found funny. When the Spanish ambassador spent an evening on the royal barge with Elizabeth and Dudley, he recorded how 'they began joking, which she likes to do much better than talking about business'. Any hope of negotiating serious matters was pointless; in the end, he decided 'to let them jest for a while'.[13] Though frustrating for the ambassador, such moments were especially precious to Elizabeth; 'in this world', she told Catherine Ashley, 'she had so much sorrow and tribulation and so little joy'.[14]

Dudley was never in any doubt that he owed everything he had to the queen. In a pun on his emblem, a bear tied to a ragged staff, he wrote to her in January 1570 that he was her 'ursus major' – her great bear – who was 'tied to your stake'. He would 'forever remain in the bond-chain of dutiful servitude, fastened above all others by benefits past, and daily goodness continually showed'.[15]

When the pair were apart, they kept up a regular correspondence. Dudley would send Elizabeth a constant stream of letters, though these were perhaps as much demanded as expected: 'her majesty doth accept in good part your lordship's often sending unto her sithence your departure,'

Francis Walsingham reminded the earl on one occasion: 'therefore your lordship will do well to continue that course until your return.'[16] At least twenty of Dudley's more personal letters to the queen have survived, preserved by Elizabeth. Tied up in a packet wrapped with ribbon in her private writing desk, they were only discovered after her death. They reveal the intimate, conversational style that existed between them. Dudley was, as ever, her 'eyes', Elizabeth's nickname for him, depicted by a double O. One letter reads:

Thanks for sending so graciously to know how your poor OO doth; I have hitherto so well found myself after my travel, as I trust I am clearly delivered of the shrewd cold that so hardly held me at my departure from you. I have always found exercise with open air my best remedy against those delicate diseases gotten about your dainty city of London, which place, but for necessity, I am sorry to see you remain about, being persuaded it is a piece of the sacrifice you do for your people's sake, seeing it is not profitable for your own health or to prolong your life, which ought to be most dearest to us, your poor servants, how little soever esteemed of yourself. My daily prayer shall be that God will make us that way blessed, and I trust you will use those means by which it may be hoped for. I would gladly wish you were ever where your OO are, but the ways are too foul for your travel; a few fair days will amend this want; if when the season shall serve, your determination holds to spend some time abroad further from London, it shall be well begun now, but I wish it had long before been put in proof. God grant you may find as much good thereof as hereafter to reap the benefit of the good continuance of your desired health.

You see, sweet lady, with how weighty matters I trouble you withal; if there were other matters in me than well-wishing, I would be as ready to pour it out to do you the least good as I will ever have a most dutiful heart to wish you the most and greatest blessings that God can give his anointed; so with humble pardon craved for your poor old OO, they reverently offer themselves as your vassals and creatures, praying the almighty to prolong your days with the longest that ever lived, and bless your reign with the happiest that ever he made most happy ... [17]

Elizabeth had nicknames for many of those close to her at court: Cecil was 'Sir Spirit', the courtier Sir Christopher Hatton her 'lids'. In many of Dudley's letters to Elizabeth, he signed himself with the symbol OO:

'Touching this poor soil,' he wrote to her in 1570, 'I can satisfy no good thing, but only here be your OO with much cold and scarcity; I would they may be ever so yours, and then have they plenty enough.'[18]

In one sense the meaning of Dudley's pet name was clear. He was her eyes at court, her guardsman keeping watch over her. But it also points to the intensely private bond between the pair. For Elizabeth the eyes were also the window into one's soul. Indeed, it was the Renaissance ideal that love enters in through the eyes, creating a union of two souls. This kind of love, however, was not a sensual one, but a love of the highest spiritual form. In the fourth book of *The Courtier* by Baldassare Castiglione, something of a bestseller in its day and translated into English by Elizabeth's own ambassador, Sir Thomas Hoby, in 1561, the character Cardinal Bembo discusses the difference between the two types of love, sensual and spiritual, and advises the Courtier to put aside 'the blind judgment of the senses and enjoy with his eyes, the brightness, the comeliness, the loving sparkles, laughters, gestures and all other pleasant furnitures of beauty – so that he with most dainty food feed the soul'.[19]

Castiglione's description of platonic love perhaps seems to come closest to describing Elizabeth's affection for Dudley. Their relationship was almost like that of siblings; Elizabeth told one ambassador that he should 'regard and honour him as my own brother, for thus do I love him and will love and regard him all my life long; for he deserves it.'[20] William Cecil was also convinced that Elizabeth's fondness for Dudley was based upon an imperceptible bond that set her Master of the Horse quite apart from the rest of her suitors. 'I see and understand,' he wrote to a friend several years later, 'that there is nothing more in their relations than that which is consistent with virtue and most foreign to the baser sorts of love.' Others might think differently, Cecil admitted, but 'they ... do not know the Queen as she really is'.[21] For her part, Elizabeth was unashamed to admit her affection for Dudley; he was, she told the Scottish ambassador William Melville, 'her brother and best friend, whom she would have herself married, had she ever minded to have taken a husband'. When she invited Melville to inspect her bedchamber, she opened a little desk, 'wherein were divers little pictures wrapt within paper, and their names written with her own hand upon the papers'. The ambassador was intrigued. 'Upon the first that she took up was written 'My Lord's picture'. Holding a candle up to get a closer look in the shadows of the room, the ambassador 'pressed to see that picture so named'. 'She was loath to let me see it,' Melville admitted, but eventually she allowed him a look: the face was Dudley's.[22]

It was perhaps unsurprising that for most of her reign, rumours circulated as to the exact nature of her relationship with Dudley. 'I am insulted both in England and abroad for having shown too much favour to the Lord Robert. I am spoken of as if I were an immodest woman,' Elizabeth told the Spanish ambassador in 1564. 'I ought not to wonder at it ... but I am young and he is young and therefore we have both been slandered.'[23] Within months of her accession, Elizabeth's closeness to Dudley would lead to gossip that they might secretly be conducting an affair, with ambassadors talking of how 'her Majesty visits him in his chamber day and night'.[24] This would have been scandal enough had Robert Dudley been single. Except he was not; he was a married man.

Robert Dudley arrived at Hatfield on a snow-white horse as soon as he had discovered news of the new queen's accession. Elizabeth issued him with one of her first royal warrants supplying him with cloth that he needed to fulfil his new role as Master of the Horse on 23 November, five days after her accession, the same day that she had travelled down to London via Hadley and Barnet.[1] From that moment on, Dudley was securely ensconced at court, rarely to leave the queen's presence. Yet where was his wife Amy?

Since her letter to John Flowerdew in 1557, written from William Hyde's 'mansion house' in Throcking, Hertfordshire, Amy's movements remain something of a mystery. The only other piece of evidence that gives a sense of her existence are two legal documents arranging the conveyance of the manor of Hales Owen, dated 27 March 1558. Amy's and Robert's signatures appear side by side on the documents, suggesting that they were both together on the day, though this provides no confirmation of their whereabouts. Possibly the documents could have been signed at Throcking, though Amy could have travelled to London, where she might have stayed at Dudley's London residence at Christchurch.[2]

Otherwise there is precious little else to indicate where Amy was living or what she might have been doing during this time. Perhaps Amy continued to live at William Hyde's during these years; she certainly stayed there during the first year of Elizabeth's reign. It is not until then that we get a brief glimpse into Amy's world, preserved in several entries in Dudley's household accounts for the period beginning 20 December 1558 to September 1559, drawn up by his financial officer William Chauncy. Some of its first entries refer to Amy, mentioned as 'my ladye' in the accounts:

> Given to Gowre for his charges riding into Lincolnshire to my ladye xxs
> Item paid for hire of certain hackneys for my ladye by Mr Blunt's command lxis

Item to John Forest for his charges riding to Mr Hides to my ladye iiis
iiiid

Item paid to Gower for his charges riding to my ladye over and besides
the xxs which is before written per bill xxvis viiid

Item paid to Mr Gower for parcel charges of my lady's coming out of
Lincoln as appeareth upon a bill before mentioned xxvis viiid.

It seems clear that at the beginning of Elizabeth's reign, Amy was residing at an unspecified location in Lincolnshire. We do not know how long Amy had been there, or where exactly she might have been staying, although the mention that she was 'coming out of Lincoln' suggests that she had been lodging within the city itself. A Mr 'Gowre' or 'Gower' sent up to collect Amy was most likely Edmund Goove, one of the men who had been arrested with Dudley during his attempt to proclaim Jane Grey queen in July 1553. His initial payment of 20 shillings suggests that he rode approximately 120 miles, based on the calculation of charges of the standard rate of two pence a mile (later on in the account, one of Dudley's servants John Forest would also be required to ride to Kew at a cost of 12d); this was roughly the distance from London to the city of Lincoln.[3] The 'hire of certain hackneys' for Amy's departure at the fairly significant cost of 61 shillings indicates that the move must have been a major one, involving several packhorse loads of household goods. Amy then seems to have returned not to London, but instead to Throcking, where she was soon visited by John Forest.

These payments are but fragments, yet they provide a fascinating glimpse into a period in Amy's life we are unlikely ever to know more about. Why did she travel to Lincolnshire? How long she was there? Who was she visiting? The answers to these questions remain a mystery. What is clear, however, is that Dudley was certainly in control of his wife's movements, ordering her carriages and sending his men to collect her. The hackneys hired to collect and bring Amy to Throcking were ordered 'by Mr Blunt's command'; 'Blunt' is likely to have been Thomas Blount of Kidderminster, a cousin of Dudley's mother who by 1553 had been appointed as Northumberland's comptroller. By October 1556 he was back in Dudley's service, where he remained until his death in 1568. Blount became a key household officer in the forthcoming years, and performed various services for Dudley including auditing the Chauncy accounts.

If Blount was merely following his master's orders in arranging for Amy's collection from Lincoln, the timing of her travels raises fresh questions. Two entries in the household accounts reveal that Dudley himself had most likely been staying at Throcking with his wife shortly before Elizabeth's accession: one records a payment of 30s 6d to one of Dudley's servants for the 'livery of your lordships horses lying at Enfield mensis November'; the other mentions the 'carriage of your lordship's tents from Hunsdon'.[4] Enfield was not on the route from London to Hatfield, but it was on the road from Throcking, as was Hunsdon. But if Dudley had been based at Throcking with Amy, this raises the question of why he felt the need to move his wife into Lincolnshire in the first instance. One plausible reason might be that he feared the uncertainties the new reign brought with it. Although Elizabeth's accession proved to be a smooth one, those closest to her were taking few chances. Her own household officer Thomas Parry sent messages to the commander of the Berwick garrison, the largest military force outside London and Dover, arranging for the equipping of 10,000 men from the north if necessary.[5] Under these circumstances, Dudley probably considered that his wife would be best placed far from the court. But one suspects that this was not the only thought in Dudley's mind.

# Young folks, heretics and traitors

On 23 November, together with a throng of gentlewomen, councillors and retainers, Elizabeth left Hatfield for the capital, where she stayed at Charterhouse, the town house of Lord North. People had travelled miles out of the city to see their new queen. Elizabeth did not disappoint. 'All her faculties were in motion,' one chronicler wrote, 'every motion seemed a well guided action; her eye was set upon one, her ear listened to another . . . distributing her smiles, looks and graces so that thereupon the people again redoubled the testimonies of their joys.'[1]

Five days later she made her procession to the Tower along newly gravelled streets, through the Barbican, past Bishop's Gate and along Fenchurch Street where 'there was such shooting of guns as never was heard afore'.[2] The scene impressed Londoner Henry Machyn, who recorded in his diary how the queen's train included 'gentlemen, and many knights and lords, and after came all the trumpets blowing, and then came all the heralds in array'. Ahead of Elizabeth, the Earl of Pembroke carried the ceremonial sword. Elizabeth was on horseback, dressed in purple velvet with a scarf around her neck. Behind her, in his new office as Master of the Horse, rode Dudley.

These were joyous times, times of hope in which people looked forward to the future, happy to forget the past. But first, of course, the traditional solemnities of Mary's funeral had to be observed. The dead queen was buried in Westminster Abbey on 14 December 1558, after an elaborate procession featuring a life-sized papier-mâché model of Mary, complete with the royal regalia of the crown, sceptre and orb and bejewelled with 'many goodly rings'. The model was placed on top of the coffin in a wheeled chariot, and then disinvested of its royal regalia in reverent ceremony.[3] As Mary's body was lowered into the ground, the officers of her household snapped their staves and threw them into the burial pit, symbolising the end of their allegiance to their former mistress. The old queen was dead – there was now a new queen to serve.

John White, the Bishop of Winchester and an affirmed Catholic, had been chosen to officiate over the ceremonies and deliver the funeral sermon. His comparison between the two queens, the living Elizabeth and the deceased Mary, could not have angered the new queen more. By taking his text from Ecclesiastes, 'I can commend the state of the dead above the state of the living', he was already taking a grave risk. White praised Mary for her piety and generosity, her duty to the realm and to purging the nation of Protestant heresy. For Elizabeth, all he could muster was that she was queen 'by the like title and right'. But it was his choice of proverb, 'a living dog is better than a dead lion', that was to prove his undoing. 'What beast is more vile than a dog, more worthy than a lion?' White asked.[4] Elizabeth was not interested in the answer. Shortly afterwards, White was placed under house arrest.

The episode was indicative of the religious problems confronting Elizabeth. It had been twenty-five years since her father's break with Rome and his creation of the Church of England. The resulting tumultuous times mirrored the religious strife on the Continent, where Martin Luther and then Jean Calvin attempted to establish a reformed Church based on the Gospels without the pope as its figurehead. Henry VIII's own religious faith remained dangerously ambiguous; he made himself Supreme Head of the Church, denying the pope's authority, whilst continuing to execute those who denied the mass and the miracle of transubstantiation. Edward's reign marked a new, more drastic, stage in the Reformation, as saints' images, stained-glass windows and altars that had been allowed to stand during his father's reign were smashed and broken up.

Mary's accession to the throne – and her defeat of Jane – might have meant the end of Protestant faith: the nation was returned to Rome and Catholic services were restored. Yet the Reformation had gone too far to return to the old medieval traditions. In many places, the very fabric of the past had simply disappeared. The new faith had also taken root, not least in Elizabeth, who remained steadfast to her beliefs during Mary's reign. Mary's programme of burnings also served merely to radicalise those Protestants who survived. Now Mary's premature death had finally closed a chapter in England's past. Elizabeth, whose Protestant convictions were well known, was widely expected to return to the new faith and to the religious position adopted during her brother's reign. But the new queen proved to be more cautious. She recognised that if she was to end decades of schism, a new religious settlement would need to be found. Elizabeth disliked religious debate; she hoped to achieve a consensus within her Church, to move away from the bitter years of division and destruction that marked the reigns of her brother and sister. 'There was only one Jesus Christ, and one faith,' she told the French ambassador as she was nearing the end of her life, 'and all the rest they disputed about [was] but trifles'.[5]

Elizabeth's own religious beliefs were somewhat more complex. Sir Francis Bacon's words, that 'Her Majesty not liking to make windows into men's hearts and secret thoughts, except the abundance of them did overflow into overt and express acts or affirmations', have frequently been cited as testament to the moderate course that Elizabeth preferred to take regarding religion. She had little time for the hair-splitting of theological arguments which, she once declared, were nothing but 'ropes of sand or sea-slime leading to the moon'.[6] Instead she preferred to base her faith on more personal grounds; she only attended chapel once a week, and had little taste for sermons, confessing that 'she had rather talk with God devoutly by prayer than hear others speak eloquently of God'. She liked her clergymen to wear vestments, albeit not too elaborate, preferred crucifixes and candles in her private chapels, and was especially fond of music at chapel, declaring that the practice 'should not be of less reputation in our days, but rather augmented and increased ... no singing men or boys shall be taken out'.[7]

Yet there can be little doubt that Elizabeth, as someone who shunned the belief that Christ's real presence was in the bread and wine of the service, would have nothing to do with the actual consecration of the mass; when the Bishop of Carlisle celebrated the mass by elevating the host in the traditional manner in her private chapel on Christmas Day, Elizabeth simply got up and walked out. She would insist too that services were held in English, not Latin, and on 28 December issued a proclamation stating that the gospels, the epistles and the ten commandments were to be read in English. Other Catholic rites might remain in use, but there was a hint that further reformation was to come: the present position would only be maintained 'until some consultation may be had by Parliament ... for the better conciliation and accord of such causes as ... her Majesty most desireth'.[8] It was this curious blend of different elements of both Catholicism and Protestantism that allowed the Spanish ambassador to believe that Elizabeth 'differed very little' from the Catholic faith, 'as she believed that God was in the sacrament of the eucharist, and only dissented from three or four things in the mass'.

It was the sense that the new queen's reign had ushered in a new era that disturbed most commentators. Change was seen to be everywhere, not least in the men and women whom Elizabeth surrounded herself with. 'The kingdom is entirely in the hands of young folks, heretics and traitors,' the alarmed Spanish ambassador Feria wrote to Philip II. 'The old people and the Catholics are dissatisfied, but dare not open their lips.' This was not necessarily true: at 38, William Cecil was the youngest member of her Privy Council, and only three others were under 50. But the ambassador was correct to notice the sea-change in Elizabeth's administration. Less than a third of Mary's old Council were retained, and most of these nobles were key to maintaining the loyalty of the northern parts of her country. In the royal household too, thirty-eight out of a total fifty positions were new appointments; and nowhere was the change more keenly felt than in the queen's own Privy Chamber where the Protestant ladies Ashley, Cary, Cecil, Knollys and Throckmorton replaced the Catholic Dormers, Cornwallises, Babingtons, Southwells, Waldegraves and Whartons. Elizabeth had already begun to make an indelible mark on the stage that she was to occcupy for nearly the next half-century, a fact not lost on the Spanish ambassador, who ended his dispatch: 'She seems to me to be incomparably more feared than her sister, and has her way absolutely as her father did.'[9]

# The court

For the first time, the court was Elizabeth's. For someone who had never expected to become queen, the change was bewildering. She later admitted that she owed much to God, who had 'deliveredst [her] out of the den from the cruelty of the greedy and raging lions'. She had gone from prisoner to prince, the sovereign ruler of her realm – a transition that even Elizabeth confessed had left her 'overwhelmed'.

It was easy to understand why. The Tudor court that she had inherited was vast: the major royal palaces within the capital included Richmond, Hampton Court, Greenwich, St James's and Whitehall. Richmond had been built by her grandfather, Henry VII, and covered 10 acres, with a vast number of towers and golden pinnacles and with so many rooms that astonished Spanish visitors believed it to be 'better than the Alcazar of Madrid'. Hampton Court was the largest of all the 'standing houses' on the outskirts of the capital. With its impressive throne room hung with an enormous Persian tapestry, a 28-foot table covered in velvet and set with pearls, a throne of brown velvet covered with jewels, including three large diamonds, the palace was mainly used for ceremonies and court festivities, especially at Christmas, Easter and Whitsun. Up the river, Greenwich was used to receive ambassadors and state visitors, who were rowed there in an eight-oared barge, fitted out with red satin seats and a cloth-of-gold bolster upon which dignitaries were invited to sit. Elizabeth had her own more impressive personal barge with twenty oarsmen, with enough room to hold parties in as it rowed down the Thames, sometimes even as far as Windsor.

While the queen was at Greenwich, royal ships would often carry out exercises on the river, displaying the nation's military capabilities to awed visitors. In the great park, a vast stretch of turf of which Elizabeth could take the view from a detached gatehouse, military drills were conducted. It was here that, on the first visit of her reign in July 1559, Elizabeth watched a mock battle: 'Guns were discharged on one another, the morris pikes encountered together with great alarm; each ran to their weapons again, and then they fell together as fast as they could in imitation of close fight'.[1]

On the other side of the river, in the cities of London and Westminster, Elizabeth was now the owner of a vast collection of buildings, including many that were leased to her noblemen and courtiers. The Charterhouse, where she stayed on her journey from Hatfield, was in fact hers, leased out to Lord North; Durham House was conventionally used as the residence for the Spanish ambassadors, while Somerset House on the Strand was occupied by various visiting foreign dignitaries. St James's Palace had been the favourite residence of her sister Queen Mary, but, perhaps with that memory in mind, and the fact that due to its size it was more befitting of a country residence than a royal palace, for most of her reign Elizabeth usually remained at her favourite London palace, Whitehall.

Sprawling across 23 acres, Whitehall was the largest palace in the whole of Europe. Over the centuries, layer upon layer had been added to the building so that in the complex maze of chambers and corridors there were now over 2,000 rooms. Some of its wall paintings dated back to the reign of Henry III, though the main room of the palace, the Privy Chamber, was dominated by Hans Holbein's mural of Elizabeth's father Henry VIII, his giant figure painted with such fine detail that it seemed almost lifelike. 'The King as he stood there,' wrote one visitor, 'majestic in his splendour, was so lifelike that the spectator felt abashed, annihilated in his presence.'

The establishment that made up the court Elizabeth inherited was huge; over 2,000 servants and attendants were employed to keep it running, making it the largest court in Europe. Its expense was enormous: the dining hall alone held 1,500 at a single sitting, while household accounts, meticulously kept by the Board of the Green Cloth, reveal the massive annual expenditure: in one year the court consumed 1,240 oxen, 8,200 sheep, 13,260 lambs, 33,024 chickens, 60,000 lbs of butter and over 4.2 million eggs, washed down with 600,000 gallons of beer and 300 tons of wine. The food bill alone came to a staggering £21,096 10s 4¼d.*

Elizabeth took her own meals alone in her chamber, since it was considered unbecoming of the queen's royal dignity to be seen eating,

* Just over £5 million in today's money

except by her ladies. She rarely stuck to regular meal times anyhow, 'but when her appetite required it'.[2] Everyone knew when the queen was dining, however, for musicians played outside in the hall when her meal was being served; one foreign visitor recalled how 'twelve trumpets and two kettle drums made the hall ring for half an hour together'.[3] Available records reveal that Elizabeth's breakfast cost 8s 6½d, her dinner 45s ½d and her supper 32s 9d. In her diet, Elizabeth was 'very temperate'; she preferred chicken or game to red meat, though she retained a soft spot for rich cakes made from Corinth currants, especially imported wholesale from Greece. The queen also disliked the strong beer served at the court, known as 'March ale' (one contemporary referred to it as 'old beer that will make a cat speak and a wise man dumb'). According to John Clapham, Elizabeth preferred instead to drink light wine 'mingled with water, containing three parts more in quantity than the wine itself'.[4]

The queen's apartments were the nexus of the court. They lay protected behind several layers of antechambers in which Elizabeth met visitors and conducted her daily business. The Great Hall led through to the Guard Chamber, then on to the Presence Chamber and the Privy Chamber. Admittance to the first three was fairly easy for anyone suitably dressed, but the Privy Chamber was heavily guarded, with 146 yeomen of the guard on duty, each paid £2 a month for their services.[5] Its door was guarded by an usher of the Black Rod, and only peers and those trusted by the queen were allowed to pass by. Access to the queen's person was all-important, for whoever held Elizabeth's ear was likely to have her favour also. The position of usher became a coveted role, not least for the bribes that could be won: access to the queen could always be sold at the highest price.

Robert Dudley was to learn that it was a position whose control he could not afford to lose if he was to retain the queen's favour. When a servant of his was refused permission to enter the Privy Chamber by the usher then on duty, Simon Bowyer, Dudley was furious at what he considered a personal slight, and, calling Bowyer a 'knave', marched into the queen's apartments to get him dismissed. But Bowyer was a quick thinker; rushing past Dudley he threw himself at Elizabeth's feet, asking the one question he calculated might win him a reprieve: was she queen or was Dudley really king?

When Elizabeth realised what had been going on and how her favourite was attempting to dictate who served her, she was apoplectic with rage.

'By God's death, my Lord,' Elizabeth exploded at Dudley, 'I have wished you well, but my favour is not so locked up in you that others shall not participate thereof, for I have many servants unto whom I have, and will at my pleasure, confer my favour, and likewise resume the same; and if you think to rule here, I will take a course to see you forthcoming. I will have here but one mistress and no master.'

Still Dudley would get his way eventually, with the appointment of Robert Laneham, a member of his own retinue, as gentleman usher, zealously guarding who could or could not venture past the chamber door. Laneham considered himself particularly good at his job, keeping those he disliked (his master's enemies) from the queen's presence, while favouring his friends. He later boasted how:

> If the Council sit, I am at hand, wait an inch, I warrant you. If any make babbling, 'Peace!' say I, 'wot where you are?' If I take a listener, or a prier-in at the chinks or at the lockhole, I am by and by in the bones of him. But now they keep good order; they know me well enough. If there be a friend, or such one as I like, I make him sit down by me on a form or a chest; let the rest walk, a' God's name![6]

There was, of course, another means of gaining access to the queen. Elizabeth employed fourteen ladies-in-waiting who held permanent positions within her bedchamber. In addition, there were six maids of honour, unmarried girls, usually the daughters of noblemen. The duties of the queen's ladies included looking after her vast collection of clothes and jewellery, which by the end of her reign included nearly 700 gowns and cloaks, encrusted with pearls, precious stones and embroidered with gold and silver. The ladies included Catherine 'Kat' Ashley, who had been Elizabeth's chief gentlewoman since her childhood, but the queen also had her other favourites, including Dudley's own sister, Lady Mary Sidney, and Lady Knollys, who despite being married to the Viscount of Hereford was refused permission to see her husband since the queen 'loved Lady Knollys above all other women in the world' and would not be parted from her. It was a demanding position; Elizabeth occasionally lost her temper with them, and swore at the younger ones if they put a step wrong – she once called Lady Mary Howard a flouting wench for not being prepared to carry a cup during dinner. Lady Cobham attempted to get leave from the court 'to rest her weary bones awhile', though this was not forthcoming. Yet the office did have its benefits; in return for promises to 'procure ... private speech with her Majesty' they might be offered gifts or rewards. 'You are much beholden to Mistress Radcliffe,' the Earl of Rutland was told by a friend in 1587, 'she daily doth good offices for you. She is worthy to be presented with something.' Unsurprisingly, many a young noblewoman would jump at the chance to serve the queen.[7]

Hidden behind these layers, at the centre of the hive, was Elizabeth's own bedchamber. For those few who were allowed to visit it, it came as something of a disappointment. The room was small and dark, but had at least one window overlooking the Thames, from which one May morning in 1559 the queen watched a mock battle between two ships, which happened to end in tragedy when a barrel of gunpowder accidentally blew up, destroying one of the battleships and drowning one of its sailors.

Elizabeth's bedroom was plainly furnished. There was a little closet, 'ornamented all over with pearls', in which Elizabeth kept her bracelets, earrings and 'other things of extraordinary value'. There was a silver-topped writing desk, and a bathroom next door, lined from floor to ceiling with mirrors, like her bathroom at Windsor. When she first arrived, Elizabeth insisted that certain personal items of furniture be delivered from Hatfield, including her royal bed, framed in a gilded bedstead six yards square and carved with 'eight beasts of wood'. There could be little doubt that the bed was solely for the use of a member of the royal family. Its valance of purple velvet laced with gold and 'garnished with a thin fringe of Venice gold' was surrounded by thirty-four gold silk tassels hanging down from curtains of purple damask, with a bedhead of purple velvet to match.[8]

Elizabeth admitted that she was not 'a morning woman'; often she would remain in a state of undress in her nightgown, sometimes hanging out of her bedroom window, listening to gossip. This could on occasion lead to considerable embarrassment. Once a carter remarked how he had seen her only partially clothed, and now 'knew the Queen was a woman'. Elizabeth sent him an angel (10 shillings) 'to shut his mouth'. She would often go for brisk morning walks, still not fully dressed; to compensate for this, a wall at Windsor was heightened – 'to prevent persons in the dean's orchard seeing into the Queen's walk'.[9]

At Whitehall her bedroom had a secret entrance, leading into the garden where there was a walkway down to the gatehouse on the river, from which the queen might depart on a barge. Travelling by barge was a perfect way for Elizabeth to display herself to her people. In June 1559, Baron Bruener, envoy to Archduke Charles, wrote how the queen 'recognised and summoned me. She spoke a long while with me, and invited me to leave my boat and take a seat in the Treasurer's barge. She then had her boat laid alongside and played the lute.' She was an accomplished player and practised regularly (during the first ten years of her reign she spent £75 on broken lute strings). Elizabeth claimed that 'she used not to play before men, but when she was solitary, to shun melancholy', though she would give regular recitals over the years to assembled ambassadors, one of whom remarked how she 'played very sweetly and skilfully'.[10]

Elizabeth brought a new atmosphere to court, where music, masques and dances began to light up the royal palaces once more. 'The Queen's daily amusements are musical performances and other entertainments and she takes marvellous pleasure in seeing people dance,' the Venetian ambassador observed. He was less than impressed. 'They are intent on amusing themselves and on dancing until after midnight,' he reported, scandalised at such a display of 'levities and unusual licentiousness'.[11] Elizabeth especially liked the galliard, a difficult dance, which, in its simplest form, involved five steps followed by a leap in the air, known as the caper, and the clapping of one's feet together in mid-air after the fifth, known also as the cinquepace. According to one observer, Elizabeth might regularly perform 'six or seven galliards of a morning, besides music and singing' for her 'ordinary exercise'. She took particular pride in her ability to dance the galliard more 'high and disposedly' than anyone she knew. For some, the complexities of the dance were simply too much. 'Our galliards are now so curious', one old soldier Barnaby Rich complained, 'that they are not for my dancing, for they are so full of tricks and turns that he which hath no more than the plain cinquepace is no better accounted of than a very bungler'.[12]

There was one man whose ability to master the complicated and rigorous modern dances impressed everyone, not least the queen. Robert Dudley leapt high into the air, 'after the Florentine style, with a high magnificence that astonished beholders'.

# Becoming queen

On 22 December 1559 the court moved to Westminster for Christmas and New Year.[1] Dudley remained by the queen's side in a 'new lodging' that had been 'trimmed up'. His household accounts show how he spent liberally on gifts for those at court: 25s 4d to the queen's guard, and even rewarding a poor woman who had brought him apples when he was at Hatfield with 3s 4d.[2] He also spent £35 14s 4d for 'sundry jewels' bought from the jeweller Hans Frank on 29 December, including £10 worth of pearls, which may have made up part of his present for the queen.[3] In reward for his New Year's gift, Elizabeth gave Dudley a gilt cup worth 35 shillings. She also granted him a house in Kew, described as 'the capital messuage of Kew', which was to become Dudley's principal London residence when he was rarely departed from court. It was the first of her many grants of land and property that Elizabeth was to bestow on her favourite over the years.[4]

Dudley's wife was nowhere to be seen. Amy almost certainly did not see her husband at Christmas, having spent the holiday at Hyde's in Throcking. But she was not forgotten. Dudley sent Thomas Blount to visit her instead; 6s 8d was paid for the hire of the horse 'when he rode to my lady in the Christmas'.[5] It is likely that John Forest, who also rode up to Hyde's at a cost of 3s 4d, delivered Dudley's gift to Amy: six gold buttons 'of the Spanish fashion' and a little chain, designed by the goldsmith William Gilbert and costing £30.[6] Dudley remained in regular written contact with Hyde, who sent him a gift of partridges from the estate.[7] He also received hawks from Amy's half-brothers John Appleyard and Arthur Robsart.

Dudley's preoccupations lay elsewhere. There was one particular reason why he was unable to leave court that Christmas. In his new position as Master of the Horse, he was now heavily involved in the arduous preparations for the queen's coronation. Elizabeth had wanted to make sure that everything was right for the occasion, and that the date of the most important event of her entire reign was chosen correctly. For this, she asked Dudley to search out the astrologer John Dee to examine her charts. He returned with the news that the coronation should take place on 15 January 1559.

With barely weeks to spare, Dudley threw himself into organising the traditional procession from the Tower to Westminster, planning and rehearsing the route and its timings – ensuring, for example, that the queen's canopy bearers moved in step with the movement of the horses carrying the royal chariot. He stayed in the Tower, sending his servant Roger Oswald ahead to prepare his lodgings there, with his 'stuff' sent from Whitehall at a cost of 8d.[8] Another servant, Powell, was paid 25 shillings 'for the making clean of the Coronation stuff' while another of his retainers, Robert Curson, was paid four shillings to watch over 'the stable stuff' in preparation for the coronation.[9]

The capital buzzed with activity. All the best silks and cloths of gold that arrived at London's docks were compounded for royal use by customs officials. As one Italian visitor reported, 'They are preparing here for the coronation, and work both day and night, on holidays and weekdays.'[10] The scale of the task was phenomenal: this was to be the most spectacular and costly ceremony not merely of the decade, but in the history of the Tudor age. No expense was spared. The total cost of the coronation, the ceremony and the festivities that followed, has been estimated at almost £20,000, just over 10 per cent of the entire revenue of the Crown.[11] The organiser of the festivities, the Marquis of Winchester, had been given an initial budget of £3,000, though looking through the detailed accounts that survive it is easy to see how that sum was quickly spent. The cost of silks, in a multitude of hues and colours, and cloths of silver alone came to £3,942 0s 9d.[12] Forty crimson-covered velvet saddles for ladies and gentlemen of the court were ordered, at a cost of £983 17s 8d.[13] More costly still were the fabrics used to spruce up Elizabeth's coronation robes, inherited from her sister: 22 yards of cloth of gold and silver tissue for the mantle of estate costing £132, 11 yards of gold tissue £66 and a fur of powdered ermines £26 3s 4d.[14] No detail was unaccounted; every item, down to a single nail, was comprehensively documented. One entry, for instance, records that seven workmen used 40,000 nails, 8,000 of them made from silver gilt, to fasten gold-striped crimson satin coverings, with no less than an extra 20,000 hooks to attach red ribbons and lace of golden silk, to cover the steps up to the coronation throne and St Edward's chair.[15]

Three days before her coronation, Elizabeth travelled from Whitehall by barge to her apartments in the Tower, in preparation for the traditional coronation procession through the streets of London. Once the river was at high tide, the queen and her household departed in a barge 'covered with its usual tapestries, both inside the cabin and outside'. To the sound of drums and fife players, 'as is the custom when she goes by water,' the Venetian ambassador observed, the barge slowly made its way across the icy waters of the Thames, pulled by a galley of forty rowers. Though the coronation was still three days away, festivities had already begun. 'Ships, galleys, brigantines, caravels, barges and skiffs had been prepared with the most elaborate decoration possible of flags, artillery, drums, fifes, trumpets and other kinds of joyful instruments to accompany her Majesty and her court ... After her Majesty passed the bridge and was in sight of the Tower some pieces of artillery were fired.'[16] But as the barge pulled up alongside the Tower, Elizabeth chose to enter the fortress inauspiciously 'by a little private bridge, [and] was seen only by very few persons'. It was the same entrance she had been taken to when she was princess; only then she had arrived as prisoner.

The irony was not lost on Elizabeth. As she left the Tower several days later to depart for Westminster, her retinue passed in front of the lions that were then held in the Tower's royal menagerie. Looking up to the skies in a carefully choreographed moment, she remarked how she, like the prophet Daniel, had been saved by God from the den of raging lions.[17] To those listening, many of whom would have been the Council members who had signed the warrant for Elizabeth's arrest during her sister's reign, the point was clearly made.

It had begun to snow as Elizabeth entered her litter to begin her coronation procession from the Tower, winding through the streets from Blackfriars, to St Paul's and on to Westminster. Whereas the formalities and sacred rituals of the coronation itself would take place behind closed doors at Westminster, the procession itself provided an opportunity for Elizabeth to be shown to the people. It was a sight to behold. Elizabeth herself wore 'a very rich royal mantle of gold with a double-raised stiff pile, and on her head over a coif of cloth of gold the plain gold crown of a princess, without lace but covered in jewels, and with nothing in her hands but gloves'; in addition, her dress had been specially embroidered with over a thousand extra 'powderings', shiny metal ringlets that glinted in the winter light. The Venetian ambassador was stunned: 'the whole court so sparkled with jewels and gold collars that they cleared the air'.

A copy of a portrait of Elizabeth posing in one set of her coronation robes survives. It shows the new queen holding the orb and sceptre, dressed in a tightly corseted, patterned bodice, her waist no wider than her head. Her smooth face glows white, and her auburn hair, long and worn loose, falls down the back of her ermine cape as a sign of her virginity. Elizabeth's dark eyes stare straight ahead. 'She had a piercing eye,' wrote one early historian, 'by which she was used to touch what metal strangers were made of that came into her presence.' Elizabeth's eyes were in fact golden, but her short-sightedness caused her pupils to enlarge, making them appear as large black discs. The portrait presents a quite different image of the queen to the made-up, alabaster face with which we are familiar; it is the face of a young woman, fresh and naturally composed, about to confront the challenge of becoming queen.

➤ 20 ⤛

# Coronation

As the procession left the Tower, the deafening sound of over four hundred guns boomed overhead, continuing for over half an hour. Along the streets, wooden barricades had been erected to marshal the crowds, while, as a result of the 'deep mud caused by the foul weather', the entire route had been covered with sand and gravel. At the sides of the road, 'merchants and artisans of every trade leant in long black gowns with linings,' the Venetian ambassador wrote, 'their hoods of red and black cloth thrown back, like those usually worn by the rectors of universities in Italy. All their ensigns, banners, and standards, which were innumerable, made a very fine show.' It had been the task of the craftsmen and merchants, together with the City's guilds and aldermen, to organise the traditional coronation pageants that adorned set points along the route. Long before the date of the coronation had been announced, the Court of Aldermen had appointed representatives to ensure that all places 'be very well and seemly trimmed and decked for the honour of the City . . . with pageants, fine painting and rich clothes of arras, silver and gold'.[1] Monuments were dusted down and the protective fencing was removed from around the cross at Cheapside.[2] The Great Conduit, which traditionally flowed with wine on such occasions, was instead covered over with 'cloths of arras and other rich cloths',[3] as the company of painters 'did utterly refuse to new paint and trim' the fountain, for what they must have considered the paltry sum of 20 marks.[4] Other preparations included a wooden scaffold erected in St Dunstan's churchyard in Fleet Street so that the poor children of Christ's Hospital could view the procession.[5] Not that all this came without charge. To pay for the celebrations, a tax of two-fifteenths was levied on London's citizens.[6]

As the procession began its snaking course, the Venetian ambassador was less than impressed by its organisation: 'Nobody kept his place,' he wrote, 'nor could they do so because of the multitude of people.' The entire spectacle had been so 'gracelessly and badly put together, so much so they made one laugh'. The procession, which the ambassador estimated must have numbered a thousand horses, continued in order of precedence. Sixteen trumpeters dressed in scarlet led the way for the mace-bearers and the carriers of the royal insignia, followed by the two most senior members of the nobility, the Earl of Arundel 'beautifully dressed on a charger very richly adorned', and the Duke of Norfolk, 'with the silver baton of his office'. Then came the queen herself, 'in an open litter, trimmed down to the ground with gold brocade with a raised pile' surrounded by footmen in crimson velvet jerkins with the arms of a white and red rose and the letters E.R. embroidered on their backs, the sight of which, even the ambassador had to admit, 'makes a most superb show'.

A sketchbook depicting the order of the procession still survives, perhaps created as a guide to those taking part in the ceremonies, for it includes detailed drawings of the procession from the Tower to White-hall, and the following day's procession to Westminster Abbey, showing the layout for the coronation. Above each picture there is a running commentary of the names of participants and their specific duties. Among its pages is a drawing of Elizabeth's own litter, surrounded by four gentlemen pensioners and pulled by two horses decorated with large feathered plumes, one at the front and one behind, the first led by Giles Paulet, the second by Ambrose Dudley, both walking on foot.[7] The picture makes clear exactly how close the Dudleys were to Elizabeth at the start of her reign, for behind Ambrose came Robert Dudley himself, riding upon a tall horse, in his hands the reins of a riderless horse beside him, the 'palfrey of honour'. The Venetian ambassador watched as Dudley passed by him, making an impression upon the diplomat, who recorded that he was 'mounted on a very fine charger and leading by the hand a white hackney covered with cloth of gold'. During the procession, Elizabeth was presented with the spectacle of a series of allegorical pageants, acted out for her amusement. They portrayed, however, a far more serious message: on the rare occasion that the people would ever come this close to their monarch, this was their moment to explain their hopes and desires for the new reign.

We know the specific details down to every last turn of the procession thanks to a unique printed work – the official version of the coronation procession, recorded by Richard Mulcaster in a pamphlet entitled *The Passage of Our Most Dread Sovereign Lady Queen Elizabeth through the City of London to Westminster the Day Before Her Coronation*[8] – essentially an exercise in propaganda drafted to bolster the new regime. Above all,

Elizabeth is presented as very much a queen among her people, rich or poor. 'If the baser personages had either offered her grace any flowers, or moved her to any suit, she most gently, to the common rejoicing of all the lookers-on and private comfort of the party, stayed her chariot and heard their requests.' Much of the description was undoubtedly true. 'How many nosegays did Her Grace receive at poor women's hands,' George Ferrers, an officer in the procession, wrote to a friend, remembering one particular moment: 'That bunch of rosemary given to Her Majesty with a supplication about Fleet Street Bridge, was seen in her chariot, when Her Grace came to Westminster not without the wondering of such who knew the presenter, and noticed the queen's reception of the same.'

In Mulcaster's version of events, Elizabeth could do no wrong. Unlike her sister's coronation procession, which had descended into something of a farce when the Bishop of Winchester, Stephen Gardiner, had ordered a banner portraying the Protestant message of 'Verbum Dei' to be ripped down and its owners arrested, or her brother Edward's, when the young king had been unable to carry the weight of £1,000 in gold coins presented to him by the Aldermen of the City of London, Elizabeth's journey was entirely successful. As she received the same purse of crimson satin containing the City's contribution, she took the gift firmly with 'both hands' and said:

> I thank my lord mayor, his brethren, and you all. And whereas your request is that I should continue your good lady and queen, be ye ensured that I will be as good unto you as ever queen was to her people. No will in me can lack, neither do I trust shall there lack any power. And persuade yourselves that for the safety and quietness of you all I will not spare, if need be, to spend my blood. God thank you all.

Elizabeth's words, memorised and rehearsed, were apparently considered 'so pithily that the standers-by, as they embraced entirely her gracious answer, so they marvelled at the couching thereof'.[9] And yet the smooth running of the queen's procession was indicative of something far greater, for the regime wanted to press home that her reign would inaugurate a new era, rising from the tumultuous years of her brother's and sister's reigns.

Under Elizabeth, unity and concord had returned. The Tudor regime was reborn. Mulcaster's text worked closely with the pageant makers, whose painted tables emboldening the route contained religious texts that could have been taken from any firebrand Protestant sermon. Whether or not any words were heard amidst the noise of the crowd and the constant thunder of gunfire from the Tower, what must have struck Londoners watching the spectacle was the visual force of the pageants and the allegorical statements contained within them. Along the route, five separate pageants had been constructed upon scaffolds. The first of these was a huge triumphal arch, divided upon three levels. On the first level was Henry VII, Elizabeth's grandfather and founder of the Tudor dynasty, together with his wife, Elizabeth of York. Below them was her father Henry VIII, with the Tudor emblem of the red and white rose in front of him; and beside him his queen, Anne Boleyn, whose own emblem of a white falcon, wearing a gold crown and carrying a gilt sceptre in its talon, lay at her feet.

The moment could not have been more significant; and it was one which Elizabeth would have fully appreciated. For the first time since Anne Boleyn's execution twenty-two years before, Elizabeth's mother was acknowledged as Henry VIII's legitimate queen – something for which her daughter had waited a lifetime. Looking upon the portraits of her parents, Elizabeth would have understood entirely the imagery before her. On the third and final level sat an effigy of Elizabeth herself, highlighting her direct descent and true legitimacy. It was as if her brother Edward and sister Mary and their reigns had never existed.

As the procession continued, at Cheapside Elizabeth was seen to smile once more. Asked why, she replied that she had just heard an old man say in the crowd that he remembered 'old King Harry the Eighth'. Elizabeth saw herself as very much her father's daughter. 'She prides herself on her father and glories in him,' the Venetian ambassador had written in May 1557, observing how she bore a far greater resemblance in appearance to Henry than had her sister Queen Mary.[10]

The most impressive of all the displays was at the fourth arch, where two hills had been constructed. One was green, fertile and alive, and on it sat a young child beneath a laurel tree. The other was covered in sterile, dead grass, and a child dressed in black sat under a dry and leafless tree. Between the two hills was a grotto and a doorway, from which an old man carrying a scythe appeared, with his daughter by his side, expressing his desire 'to mow and reap the grass on the pleasant mount'. As she watched, Elizabeth asked who the old man was. 'Time' came the answer.

'It is Time,' she replied after some consideration, 'that hath brought me here.' What remained unsaid was witnessed and understood by all. The barren hill was intended to represent Queen Mary, who had died childless. Time and its daughter was a direct allusion to Mary's own motto, *Veritas temporis filia* – 'truth is the daughter of time'. The powerful imagery of the green, fertile hill in contrast to the sterile hill of the past could not be missed. Time, with scythe in hand, would eventually come to reap, as it had done for Mary. While Elizabeth remained young, she could not afford to let Time leave her barren.

The procession over, the new queen returned to Whitehall Palace. After she had attended a banquet and enjoyed 'a little dancing', she retired to bed 'at an early hour'. It had been a long day, and she had to prepare for the next – the most important day of her reign.

All the preparations were now in place. Westminster Hall had been 'decorated with the handsomest and most precious tapestries that were ever seen, they having been purchased by King Henry the Eighth'. To the side, a lavish buffet had been prepared, 'on which were 140 gold and silver drinking cups'.

Once the members of the nobility had again assembled according to their rank and file, Elizabeth walked the few hundred yards to Westminster Abbey for the official coronation ceremonies to take place. A special carpet had been laid for her route. In all, twenty-nine pieces of blue cloth, each 24 yards long, were stitched together to form a path almost a third of a mile in length for the queen to walk on from 'the marble chair in Westminster hall' to the choir door in Westminster church and up to the coronation throne.[11] As Elizabeth passed, her long train carried by the Duchess of Norfolk, the cloth was almost torn up from beneath her feet, 'by those who could get it', in a frantic rush for souvenirs or scraps to sell.

When Elizabeth reached the Abbey, to the sound of 'all the bells in London ringing', she was presented to the people from a 'lofty tribune' constructed for the occasion. After she was exhibited to her subjects from four separate corners, they were asked if they wished her to be crowned queen. 'Whereupon they all shouted "Yes!" and all the organs, pipes and trumpets and drums playing, the bells also ringing.' According to the Venetian ambassador, 'it seemed as if the world would come to an end'.

Elizabeth was then led up the steps to St Edward's chair, where, after mass was heard, the traditional anointing ceremony took place. For the moment, there would be little change in the actual ritual that had informed the coronations of kings for centuries. The coronation service itself was the last to be conducted using the medieval Latin ceremony, though parts of it were also read in English, at Elizabeth's insistence.[12] She even allowed the anointing chrism that had been obtained specially by her sister to be used, though she complained that it 'was grease and smelt ill'.

As Elizabeth returned to Westminster after the coronation ceremonies, she continued to indulge her fondness for displays of public affection. The stiff and formal Venetian ambassador looked on with disdain: 'She returned very cheerfully with a most smiling countenance for everyone, giving them all a thousand greetings, so that in my opinion she exceeded the bounds of gravity and decorum.'[13]

Back at Westminster Hall, the traditional coronation banquet lasted from 3 o'clock in the afternoon until 1 in the morning. It was hardly surprising that, the following day, 'Her Majesty was feeling rather tired' and found to be suffering from a heavy cold. Elizabeth cancelled a tournament arranged for the next day, though even in her absence the masques, banquets and tournaments that had been planned lasted well into the week.[14]

# God send our mistress a husband

Elizabeth's accession may have seemed an unusually smooth transition of power, but the fate of the House of Tudor could not have been more uncertain. The queen remained unmarried, and without a male heir she had no natural successor. The complicated tangle of family trees, lineages and lines of succession that the dysfunctional Tudor family had created made it almost impossible to decide who should inherit the throne if Elizabeth died. Already people had begun to argue over whether her cousin, Mary Queen of Scots, or Catherine Grey, the sister of Lady Jane, had the stronger claim.

Yet under no circumstances would Elizabeth be forced into naming her successor. Fearing that she might only set her own 'winding sheet' before her eyes, she understood that appointing an heir risked sparking a bloody power struggle, perhaps even civil war. Her own experience under her sister's reign, when plotters had sought her out, taught her a painful lesson. To decide upon, or 'limit', the succession, could only disinherit those who competed for the Crown, causing dejection and possible disruption.

Of course none of these claims would matter if Elizabeth bore the nation a natural successor – a male heir. But first she would have to marry. Her councillors assumed that, at 25, she would wish to marry sooner rather than later. As the Imperial ambassador noted, 'The Queen is of an age where she should in reason, and as is woman's way, be eager to marry and be provided for ... For that she should wish to remain a maid and never marry is inconceivable.'[1]

Over the years the image of the Virgin Queen, determined never to marry for the sake of her realm, grew stronger. It became Elizabeth's own particular brand, one that she exploited to the full in portraits and in literary comparisons to Diana, the chaste goddess of the hunt, establishing with it a reputation that has survived into posterity. It is an image with which we are all familiar; her famous declarations – that she would prefer to be a 'beggarwoman and single, far rather than queen and married',[2] or that she found 'the celibate life so agreeable ... she would rather go to a nunnery, or for that matter suffer death' – are well known. But they do not tell the whole story. During the first decade of her reign and beyond, while the queen remained of childbearing age, she made an equal number of contradictory statements that she would marry for the sake of her people. Elizabeth knew too well that the entire Tudor succession depended on it. 'She was the last issue of her father left,' she told the Duke of Württemberg, 'and only of her house.' She recognised that she would have to wed, which she promised to do: 'the care of her kingdome, and love of posteritie did ever councell her to alter' her single 'course of life'.[3] Earlier in the year she also informed her Parliament that, if any of them believed that she would remain single, they were mistaken. 'If any here doubt that I am as it were by vow or determination bent never to trade that life, put out that heresy; your belief is awry,' she said to the surprised onlookers; 'for as I think it best for a private woman, yet do I strive with myself to think it not meet for a prince. And if I can bend my liking to your need I will not resist such a mind.' Whatever Elizabeth privately wished for as a woman, she recognised it was her princely duty to marry.[4] This important distinction between her private thoughts and her public duties embodied the contradictions in Elizabeth's own personality. 'She had inwardly resolved,' she told the Imperial ambassador, 'that if ever she married it would be as a queen and not as Elizabeth.'[5] But it was clear to her contemporaries that Elizabeth's duty was to marry, and marry she would. To think otherwise was simply inconceivable.

It was only as Elizabeth grew older, and people began to question why the queen remained unmarried and without an heir, that there were concerns that Elizabeth had other, more personal, reasons against marriage. The first was quite obviously the risks involved with childbirth. At a time when one in five women lost their lives in having children, the dangers of marriage and sex must have crossed Elizabeth's mind. She might have recalled as a child the pain and anguish when her father's third wife, Jane Seymour, died in childbirth; she would certainly have been able to recall the death of Catherine Parr when Elizabeth was 14. 'Two examples so near,' one tract recalled, 'and in fresh memory, that they must needs make much indeed to the terror of mischance.'[6]

'What number of women every hour, even in their travail, or shortly after, be dispatched, and sent from their childbed to their burial?' the tract continued. 'Not only poor folk's wives, in whom negligence or poverty might have some excuse, but Countesses, Duchesses, Empresses, and Queens.'[7] It was surely best, according to the same tract, that 'Her Grace should never enter into that danger and battle, wherein she herself, hand to hand without aid, must fight with Death himself a more perilous fight than any set battle'. Against this, it was argued that 'So many fair ladies, so goodly gentlewomen, so fine and trim maids, pass these pikes so well … so easily, so merrily, so quietly in their fine beds of down … and after it look so fair and ruddy and so beautiful that it would make any man in the world enamoured of them,' and, notwithstanding, 'what haste they make to go to the battle again'. In addition, the 'bringing forth of children doth not only preserve women from many diseases, and other inconveniences, but it doth also clear their bodies, amend the colour, prolong their youth'.[8] But there was no getting away from the fact that, as the queen grew older, the risk would only increase. Later, when drawing up a memorandum setting out the arguments for and against marriage, against the sentence marked 'the peril of childbirth', William Cecil wrote simply: 'In God's hands.'

As Elizabeth continued to remain single, less salubrious rumours had begun to surface. 'If my spies do not lie, which I believe they do not,' the Spanish ambassador Feria reported in 1560, 'for a certain reason which they have given me, I understand she will not bear children.' The Venetian ambassador had also heard the same, having been told secrets that he did 'not dare to write'. 'The common opinion, confirmed by certain physicians,' de la Quadra considered, 'is that this woman is unhealthy, and it is believed certain that she will not bear children.'[9]

It was a rumour that would not go away. During the 1566 session of Parliament, certain members of the House of Commons were alleged to have searched out Elizabeth's physician, Dr William Huicke, cursing him 'as a dissuader of marriage'. The story was told by Camden, who was unable to give any further details on the matter ('for I know not what womanish impotency'). And near the end of Elizabeth's reign, the queen's own godson Sir John Harington added to the speculation over the reasons for Elizabeth's refusal to marry, arguing that 'in mind she hath ever had an aversion and (as many think) in body some indisposition to the act of marriage'. After Elizabeth was dead, some went even further; the dramatist Ben Jonson wrote to a friend of his that he had discovered Elizabeth 'had a membrane on her, which made her uncapable of man, though for her delight she tried many'. Jonson did not divulge where he had garnered his information, and in any case it was easy to make such accusations without fear of facing punishment now that the queen was dead. But even during Elizabeth's own lifetime, similar reports persisted: when one of Elizabeth's own gentlewomen of the Privy Chamber, Bess of Hardwick, alleged that the queen was 'not like other women' it was seized upon as evidence that perhaps Elizabeth did have some kind of medical complaint that made her unable to have children.

Many of these accusations can be dismissed: in 1566, Elizabeth's own doctor, claiming that 'there is not a man in the kingdom who knows her constitution better that I', told the French ambassador that she was perfectly capable of bearing children, perhaps even as many as ten.[10] Thirteen years later, having questioned the queen's physicians, her maids and her laundresses for evidence that Elizabeth was still having her regular monthly period, William Cecil noted with great satisfaction:

> Considering the proportion of her body, having no impediment of small-
> ness in stature, of largeness in body, nor no sickness nor lack of natural
> functions in those things that properly belong to the procreation of
> children, but contrariwise by judgment of physicians that know her estate
> in those things, and by the opinion of women, being more acquainted
> with Her Majesty's body in such things as properly appertain, to show
> probability of her aptness to have children.[11]

While the queen remained young enough to have children, she was constantly pressed from all corners to marry as soon as she possibly could. The subject of the queen's marriage and her succession became a kind of national obsession; there were times when it seemed William Cecil could think of little else. 'I am most sorry of all that her Majesty is not disposed seriously to marriage,' he later lamented, 'for I see likelihood of great evil both to this State and to the most of the good particular persons, if she shall not shortly marry ... God send our Mistress a husband, and by time a son, that we may hope our posterity shall have a masculine succession. This matter is too big for weak folks, and too deep for simple. The Queen's Majesty knoweth of it, and so I will end.'[12] Hundreds of books, poems and tracts survive, all urging the queen to take a husband and provide the realm with an heir. For his New Year's gift in 1560, Sir Thomas Challoner had presented Elizabeth with a book praising Henry VIII, but he could not resist ending the work with a sentimental plea for Elizabeth to marry and 'to bestow the bonds of your modesty on a husband ... For then a little Henry will play in the palace for us'.[13] Even her own bishops, whose faith should have been sympathetic to Elizabeth's private desire to remain single, stood against her. 'Single life, for many causes, is the best, I grant,' wrote Bishop Jewel of Salisbury, 'yet it is not best for everybody.' Later she would be approached by a delegation of bishops led by Matthew Parker, the Archbishop of Canterbury, who told her that they 'thought it our parts for our pastoral office, to be solicitous in that cause which all your loving subjects so daily sigh for and morningly in their prayers desire to appear to their eyes', namely for Elizabeth to give birth to an heir. If she continued to refuse to marry, they warned the queen that they would 'fear that this continued sterility in your Highness's person to be a token of God's displeasure towards us'.[14]

The debate was not so much about whether Elizabeth should marry, but whom she should take as her husband. Should she marry an Englishman and a subject, or a fellow royal and a foreigner? For many members of her court, there was no greater question that desperately needed an answer. For her subjects, there could be little doubt that they wanted the queen to marry a natural-born Englishman. 'We are all of us in favour of one of our own countrymen in preference to a stranger', Elizabeth's former tutor, Roger Ascham, told a friend. Memories of her sister Mary's marriage to the Spanish King Philip were still painful; Elizabeth herself had told the Spanish ambassador Feria before her accession that Mary 'had lost the affection of the people of this realm because she had married a foreigner'.[15] The dangers of a foreign match were manifold. The country might be drawn into war abroad, just as it had been in the disastrous campaign of 1558 that had witnessed the loss of Calais; 'they fear he will want to recover his estates with English forces and will keep them constantly at war', the Spanish ambassador warned of the problems with any foreign match. Her subjects, he wrote, would prefer her to marry one of them rather than the Spanish king, since 'what the English needed in England was a King who would stay in the country and govern'.[16]

There was also the obstacle of religion. Elizabeth instantly ruled out any prospect of marriage to a man who did not share her religious beliefs. This was to become a major sticking point for the various suits of marriage from the Hapsburg family, who also refused to give ground on the issue. 'I do not think it necessary to enumerate the thousand and one difficulties which would result if husband and wife held different conscientious views,' she wrote. 'What worse lot could befall a realm than division into two parties, one championing him and the other espousing her cause. That would be like a span of horses with various paces which could never pull together. What should be one will working in harmony would then be converted into a mutual hate.'[17]

But, perhaps most importantly, there was the question of whether Elizabeth would ever get to meet a potential foreign husband before their marriage. Traditionally, dynastic match-making precluded the couple being able to meet beforehand, instead having to make do with the miniatures and oils of portrait painters. Yet Elizabeth, perhaps mindful of her father's disastrous experience of trusting the sympathetic brush-strokes of his court painter Hans Holbein's portrait of Anne of Cleves, the 'Flanders Mare', was determined that she would meet the man she would marry; she had, she told ambassadors, 'taken a vow to marry no man she has not seen, and will not trust portrait painters'. It was a convincing argument, and one that supporters of an English match sought to play upon. If Elizabeth married a foreign suitor, one tract argued, she would be taking 'a pig in the poke'. In contrast, 'The Englishman is here at home, not his picture or image, but himself. His stature, colour, complexion, and behaviour, is to be seen face to face. And not only that, but his education and his bringing up, his study, exercise, and what things he hath a delight in, what things he doth refuse, every fault, imperfection, deformity, and whatsoever should be to his hinderance, is apparent and clear.'[18]

There were those who argued that it was improper for a queen, of the blood royal, to marry a subject, her inferior. Yet historical precedent stood against this. If it had been acceptable for English kings in the past to take subjects as their wives, then why not for a queen? 'Is it a disparagement for the Queen of England to marry an Englishman?' one tract asked. 'Why more than to the King of England to marry an English woman? The authority is all one; and as well is the English woman a subject to the crown as the English man. Do you think that King Henry VIII, her majesty's father, was disparaged, when he married her highness' mother, or Queen Jane, or Queen Catherine Parr ... and think you that all the rest of the Kings of England, of whom a great number married their subjects, were disparaged?'[19]

The nobility, however, had different ideas. They were highly suspicious of Elizabeth marrying a man from their own rank, not merely through jealousy but also through fear. As Cecil aptly put it, they were afraid that 'the novus homo who rose to kingship from their midst would favour his own family and oppress the others'. Even if Elizabeth were to marry a Catholic and a foreigner, they 'would much liefer [rather] have him as King than a native-born Englishman, who would only increase his faction, while they would fall from their high estate'.[20]

It was a sentiment shared by the Earl of Sussex, one of the members of the ancient nobility who was encouraged by 'the great amity ... the great riches that might be gotten by foreign marriages'. But above all he feared the revenge that an English husband might exact on his fellow nobles, knowing full well 'the desire of domestical persons to exalt or overthrow old friends or foes according to their affections'.[21] In time, it would be the candidacy of one particular Englishman for Elizabeth's hand in marriage that the earl would come to especially detest.

For now, however, that hand appeared to be open to all comers. Men waited, expecting an announcement sooner rather than later; the security of the realm depended upon it. 'The more I think over this business,' Feria wrote to Philip II in early December 1558, 'the more certain I am that everything depends upon the husband this woman may take.'[22]

# PART THREE

+>-<+

## A great resort of wooers

# Many great difficulties

Already English candidates for the queen's hand in marriage were accumulating. Among the names being talked of were some of the leading members of the nobility, including the Duke of Norfolk and the Earls of Westmorland and Arundel. Only Arundel considered himself a serious candidate for Elizabeth's hand. Coming from the oldest noble family, Arundel was a traditional Catholic who had risen to become one of the main conservative figures in Henry VIII's Council. After being imprisoned by the Duke of Northumberland during Edward VI's reign on trumped-up charges of conspiracy against the state, Arundel was later released and turned against the duke, deserting him during his attempt to keep Lady Jane Grey on the throne. He once again became a leading councillor under Mary. The Spanish ambassador Feria considered that the earl, approaching his fifties, stood little chance of success. Not only was he old enough to be Elizabeth's father; he was dismissed as 'a flighty man, of small ability'; he was 'somewhat advanced in years and also rather silly and loutish, is not well-favoured, nor has a handsome figure'.

Arundel had a more optimistic view of his chances. Despite being a generation older than the queen, as one of the premier peers of the realm, Arundel believed that he had a strong chance of winning Elizabeth's hand in marriage. He was soon seen at her court 'very smart and clean, and they say he carried his thoughts very high'. The Spanish ambassador observed that he had 'been going about in high glee for some time' and it was rumoured that he had been bribing Elizabeth's ladies-in-waiting to speak well of him, whilst it was reported that he was about to sell 'all he has' to spend on banquets and a jewel as a New Year's gift for the queen.[1]

Feria had other plans. He had grown attracted to the idea that Elizabeth might be married to an ally of the Hapsburg family in order to keep a toehold in English affairs. His initial choice was to marry Elizabeth to Philip II's cousin, the Duke of Savoy. Feria laid down his plans for dealing with the reluctant queen. 'The best course of action,' he considered, would be 'to get my foot into the palace, so as to speak oftener to the Queen as she is a woman who is very fond of argument. Everybody thinks she will not marry a foreigner and they cannot make out whom she favours, so that nearly everyday some new cry is raised about a husband.'[2] Feria's strategy was carefully crafted. 'We must begin by getting her into talk about your Majesty, and run down the idea of her marrying an Englishman', not forgetting to remind her that her sister Mary would never have married a mere subject. 'After that we can take those whom she might marry here and pick them to pieces one by one, which will not require much rhetoric, for there is not a man amongst them worth anything, counting the married ones and all.'[3]

But Feria did not find Elizabeth or her councillors receptive to his diplomatic charms. Philip's ill-fated marriage to her sister Mary had cast a long shadow over the Spanish king's reputation. 'They are glad to be free from your Majesty,' Feria wrote back, astounded, 'as though you had done them harm instead of good.' He continued: 'I am so isolated from them that I am much embarrassed and puzzled to get the means of what is going on, for truly they run away from me as if I were the devil.' Where once he had resided in a suite of rooms inside Whitehall Palace, he now found himself suddenly ejected. 'In return for all my efforts to please I believe they would like to see me thrown in the river.'[4]

To begin with, Philip had also been keen to go along with Feria's scheme, especially if it might persuade Elizabeth 'that it was not to her interest to marry a subject'. It soon became clear, however, that Savoy would be needed to broker a deal elsewhere, for the French had demanded his marriage to a French princess as part of the terms of a peace settlement that was currently being negotiated. There was little choice but for Philip, less than two months after his wife's death, to offer his own hand in marriage to her sister. Philip was reluctant from the outset. Having carefully considered the marriage with his councillors, he admitted: 'Many great difficulties present themselves and it is difficult for me to reconcile my conscience to it as I am obliged to reside in my other dominions and consequently could not be much in England, which is apparently what they fear.' This was not the only sticking point. Elizabeth's Protestantism presented another substantial obstacle that would not be overcome unless she became a Catholic. Besides this, there was 'the heavy expense I should be put to in England by reason of the costly entertainment necessary to the people there'. But, despite near bankruptcy, Philip was determined to press on:

I nevertheless cannot lose sight of the enormous importance of such a match to Christianity and the preservation of religion which has been restored to England by the help of God. Seeing also the importance that the country should not fall back into its former errors which would cause to our own neighbouring dominions serious dangers and difficulties, I have decided to place on one side all other considerations which might be urged against it and am resolved to render this service to God, and offer to marry the queen of England.[5]

Privately, Philip was deeply uncertain if he had made the right decision. In a secret letter written on the same day, he described himself as 'a condemned man, awaiting his fate'. 'If it were not to serve God, believe me, I should not have got into this ... Nothing would make me do this except the clear knowledge that it would gain the Kingdom [of England] for his service and faith.'[6]

By the end of January, speculation and rumour were rife about whom the queen would choose to be her husband, with an announcement expected imminently. 'Some persons declare,' the Venetian ambassador observed in a letter, 'that she will take the Earl of Arundel, he being the chief peer of this realm, notwithstanding his being old in comparison with the queen. This report is founded on the constant and daily favours he receives in public and private from her majesty.' But this was only gossip, he wrote, and could certainly not be confirmed. His final words echoed the thoughts of many an Englishman: 'There may God give her a good and Christian husband, that the affairs of this kingdom may not continue to grow worse.'[7]

One of the first tasks of the new Parliament immediately after the Queen's coronation was to establish Elizabeth's legitimacy to the throne and end the years of uncertainty surrounding her royal title. A statute was passed which declared the queen 'rightly, lineally, and lawfully descended from the blood royal' at the same time as pronouncing 'all sentences and Acts of Parliament derogatory to this declaration to be void'. The ghosts of Elizabeth's childhood had been put to rest, as had her mother Anne Boleyn's attainder and execution, her disinheritance under the reigns of both her father and her brother, and her own sister's refusal to even recognise her as a sibling, let alone her lawful heir.

Mindful of the turmoil of the previous years, it was perhaps not surprising that in the same session, members would seek security as their chosen course for the future. It was not long before the issue of Elizabeth's marriage surfaced in Parliament. 'Arguments that a request may be made to the Queen's Highness for marriage,' the clerk noted in the journal of the House of Commons, recording the proceedings of Parliament just days into the session on 4 February. According to the Venetian ambassador, during the debate its members urged that Elizabeth should marry 'within her realm', in other words, marry an Englishman and a loyal subject.[8] Given the lessons of Mary's disastrous marriage this was understandable. A decision was reached to approach the queen and make a humble suit to her to marry as soon as she could.

On the afternoon of 6 February the speaker, Thomas Gargrave, together with members of the Council and a delegation of thirty MPs, was granted an audience with Elizabeth where the speaker made 'request to her highness for marriage'. According to Elizabeth's first biographer William Camden, Gargrave delivered a stinging threat, demanding that Elizabeth renounce her single life: 'Nothing can be more repugnant to the common good,' he said, 'than to see a Princess, who by marriage may preserve the Commonwealth in peace, to lead a single life, like a vestal nun.'[9] They were powerful words, though whether they were actually spoken is unlikely. Writing over fifty years after the event, Camden was prone to the occasional elaboration of the truth when it suited, and in any case the remarks do not fit with the account given by Richard Grafton, who was present in the audience and who recorded that the speaker 'solemnly and eloquently set forth the message'.

After a considered pause, Elizabeth delivered her reply. She liked their petition, she told them, 'and take it in good part' since it 'containeth no limitation of place or person'. 'If it had been otherwise,' she continued, 'I must needs have misliked it very much and thought it in you a great presumption, being unfitting and altogether unmet for you to require them they that may command.' Nevertheless, she told them, 'whensoever it may please God to incline my heart to another kind of life', she would do nothing against the interests of her realm. 'And therefore put that clean out of your heads.' Whatever the future held, she was determined to protect the safety of her nation, 'whereof I will never shun to spend my life'. With that in mind, she insisted that 'whomsoever my chance shall be to light upon' as her husband, she trusted that above all 'he shall be as careful for the realm and you as myself'. She continued:

And albeit it might please Almighty God to continue me still in this mind to live out of the state of marriage, yet it is not to be feared but He will so work in my heart and in your wisdoms good provision by His help may be made in convenient time, whereby the realm shall not remain destitute of an heir that may be a fit governor, and peradventure more beneficial to the realm than such offspring as may come of me. For, although I be never so careful of your well doings and mind ever so to be, yet may my issue grow out of kind and become perhaps ungracious. And in the end, this shall be for me sufficient, that a marble stone shall declare that a Queen, having reigned such a time, lived and died a virgin.[10]

'And here I end, and take your coming unto me in good part, and give you all eftsoons my hearty thanks,' Elizabeth added, though she ended with the barb: 'more yet for your zeal and good meaning than for your petition.'

It was a speech full of complexities and mixed meanings, one that threw up more questions than it did answers. Did Elizabeth really believe that she would live out her days, as she hoped she might, a virgin never to marry or conceive children? According to William Camden, Elizabeth had supplemented the drama by removing her coronation ring from her finger and showing it to the MPs gathered, saying, 'Yea, to satisfy you, I have already joined myself in marriage to an Husband, namely, the Kingdom of England. And behold, which I marvel ye have forgotten, the pledge of this my wedlock and marriage with my kingdom.'[11] Camden's version of events, however, bears no relation to the original version of Elizabeth's speech, written in her own handwriting and stored away in Cecil's papers.

To those listening, Elizabeth's words seemed clear. The queen had, hadn't she, taken heart from their petition? They had been careful not to prescribe to her the details of her marriage – a wise move indeed. Elizabeth had in return spoken plainly that it was more a question of *when* rather than *if* she should marry. She had, hadn't she, said that 'whomsoever my chance shall be to light upon', she trusted '*he* shall be as careful for the realm ... by my good will *he* shall be such as be as careful for the realm and you as myself'? All this pleased the Commons immensely. There may have been some reservations about providing the realm with an heir, but she had, hadn't she, pledged that with God's help 'in convenient time' the realm might have 'such offspring as may come of me'? As they departed the chamber content with the outcome of their efforts, Elizabeth's words only fuelled speculation that she would marry, and marry soon.[12]

Elizabeth was beginning to take a religious course which ensured that Philip's suit was doomed to failure from the start. Despite Feria's insistence that the queen 'differed very little' from Catholics, 'and only dissented from three or four things in the mass', the first sign that Elizabeth was not content with maintaining the Catholic faith bequeathed to her by her sister came on Christmas Day 1558, when she had walked out of the divine service after her orders that mass should not be heard were ignored. Three days later, a proclamation was issued, allowing for the gospel, the epistles and the Ten Commandments once again to be read out in English, a move that restored worship to its former state under Henry VIII. There were to be further changes. Already, in the early days of Elizabeth's reign, a document named the *Device for Alteration of Religion* was circulating urging religious uniformity based upon the 1552 Book of Common Prayer, the text that represented the high watermark of the Reformation in Edward VI's reign, though it advised caution at the pace of religious change.[13]

William Cecil, however, was unashamed of his dedication and attachment to the Protestant cause. When he was charged with being the author of religious change under Elizabeth, he did not deny it. 'I must confess,' he admitted, 'that I am thereof guilty but not thereby at fault and thereto I will stand as long as I shall live.'[14] This became manifest when Cecil introduced a Bill of Supremacy into Parliament during the second week of February, re-establishing the queen as Supreme Head of the Church of England and, in so doing, removing any semblance of papal authority. Only after some months of severe wrangling and disputes in the House of Lords was it eventually passed.

There were also significant shifts in foreign policy. The Treaty of Cateau-Cambrésis, signed with France on 2 April 1559, brought peace between the two nations. Commissioners on both sides had been working on the settlement since the last weeks of Mary's reign. Principal to the negotiations was the fate of Calais, England's only toehold on the Continent, which had been lost to the French in 1558. Elizabeth insisted that it should be returned to England; 'she would have them [the commissioners] beheaded if they made peace without Calais,' she told

Feria. But the queen knew that she was in no position to bargain. In the end, the French agreed to hand over Calais after eight years, or else compensate the English financially. Few believed that this would ever take place, but it at least allowed the honourable peace for which both sides, exhausted, were desperate.

These developments formed the backdrop to Feria's negotiations with Elizabeth over the question of her marriage, which he still hoped might be to Philip. Feria ignored the religious direction Elizabeth was taking and hoped that the proposed changes would come to nothing. He wrote back to Philip, 'If the marriage is carried out the rest will be soon arranged, and all will proceed in accordance with the glory of God and the wishes of your Majesty.'[15] This was seriously misleading.

Between January and March, the ambassador had an audience with Elizabeth on at least three occasions, raising Philip's proposal of marriage. She replied that although she understood the marriage 'would be advantageous to her honour', she hoped this could be obtained through friendship, as 'she had no desire to marry, as she had intimated from the first day'. Elizabeth set out her reasoning. To Feria's horror, she took the opportunity to deny 'point blank' the authority of the pope, 'which she had previously only pointed out indirectly'. Added to this, the queen raised a new, compelling, argument against marrying Philip. As he had married her sister, he was still her brother-in-law, so any marriage to him was invalid and forbidden by the Scriptures. In such cases, it was always possible to obtain a dispensation from the pope, but to do so would recognise the validity of Henry VIII's marriage to Catherine of Aragon, and hence her own illegitimacy, since Henry's marriage to Anne Boleyn would then be considered a bigamous one. It was a sound point, already noted by the French, and one to which Feria had no answer.[16]

Elizabeth also made it clear that she would only listen to her people, who 'did not wish her to marry a foreigner'. To round off her dismissal of Philip's suit, she said that 'several persons had told her that your Majesty would come here and then go off to Spain directly'. 'This she said with great laughter,' the ambassador noted, 'as if she could read [his] secret thoughts.' Feria was alarmed. 'She is so well informed about this that it looks as if she had seen His Majesty's letters. This should be taken good note of.'[17]

Feria nevertheless persisted, eventually forcing Elizabeth to make her feelings known – and admit the truth about her religious leanings. At a meeting with the ambassador in mid-March, Elizabeth seemed 'disturbed and excited', telling Feria 'after a time that she could not marry your Majesty as she was a heretic ... she kept repeating ... that she was heretical and consequently could not marry your Majesty'. Still, Feria refused to believe her. 'I said that I did not consider she was heretical and could not believe that she would sanction the things that were being discussed in Parliament, because if she changed the religion she would be ruined.' The emperor, he warned her, would not allow it, for he 'would not separate the union of the church for all the kingdoms of the earth'. Elizabeth was quick to display her sharp tongue. 'Then much less you would do it for a woman,' she replied. Feria was somewhat taken aback, and could only reply that 'Men did more for a woman than for anything else'.

As if to drive a wedge further between Philip's ambitions and her own sensibilities, Elizabeth continued her impassioned attack on the Catholic faith. Each year so much money had been pouring out of the country into the pope's coffers, she said, 'that she must put an end to it'. For good measure, she added that the bishops were 'lazy poltroons'.[18] Feria was astounded. As he was being ushered out of the chamber, he ended by saying that 'she was no longer the Queen Elizabeth' he had known before, 'and that if she went on thus she was a lost woman'.

Philip was left with little hope. He had now convinced himself that he had no wish to marry Elizabeth. Days later, before he had in fact heard of her final rejection, he arranged a marriage with the 14-year-old Elisabeth de Valois, the eldest and most beautiful daughter of Henry II and Catherine de' Medici. The Duke of Alba stood as proxy for Philip at the ceremony, and somewhat more bizarrely, at the official consummation ceremony in the marriage bed that same night.[19] Hearing the news, Elizabeth 'affected one or two little sighs, and then observed, with a smile, that her name was a fortunate one'. 'I told her', wrote Feria, 'I was very sorry, but the fault was more with her than with Your Majesty; she knew how unwilling I had been to accept her refusal.'

'It was your Majesty's fault it had fallen through and not hers,' Elizabeth snapped back, 'as he had given me no reply', adding, 'your Majesty could not have been so much in love with her as I had said, as you had not had patience to wait four months for her.'[20]

Despite her piquant display of rejection, Elizabeth was privately relieved. From the start she had consistently displayed her opposition to

Philip's suit, and was glad that it had been he who had chosen to break it off.

The threat still remained, however, that Philip, in fresh alliance with the French, might punish her for her religious changes and abolition of the Catholic faith. But Elizabeth had gambled that, despite the new treaty, France remained for Philip too great a rival to leave her undefended against the French, even if she did reintroduce Protestantism to England. She was right. Though Philip had failed to obtain Elizabeth's hand, he still hoped that a member of his Hapsburg family might do so. The family motto was 'Others make war: you, fortunate Austria, marry'. And it was his first cousin, Emperor Ferdinand of Austria, to whom Philip turned for support. Since Charles V's abdication in 1556, when the title of emperor had passed to his brother and Ferdinand's father, Maximilian, relations between the two separate branches of the Hapsburg family had not been close. As a result, when the prospect of Philip's marriage to Elizabeth was still a possibility, Feria had not been well disposed to the idea of a match with Ferdinand. 'It would be inconvenient enough for Ferdinand to marry here even if he took the titbit from Your Majesty's hand, but very much worse if it were arranged in any other way.'[21]

Now that the diplomatic light had shifted, the ambassador saw matters rather differently. 'If Ferdinand is a man,' he wrote, 'backed up as he will be by Your Majesty, he will be able not only to reform religion and pacify the country, but, even though the Queen may die, to keep the country in his fist.' Soon, with the idea having firmly taken root, Philip was committed to protecting Elizabeth as if she was his own sister, telling Feria to 'banish any shadow of doubt she may have that because she did not marry me and I have entered the French alliance I shall take any less interest in her affairs.'[22] Indeed, over the course of the next thirty years, Philip would maintain a close watch on the English queen.

Ferdinand was undoubtedly interested in investigating the idea of marriage, if not for himself, then for one of his two sons, the archdukes Ferdinand and Charles. Rumours that the King of Denmark had also been expressing an interest in marrying Elizabeth spurred him on. In February 1559 he sent his ambassador, Count Georg von Helfenstein, to discover 'whether this Queen and the Lords of her realm have a preference for one of our sons'.[23]

Upon meeting the queen, Helfenstein was overwhelmed by Elizabeth's charisma, 'speaking extempore and with many brilliant, choice and felicitous phrases and rare benevolence' and reported back that Elizabeth certainly seemed interested in the prospect of marrying one of the archdukes. There was one problem, however. Elizabeth had been explicit that she would only agree to marriage with a suitor if she could actually meet them in person, claiming that she had taken a vow to marry no man whom she had not previously seen, 'and will not trust portrait painters and a thousand things of the usual sort'.

In any case, Elizabeth had high physical expectations of her suitors. She told the Spanish ambassador: 'Amongst other qualities which she says her husband must possess is that he should not sit at home all day amongst the cinders, but should in time of peace keep himself employed in warlike exercises.'[24] Ambassadors were quick to exploit the queen's desires, taking care to describe the physical attractiveness of their masters and to discredit the features of their rivals. For instance, Elizabeth had apparently been told that the Archduke Ferdinand 'had a bigger head than that of the earl of Bedford, and was unfit to govern'.[25]

When it came to physical prowess, however, there was one man who stood shoulders above the rest of the court.[26] The ambassadors observing court life could not help but speculate about Elizabeth's relationship with her favourite, Robert Dudley. Soon rumours began to fill the court. The Venetian ambassador, Paulo Tiepolo, wrote that Dudley was 'in great favour and very intimate with Her Majesty', though he stopped short of making any accusations of improper behaviour that could damage his own diplomatic relations with the queen, merely stating with enough suggestion that: 'On this subject I ought to report the opinion of many, but I doubt whether my letters may not miscarry or be read, wherefore it is better to keep silence than to speak ill.'[27]

# God hath increased you with honour

Gossip was rife. Despite Elizabeth's promise to her Parliament that she would marry, no change in the situation had been forthcoming. The queen remained single; the realm remained without an heir. It seemed clear to many looking on that one man was responsible for distracting the Queen's attention from her duty. 'During the last few days', the Spanish ambassador Feria wrote in mid-April, 'Lord Robert has come so much into favour that he does whatever he likes with affairs and it is even said that her majesty visits him in his chamber day and night'. Though some dismissed such talk as tittle-tattle, the queen's next move just days later surprised everyone. On St George's Day, 23 April 1559, Elizabeth bestowed her first sign of significant reward upon her Master of the Horse, and nominated Dudley as a Knight of the Garter.

Elizabeth could not have made a greater public statement. The honour, established by Edward III in 1348, was considered a deeply prestigious one, usually reserved for the highest orders of the nobility. The number of knights was limited to twenty-six, with vacancies made available only through either death or disgrace. Dudley was to become only the 342nd person to be awarded the honour in the two centuries of its existence (Prince William was created the 1,000th Knight in 2008). The Knights of the Order were regarded as the monarch's closest companions, men who were to be distinguished from the rest of the nobility not only by having the title KG after their name, but also by being allowed to wear the insignia of the Order, in the form of a small, round, enamelled gold pendant depicting St George on horseback slaying the dragon, encircled by a garter belt, and hung from a ribbon tied around the neck, known commonly as the 'lesser George'. It was a badge of superiority, flashed around the court by those lucky enough to own one.

Dudley was evidently proud of his new honour, purchasing a case for his garter worth 2s 6d.[1] He also had his seal engraved with a new coat of arms encircled by the garter belt and its motto, '*Honi soit quy mal y pensé*' – shame upon him who thinks evil upon it – at a cost of 30 shillings.[2] No expense was spared. The queen's own goldsmith John

Everard designed and made Dudley's 'lesser George', which hung on a gold chain 'set with diamonds' for £70. Spanish ribbon costing 12d was also specially purchased to hang the award around Dudley's neck.[3] The George and its jewelled chain features in all of Dudley's portraits, hanging proudly down on the front of his doublet.

The Duke of Norfolk and the Earl of Rutland were also nominated as Knights of the Order alongside Dudley. Their promotions were entirely understandable. Both were members of the 'ancient' nobility as opposed to those nobles recently raised to the peerage (as Dudley's family had been); Norfolk, the only surviving duke in the ranks of the nobility, was also Earl Marshal, while Rutland had already carved out a distinguished career as a soldier and diplomat. But for Robert Dudley, who still ranked beneath the nobility and whose father many still regarded as a traitor, to receive the award was contemptible. Both John Dudley, created a Knight of the Order in 1543, and Robert Dudley's uncle, Sir Andrew Dudley (made a Knight in 1552) had been degraded from the Order. Many considered Dudley was permanently tarnished by their disgrace. The only basis for Dudley's appointment seemed to be his closeness to the queen. The more traditional members of the Order were outraged; the historian William Camden later wrote how the award aroused 'the admiration of all men' – 'admiration' used here to mean 'wonder'.

In spite of his loyal service to both Mary and Elizabeth, Robert Dudley had found it impossible to rid himself of the stigma of his traitorous background. That year he had purchased, for 6s 8d, a copy of the Act repealing his attainder that had been passed in the 1558 Parliament.[4] He had sought to rehabilitate himself slowly, making amends for past misconduct, but he could never escape the taint of dishonour that his father, and his grandfather, Edmund Dudley, had bequeathed him, having both been executed for treason.

Members of the nobility, proud of their own unbroken lineages and loyalty to the Crown, were certainly not going to allow him to forget it. The Earl of Sussex was a friend of Dudley at the beginning of the queen's reign, playing dice with him or even sharing sides on the tennis court, but when he fell into an argument with Dudley several years later, he ended with the pointed jibe that 'neither he [Sussex] nor any one of his family had been traitors to their sovereign'. Sussex and Dudley were to fall out drastically over the question of the queen's marriage. On his deathbed, Sussex warned his friends to be wary of the man he called 'the gypsy'. Dudley had earned the nickname through his slightly tanned complexion, probably gained through spending his days outside hunting and on horseback. Although his olive skin would go unnoticed today, it stood out in sharp contrast to the pale visages of his contemporaries.

But the name was also deliberately intended as a slur upon Dudley's character and his lifestyle. Gypsies, or 'Gipeyans' as they preferred to term themselves, had first arrived from the Continent at the beginning of the sixteenth century. They were widely detested for their alternative lifestyle, which many viewed with suspicion. Soon they became associated in the common imagination with a range of every imaginable crime from selling poisons to stealing horses and kidnapping children. They were also regarded as sexually promiscuous. Henry VIII considered them 'lewd persons', though on one occasion he pardoned a group for 'a most shameful and detestable murder'.[5] Elizabeth shared her father's views. In 1559 she wrote thanking one of her noblemen, Lord Mountjoy, for arresting a group of gypsies. They had, she wrote, a 'horrible and shameful life that these kind of people do haunt' which 'from their youth of long time harboured this lewd life'. By all laws of the realm, they were 'to be used as felons'. 'Heretofore in our late sister's time some example of them was made by execution of some of the like'.[6]

Still there were those, family and friends alike, who were pleased for Robert Dudley's rapid promotion through the ranks. Dudley's sister Catherine, Countess of Huntingdon, wrote congratulating him on his promotion: 'I hear God hath increased you with honour since my departure. I pray let me desire you to be thankful unto him that showeth himself so gracious unto you. I am bold to write this because I know honour doth rather blind the eye than clear it.'[7] Catherine went on to ask a favour of her brother for her husband, who, despite being troubled with debts, 'useth not such flattering behaviour as many will do unto prosperity'. Others were more forthcoming. Dudley was inundated by requests for help and assistance, messages of goodwill and support, as nobles, gentlemen, ladies, merchants and the poor looked to secure their future through the queen's new favourite. Typical were letters asking Dudley to intercede on the writer's behalf, using his influence with Elizabeth to ensure that their suits were dealt with quickly – and favourably. Such was his sway over the queen, many seemed either to hope or to believe that all Dudley needed to do was speak to Elizabeth or pass on a letter to ensure a speedy success. Dudley's surviving papers are filled with examples of these requests, each pledging the writer's dedication to Dudley's cause. 'Seeing the great affairs whereat your honour is continually travailed', wrote George Gilpin, a gentleman who was having problems securing a grant of land, he had 'been afraid to trouble you with my humble suit but now am of pure necessity constrained to beseech your honour to stand my good lord to further this my suit where of I have here enclosed a brief note unto the Queen's Majesty'.[8] Many were simply desperate; Thomas Benger, a former member of the royal household who had recently been dismissed, wrote to Dudley begging to be restored to his former position. 'I am in her highness' displeasure,' he wrote, 'and so doth all men think, for that I only am forgotten and no man else. For such my shame and grief as I would to God the rack had torn me in a thousand pieces.' He asked for Dudley to intercede and to tell the queen that 'although I live from her highness as I take it, like a banished man, yet would no man fayner to creep to his food, than I on the knees of my heart desire to serve and follow her'.[9]

With the Dudley name restored to power and influence once again, requests frequently involved former servants of the family, men and women who had served in the Duke of Northumberland's household, but had fallen on hard times during Mary's reign. In early April 1559, Sir James Croft wrote to Dudley, asking him to help an unnamed 'gentleman's widow, whom my lord your father (whose soul God pardon) favoured well'. Croft trusted that she would be treated well, given the knowledge he had of 'the goodness of your own nature which I have known always to be favourable to women'.[10] Shortly afterwards, Lady Joan Poyntz contacted him requesting a prebend for 'my man Freeman, the which was once servant to my lord your father, whom I think your lordship knoweth well ... speak to the Queen's Majesty that for my sake he may have it'.[11] William Lord Eure sought Dudley's help in obtaining a stewardship that had been 'granted me in King Edward's times under him and my lord your father'.[12] Dudley's household accounts reveal that he was at pains to take care of his father's former servants, and sent them money and rewards. 'To an olde man sometime your lordship's porter upon a supplication delivered' he sent 19 shillings, while to 'a poor woman that named herself your lordship's father's nurse' he sent 2s 8d.[13] Despite John Dudley's notoriety, there were still those prepared to defend his honour. One supporter, Thomas Trollope, even wrote to Dudley proposing to publish a tract to 'take away the infamies passed against your father and grandfather', which he believed 'shall win you the hearts of all the nobility and commons of the realm without grudge' and give 'a probable reason to prove their unjust and innocent deaths procured through envy and malice'.[14]

Even the most unlikely sought favour at Dudley's hands. Sir Thomas Cornwallis was an ardent Catholic and had been a member of the Council that presided over Dudley's imprisonment in the Tower. By 1557 he had been made Comptroller of the Household, demonstrating frequently his hostility to Mary's opponents, not least Princess Elizabeth herself. Upon Elizabeth's accession, fortune's wheel had turned and Cornwallis had been placed under house arrest since November 1558. Desperate to secure 'my further liberty' he wrote to Dudley in July, having heard from his wife and brother 'your Lordship's great courtesy in suffering them to have recourse unto you in the time of their suits . . . although it is not in me to deserve any part of this your goodness, yet hath your own good nature in this point emboldened me to use your friendship further'.[15] Cornwallis may have expected nothing in return given his treatment of Dudley six years earlier, but his supplication worked: he was shortly given leave to retire peacefully to his estates in Suffolk, where he remained for the next forty-five years, outliving the Queen, until his death at the age of 86.

Like Cornwallis, few suitors were to be disappointed in their approaches to Dudley. He was keen to satisfy as many requests as possible, and those who were emboldened enough to write frequently found themselves rewarded with the grants of land that they had asked for, and, if not the exact political office or ecclesiastical patronage they had desired, Dudley was often able to find some other position on their behalf. It was a clever game to be playing; as Dudley well knew, a favour done might one day be a favour returned. As he built up his network of supporters, each day his influence at court grew stronger and more widespread. He had become the focal point for patronage, the person through whom people might gain crucial access to the queen. And yet his privileged position would continue to stoke jealousy among the nobility and his enemies, envious of his increased power and closeness to Elizabeth. 'He does whatever he likes with affairs,' the Spanish ambassador was soon to grumble.

Dudley was also well aware of how his position as Master of the Horse might also be used to his advantage to build up his network of patronage amongst the nobility and create his own separate power base if ever he needed its support. He had at his disposal a number of positions within the Royal Stables, which he distributed to great effect, using them to reward favours or win support. For instance, Thomas, Earl of Ormond wrote to him in July, requesting that his man 'have a room of a groom of the stable, according to your promise, so doing you shall mind me to requite the same'. Dudley quickly obliged.[16] In particular, Dudley sought to gather young sons of the nobility within his network, men who one day would become the leaders of their houses. Elizabeth, Lady Darcy, the widow of Thomas, Lord Darcy, a nobleman who had served as Lord Chamberlain under Dudley's father during the reign of Edward VI, wrote to thank him for accepting her son Robert into his service, 'into ye house that my Lord his good father bear so earnest good will unto ... showing your most honorable favour towards him divers ways for his honorable father's sake'.[17] The same month Henry Lord Stafford also wrote thanking him, being 'so much bound for taking my poor son into your service that all the days of my life I shall think myself bound from the bottom of my heart to do your service as any servant that you have this day living'.[18]

Dudley was always especially keen to bolster his network of supporters, inviting men to join him at court as part of his retinue, a group of men loyal to their master who would wear his heraldic badge or particular colour (their 'livery') as testament to their allegiance. Many of them were long-standing members of the family circle, dedicated to the Dudley name; men such as Thomas Blount, William Hyde, Richard Verney and Anthony Forster were willing to aid him financially, offering loans and even their own houses for his convenience. Yet Dudley remained on the lookout for new recruits: a few months later, he would write to one gentleman, Francis Yaxley, promising him his support if he came to court: 'I must say ye are very welcome always unto me, and will be glad to have you there.' Dudley admitted that joining his company would hardly involve the quiet life, but he promised that it would be worth it. 'The trade of court you know is such as presence with diligence helpeth much. And where the benefits thereof are gotten with less quietness than you now enjoy, I would be loathe to persuade you from your best liking, yet if the other can content you, there is no cause to discourage a great good hope of you very well doing, considering what you can deserve.'[19]

\*

Two days after Dudley's surprise promotion as a Knight of the Garter, on St Mark's Day, 25 April, the Earl of Pembroke held a celebratory dinner for the queen at his residence at Baynard's Castle, his imposing medieval residence overlooking the Thames between Blackfriars and London Bridge. It was here that the Lords of the Council had met in secret and taken their decision to desert Dudley's father and Queen Jane in July 1553. Having spoken out in person against John Dudley, Pembroke himself had thrown a cap full of gold coins into the air in celebration. Despite this, he had remained a constant and loyal friend of Robert's; their bond of friendship was secured during Dudley's committed service at the siege of St Quentin.[20]

That evening, as the sun set, Elizabeth rode down the river on a barge; crowds in their thousands gathered on the banks to catch a glimpse of their new queen as she crossed the water with 'hundreds of boats and barges rowing about her'. It was a spectacle worth waiting to see: 'Trumpets blew, drums beat, flutes played, guns were discharged, fireworks rose into the air.' Dudley accompanied the queen at the banquet, where he gave her a pair of perfumed gloves set with gilt buttons that had cost 18s 4d to have made.[21]

He had assumed the role of her consort in all but name. Many were shocked by their behaviour; the queen should have been entering into serious marriage negotiations with the Hapsburgs, and Dudley was a married man, despite the fact that there was still no sign of his wife at court.

Amy's constant absence bred uncertainty and demanded that further questions be asked. Why was Dudley's wife never present at court? And what were her reasons for hiding away in the shadows? A new, more shocking, rumour had begun to circulate, this time involving Amy herself. Feria reported what he had heard back to the Imperial court:

> People talk of this so freely that they go so far as to say that his wife has a malady in one of her breasts and the Queen is only waiting for her to die to marry Lord Robert. I can assure your Majesty that matters have reached such a pass that I have been brought to consider whether it would not be well to approach Lord Robert on your Majesty's behalf promising your help and favour and coming to terms with him.[22]

The ambassador wrote again four days after the banquet at Pembroke's residence, equally concerned by fresh gossip that he had encountered:

'they say she is in love with Lord Robert and never lets him leave her.'[23]

Feria was not the only one who had picked up the news that Robert's wife Amy was unwell. The Venetian ambassador sent his own report back to Italy on 4 May: 'Robert Dudley,' he wrote, was 'a very handsome young man towards whom in various ways the Queen evinces such affection and inclination that many persons believe that if his wife, who has been ailing for some time, were perchance to die, the Queen might easily take him for her husband.'[24]

# A visit

Amy may not have been seen at court, but she had in fact remained at William Hyde's in Throcking for the early months of 1559, receiving the occasional payment from her husband, who also sent up members of his staff to visit her there. Dudley's household accounts record that his servant Thomas Jones visited Amy at Hyde's on at least two occasions, for which he was paid 3s 4d and 5 shillings respectively.[1] On one journey he took with him 66s 8d, 'for my lady', and it was perhaps on another of his journeys that he took with him a hood specially made for her, costing 36 shillings.[2] Dudley's other servant Edmund Goove was sent to see her twice, on the second occasion delivering 100 shillings to her 'by your lordship's commandment'. Dudley also ensured that his wife's household was well fed and sent venison to Hyde's.[3]

That Easter, Dudley himself came up to Throcking to visit his wife, taking advantage of the parliamentary recess that lasted from 24 March to 4 April.[4] Three days earlier he had paid for a lavish banquet for the queen in St James's Park, at which Morris games were performed.[5] He departed soon after, stopping off overnight at Ware where he spent 12d on drink and enjoyed a rather expensive meal costing 34s 8d, and was entertained by a juggler and a blind harpist, whom he rewarded with 3s 4d each.[6] The next morning Dudley enjoyed breakfast costing 35 shillings, before journeying on, stopping briefly for supper at Waltham.[7] Dudley had planned for a comfortable Easter holiday with his wife, including something of a feast to mark the celebrations. He brought food, cooks and expensive spices from London especially for his visit to Throcking.[8] There is, however, little evidence that Dudley spent time with his wife on this occasion. He was an inveterate gambler: he relaxed by placing frequent and not insignificant wagers at dice and card games, if somewhat unsuccessfully. At court he entertained himself in his chamber playing cards with John Fowler, one of the grooms of the queen's Privy Chamber, and his friend Sir Ralph Bagnall, a close associate and MP during the 1559 Parliament. The sums needed to pay for his gambling debts were large: during Elizabeth's first year on the throne, Dudley gambled away a total of £109 7s 10d. The most significant of his losses came when he lost £40 in a dice match against the son of his father's enemy the Duke of Somerset, the recently restored Earl of Hertford.[9] A rare visit to his wife was hardly enough to make him desist from this habit. In the course of one game of cards or dice during his stay at Hyde's, Dudley had to borrow 40 shillings from his host to pay off his debts. Over the next few days, his run of bad luck continued: his household accounts record three separate occasions when money was 'delivered to your Lordship at Mr Hide's at sundry times' – on one occasion 20 shillings, 11 shillings on another and 28 shillings on a third.[10]

It was only to be a brief visit. By 8 April, Dudley was back at court in London, where his household accounts reveal that he remained as unlucky as before, losing 20 crowns playing cards in his chamber with the Duke of Norfolk and the Earl of Sussex.

Gambling debts were just one of the prices to pay to keep up with the rest at court. Games of dice or tennis were frequent pastimes, both of which were made more entertaining by placing wagers upon the outcome. During his first year in office, Dudley saw his expenditure rise astronomically. One of the largest bills among his accounts was for 'apparel and goldsmith's work' amounting to £824 17s 5d, a sizeable proportion of his total personal expenditure, which for the first year of Elizabeth's reign amounted to £2,589 2s 1½d.[11] No expense was spared; new clothes were ordered, furnishings for his rooms at court and his new house at Kew fitted, his men rewarded, noblemen sent gifts; as the queen's favourite, Dudley was now part at the centre of court life, and he was expected to live the part. He frequently dined out with influential members at court, including with the Earl of Westmorland, when he spent 13 shillings at the Earl of Pembroke's (costing 21 shillings for his servants' dinner alone) and at Sir William Pickering's house.[12] One of Dudley's favourite dining spots was Arundel's tavern, near St Lawrence Pountney. The tavern had a chequered history; often the scene of drunken antics and boisterous behaviour, it was here that the Earl of Surrey drank before launching his riot in 1543. It was also where dissidents would gather, and it is perhaps more than coincidence that the tavern featured in Wyatt's rebellion and in further plots to place Elizabeth upon the throne.

Dudley's constant socialising, gambling and tennis-playing began to take its toll on his work. As Dudley remained at court, frequently spending his time on the tennis court (where he spent 18d on tennis balls) he found it increasingly difficult to keep on top of his official role as Master of the Horse, especially the control of the export of horses from the realm, a task which required him to be away from the court and the queen. On 27 May he issued a commission allowing Thomas Keys to deputise for him.[13] From now on Dudley would rarely travel far beyond where Elizabeth chose him to be – by her side. 'I cannot live without seeing you every day,' she would tell him six years later. 'You are like my little dog. As soon as he is seen anywhere, people know that I am coming, and when you are seen, they say I am not far off.'[14]

# She is well worth the trouble

For now, Dudley's presence only added to the theatre of Elizabeth's proposed marriage, as more candidates from across the Continent piled on to the stage, including Prince Eric of Sweden, the King of Denmark's brother, Duke Adolphus of Holstein, and William, Duke of Savoy. 'Be you most assured,' the Spanish ambassador wrote, 'that there be at this day many eyes over England, and, as Her Grace doth match herself in marriage, so shall she see things fall out, which as yet are hidden. And, to make a lewd comparison, I may liken England to a bone thrown betwixt two dogs.'[1]

Rivalries between English candidates were also growing. The return of an English courtier, Sir William Pickering, from France in early May seemed to bring yet another suitor into the game. Unlike Arundel, Pickering had been unable to hurry back to court at the queen's accession, as he had fallen ill and was obliged to remain at Dunkirk until the spring. His absence merely helped to stir gossip that when he returned, Elizabeth would marry this 'very handsome gentleman' who, it was understood, 'is a great favourite of the Queen'. Earlier in the year, the Venetian ambassador had reported that it was common gossip that 'she will marry an individual who till now has been in France on account of his religion, though he has not yet made his appearance, it being known how much she loved and loves him'.

A bachelor in his forties, Pickering's reputation with the ladies was well known. He was, one ambassador remarked, 'of tall stature ... and very successful with women', and it was rumoured that he had 'enjoyed the intimacy of many and great ones'. During his youth, Pickering had led a hell-raising life with his compatriot Henry Howard, the brash Earl of Surrey, whom Pickering had joined on a riotous night of debauchery through the streets of London in spring 1543, leading to a brief spell of imprisonment in the Tower. Sharing his cell was another drinking companion, Thomas Wyatt the younger, son of the poet and reputed lover of Anne Boleyn. Their shared experience formed a strong bond of friendship between the pair, who eleven years later joined forces in plotting together to place Elizabeth and Edward Courtenay upon the throne as part of Wyatt's ill-fated and short-lived rebellion. When the rebellion failed, Pickering fled to the Continent. Despite the obvious threat to her own life that his actions had caused, Elizabeth never forgot that Pickering had risked his own safety for her cause. His return to England five years on was welcomed by the Queen, who greeted him at court and 'saw him secretly two days after his arrival', the Spanish ambassador reported, 'yesterday he came to the palace publicly and remained with her four or five hours.'[2]

The arrival of another supposed suitor revived popular interest in the queen's marriage once more; soon Londoners in the city were even waging '25 to 100 that he will be king'.[3] This was much to Dudley's chagrin. 'They tell me Lord Robert is not so friendly with him as he was', the Spanish ambassador reported. Yet this was not necessarily true – Dudley dined at William Pickering's home at St Mary Axe shortly after his return, and rewarded Pickering's servant with 20 shillings for bringing him a horse.[4] If Dudley perceived Pickering as a threat to his ambitions, however, they soon became friends, with Dudley sending him books as presents during the 1560s.[5] Pickering's appearance on the scene caused particular consternation to the Earl of Arundel, who was still 'labouring hard' to win Elizabeth over. It was rumoured that the earl had already decided to sell his lands for ready money since he was 'thinking to flee out of the realm because he could not abide in England, if Mr Pickering should marry the Queen, for that they were enemies'.[6]

Despite his relative poverty, there were others ready to consider Pickering a strong candidate for Elizabeth's hand. 'It is said that the Queen prefers him to all others that are in England,' an Imperial envoy wrote back to Ferdinand. 'Despite his small fortune, he lives at times in great state. When the whim seizes him he lives like a prince all alone in a stately house. But many of the eminent men of the land are against this marriage, and it is to be feared that if the Queen do not soon declare whom she will take, there will be a broil in England between the various factions.'[7] Pickering's case acutely summarised the problems with an English marriage. 'If the Queen were to take the noblest and fittest man in her realm, she would affront one-half of the Kingdom, for there are thousands who deem themselves worthy to be made the Queen's consort ... should the Queen, however, wed a nobleman or knight, such as

Pickering, in less than a month both the Queen and the new King would be slain.'[8]

The archduke, however, remained the strongest and most realistic candidate in most people's minds. Ferdinand, the eldest son of the Holy Roman Emperor Ferdinand I, was second to Philip II, the most powerful suitor Elizabeth might have married. 'It is the general talk of the town in London,' a German envoy reported, 'that the Archduke Ferdinand will marry the Queen, but I do not know how the matter already comes to be in everyone's mouth . . . almost everybody else has pronounced in favour of it.'[9] Inside the court it was a very different story. The Spanish ambassador Feria was growing impatient at the lack of progress. He had run out of time and was due to travel back to his native country. 'I want the matter pressed,' he insisted, barely concealing his frustration, 'so as to make this woman show her hand. Sometimes I think she might consent to it, and at other times that she will not marry and has some other design.' When he was called back to Spain, handing over his position to Alvaro de la Quadra, Bishop of Aquila, he was glad to leave this thankless task behind. It had been, he considered, 'very troublesome to negotiate with this woman, as she is naturally changeable, and those who surround her are so blind and bestial that they do not at all understand the state of affairs'.[10]

Encouraged by his envoy Helfenstein's earlier reports, Archduke Ferdinand had sent a second Imperial ambassador, Baron Caspar Bruener, to begin the marriage negotiations. Arriving on 26 May, he sought out the new Spanish ambassador's help. De la Quadra, a skilled diplomat well versed in the art of intrigue, judged that Bruener was 'not the most crafty person in the world', but nevertheless agreed that he would try to arrange an audience with the queen. Arriving at the royal palace at one o'clock on a Sunday, they found Elizabeth in her Presence Chamber 'looking on at the dancing', where she kept them waiting a good while.

De la Quadra realised that Elizabeth was by now growing weary of Archduke Ferdinand's suit, having been unimpressed by his physical appearance. To revive her flagging interest, he played a masterstroke by suggesting that it was not Ferdinand at all that Bruener had come to offer, but rather Ferdinand's 21-year-old younger brother, Charles of Austria. Elizabeth's interest began to flicker once more. After some 'demurring and doubting', the queen admitted that Charles was indeed 'the younger and more likely to please her'. Elizabeth, having been shown a picture of the Imperial family, had already 'conceived a greater liking for the younger'.[11] Charles was also more acceptable to the English as a candidate for Elizabeth's hand; he was endowed with suitable royal connections, yet as the younger son, he could be based permanently in the country and dedicate his time to domestic affairs since the Imperial title was unlikely to pass to him. 'He is not a Philip,' an English diplomat admitted, referring to the Spanish king's earlier failed suit, 'but better for us than a Philip.'[12]

The marriage negotiations opened up in earnest. On 28 May, Bruener was granted a separate audience with Elizabeth where, 'breathing a prayer to the Almighty', he delivered a letter outlining a proposal giving her a choice of Emperor Ferdinand's two sons, Ferdinand and Charles of Austria. Elizabeth was delighted, yet, although she was grateful for 'the honour shown to her in deeming her worthy to marry one of your sons', she refused to commit herself either way. Her words were by now familiar ones. 'She had been desired in marriage by many during and after her imprisonment,' she told Bruener, while 'her council and her loyal subjects daily and hourly begged and exhorted her to marry whom she would, so that they might hope to have heirs ... Whenever it should be possible, she would not only fulfil the wish of her faithful subjects, but also,' she said, in a veiled reference to childbearing, 'if the need arose and they thereby were served and helped, hazard her life.' For the moment, however, she would swear 'by the salvation of her soul' that 'to this hour [she] had never set her heart upon, nor had come so far as to wish to marry, anyone in the whole world'. But neither had she ruled out marriage entirely, for 'she was but human and not insensible to human emotions and impulses, and when it became a question of the weal of her Kingdom, or it might be for other reasons, her heart and mind might change'.[13]

A month later Elizabeth had indeed changed her mind. She was in no mood to consider the possibility of marriage. She wrote to Archduke Ferdinand in June that 'when however we reflect upon the question of this marriage and eagerly ask our heart, we find that we have no wish to give up solitude and our lonely life, but prefer with God's help to abide therein of our free determination'. There was a time, certainly, she wrote, 'when a very honourable and worthy marriage would have liberated us from certain great distress and tribulation (whereof we here will not speak further) but neither the peril of the moment, nor the desire for liberty could induce us to take this matter into consideration. But even as we can give account for our resolves both past and present, even so we cannot safely assert anything for the future nor wilfully predicate anything rash.'[14]

They were determined words, but the ambassadors would not give up. A few days later, Bruener wrote to Archduke Charles that despite three audiences with the queen, he had 'been unable to obtain any answer except her excuse that she has not yet made up her mind to marry anyone in this world'. Nevertheless, the prize was still worth waiting for. As Bruener reported:

> There is no Princess of her compeers who can match her in wisdom, virtue, beauty and splendour of figure and form. Furthermore I have seen several very fine summer residences that belong to her, in two of which I have been myself, and I may say that there are none in the world so richly garnished with costly furniture of silk, adorned with gold, pearls and precious stones. Then she has some twenty other houses, all of which might justly be called royal summer residences. Hence she is well worth the trouble.[15]

Then at some stage Bruener learned of the gossip that had been doing the rounds at court concerning Elizabeth and her Master of the Horse. He was shocked and horrified at the news. What if Elizabeth was no longer a virgin? He was not prepared for his master to be ridiculed as a cuckold, and would better discover the truth now than wait until any marriage contract had been sealed. Bruener decided to launch his own investigation, paying for a secret agent named Francis Borth who was apparently 'on very friendly terms with all the ladies of the bedchamber' to discover the exact nature of Elizabeth's relationship with Dudley – had they been sleeping together? He was soon assured by Borth that no improprieties had ever taken place between them. 'They all swear by all that is holy that her Majesty has most certainly never been forgetful of her honour,' Borth reported back. He remained wary of the queen's closeness to her favourite nevertheless: 'And yet it is not without significance that Her Majesty's Master of the Horse, Mylord Robert, is preferred by the Queen above all others, and that Her Majesty shows her liking for him more markedly than is consistent with her reputation and dignity.'[16]

It was not to be the last time that Elizabeth was to be either accused of, or investigated for, having sexual relations with Robert Dudley or other courtiers. The rumours were to follow her for her entire life, even decades later. The French ambassador reported that Elizabeth had slept with Dudley on New Year's Eve 1566; in September 1572, Elizabeth Massie testified that the Earl of Southampton, while a prisoner in the Tower, had told his fellow inmate that 'there was a privy stairs where the Queen and my Lord Leicester [Dudley] did meet, and if they had not used sorcery, there should have been young traitors 'ere now begotten'. That same year a violent and thoroughly unsavoury character named Berney admitted under torture that he had claimed that Elizabeth 'desireth nothing but to feed her own lewd fantasy, and to cut off such of her nobility as were not perfumed and courtly-like to please her delicate eye.' Instead, he claimed, Elizabeth only preferred and advanced good dancers such as Dudley whom she might use 'for her turn'. In 1581 Henry Hawkins was punished for insisting that Elizabeth had as many as five illegitimate children with Dudley, since 'she never went into progress but to be delivered'.[17]

In time, Elizabeth's virginity became the topic of everyday conversation. Gossips began to speculate that one reason why the queen had remained unmarried was because one man alone would be unable to satiate her lusts and sexual desires for more than one partner. According to Mary Queen of Scots, the Countess of Shrewsbury, Bess of Hardwick, told her that Elizabeth had slept with her courtier Sir Christopher Hatton and had taken 'various indecent liberties' with the French envoy, Jean Simier. Hatton was shocked by the accusations. He denied it to Elizabeth's godson, Sir John Harington, and 'did swear voluntarily, deeply and with vehement asseveration that he never had any carnal knowledge of her body'.[18] Even when Elizabeth had entered her sixties, the gossip failed to die down. In 1598, Edward Francis of Dorset was summoned before magistrates for attempting to persuade a woman named Elizabeth Baylie to sleep with him, saying 'that the best in England had done so, and had three bastards by noblemen of the court, and was herself base-born'.[19]

The reality, however, was somewhat different. There is no evidence that Elizabeth ever entered into a physical relationship with any man. Her public displays of affection certainly raised eyebrows, including several years later when she kissed Dudley openly in public, to the amazement of those watching. 'She cam owt of hir coche in ye highe way', one bemused observer wrote, 'and she imbrased [Dudley] and kyssed hym thrise'.[20] But as for anything more serious taking place, this was highly unlikely. That risk would have been far too great to take, and besides, the queen was so rarely left unattended that any such trysts would have been nearly impossible. As Elizabeth herself noted, 'she was always surrounded by her ladies of the bedchamber and her maids of honour': 'My life is in the open,' she told the Spanish ambassador, 'and I have so many witnesses . . . I cannot understand how so bad a judgment can have been formed of me.'[21]

As for the rumours that she and Robert Dudley were lovers, Elizabeth was also quick to dismiss these and hoped in time that they both would be proven innocent of such charges. 'God knows they do us grievous wrong, and the time will come when the world will know it also. A thousand eyes see all that I do, and calumny will not fasten on me for ever.'[22] The ambassador privately agreed; Elizabeth had been watched 'with Argus' eyes'; he was sure that 'there could never be found any manner of suspicion that could once touch her honour'. Others were in agreement. 'I saw no signs of an immodest life,' wrote Nicholas Guildenstern, the chancellor of Eric XVI of Sweden, who was tasked with attempting to arrange a match with Elizabeth and his master in 1561, 'but I did see many signs of chastity, of virginity, of true modesty; so that I would stake my life that she is most chaste'.[23] 'I can say with truth,' wrote Michel de Castelnau, Sieur de Mauvissière, who had been appointed French ambassador by Henri III in 1575 and who remained in constant contact with Elizabeth until her death, 'that these [stories] were sheer inventions of the malicious, and of the ambassadorial staffs, to put off those who would have found an alliance with her useful.'[24]

If there was one thing Elizabeth was protective over it was her honour. 'She would fain vindicate herself,' she told an Imperial envoy several years later, 'against all the slander that had been cast at her, and she hoped that Your Imperial Majesty would find that she had all the time acted in all matters with due decorum and attention.'[25] On this point, the envoy was convinced. Just as Bruener had done before him, he once again investigated the claims that Elizabeth was no longer a virgin and that she led an 'immodest life' with Dudley. 'I have through several persons made diligent inquiries concerning the maiden honour and integrity of the Queen, and have found that she has truly and verily been praised and extolled for her virginal and royal honour, and that nothing can be said against her, and all the aspersions against her are but the spawn of envy and malice and hatred.' He was certain, too, that there was nothing improper taking place between the queen and her favourite. Dudley was a 'virtuous, pious, courteous and highly moral man' who Elizabeth 'loves as a sister her brother in all maidenly honour, in most chaste and honest love'.[26]

Rather than attempting to prevent the gossip about her relationship with Dudley going unchecked, Elizabeth seemed to delight in the attention that it brought her. On one occasion, she spotted a group of her gentlewomen of the chamber chatting in the corner of the Privy Chamber with some gentlemen of the court. Asking them 'what the subject of their conversation was', they answered 'that they were talking about whom the Queen would marry and had mentioned four or five Englishmen, one of whom, so the courtiers thought, the Queen would choose.' With her customary sense of mischief, Elizabeth replied that 'they were forsooth very intelligent people to propose her such a magnificent match among her compatriots, but in the number of candidates they should have included one of her halberdiers'.[27] It was obvious to all whom she had in mind.

It was not only the foreign ambassadors who had grown disturbed by the rumours at court that Elizabeth was in love with Robert Dudley. Her closest friends sought to limit the damage that the gossip seemed to be doing to her reputation, both at home and abroad. Elizabeth's most trusted confidante and senior gentlewoman of her chamber, Catherine Ashley, had fallen at the queen's feet begging her 'in God's name to marry and put an end to all these disreputable rumours'. Catherine went on to reveal the full extent of what others had been saying about Elizabeth's relationship with Dudley, 'telling Her Majesty that her behaviour towards the said Master of the Horse occasioned much evil speaking; for she showed herself so affectionate to him that Her Majesty's honour and dignity would be sullied, and her subjects would in time become discontented'. This, Catherine implored, would 'be the cause of much bloodshed in this realm' for which Elizabeth would have to give account to God and 'by which she would merit the eternal curse of her subjects'. She ended by saying that 'she would have strangled Her Majesty in the cradle' if she had known then how Elizabeth would have later behaved.

They were words that could only have been uttered by a woman with the utmost familiarity with the queen, who had known her since birth.

For, faced with an outburst that might have been considered treasonable, Elizabeth did not lose her temper. Instead, she replied calmly that she knew Ashley's anger came from her 'good heart and true fidelity'. She was quite willing to marry, she told her, 'in order to console her and all her subjects'. Until now she had had 'no wish to change her state' but she was considering changing her mind, though she insisted that before she did so 'such a marriage must be well weighed'.

Ashley interrupted, pleading to Elizabeth that 'for the love of God, where she had so many and worthy offers of marriage to resolve upon one, lest God, to punish her, call her away from this world before her time'. To this, Elizabeth gave a fascinating and revealing response. She hoped that God, 'who had freed her from the violence of her enemies and suffered her to rise to her exalted dignity', would continue to preserve her. As to the gossip concerning herself and Dudley:

> she hoped that she had given no one just cause to associate her with her Equerry or any other man in the world, and she hoped that they would never truthfully be able to do so. But in this world she had had so much sorrow and tribulation and so little joy. If she showed herself gracious towards her Master of the Horse, he had deserved it for his honourable nature and dealings. She had also never understood how any single person could be displeased, seeing that she was always surrounded by her ladies of the bedchamber and maids of honour, who at all times could see whether there was anything dishonourable between her and her Master of the Horse. If she had ever had the will or had found pleasure in such a dishonourable life, from which may God preserve her, she did not know of anyone who could forbid her; but she trusted in God that nobody would ever live to see her so commit herself.[28]

'She did not know of anyone who could forbid her.' Elizabeth the woman knew her rights as Elizabeth the queen.

Of course there should have been one woman who stood in Elizabeth's way. 'This Master of the Horse is, I hear, married to a fine lady, from whom he has always had nothing but good,' Bruener wrote in his dispatch containing news of Ashley's confrontation with Elizabeth. 'Nevertheless since the Queen was crowned he has never been away from Court. Moreover they dwell in the same house and this it is which feeds suspicion.'

# A journey

It was in early June 1559 that Amy finally left William Hyde's home at Throcking. She did not return. A servant, Elmby, was sent to collect her, having been paid £10 'for my lady's charges from Mr Hides to Camberwell'.[1] Camberwell was where her mother's family, the Scotts, had their family home, and where Amy had most likely last stayed when her husband was imprisoned in the Tower during Mary's reign. It was clearly a significant move. The departure involved her whole household, for Amy travelled down from Hyde's with an entourage of twelve horses, hired at a cost of 60 shillings.[2] The trip to Camberwell had been carefully planned: all the necessary preparations were made for her visit in advance, with beddings and hangings being sent over to Camberwell several days before Amy arrived.[3]

Arriving in the capital, Amy first lodged at Dudley's London home Christchurch for two days, where she was attended by his servant Edward Langham.[4] Amy then journeyed to her family home at Camberwell, where she was accompanied by Thomas Jones 'and his fellows', purchasing some cherries – perhaps as a small token of thanks for her stay – at a cost of 12d.[5] It seems that she also did some shopping while she was there, ordering a gown of russet taffeta worth 35 shillings. Dudley certainly supplemented some of her spending, sending 66s 8d 'to my Lady at Mr Scott's'.[6]

London was not the only place that Amy had visited in recent months. At some stage, though it is uncertain when, she also made a journey into Suffolk. Considering its position, it seems likely that she was then residing at Throcking. Where she travelled to, or whom she called upon, is unknown, though perhaps she went to visit relatives or family friends there. On her journey she had been accompanied by her maid Mrs Picto, William Huggins, the brother-in-law of her half-brother John Appleyard, and Thomas Blount. The reason for the journey is also unknown, though Dudley gave Huggins 40 pistoles 'to put in her ladyship's purse', with another 20 shillings to Picto. In total, the cost of Amy's charges came to £25 13s 4d.[7]

Amy's movements seem unusual if only for the fact that, if ambassadors' reports are to be believed, she was meant to be seriously ill. Such intensive journeying certainly does not seem in keeping with earlier reports from the Spanish ambassador de la Quadra that Amy was suffering from 'a malady in one of her breasts', an illness that was considered serious enough that 'the Queen is only waiting for her to die to marry Lord Robert'. The Venetian ambassador had also picked up on the rumours that Amy was ill, and had discovered that she had in fact 'been ailing for some time'.

Both comments have been pored over by historians determined to prove that Amy must have been suffering from some form of terminal illness, cancer perhaps, and that this was one of the reasons why she had retired from court. But there exists another statement from de la Quadra which he made in a little-known dispatch of 6 June 1559, possibly shortly after Amy had arrived in London. It has been relatively ignored since it was omitted from the English translations of his dispatches, but is nonetheless a crucial piece of evidence.[8] According to the ambassador, Amy had recovered from her illness – this would certainly accord with the timing of her journey to the capital. But de la Quadra also had some revealing news to add: '*Su mujer de milort Robert esta ya Buena, y dicen que muy sobre el aviso en no comer cosa que no sea con mucha salva.*' [The wife of the Lord Robert is already better, and it is said that she has been warned not to eat anything that is not very safe.] De la Quadra did not explain precisely what he meant by his words. Perhaps Amy, so recently recovered, had been warned by her doctors to take care over what she ate in order to facilitate a full recovery. One gets the impression that Amy's situation was precarious at best.

It is equally strange that her husband was not there to greet her on her visit to London. She arrived only after Dudley had left for Windsor with the court, where, following his nomination in April, he was to be officially installed as a Knight of the Garter. As his wife entered the capital, Dudley instead first journeyed to Kew, where he was entertained by his players, whom he paid 4 shillings in reward. Dudley was one of the first members of the nobility to keep a group of players, a sign of his interest in patronage of the arts. Aside from occasionally rewarding them with gifts of money, he allowed them to use his name so that they might travel across the country to perform. Just before travelling to Windsor, he wrote to the Earl of Shrewsbury requesting that his players be given the liberty to tour Yorkshire.[9]

Hiring a number of hackneys at a cost of £8 6s 4d, Dudley rode on to Windsor where, on 6 June, the ceremony took place in St George's Chapel. The herald's fees for the occasion cost him £37 5s 4d, on top of the total of 19 shillings he paid in rewards to the servants of the house in town in which he had lodged. The official ceremony was probably something of an anticlimax after his initial elevation in April, and it came at a particularly bad time for Dudley, who was also recovering from a unspecified, though fairly serious, illness. Both his sister Catherine Hastings and the Earl of Pembroke had written to him in May, wishing him a speedy recovery from his ailment, which was described as a 'quatrain ague', an acute fever that was believed to strike on every fourth day.[10] The ailment seems to have caused Dudley some distress for which he sought professional medical help; his household accounts record that, for the payment of 10 shillings, a surgeon was employed 'for letting your lordship's blood'.[11]

On his return to London, Dudley spent a few weeks with his wife before the court moved to Greenwich for the start of the queen's progress on 21 June. But wives were not invited when the court made its progress, and this marked the end of Amy's stay with her husband. While Dudley departed for the court, his accountant William Chauncy was left to travel by barge to Dudley's home at Christchurch, 'being sent thither about the dispatch of my ladye'. The final preparations for Amy's departure were made, with some hose being purchased 'for my ladies boye', presumably one of her servants, and an extra trunk and saddle bought, costing 20 shillings, 'for carriage of my ladye's apparel'.[12]

From this point there is little information about where Amy was currently residing or what she was doing. Yet there is a single clue in Dudley's household accounts that summer which may point to her whereabouts:

Item ii peir of hose sent to my ladye by Sir Richard Vernies servant viiis.[13]

Sir Richard Verney was one of Dudley's trusted supporters, whose family lived at Compton Verney in Warwickshire. Although it is not clear why Amy would have been sent into Warwickshire at that time, the most likely reason was that during that summer, Dudley had been appointed as joint Lord Lieutenant of the county, alongside local magistrate Sir Ambrose Cave. The county had strong links with the Dudley family, and Robert Dudley himself would later claim that 'I am of that countrye & mynde to plant myself there'.[14] His father, John Dudley, had been created Earl of Warwick in 1547, a title which he claimed by descent on his mother's side to the original fifteenth-century Beauchamp earls of Warwick, taking their family crest of the bear and ragged staff as his own. Dudley retained his interest in Warwickshire through the manor of Hales Owen; although he sold it in 1558, by the autumn of 1559 he was actively seeking to purchase lands in Warwickshire from Lord Dudley, a nobleman from a separate line of the Dudley family, a proposal which was rejected since Lord Dudley refused to part with 'mine ancient inheritance'.[15] Undeterred, Dudley sought successfully to purchase the constableship of Warwick Castle and the stewardship of the lordship there, offices that had been confiscated from his father during Mary's reign.[16]

Sir Ambrose Cave wrote to Dudley in July 1559, upon his appointment as joint Lord Lieutenant, providing a report of the 'state of this county which appeared to me', while at the same time recommending 'certain gentlemen to be officers unto us'. One of these men included 'Sir Richard Varney, a gentleman meet to serve in that behalf' and who Cave believed 'would willingly endeavor himself for Warwickshire if it please you to appoint or require him by your letters'.[17] Dudley did not need persuading of Verney's abilities. He was well known to him as a close associate of his family's since the reign of Edward VI, and may have been part of his elder brother John, Lord Lisle's household, as he featured in his accounts, and was granted lands worth £46 13s 4d by the Duke of Northumberland in January 1553.[18]

Of Amy's stay at Compton Verney, we know almost nothing. Yet two months later, the records reveal that Amy suddenly moved once more. Under the entry for December 1559, Amy was sent a looking glass worth 6s 8d and two yards of 'blue sowing silk' costing 4 shillings, both 'by Mr Forster' – Anthony Forster, Dudley's associate, who lived at Cumnor Place in Berkshire. It was here that Amy resided for the next nine months with her small household entourage, including her maid Picto. She never saw her husband again.

# Te stante virebo

## 'You standing, I will flourish'

By the summer of 1559, less enthusiastic suitors for Elizabeth's hand in marriage, wary of their dwindling resources, began to peel away. The first was Sir William Pickering, who was probably always surprised to be considered one of the queen's suitors. Since his return to court from France, he remained as extravagant as ever, and made a point of dining separately from the court to the accompaniment of music. It was a lifestyle he struggled to maintain. 'At first they made much ado about him,' the Spanish ambassador reported, but now observed that 'this cry is now stilled, he being ill and much in debt. I think he would be glad if he were rid of his debts and let who will be King.' When asked if he still hoped to propose to Elizabeth, Pickering shrugged, saying, 'The Queen would laugh at him, and all the rest of them as he knew she meant to die a maid.'[1]

Others were not so perceptive. The Earl of Arundel clung to the possibility that, if the queen decided to marry within the country, as one of the premier noblemen of the realm he would stand the best chance of success. Most observers had already long dismissed his prospects. 'He and he alone entertains the hope,' one ambassador reported. Not to be deterred, Arundel entertained Elizabeth lavishly at his residence during the queen's first summer progress.

The progress was a massive undertaking as the queen and her entire court moved around the country. One contemporary estimated that the entourage, travelling at its average speed of ten to twelve miles a day, required the use of 400 carts and 2,400 packhorses.[2] Many followers-on struggled to meet the cost of keeping their own lodging; Sir Nicholas Poyntz wrote to Robert Dudley in July 1559, excusing his absence from the progress: 'suspend any ill judgment that may be thought by my departure, for I do most truly ascertain your lordship that extreme want forceth me thus to do'.[3]

Dudley had other concerns. In his role as Master of the Horse, he remained in control of the entire progress. Distances and times would need to be calculated, places for accommodation booked in advance, hundreds of men and horses needed to be fed. Even though the great banquets Elizabeth was treated to were paid for out of her host's pockets, there was still the need to requisition items from the royal stables. One such list survives from 1567:

A rich litter covered with velvet laid upon with gold lace.

A litter for the ladies.

Saddles for my lord swathed and guarded with velvet and spare furnishings.

Saddles of calves leather for the gentlemen.

Three pairs of gilt stirrups.[4]

Not least, Dudley would need to gather together the hundreds of horses that were needed for the journey; once the stables were empty, horses would be seized from whoever had colts or mares to hand. A visiting Italian, Donato Rullo, complained to Dudley in July that 'two officials of yours have seized two of my horses for the Queen's stable ... I appeal to you directly; as a native of the Kingdom of Naples, I know where to get good horses there, and will let you know of any'.[5]

The offer would have caught Dudley's interest: Elizabeth often demanded that she have the fastest and best horses that might match her desire for speed and agility when riding out on the hunt. She never tired of the excitement of the chase, which became her chief occupation during each progress. From morning until night, she would take to the field. A herd of deer would be driven into an enclosure, the queen would follow on horseback; when the animals were trapped in a corner or wood, Elizabeth would kill three of four with her crossbow, or else allow her greyhounds to tear them to pieces. On one occasion she spared a stag, but even then ordered that it 'lost his ears for a ransom'.[6] Her stamina was unmatched. The Spanish ambassador recorded a few years later how when at Windsor, 'the Queen went so hard that she tired everybody out, as the ladies and courtiers were with her they were all put to shame. There was more work than pleasure in it for them.'[7]

At the beginning of August, after nearly a month's slow journey, the royal progress reached the Earl of Arundel's residence of Nonsuch, the royal palace built by Henry VIII. It was a splendid setting to mark the culmination of the summer festivities, and Arundel, his marriage suit still at the forefront of his mind, was determined to impress. The end result was one of the most expensive celebrations ever to be staged in England. The entertainment included 'a great banquet at his cost ... as ever was seen,' one observer recalled, 'for supper, banquet and masque, with drums and flutes, and all the masquing that could be, till midnight; and as for cheer has not been seen or heard'.[8] According to the French ambassador the cost of the Queen's stay there came to a staggering 25,000 ducats, though records in the State Papers reveal that the actual cost was £951 14s 5d.[9] In doing so, Arundel set a trend that was to continue for the rest of Elizabeth's reign. 'It cost him ten thousand marks at the least by report,' an anonymous chronicler commented, 'wherefore afterword he was constrained to sell a great part of his lands. For this precedent the earl had many curses of many.'[10]

Upon Elizabeth's return from her progress, the issue of the day remained unchanged. The pressure was beginning to take its toll on the queen. When Bruener paid Elizabeth a visit in late August, he found her 'somewhat dejected', telling him that she was being pestered daily by petitions from her subjects to marry. She would 'rather be dead than that her realm should suffer harm or loss' and was prepared even to marry 'the vilest man in her Kingdom rather than give people occasion to speak ill'.[11] The spy employed by the Imperial envoy Bruener had also learned from the queen's maids-of-honour that she had been 'quite melancholy alone in her room of nights and had not slept half an hour'. In the mornings, Elizabeth looked pale and weak, and was plagued with a burning fever.[12]

Elizabeth suffered frequent bouts of illness throughout her youth, which tended to coincide with some of the most stressful periods in her life. Though early biographers such as William Camden were keen to claim that Elizabeth 'had enjoyed very perfect health', ascribing her fitness to regular exercise, 'abstinence from wine' and 'most temperate diet' (according to Camden, Elizabeth 'never eate meate but when her appetite served her', clearly somewhat of a rarity among the carnivorous appetites of the Tudor court) this was not the case. Ever since puberty Elizabeth had been struck down with poor health, suffering frequent and crushing headaches that often incapacitated her for weeks at a time. 'The pain in my head precluded all modes of writing,' the young princess wrote to her brother Edward VI in July 1549; six months later, she apologised again for not writing to him more often, yet 'some ill health of body especially headache recalled me from the attempt'.[13] Of course, illness might be used as convenient cover and pretence to avoid a meeting or confrontation, as Elizabeth's sister Mary suspected, when during the first year of her turbulent reign Elizabeth, accused of complicity with Wyatt's rebels, was summoned to appear before the queen. When she refused, Mary sent her commissioners to investigate. They found her 'so sicke in hir bed, and verie feeble and weake of bodie'; her body was 'almost entirely swollen', particularly in her face. 'Those who have seen her do not promise her long to live', the French ambassador De Noailles remarked.[14] According to her physician Dr Owen, Elizabeth was 'trobled with ye swellyng in her face, & also of her armes and hands'; the reason for this, Owen believed, was that 'her graces body ys replenished with mannye colde and waterish humours'.[15] The princess was bled in the arm and the foot to help alleviate the symptoms, which were to eventually clear.

It has been suggested that Elizabeth suffered from nephritis, an inflammation of the kidneys that can cause amongst other symptoms searing headaches and swelling of body tissue.[16] Whatever her exact condition, there was clearly some concern at court for the state of the queen's health. It was to Dudley that many turned to discover the true nature of her ailment. In July, Lord Grey wrote to Dudley praying for the queen's good health, 'wishing that she would not too much presume of her own strength as to be let blood both in the foot and arm all at one time, because it was more than ever I heard done to any'.[17] Dudley's sister-in-law, Lord Ambrose's wife, Elizabeth, wrote in August to inform him that she had heard 'that her Majesty is not in such health' and had delayed her return to Hampton Court.[18] It was serious news: according to the French ambassador, who described the sickness as a 'fiebre quarte' – a quatrain fever similar to that Dudley had himself suffered a few months before – the doctors had 'great doubt of her convalescence'.[19] Already rumours had begun to leak from the court. 'I have punished several,' Sir John Chichester wrote to the Earl of Bedford in mid-August 1559, 'for bruiting the death of the Queen's Majesty and so hath others been in other parts of the shire as I hear.'[20]

For her councillors and advisers, it was an all-too-clear reminder of the queen's own mortality. The spectre of the succession seemed to loom once more. Who would inherit the throne if the queen was to die? For now, that horrifying prospect was not worth giving too much consideration. Instead, some believed, ways should be found to insist that Elizabeth marry as soon as could be permitted.

The Duke of Norfolk wrote as soon as he had heard of her illness, but by then Elizabeth's health was already fast improving and with it the mood of the court. 'Had I been advertised of the Queen's Majesty's sickness before the recovery again of her highness,' he wrote to Cecil at the end of August 1559, 'it must needs have been very great grief unto me . . . that the sickness is past, it putteth away the heaviness that might have grown.'[21] While Elizabeth recuperated from her illness, Dudley remained at her side. The Earl of Huntingdon thanked him in October for informing him of the 'first and best news' of the queen's recovery and her 'good and prosperous health'.[22]

By early September, after the court had returned to the capital from its progress, there was to be little change in the queen's mood towards the prospect of marriage. Elizabeth continued to twist and turn her words, keeping foreign ambassadors at bay. She had not ruled out marriage, but neither did she want to marry personally; only for the sake of her realm would she be prepared to renounce her single life. 'Though she had never purposed never to marry,' she told the Imperial envoy Bruener, 'yet I might believe her when she said that she had never had a mind to marry; nevertheless she hoped that if it were the Lord God's will He would inspire her with the wish.' He might also be 'quite sure that if she ever married, she would do so only for the profit and weal of her realm'.[23] That was enough to keep Bruener content that the suit was worth pursuing, though for Emperor Ferdinand, hearing the rumours of Elizabeth's affection for Robert Dudley, doubts had begun to grow. Now he was no longer sure if he wanted 'to give her my son even if she asked for him'.[24]

It seemed to de la Quadra that the marriage would never take place. But then there was a sudden change that made him reconsider. Lady Mary Sidney, one of Elizabeth's ladies of the bedchamber and Dudley's sister, paid him a surprise visit. She had some remarkable news to impart. Informing him that Elizabeth had changed her mind and now wanted the proposed match to the archduke 'speedily settled', Mary advised him to visit the queen. He should 'not mind what the Queen said, as it is the custom of ladies here not to give their consent in such matters until they are teased into it'. The negotiations would only be expected to take a few days, for the council 'would press her to marry'. Elizabeth had also expressed her wish for the archduke to visit in person at once. Mary urged de la Quadra to write to the emperor asking him to make arrangements for his son to do so. 'On her honour and word,' she told him, she would 'never dare to say such a thing as she did … unless it were true.' Mary further assured the ambassador that she was acting with the queen's full consent, but Elizabeth herself 'would not speak to the Emperor's Ambassador about it'.[25]

The remarkable turnaround in the situation seemed almost too good to be true. But after further investigation, de la Quadra was convinced of Elizabeth's sudden change of heart. A plot had been discovered, he wrote, to have Dudley assassinated at the Earl of Arundel's banquet. Elizabeth was to have been poisoned. In fear for her life and for the safety of her realm, Elizabeth wished to settle her marriage immediately. Even then, de la Quadra was taken aback by his new-found favour. 'They cannot make too much of me here at Hampton Court now. It is curious how things change.' He sought a second opinion from Thomas Parry, the Treasurer of the Queen's Household and one of Elizabeth's dedicated servants, who agreed with what Mary had said, saying that when the ambassador next went to the palace, 'he hoped to give some good news'. Parry confirmed that Elizabeth herself had summoned both Mary and himself to her bedchamber the previous night, telling them 'that the marriage had now become necessary'.[26] De la Quadra was buzzing with excitement at the prospect of having settled Elizabeth's match with Archduke Charles. He was equally flattered by the attention. 'Lord Robert and his sister are certainly acting splendidly, and the King will have to reward them well, better than he does me.' Dudley, too, had confirmed the queen's desire to marry the archduke, and had told him that 'in this as in all things,' he was at Philip's disposal 'to whom he owed his life'.

At the same time, Mary Sidney passed the same message to Bruener, swearing 'by all that is sacred that she would not under pain of death have informed me, nor durst inform me, if the Queen had not commanded her to do so'. With expectations riding high, Bruener took a barge down to Hampton Court to visit the queen, where he expected a warm welcome. It was not to be. Instead he found Elizabeth unreceptive to any proposal of marriage. 'The only answer I received was that she had not yet decided to marry, but should she ever do so, I might be quite sure that she would marry only the highest and the best.' Somewhat aghast, Bruener reported back to Mary Sidney news of Elizabeth's answer. He was 'astonished that, considering what had been brought to my notice, Her Majesty had not spoken more explicitly, and I expressed my fear that Her Majesty was deceiving me with fair words'. Yet Mary was quick to reassure him, and replied that if he knew 'how often she had heard the Queen say that my affair was promising well,' the ambassador would think differently.[27]

At a meeting with the queen three days later, de la Quadra met with the familiar response that Elizabeth was not prepared to marry: 'Her answer was that she did not want to marry him or anybody else.' However, Elizabeth went further than she had gone before in dismissing the archduke's suit on the grounds that he was a foreigner. 'If she married at all,' she added, it would certainly not be the archduke, but rather 'it would only be to a man whom she knew.' Elizabeth especially did not want the archduke to visit, 'by any means, as she did not wish to bind herself even indirectly to marry him'.

For a long time the discussions seemed to be going around in circles, with each party 'wasting words' until Elizabeth finally snapped. 'Shall I speak plainly and tell you the truth?' she interjected. 'I think that if the Emperor so desires me for a daughter he would not be doing too much by sending his son here without so many safeguards. I do not hold myself of so small account that the Emperor need sacrifice any dignity in doing it.'[28]

This was not what the ambassadors had come to hear. Yet, thanks to Mary's determined efforts, they had convinced themselves that Elizabeth was only putting on a display for the sake of her modesty and that if the archduke would only visit the queen in person, she would agree to marry him. De la Quadra pressed Elizabeth to admit whether she should be pleased if the archduke visited her, in public or in secret, but Elizabeth 'retreated into her shell very quickly', saying 'she did not wish to be pressed any more; he should do as he thought fit, and she did not want to know anything about his coming'.

De la Quadra remained convinced that the only solution was to press on regardless, forcing Elizabeth into a situation from which she could not back down. 'By these words and her manner of saying them,' de la Quadra reported, 'I understood that she made no difficulty as to the conclusion of the business, but only in the procedure to bring it about.'[29] He went on:

It is known that she is determined to marry, and will do so before Christmas according to the general opinion; indeed, she told me herself that the people were troubling her about it so constantly that it was impossible for her to avoid satisfying them. The necessity being admitted for her to marry, and to marry wisely, there can be no doubt that she has not consented to receive the Archduke for the purpose of refusing him and offending your Majesty ... It can hardly be believed, moreover, that if she did not mean to marry she would condescend to such vanity as to bring a son of your Majesty here to no purpose.

If they were not careful to act swiftly, the queen might marry 'some other heretic, which is exactly what the people around her advise her to do'.

He urged that the archduke be sent immediately. 'His coming would involve no loss of life, danger to property, nor sacrifice of dignity,' de la Quadra wrote to the emperor. 'His failure to come, on the other hand, would be evidently followed by his losing this woman, and with her, all the advantages which I have recounted.' As to Elizabeth's apparent unwilling demeanour, de la Quadra judged, 'in pure reason that is so, but as she is a woman, and a spirited and obstinate woman too, passion has to be considered'.[30]

Once again, the ambassador had underestimated Elizabeth. She had no intention of marrying the archduke; the entire episode had been of her own fabrication, using Mary Sidney as the innocent messenger to raise the ambassadors' hopes and reopen the marriage negotiations without wishing to seem over-committed to the match.

There had been no plot to kill Dudley or the queen, either. Admittedly, a courtier named Sir William Drury (who had been captain of Calais between 1557 and its fall in 1558 and was now captain of the fortifications at Berwick on the northern borders) had been arrested in late November after his return from a mission in Scotland since, as one observer recorded, 'it was suspected leste he would have slayne the Lord Robert, whome he thought to be uncomly to be so grete with the queen'.[31] Yet Drury confessed that his crime was only words, not deeds, which he admitted 'with most sorrowful heart, and humble voice, I acknowledge and confess that I have in lewd, disordered sort offended the Queen's most royal majesty'.[32] Released in October 1560, Drury later wrote to Dudley, requesting his forgiveness and expressing his regret that Elizabeth 'hath taken with displeasure those rash words which only I meant and spoke of your Lordship'. 'I was moved by nature and not by malice,' he confessed, 'I spoke rashly and unadvisedly ... I wish the same unspoken with the loss of my blood.'[33] It seems highly likely that the charges against Drury had been trumped up to validate Elizabeth's claims that an assassination attempt was indeed imminent.

What exactly had been going on? And what had been the purpose of it all? Elizabeth's reasoning was simple. After the death of the French king Henri II in July, relations with France had deteriorated. Francis II was now King of France; his wife was Elizabeth's cousin Mary Stuart, who was also legally the Queen of Scotland even though she resided at the French court with her husband. The Guises, the ruling dynasty of France, had decided that this would be the time to rip up the Treaty of Cateau-Cambrésis they had signed just six months earlier, and prepare for war with England along its Scottish borders, on Mary's behalf. England suddenly seemed dangerously isolated. In anticipation of conflict, Elizabeth needed to neutralise the Hapsburgs and, she hoped, ensure their support against France.

Her double dealing paid off. While hope remained of a match between the queen and Archduke Charles, Elizabeth's hand against the French was strengthened. De la Quadra told the Spanish ambassador in Rome that 'he must take care the French do not get at the new Pope [Pius IV] and cause him to proceed against the Queen on the Scotch queen's claims. It would do much damage both here and elsewhere before the marriage.' The possibility of Elizabeth's marriage to the archduke, of which the French were well aware, forced them to proceed cautiously with any plans for military action.[34]

There had also been some seriously wishful thinking on de la Quadra's part. Keener than his predecessor Feria to arrange the match, he had come to the conclusion in mid-October that Elizabeth 'is really as much set on this marriage as your Majesty is'.[35] Still naive and new to the English political landscape, with its intrigue and deceit, de la Quadra had been too trusting of Dudley. Feria, writing from Spain, remained sceptical. 'As to what Lord Robert and his sister say I do not believe more than the first day that the only thing the Queen stickles for is the coming of the lad [Archduke Charles].'[36]

But it does seem that Dudley's sister Mary was simply a pawn in a game devised by her brother and the queen. She had been used by both to give a false impression to both ambassadors, and trusting them wholeheartedly, she had gone along with their scheme. Upon discovering how she had been taken advantage of, Mary was both horrified and furious. She demanded immediately to see the queen in person. Despite being warned against doing so by a friend, since Elizabeth was in an 'ill humour', Mary replied that she was 'not asking anybody's opinion and would go to the Queen just to spite them all ... she would speak to her in plain English'. Mary was just as horrified by her brother's behaviour. Dudley had quite consciously used his own sister as bait. She complained bitterly to de la Quadra that even if she was sent to the Tower 'she will not cease to proclaim what is going on, and that her worst enemy is her brother'.[37]

From Dudley's point of view, the promotion of the archduke's suit could not have been better news. For one, it helped counter another suit that he considered the most dangerous threat to his putative chances of ever marrying the queen. Over the summer months, new proposals had been aired that Elizabeth should marry the Protestant James Hamilton, Earl of Arran, the heir to the rival ruling family to the Stuarts in Scotland.[38] Arran seemed a perfect match for the queen; not only did he share her religion, there was the possibility that marriage might one day bring the union of Scotland and England closer. Among Arran's supporters was Cecil. Arran had been living in France, but was forced to flee the kingdom after the Guises returned to power. Elizabeth had ordered her servants to bring him to England in disguise, but by mid-June Arran had arrived in London by his own means.[39] Though the details of his visit are shrouded in mystery, Cecil seems to have gone out of his way to assist the earl, hiding him in his London home – even lending him two hundred crowns.[40] Soon there was talk that a match would be made between Elizabeth and Arran, though it was reported that 'she shows the same indecision in marrying ... as with the rest'.[41]

By lending his support to the archduke's suit, Dudley was able to neutralise any attempt to promote Arran as a possible match, for the time being at least. While there remained more than one candidate vying for Elizabeth's hand, the field remained open. So long as Elizabeth remained uncommitted, Dudley might, despite the small matter of his wife, hold out hope that the queen might one day be his. It would not be the last time that he would resort to such tactics, and the strategy of divide and rule became a familiar one in his efforts to win Elizabeth's favour. It was not a strategy that readily earned him many friends.

For Elizabeth's part, reopening negotiations with the Hapsburgs had the added advantage of placating the more conservative members of her own nobility, who favoured closer ties with Catholicism, and drawing attention away from the growing furore over her relationship with Dudley. Gradually, however, the ambassadors began to realise what was going on. 'She is not in earnest,' de la Quadra wrote wearily in mid-October, 'but only wants to amuse the crowd with the hope of the match in order to save the life of Lord Robert, who is very vigilant and suspicious, as he has again been warned that there is a plot to kill him, which I quite believe, for not a man in the realm can suffer the idea of his being king.'[42]

Principal among Dudley's enemies, de la Quadra reported, was Thomas Howard, Duke of Norfolk. Several years younger than Dudley, Norfolk was the pre-eminent nobleman in the realm, the only remaining duke and a member of the ancient nobility. He was also a cousin of the queen, while his palace at Kenninghall rivalled that of Hampton Court in scale and grandeur. He considered Dudley an upstart, base-born son of a traitor, whose attempts to win Elizabeth's heart threatened the position that was his by right.

Tensions between the two had been growing for some time since they had both been made Knights of the Garter, an honour that Norfolk nearly turned down once he discovered who his fellow knight would be. There had been further points of contention since then that had drawn the two men apart. That autumn, when the position of High Sheriff of Norfolk and Suffolk fell vacant, a position whose patronage was normally in Norfolk's pocket, Elizabeth awarded it to John Appleyard, Amy Dudley's half-brother.[43] On top of this snub, when the tax collectors demanded £160 from him in income tax, Norfolk was enraged to learn that Dudley had managed to get away without paying a single penny, producing a writ of discharge signed by the queen.[44]

Dudley's behaviour at court aggravated matters further. On 5 November, he decided to display his chivalric prowess to Elizabeth in a series of staged tournaments at the tilt. This was traditional aristocratic turf, something of which Norfolk would have been acutely aware. Scooping up the challenger's prize while his brother Ambrose won the defender's, Dudley followed his victories by having a special manuscript drawn up for the occasion, complete with illustrated pictures of the winning performances, detailing each triumph down to every blow, 'to shew the maner of the breking of the speres'. Dudley had a new shield created especially, with a particular design showing a vine clinging to an obelisk.

This could be interpreted as a symbol of his relationship as a subject with the monarch, but could just as equally be read as the lover's dependence upon his beloved. Beneath was the motto: *Te stante virebo* – 'you standing, I will flourish'.[45] It was the kind of ambiguous presumption and arrogance that drove Norfolk mad with anger. 'If Lord Robert did not abandon his present pretentions and presumptions,' the duke was overheard to have said, 'he would not die in his bed.'[46]

By late October, de la Quadra was reporting some sensational news. 'A plot was made the other day to murder Lord Robert, and it is now common talk and threat. The plot was headed by the Duke of Norfolk, the Earl of Sussex, and all the principal adherents of the archduke. The queen and Robert are very uneasy about the Duke of Norfolk, as he talks openly about her lightness and bad government. People are ashamed about what is going on, and particularly the duke, as he is Lord Robert's enemy.'[47] This time, it seemed there was no fabrication. Dudley took to wearing a 'privy coat' made especially by the armourer at Greenwich – a coat of chain mail that was worn underneath his usual attire – clearly he took the rumours of plots against his life very seriously.[48]

De la Quadra sensed that Norfolk was a man he might be able to do business with. He sent a delegation to discover what the duke thought about the archduke's suit. Norfolk replied that he would 'rejoice greatly if the affair could be brought about'. He knew, however, that one man would continue to stand in the way of the marriage going ahead. In a separate conversation with the Imperial envoy Bruener, Norfolk said he believed that Dudley was the biggest obstacle to the archduke's match, and 'will place as many impediments in our path as possible'. Elizabeth also had kept them in 'absolute ignorance' about her dealings, he stated, adding 'if it depended upon the Queen alone, she would never marry. But the need was so great that her marriage could not be deferred any longer, for her countrymen were no longer willing to remain passive spectators.'[49]

'This to me seems quite credible,' Bruener wrote back to the Emperor Ferdinand. 'I really do not see why she should not be compelled, if she is not willing to marry as they desire.' Norfolk had told him that he hoped that the archduke might still come to England, 'publicly and ostentatiously'. If this could be achieved, 'he would stake his right arm that he would give us the votes of all the best and biggest of the land,' and promised to meet him personally at his reception into the country.

'I think his hatred of Lord Robert will continue, as the Duke and the rest of them cannot put up with his being king.'[50]

This was perhaps something of an exaggeration on the ambassador's part. There was certainly a number amongst the nobility who recognised where true power and influence lay and were more than willing to give Dudley their full support. The Earl of Huntingdon wrote to him in early October, calling him 'one of my special friends' and requesting that 'if there be any thing wherein I may pleasure you to be likewise ... you shall find your friend to the uttermost of my power'.[51] Henry, Earl of Westmorland, wrote him a brief and sycophantic letter the following January, simply 'to declare and express my heart and good will towards your L[ordship] and the continuance thereof, I thought good to write unto you and do wish that I had that thing or might do that pleasure that might stand your L in good stead, and then my good heart and will towards your L should appear as well in act as by writing'.[52] The Earl of Bedford also pledged that 'if there is any thing I have that may do your L pleasure, I shall be as ready for you as you shall request the same', while the Earl of Derby, in addition to sending Dudley a brace of puffins as a present, wrote to him in January and March 1560, signing himself Dudley's 'very loving friend' and 'praying God to preserve your good L in health and long life with much increase of honour'.[53]

# Veracious news

The rivalry between the various parties vying for Elizabeth's hand continued to escalate throughout the autumn of 1559. 'Here is a great resort of wooers and controversy among lovers', William Cecil boasted to Sir Nicholas Throckmorton, the English ambassador in Paris, in October 1559. Privately he knew it was not a boasting matter. Confiding to a friend, he wished simply that he 'would her Majesty had one and the rest honourably satisfied'.[1]

Cecil's frustrations were shared by those around him, not least the foreign ambassadors who had now spent months at the English court with little to show for their efforts. De la Quadra was still seething over his treatment in the debacle of Mary Sidney's intervention, which had ultimately come to nothing as signs of Dudley's scheming began to unravel. 'I noticed that Lord Robert was slackening in our business,' the ambassador wrote back in mid-November. 'He had had words with his sister because she was carrying the affair further than he desired.' As for the queen, he believed that 'she must have a hundred thousand devils in her ... notwithstanding that she is forever telling me she yearns to be a nun and pass her time in a cell praying'.[2]

The field was becoming an increasingly crowded one. 'Here we are, ten or twelve ambassadors, competing for her favour,' de la Quadra complained. Aside from the Earl of Arran, the Spanish ambassador had heard that the Duke of Holstein, brother of the King of Denmark, and by all reports 'not a worse looking man than the archduke' was now too on his way to woo Elizabeth. One of the most talked about, and entertaining, suits of marriage came from Prince Eric of Sweden, the son of King Gustavus Vasa.

Eric had first attempted to present his suit to marry Elizabeth during Mary's reign; his chances quickly came undone as he had fallen foul of the diplomatic process by forgetting to inform Mary herself. Nevertheless, he had hoped that his earnestness then might hold him in good stead with the new queen. Yet in renewing his suit he displayed the same lack of tact when he asked for a reply to the letter he had sent Elizabeth back in

1558, and earned a rebuke from the new queen that 'the letter was written when she was Madam Elizabeth, and now that she was Queen of England he must write to her as Queen'. Wary of Eric's intentions, Elizabeth had declared from the outset that she did not know if he would leave his kingdom to be with her, 'but she would not leave hers to be monarch of the world'. As a result of the gaffe, the Swede received no answer for months; when he did, in May 1559, it was a definite no.

Still Eric persisted, sending over an embassy to treat with the queen which arrived in mid-July 1559 and departed in mid-August. Despite their liberality to the poor and to London merchants, whose support they earned by scattering gold and silver in the streets, the foreign manners of the Swedish dignitaries had left them to be 'made fun of in the palace, and by the Queen more than anybody'. Their dress sense was a particular source of amusement, for they purposefully wore red crimson velvet hearts on their sleeves, pierced through by an arrow, 'symbolising the passion of their sovereign'.[3] Still, they had some sense of who would need to be won over at court if the match stood any chance of succeeding; the embassy brought two 'great horses' for Dudley as a present, for which he gave the servant who brought them 37 shillings.[4]

It was all to little avail, yet Eric refused to be beaten. In September he sent his own brother Duke John to woo Elizabeth on his behalf. Duke John caused consternation from the moment he stepped ashore. His reception party was led by the Earl of Oxford and Robert Dudley, who wore a coat specially embroidered for the occasion with silver and pearls costing £30. Things did not start well when John expected his hand to be kissed.[5] He then interpreted the welcome he received as meaning that Elizabeth had now decided to marry his brother, an embarrassing mistake that was soon corrected. Elizabeth delighted in the novel attention that Duke John's visit brought. On one occasion she deliberately kept him waiting for so long that John stormed back to his lodgings. Yet Elizabeth could be charming when she wished to be. 'The Swedish ambassador was summoned the other day by the Queen, who told him she wished to show her gratitude to his master who had sought her in the day of her simplicity, and asked him to tell her whether his ambassadors were coming, as she was being pressed with other marriages,' de la Quadra reported. 'They are constantly getting presents out of them in this way.' Among the many gifts included a ring, supposed to be worth 6,000 crowns, which unusually Elizabeth refused to accept.[6]

The Swedish duke had brought with him an abundance of jewels, money and horses to impress; he was noted as being 'very liberal to the poor' and further promised 'mountains of silver' if his brother's marriage was a success. (It was quickly discovered, however, that the money had mostly been forged.)[7] According to one observer, both Duke John and other rival ambassadors were 'courting at a most marvellous rate. But the Swede is most in earnest, for he promises mountains of silver in case of success.'

The duke's 'high looks and pontificality' pleased no one, especially his rivals. Matters reached a head when the Imperial ambassador Bruener confronted the duke, telling him that his father, the Swedish king, 'was only a clown who had stolen his kingdom'. In return John threatened to kill Bruener. 'The matter has reached such a point,' the Spanish ambassador commented from the sidelines, 'the Queen is careful they should not meet in the palace to avoid their slashing each other in her presence.'[8]

They were not the only ones threatening to trade blows. Despite having given up his pretensions of marriage, Pickering continued his erratic behaviour, issuing a challenge of a duel to the Earl of Arundel, 'for having spoken ill of him at a banquet'. Perhaps as a sign of their growing friendship now Pickering had abandoned any idea of marrying the queen, Robert Dudley promised to deliver the challenge to Arundel in person.[9] On a separate occasion, as Pickering was about to enter the queen's chapel, Arundel stopped him at the door and told him that only members of the nobility might enter. Pickering replied that he knew this, but he also knew the earl was 'an impudent discourteous knave'. Arundel stormed off without saying a word, leaving Pickering to boast of his victory to the court. 'Pickering tells it in public and refrains from challenging him as he holds him of small account,' the Spanish ambassador reported.[10]

It was an amusing sideshow to what was taking place centre-stage. The man believed by most to stand the best chance of becoming the queen's husband was not even a candidate; not yet anyhow. 'I still have a more formidable enemy, who is very much in my way,' the Imperial ambassador reported in early December. 'It is Mylord Robert, the Queen's Master of the Horse. The Queen shows a marked preference for him over all others, and verily more so than it beseems such a Queen, much against the will of her subjects.'[11]

Rumour and gossip about Elizabeth's relationship with Robert Dudley was now rife across the Continent, encouraged by the pens of the affronted Hapsburg ambassadors. Sir Thomas Challoner wrote to Cecil from the Imperial court at Brussels how 'these folks are broad mouthed ... of one too much in favour, as they esteem. I think ye guess whom they named ... as I count the slander most false.' Yet Challoner still felt that he needed to add his own words of advice. The rumours might be untrue – he was sure that, if only for the queen's sake, they were – but Elizabeth nevertheless should practise caution in her behaviour and to which courtiers she showed especial favour to, in order to prevent tongues from wagging. 'A young Princess can not be too wary, what countenance or familiar demonstration she maketh, more to one, than another ... this delay of ripe time for marriage, besides the loss of the realm (for without posterity of her Highness what hope is left unto us) ministreth matter to these lewd tongues to descend upon, and breedeth contempt.'[12] Dudley's closeness to the queen was widely viewed with a mixture of hostility and fear. He was already being blamed for Elizabeth's refusal to marry; 'even his own sister and friends bear him ill-will,' Bruener reported. With his ability to lose friends and make enemies of the most powerful, it was a marvel, he believed, 'that he has not been slain long 'ere this'.[13]

In spite of the rumours about the queen's relationship with her Master of the Horse, Elizabeth still managed to maintain the archduke's interest into November, dropping suggestive hints to de la Quadra that 'she knew that this was the best marriage in Christendom for her, and I might be sure she would only take the best'.[14] But the ambassadors soon grew weary of her prevarication and could see straight through her games. Any hope of reviving the match ended with the arrival of the emperor's reply to the ambassador's pleas that his son Charles be allowed to travel to England. Furious that Bruener and de la Quadra had taken the affair this far without his permission, he wrote back: 'For if you ... think that we could have sent our son incognito ... you are greatly mistaken in thinking that it could have been done in secret. We will not say how unworthy, puerile and unseemly a journey so made would have been for us, for our son and for the whole glorious House of Austria.'[15]

While Elizabeth's flirtation with the archduke had backfired spectacularly, the cracks were also beginning to open among her nobility, driven by jealousy at the lavish favour and attention Dudley continued to receive from the queen. On 24 November, letters patent were issued appointing him to the lucrative position of Lord Lieutenant of Windsor Castle and Park. The office of Constable of Windsor Castle soon followed. It was too much for the Duke of Norfolk to bear. In late November, he confronted Dudley 'so plainly ... that they separated abruptly'. In return, Dudley told Norfolk to his face that 'he was neither a good Englishman nor a loyal subject who advised the Queen to marry a foreigner'. 'Things are very strained between them,' the ambassador commented, 'the Duke has gone home in dudgeon.'[16] As he planned to return to his ancestral home in Norfolk for Christmas, the duke perhaps hoped that by the time he arrived back in London again in January, the queen's infatuation with Dudley would have blown over. In fact, he never made it home. On Christmas Day, barely weeks after his quarrel with Dudley, the duke was suddenly appointed Lieutenant General in the North, to be posted up at the frozen garrison at Berwick. The commission must have struck the duke as more than mere coincidence. It was clear that he was being sent away from court, out of sight, perhaps out of mind. He had little alternative but to accept Elizabeth's wish with good grace. His hatred of Dudley, however, remained undiminished.[17]

It was during this fraught time that fresh revelations suddenly appeared against Dudley, making their rounds among both the Spanish and Imperial ambassadors. This time they concerned his wife, Amy. The news was breathtaking. De la Quadra reported how he had heard

> from a certain person who is accustomed to give me veracious news that Lord Robert has sent to poison his wife. Certainly all the Queen has done with us and with the Swede and will do with the rest in the matter of her marriage is only keeping Lord Robert's enemies and the country engaged with words until this wicked deed of killing his wife is consummated. The same person told me some extraordinary things about this intimacy, which I would never have believed, only that now I find Lord Robert's enemies in the Council making no secret of their evil opinion of it ...[18]

Bruener told the same tale. On 12 November, he reported how he had discovered that de la Quadra had been 'told as a fact that the Queen was not willing to contract' marriage, 'and only wished to keep both us and her realm in dalliance with mere words, until she should marry Mylord Robert'. Bruener recognised the one obstacle lying in the way. 'It is said that he seeks means to poison his wife, for he is indeed a great favourite with the Queen.'[19] Three weeks later, the rumours that Dudley was planning his wife Amy's death so that he might marry the queen were still the talk of court. As Bruener reported back on 5 December:

> Although he is married to a beautiful wife he is not living with her, and, as I have been told by many persons, is trying to do away with her by poison. For this reason I think that the Queen and he have a secret understanding, for I know full well ... that the Queen had more than once been addressed and entreated by various persons to exercise more prudence and not give people cause to suspect her in connection with this man, whereat she with many oaths exculpated herself. I now hear that the liking grows in intensity with the lapse of time.[20]

Yet despite his extensive enquiries, Bruener could discover no further scandal surrounding their relationship. 'I rather incline to believe that it is but the innocent love which at times subsists between young men and maidens, though it be unseemly for such a princess.' This he blamed on Elizabeth's own experiences during her youth:

> She has not always had the upbringing and instruction befitting a princess, for sometimes she was regarded as legitimate and at other times not ... She has been brought up at Court, then sent away, and to crown all she has even been held captive. For these reasons she has learned to be so stubborn and headstrong that she acts regardless of her own welfare and that of the Kingdom.[21]

If Elizabeth was actually considering Dudley as a possible husband, the ambassador believed, there would be serious repercussions to come. 'If she marry the said Mylord Robert, she will incur so much enmity that she may one evening lay herself down as Queen of England and rise the next morning as plain Mistress Elizabeth.' The nobility would certainly not accept a man, Bruener warned, whose grandfather and father had both been sent to the block for treason:

> I really do believe that he will follow in the footsteps of his parents, and may the Devil be his companion, for he causes me and all those who are active on behalf of his Princely Highness a world of trouble. He is so hated by the Knights and Commoners that it is a marvel that he has not been slain long ere this, for whenever they behold him they wish he might be hanged. An Englishman once asked if England was so poor that none

could be found to stab him with a poniard. But I am certain that he will one day meet with the reward he so richly merits. It is just like him to protract this marriage until he has sent his wife into Eternity.[22]

To others, if the rumours about Dudley's wife Amy's treatment were true it seemed that even Elizabeth's throne might be in danger. A few weeks later, there was supposedly new information to add to the rumours of Amy's poisoning, which the Imperial ambassador Bruener had obtained. De la Quadra wrote to Feria explaining how Bruener was going to tell him 'what he knows of the poison for the wife of Milort Robert'; it was, he recalled, 'an important story and necessary to be known'. 'I should be glad if that woman were to lose her head and bring matters to a point,' Feria replied, 'although when I think what a baggage she is and what a crew she is surrounded by, there is probability enough of my wish coming true.'

# 29

# Cumnor Place

By the end of 1559, it had been over six months since Robert Dudley had last seen his wife. During that time, as rumours snaked across the country of tales of her husband's antics with the queen, Amy was over two hundred miles away, residing briefly at Sir Richard Verney's residence at Compton Verney, Warwickshire, probably between June and December 1559, before departing from there and moving instead to the residence of another of Dudley's associates, Sir Anthony Forster, at Cumnor Place.

Dudley's decision to move his wife to Cumnor Place is perhaps more understandable in the context of his recent promotions, especially as Constable of Windsor Castle. If Dudley, still without any family home to call his own, was to spend more time at Windsor, moving his wife to a nearby location made perfect sense. Amy moved to Cumnor Place in November or December 1559, shortly after Dudley's appointment at Windsor, which was less than a day's riding distance away. Cumnor was certainly a more remote place to live away from the court than Throcking, though evidently closer than Compton Verney.

The village of Cumnor lies on high ground within the county boundary of Berkshire, three miles west of Oxford and around five miles north of Abingdon, with a fine view over the fields and across the river into Oxfordshire. In the centre of the village is the church of St Michael, where Anthony Forster lies buried. Cumnor Place was nearby, immediately to the south, the church spire rising over its quiet and unobtrusive medieval lodgings. Originally built as a summer retreat for the abbots of Abingdon in the mid-fourteenth century, probably around 1330, the building had undergone significant alterations in the mid-fifteenth century. After the dissolution of the monasteries in Henry VIII's reign, the house had passed into the hands of George Owen, who had leased the building to Forster. Forster considerably altered the design of Cumnor Place in the 1570s, though until its demolition in 1811 enough of the existing medieval building survived to imagine how it appeared when Amy was living there.

The grey stone building was set around a quadrangle 52 feet wide and 72 feet in length. There was an outer courtyard on the north side, entered from the road. The building and its inner courtyard were entered through a gatehouse, its doorway 9 feet high with a vaulted roof in the centre. Four ground-floor rooms, two on either side of the gatehouse, made up the north side of the building. Though each room was rather small, when they were last seen in the early nineteenth century they were apparently 'well proportioned, and highly finished. The door cases were described very elegant; the windows were uniform, of the Tudor fashion, composed of two cinquefoil arched lights, enclosed in square frames; and the chimney pieces were richly adorned', suggesting that the rooms had undergone modification in the fifteenth or sixteenth century, turning what may have been storerooms into domestic residences.

On the upper floor of the north range was a single apartment forming the Long Gallery. Measuring over 60 feet long by 15 feet wide, it was lit by a large gabled window and several subsidiary ones. This was accessed by a circular stone staircase, positioned in the north-west corner of the building, but accessible through both an entrance on the west side of the courtyard and also by a staircase built on to the outside of the building.

Most of the west side of Cumnor Place was taken up by the Great Hall. An engraving of this side was made by Samuel Lysons in 1805, before the building was demolished. It shows the outside of what would have been the Great Hall, with its two gabled windows made of carved stone, facing east into the courtyard. Both these now survive as part of Wytham church, having been removed and rebuilt into the church by the Earl of Abingdon in the early nineteenth century.

It was here in the hall that Amy and the household would have eaten their meals, or perhaps been entertained during the evenings. Measuring 44 feet by 22 feet, the timber roof of the hall was 'richly ornamented', being 'supported by immense arched beams of wood, carved with bold and handsome mouldings resting on stone corbels sculptured to resemble angels and other figures bearing shields, some charged with arms, and others quite plain. The principal cross beams, at their intersection, were adorned with bosses, on which were carved shields of arms and flowers; the panels of the roof were ceiled.'

At the southern end of the hall was a stone chimneypiece upon which had been carved the arms of the Abbey of Abingdon, while in the centre the letters J.H.S had been embossed 'in a curious cipher' with other carved square panels 'ornamented with circles enclosing quatrefoils'. There were three exterior entrances to the hall, one of which, eight feet high and just over three feet wide, still exists as the exterior entrance to the porch of Wytham church. One, to the north, accessed a room lighted by a square window, that was perhaps subdivided, the back room leading out to the yard at the back of the courtyard, 'where the kitchen and other offices were situated'.

A separate square doorway, in the south-west corner of the quadrangle, opened on to an enclosed staircase that led solely up to a 'spacious and elegant' apartment, the largest and 'most elaborate' in the Place. It was lit by a large pointed arched window in its gable, facing east, now built into Wytham church, and would have had a good view of the tower of Cumnor church from its vantage. The room was probably heated by the same chimney stack as the hall. It was here in this room that Amy slept during her residence at Forster's, and it 'has ever since been termed the Lady Dudley's Chamber' by villagers there, according to an early nineteenth-century account.

Most of the south range of the court was taken up by the chapel, its entrance 'formed by a plain pointed arch' with a series of plain windows facing south. Inside, the furnishings were lavish: 'the roof was finely timbered, the beams reposing on corbels grotesquely carved'. Adjoining the chapel, to the west, were a set of apartments, 'which were the most highly finished in the building', probably containing no more than two small rooms on each floor and which could only have been accessed through the ground floor of the chapel. Isolated as they were, they were perhaps intended as accommodation for a resident chaplain. There was also a doorway leading out to the grounds at the back of the courtyard, which included a pleasure garden, terraces – traces of which are still visible – a large pond and a deer park of twenty-five acres, extending to the boundary of the adjoining parish.[1]

On the opposite side of the courtyard from the Great Hall and Amy's bedchamber was the east side of the quadrangle. Its ground floor was divided by a passage linking the courtyard with the churchyard. As with the north side, there were two rooms on either side of the passage, with another five apartments on the first floor, accessed only through the adjoining Long Gallery. Part of the ruined wall of this side still survives, including an ornamental fireplace with a stone head and a series of sunken quatrefoils, testament to the fine detail and lavish features of the original building that Amy would reside in for the next nine months.

Amy brought with her her own small household, including her maid Mrs Picto, William Huggins, and three other retainers 'that wayteth upon my lady', to whom Dudley delivered three pairs of hose as part of their livery.[2] Amy was also joined at Cumnor Place by several others who had their own apartments within the walls of the courtyard. The Forsters had their own separate apartments there, which they now rented from William Owen. His elderly mother, Ann Owen, the widow of Dr George Owen, lodged in one wing of the house. Also at Cumnor Place lived Elizabeth Odingsells, the 41-year-old widowed sister of another William Hyde, unrelated to William Hyde of Throcking, who lived at the nearby village of Denchworth and whose family were close neighbours of the family of William Owen's wife, Ursula Fettiplace. Amy spent a great deal of time with these women who acted as her unofficial gentlewomen, helping her to get dressed in the morning, going for walks or attending church with her, amusing themselves in various recreations that included sewing (possibly accounting for the 'blue sowing silk' that was delivered to Amy through Forster's hands) or playing cards together, whiling away the time as one day followed another.

There were other villagers with whom Amy might have spent time, men and women of her own standing. A taxation return of the village from February 1560 reveals that there were fifteen villagers wealthy enough to be assessed on either their lands or goods above £6. Anthony Forster and William Owen were the wealthiest, with £20 worth of lands, but the list included other prosperous yeomen such as Henry Langley, John House, Robert King, all assessed as having £6 worth of goods. There were also Thomas Spene, who according to his will owned the lease on the nearby mill at Botley, John Kene, William Bounde, and Ralph Gunnell, each assessed as owning £9 of goods, though this was probably a conservative estimate: William Bounde left £210 8s 4d worth of goods in his will, which included carpets, pewter, brass, silver bowls and spoons, five houses, twenty cattle, a plough oxen, hogs, geese, ducks and poultry, while Ralph Gunnell was generous enough to leave 6s 8d to Cumnor church in his bequest, together with a bushel of wheat or malt to every poor householder in the village.[3] Perhaps Amy got to know their wives, or some of the other wealthy widows or unmarried women in Cumnor, who included Dorothy Buckner, whose husband William had died in 1558, leaving her with £105 15s 4d, and other goods that included silk damask, carpets, cushions, gold rings and a face cloth edged with red silk and gold, and Elizabeth Mutlowe, assessed as having 100 shillings' worth of goods.[4] Nevertheless, it can only have been a remote existence, isolated from the rest of the world and the daily bustle of the court.

# 30

# No reputation in the world

For their New Year's gift to the queen in 1560, the boys of Eton College presented Elizabeth with a small illuminated volume of Latin verses written on vellum, urging her to marry. A year had passed since her accession, yet Elizabeth was no closer to finding a husband.

By the end of January 1560, the marriage negotiations with Archduke Charles had collapsed, and, unable to break the religious deadlock, Bruener had left England, dejected by the failure of his mission. The Spanish ambassador was convinced that Elizabeth would, in time, become the victim of her own downfall, for without Imperial support, he considered, 'not only will the French despise her, but her own people as well, and she will be left helpless'. Others felt the same. 'Every one of the Queen's Majesty's friends wisheth,' Sir Thomas Gresham lamented to Elizabeth's treasurer Thomas Parry later in the year, 'that her highness were so far forth with Archduke Charles in the way of marriage, saying, if that might come to pass, all Christendom should be in rest and peace, wherein the will of God and her Majesty be fulfilled, and I beseech the Lord to bless her and strengthen her Highness to take a husband as well for the stay of the succession'.[1]

The failure of the archduke's suit was not the only disappointment that those still hopeful that the queen might wed shortly would have to face. The archduke's main rival had been the Swedish prince, Eric, and in mid-December his awkward brother Duke John had finally presented Elizabeth with detailed proposals for a matrimonial alliance.[2] The terms were attractive. There were few concerns about religion since Eric was a Protestant (albeit a Lutheran), but the Swedes had taken care to cover the main points of contention that arose with a foreign match. The Swedish king was prepared to pay for the expenses of Eric's royal household; Eric would live permanently in England even when he was crowned King of Sweden; he accepted that he would not interfere in English matters of state. Both countries would also continue to exist in their own sovereign right, and a military alliance was proposed, with each nation offering the support of eight thousand men where necessary.

Still Elizabeth could not be tempted. Sweden could never provide the protection against France that the Hapsburg Empire could wield, and though there were advantages in marrying a fellow Protestant, Elizabeth undoubtedly understood that this would isolate England from the rest of Catholic Europe. The Swedish monarchy was also an elective one; Gustavus himself had seized the throne from the King of Denmark, and therefore there was no guarantee that any son of his would inherit the kingdom. With all this in mind, on 25 February 1560, Elizabeth decided to write to Eric in person, once more breaking the disappointing news that she had decided not to marry him. 'We certainly think that if God ever direct our heart to consideration of marriage,' she wrote, 'we shall never accept or choose any absent husband how powerful and wealthy a Prince soever ... we do not conceive in our heart to take a husband, but highly commend this single life, and hope that your Serene Highness will no longer spend time in waiting for us.'

On finishing the letter, Elizabeth had second thoughts. What if, reading her rejection, Eric's passion turned to humiliation and to eventual reprisals? Alternatively, what if the king took the letter as a sure sign that she wished him to visit to pursue his suit? To be sure, she added a postscript: 'Concerning your coming, however earnest your desire yet we dare not approve the plan, since nothing but expectation can happen to your Serene Highness in this business: and indeed we very greatly fear lest your love, which is now so great, might be turned to another alien feeling, which would not be so pleasing to your Serene Highness, and to us also would be very grevious.'[3]

In spite of Elizabeth's letter, the Swedish ambassador continued to regale the Council with arguments in favour of the match and Duke John returned home in April, full of confidence that the marriage might still go ahead.[4] It was not the last that Elizabeth would hear from Eric; in future he would be determined to press his suit of marriage in person, encouraged by the queen's vague response. Elizabeth insisted that there was little point and that he should find a bride elsewhere, yet by June news reached the court that Eric was planning to set sail that summer with a fleet of ten thousand men and huge quantities of gold.[5]

Without any prospect of a marriage forthcoming, Elizabeth's isolation was becoming dangerous. While she remained without a husband, there was little chance of providing an heir for the throne. And while the question of the succession, of who might inherit the throne 'in the awful chance of the Queen's death', remained unanswered, to William Cecil's horror there was one candidate emerging as a dark cloud across the horizon that threatened to destroy everything that he stood for.

It had been clear from the beginning of Elizabeth's reign that Elizabeth's cousin, the 17-year-old Mary Stuart, would pose a significant threat to the realm. Based on legitimacy in blood, Mary had the strongest claim to be Elizabeth's successor. As the granddaughter of Henry VIII's elder sister Margaret, who married James IV of Scotland in 1502, she was the closest descendant of the Tudor line. Since Elizabeth had previously been declared illegitimate by her own father, it might be argued that Mary had a far greater claim to the throne than Elizabeth herself. She had already been crowned Queen of Scotland when she was six days old, on the death of her father King James V. When Mary was 5 she was sent to the French court, leaving her mother behind to rule as regent. She remained there for the next thirteen years, marrying the Dauphin Francis, the eldest son of King Henri II of France, in 1558. France now had a strong vested interest in Mary's success; shortly afterwards, the Guise family, the ruling dynasty of France, began to press Mary's claim to the English throne by demanding that the pope declare Elizabeth illegitimate. Cecil feared that Mary might become the centrepiece of an international Catholic conspiracy to depose Elizabeth, whose right to sit on the English throne was disputed on the Continent. The Guises were loyally Catholic, determinedly ambitious and, in Cecil's words, had 'a long old rooted . . . hatred against England'; Mary was, Cecil believed, a pawn in their ruthless political game.

Then a chance accident transformed the diplomatic scene entirely. In July 1559, King Henri II of France was killed when a splintered fragment of a lance pierced his left eye in a jousting accident, lacerating his brain. The 15-year-old Francis now succeeded to the French throne as Francis II, with his wife Mary becoming queen. Mary was now queen of two realms, both Scotland and France. With the full backing of the Guises, Mary now sought to claim another crown. 'As God has so provided that not withstanding the malice of her enemies, she is Queen of France and Scotland,' the English ambassador Nicholas Throckmorton overheard her say, 'so she trusts to be Queen of England also.'[6] Not only was Mary continuing to use Elizabeth's royal arms as her own – it was even stamped on her silver dinner plates; when she attended chapel, her ushers cried out before her, 'Make way for the Queen of England!'[7]

'This quarrel now begun,' Cecil wrote, 'is undoubtedly like to be a perpetual incumbrance of this kingdom.'[8] With France and Scotland inextricably bound, the Secretary knew that it would be easy for the French to build up their troops in Scotland, launching an invasion from across the border. If this was coupled with a French invasion from across the Channel, England would be hopelessly outmanoeuvred, fighting a war against its two ancient enemies on two separate fronts.

As autumn progressed, it became clear this was exactly what the French were planning, as they mobilised men ready to be sent to Scotland. The stakes rose ever higher. The Council agreed that 4,000 men should be stationed on the borders at Berwick, and an emergency debate of the Privy Council took eight days to decide what further action to take. The Council was split down the middle – should they risk military intervention, with all the costs of munitions and men that it would involve, or else ignore the growing French threat on their doorstep?

It was Cecil's policy of intervention that eventually succeeded. He decided to take advantage of the growing internal and religious dissent within Scotland. In Mary Stuart's absence, her mother, Mary of Guise, had acted as Queen Regent of Scotland. Her reign had proved unpopular, and she had fallen out with a group of Protestant nobles, the Lords of the Congregation, who now sought her demise. At first, Cecil persuaded Elizabeth to provide these nobles with financial support, but news that the French navy was preparing to set sail with 15,000 German mercenaries drastically changed the situation. The English garrison at Berwick was immediately mobilised. The Council now realised the gravity of the situation, and on 27 December produced a plan of war for an immediate strike against the French army in Scotland.[9] The scheme was presented to Elizabeth for royal approval. It was refused. On the back of the paper, the Secretary simply scrawled the words: 'Not allowed by Her Majesty.'[10]

Elizabeth's caution was understandable. Earlier, the Council had advised her that in going to war she might 'hazard not only money and men ... but also the state of the crown, the realm, and all that depend thereupon, which is too dreadful to think upon.'[11] Nevertheless, Elizabeth had seriously underestimated the threat that Scotland posed; her initial reaction was to declare that the Scots should be able 'to expel the French of themselves, without ... open aid'.[12]

Cecil knew otherwise. 'I cannot for any reason that I have yet heard, think any otherwise than I have done, but that it is meet for the Queen's

Majesty to prevent the French possession and conquest of Scotland.'[13] If France gained the advantage in Scotland, it would only be a matter of time before England faced a war against a united enemy on two fronts. In one of the greatest gambles of his career, he drafted a letter tendering his resignation 'with a sorrowful heart and watery eyes'. He was, he wrote, willing to consider 'any other service, though it were in your Majesty's kitchen or garden' but he would not give his 'unprofitable service' to any matters 'that myself cannot allow'. Elizabeth had told him at the beginning of her reign that she would listen to his advice, no matter how frank. Now Cecil believed he deserved the right to be heard.[14]

The gamble paid off. Elizabeth capitulated and agreed to enter into a formal alliance with the Lords of the Congregation. On 27 February, she signed the Treaty of Berwick, which gave the assurance that since France was intended to conquer Scotland, she would send 'with all speed . . . a convenient ayde of men of war on horse and foot'.[15] Yet Elizabeth still hoped that direct military action might be avoided. She hesitated and ordered the Duke of Norfolk to delay his departure with the English army. The Council attempted to reason with her otherwise, but were merely met with the reply that 'it is a dangerous matter to enter into war.'[16]

Elizabeth understood the risk she was taking. In its weakened state, England could barely struggle to defend itself, let alone provide troops to intervene in another nation's quarrel. Aiding the Lords of the Congregation, essentially rebels in a separate country, raised more questions than it did answers. 'Will she take upon herself to meddle with other Princes' rebels?' the former Spanish ambassador Feria asked Sir Nicholas Throckmorton. 'And the French being driven out, will she maintain the Scots in their religion? . . . What doth she think? We know well enough what her forces are . . . no friends, no Council, no finances, no noblemen of conduct, no captains, no soldiers. And no reputation in the world.'[17]

With the treaty signed, war was inevitable. The court busied itself with military preparations. 'The Queen rides out every day into the country on a Neapolitan courser or a jennet to exercise for this war, seated on one of the saddles they use here. She makes a brave show and bears herself gallantly,' the Spanish ambassador wrote.[18] Within months, Elizabeth had reluctantly allowed 8,000 English troops to cross the border, where they based themselves outside Leith, the port that Mary of Guise had blockaded with French troops. The English soldiers were woefully unprepared. When they finally attacked, it was a dismal failure. Even the ladders intended to scale the walls of the city were too short. There were over a thousand casualties.

Cecil, who had pinned his political reputation on war with the French, was aghast. It had only been with the utmost determination – and threats of resignation – that Elizabeth had been persuaded to go to war. 'The Queen's Majesty never liketh this matter of Scotland,' he wrote to a friend; he knew that he would have to face the blame for defeat. Elizabeth tore into him, and with 'the opinion of Cassandra' took the opportunity to berate her Secretary of State, castigating him for the failure of the mission. 'I have had such a torment herein with the Queen's Majesty,' Cecil wrote, 'as an ague hath not in five fits so much abated.'[19] Still, Cecil knew that his policy to contain French power in Scotland was the right one. 'You know what hangeth thereupon,' he wrote to his friend Sir Nicholas Throckmorton, who understood the consequences that would follow if Mary Stuart's authority went unchecked. It was only 'weak hearted men and flatterers', he believed, who were determined to side with the queen against him. Cecil did not have to name the man they must both have had in mind.

# Let the malicious report what they list

Since the Duke of Norfolk's sudden appointment as Lieutenant in the North, forcing his departure from court to the wintry lowlands of Scotland barely days after his quarrel with Dudley, Elizabeth's Master of the Horse now had unrestricted rule over her emotions.[1]

As a testament to this, Dudley's favour was marked with a lavish grant from the queen: in January 1560 he was given the priory of Watton in East Riding, Yorkshire, land that had once belonged to his father, the Duke of Northumberland. Dudley's interest in the East Riding area has been suggested as part of his plans to create an estate that might support a claim to the Lordship of Holderness, since contemporary pedigrees traced the Dudley descent from a Saxon Lord Sutton of Holderness, thereby paving the way to a promotion within the nobility. Dudley paid 20 shillings for a survey of the land there in the previous July, suggesting that he had considered investing in the property for some time previously.[2]

Elizabeth was prepared to go further. A few months later, in April, she granted Dudley a licence that allowed him to import 1,000 sarplers (bales) of wool 'which the merchants much grudged at, they being restrained from shipping'. Not quite understanding the nature of the grant, the Spanish ambassador reported that the queen had given him £12,000; he was correct in judging the scale of the grant that Elizabeth had bestowed upon her favourite. The profits to be had were enormous, and over the next twelve months, the privilege earned Dudley a massive £5,833 6s 8d (£1.2 million in today's prices).[3]

The money was sorely needed. Ever since he had been appointed Master of the Horse, Dudley's finances had been tested to the limit. He was now the pre-eminent nobleman at court, but this did not come without a price. His household accounts were filled with payments for goldsmiths and tailors, furniture and an endless round of banquets. He dined with John, Duke of Finland, on 10 January and 8 February, and again at the Lord Mayor's residence on 18 February; with the Marquis of Traynes on 9 and 17 March, at the Tower on 10 March, with the French ambassador two days later, with the Imperial ambassador on 24 March, and the Duke of Finland once more on 17 April. Much of his time was spent on the tennis court; aside from the court fees, Dudley purchased a dozen rackets for £12 from the racket maker Isaac Burges. On one occasion he played on the Earl of Sussex's side, winning £12 6s 8d.[4] On another he took on John, Duke of Finland. It would have been a fascinating match to watch; it is tempting to suggest that Elizabeth herself went to watch the game, for the Spanish ambassador reported that she had failed to attend an important diplomatic engagement on the same day that they played, claiming to be 'indisposed', much to de la Quadra's frustration.[5] Dudley also continued his costly gambling habit; his accounts reveal that he played cards or dice with the Duke of Holstein on 24 June, losing £6 3s 4d; on the same day he played cards with one Mr Stookes, losing yet another 76s 4d.

It was an extravagant and expensive lifestyle, funded mainly by borrowing from London merchants. The money Dudley borrowed was truly staggering, almost on a regal scale. Between December 1559 and April 1561, £14,000 was lent to him by various friends and contacts within the City of London, each expecting a reasonable rate of return – or else some other significant favour. On 22 December at a dinner with the merchant William Bird, he agreed to a loan of £1,630, and would eventually come to owe Bird £3,726.[6] Dudley also borrowed £1,410 from the grocer John Chapman and £1,093 from the merchant Thomas Aldersaye.[7]

While he still held the queen's favour, Dudley would always find creditors willing to lend a hand to solve his precarious financial situation. He remained in the ascendant, continuing to receive the usual presents from flatterers and the needy, hoping to seek his favour: a poor woman who presented him with a nosegay of flowers outside the doors of the Privy Chamber was rewarded with 3s 4d; the Lord Mayor of London presented him with a singing blackbird; in June, a gentleman named Peter Chowte sent him a sapphire, 'wishing it to be an orient diamond ... but as it is King Henry the Eight wore it in a ring'.[8] Many examples survive; there must have been countless others. Some were slow to realise where the queen's affections truly lay; Sir Ralph Sadler wrote to him craving pardon, 'for that all the times of my being here I have not done my duty sometimes to salute your Lordship with my poor and rude letters, trusting your Lordship will rather impart the same to my folly and negligence than to my lack of good will'.[9]

Men wrote seeking not only political favour, but religious patronage too. Protestant preachers sought preferment at his hands. The preacher John Aylmer had written to him in August 1559, requesting Dudley's help in securing office – Aylmer had already singled out the deaneries of Winchester or Durham. The letter demonstrates that even at this early stage in his career, Dudley was considered by Protestant preachers as a great hope for the future. 'I commit you to the Almighty', Aylmer ended his letter, 'who sent you to set up that others have pulled down'.[10] Dudley eventually managed to secure the archdeaconry of Lincoln for the prelate.[11] Sir Thomas Newenham wrote to him in April 1560 regarding the parsonage of Tewkesbury, requesting that Dudley 'stand so much my good Lord as to be a mean to the Queen's Majesty for me your poor orator and bedesman ... which done you shall not only do an almost deed to the poorest gentleman in all England, and bind him continually to pray for you'.[12] There is no evidence that he went away disappointed.

There can be little doubt too that Dudley held strong reformist sympathies, and was determined to make sure that men who shared his beliefs were promoted into positions of influence. Both of Dudley's household chaplains, Thomas Willoughby in 1559 and the Scotsman Alexander Craig in 1560, had been Protestant exiles under Mary I's reign. Both had also served under Dudley's father, the Duke of Northumberland.[13] Years later, Dudley himself would come to boast that

> There is no man I know in this realm of one calling or other that hath
> shewed a better mind to the furthering of true religion than I have done,
> even from the first day of her Majesty's reign to this ... who in England
> had more blame ... for the success that followed thereby than myself? ...
> And for proof of it, look of all the bishops that can be supposed that I have
> commended to that dignity since my credit any way served ... Look of all
> the deans ... who in England hath had or hath more learned chaplains
> belonging to him than I, or hath preferred more to the furtherance of the
> Church of learned preachers?[14]

Throughout the spring and into the summer, Dudley remained close by Elizabeth's side. The Duke of Norfolk had been removed from court, while Cecil was preoccupied with imminent war in Scotland. In their absence, his influence upon the queen had only grown stronger. His rivals had also been brushed aside: Duke John had departed back to Sweden in April; the Imperial ambassadors were shortly to follow.

The Spanish ambassador de la Quadra watched Dudley and the queen while away their time together, and was enraged:

> He is the worst and most procrastinating young man I ever saw in my life, and not at all courageous or spirited. I have brought all the artillery I can to bear upon him, and, by my faith if it were not for some fear of our own house I would soon give the historians something to talk about. Not a man in England but cries out at the top of his voice that this fellow is ruining the country with his vanity.[15]

Three weeks later, he had yet more sensational news to report:

> I have understood Lord Robert told somebody, who has not kept silence, that if he live another year he will be in a very different position from now. He is laying in a good stock of arms, and is assuming every day a more masterful part in affairs. They say that he thinks of divorcing his wife.[16]

There was no time for Dudley to visit Amy at Easter this year. Though his wife remained at Cumnor, just 30 miles from Windsor Castle, Dudley was busy preparing to take part in a tournament that had been organised to take place on two days, 21 and 28 April, first at Whitehall and then at Greenwich in front of the queen. Dudley missed the first tournament at Whitehall since the headpiece of his armour had broken and was being mended at the armory, but he returned for the second tournament at Greenwich where he broke three staves.[17]

Dudley was acutely aware of his unpopularity, and highly sensitive to the gossip and rumour that surrounded him. In January 1560, Lady Ormond, having heard that Dudley was angry with her over something she had said about him, felt compelled to write: 'My Lord, I do understand by my man ... that you are offended with me. Wherefore I am right sort, for that I assure you I never ministered any occasion whereby I should possess your displeasure, but, good my lord, let me know both what hath been reported unto you and also who they be that are my accusers, which you say are credible, but I doubt not ... I will take an oath upon a book,' she protested, 'that I for my part never said anything touching you.'[18]

It made little difference in stemming the flow of rumours and speculation. In April, the Bishop of Worcester, Edwin Sandys, wrote to Dudley urging him to ignore it – 'let the malicious report what they list' – though even the bishop felt obliged to write requesting that Dudley should set an example by maintaining his 'honest and righteous causes'.[19]

The surviving confession of Anne Dowe, named 'Mother Dowe', a 68-year-old widow from Essex, provides an insight into exactly the kind of rumours that were circulating in taverns and alehouses across the country. One day in July, Dowe happened to meet a gentleman riding on his horse. When he asked her what news there was, she had replied that she had heard that Dudley had bought the queen a new petticoat.

'Thinks thou it was a petticoat?' the gentleman replied. 'No, no, he gave her a child, I warrant thee.' Having a bottle of wine in the side of his saddle, he gave her a drink before he departed. A few days later, visiting the local tailor's shop at 8 o'clock in the morning, Mother Dowe could not help but repeat the story that she had been told by the mysterious gentleman. She told the tailor John King that 'There was things nowadays that she might say nothing of.'

'Why?' King asked.

'Marry,' replied Dowe, 'there is one now, they call him Dudley, that beareth more rule than ever did his father, for we had a queen whose name was Elizabeth.'

'So have we still, as I trust,' replied King.

'Dudley and the queen have played by Léger main together,' Dowe blurted out.

King protested, but Dowe insisted that 'he hath given her a child'.

'She hath no child yet,' King replied.

But Dowe was insistent that what she had been told must have been the truth. 'No, if she have not,' she answered, 'he hath put one to making, and that greater fools than he or she did talk of the matter.'

King bade her to hold her peace. 'Take heed what thou sayst; though thou be drunk now thou will repent these words when thou art sober.'[20]

The local JPs, Lord Rich and Sir Thomas Mildmay, were charged with investigating the case and wrote to the Council with details of Dowe's outburst. 'The words much touched her Majesty's honour,' they wrote, 'which words we thought not meet to be divulged amongst the common people.'

The Earl of Oxford wrote to Cecil for similar advice in June 1560. It had been reported to him that Thomas Holland of Little Bursted had gossiped that 'there was one gone to the Tower for saying the Queen's Majesty was with child.' It pointed to a wider flow of tales and rumours that were obviously circulating within and around the capital: under interrogation, Holland admitted to the earl that he had heard the news 'when he was last in London' where at Cheapside he had met a man claiming to be 'the sometime vicar of Stortford'. Oxford now required to know whether he should continue with the traditional method of punishing rumour-mongers such as Holland, namely by ordering that his ears be cut off.[21]

Tales such as these did little for Dudley's tarnished reputation. He could have been in no doubt that he was hated by many across the realm who held him responsible for the Queen remaining single. But soon matters began to grow far more serious than mere words. At the beginning of June 1560, he had received an alarming letter from the Earl of Rutland. Rutland wanted to apologise. The earl had intended to send him a greyhound as a present, 'by the judgment of many one of the best dogs that ever hath been in this country', but the dog had not arrived. Making his excuse, Rutland had to confess that while the dog was being transported from his estate to Dudley's residence, a group of men 'for the enmity that some beareth your Lordship', had 'found the means to steal the same dog, so as in ten days he could not be heard of'. When the dog was finally discovered, still alive, the creature's fur had been dyed 'with sundry colours'.

'I hear also there is wagers laid in the court that I should not keep promise with your lordship in sending him unto you', Rutland ended his letter. 'But whosoever saith, I wish they were as honest in their deeds as I am and will be in keeping my promise.'[22] For Dudley, reading the letter in his hands, they were small words of comfort.

# A deep dungeon of sorrow

As summer approached, the situation in Scotland seemed to be turning from bad to worse. After the English defeat, the French had continued to hold the Scottish port and stronghold of Leith, despite incessant bombardment. Few could predict how the military operation might end. 'My Lords here are in a marvellous perplexity that there is no more to be done,' one observer wrote from the English court. They were simply unable to understand how the French at Leith had managed to withstand the siege, which had gone on far longer than when Calais had fallen.[1]

Elizabeth was determined to finish what she had begun, ordering that 'nothing shall be spared' and reinforcements should be sent 'with all possible speed'. She had already acquired a thirst for victory. 'We be sorry that the success was no better,' she consoled her cousin Norfolk, 'but considering the importance of the matter ... the enterprise must needs be achieved.'[2] The siege continued, with fresh troops sent into Scotland. Before long, dwindling supplies forced the French to request the reopening of negotiations to end the stand-off.

Elizabeth chose William Cecil to make the long and arduous journey up to Scotland to conclude a peace settlement. It was his war, Elizabeth considered; now he could finish it. The Secretary of State was understandably anxious as to what settlement he might actually be able to achieve. 'What shall follow of my going towards Scotland, I know not, but I fear the success ... the Queen's Majesty is so evil disposed to the matter, which troubleth us all.'[3] Cecil was also concerned about leaving the queen alone under Dudley's influence for too long. He could not help thinking that his departure from the court had in some way been engineered by his enemies who wanted rid of him. A few days before he left London, he wrote to Sir Nicholas Throckmorton: 'My journey is to me very strange and diversely judged of. My friends in Council think it necessary for the matter and convenient for me; my friends abroad think I am herein betrayed to be sent from the Queen's Majesty. Whatsoever it is, I content myself with service ... If I may do good I shall be glad; but this is so difficult as I rather despair.'[4] With some exceptions, Cecil knew he could trust few men at court, and urged Throckmorton 'to write circumspectly, for how he should be judged of in his absence, he knew not'.

Three weeks into the negotiations, it seemed little progress had been made. 'We can get nothing but with racking and straining,' Cecil wrote back from Scotland. Promises were made, only to be quickly taken back again; when 'we have it in words', the Secretary deplored, 'they always will steal it away in penning and writing'.[5] But then there was an unexpected breakthrough. It came not around the negotiating table, but with the death of the Scottish regent Mary of Guise at midnight on 10 June 1560, after months of failing health. A peace settlement between the two countries was now quickly sought.

On 8 July, after sixteen days of difficult negotiation, the Treaty of Edinburgh was signed. According to its terms, the French forces were to be withdrawn immediately, while Mary Stuart and her husband Francis II were to give up their claim to the English throne – including quartering the arms of England with their own. Elizabeth had been determined that the return of Calais, so humiliatingly lost under her sister's reign, should be part of the bargain, though Cecil recognised this was wholly unrealistic, telling her that he could not 'give your Majesty counsel to embrace things so far'. As the ink lay drying on the treaty, however, Elizabeth sent a messenger with a letter ordering Cecil not 'to abandon the demand and restoration of Calais'. The contents of the letter plunged Cecil into deep despair. Fortunately, it contained the saving clause that would come to typify Elizabeth's indecision: 'If you shall have concluded for us with the French Commissioners before the receipt of these our letters, we mind not you should vary in any point agreed upon by you.'

What could Elizabeth possibly have wanted Cecil to do? He wrote back on 9 July: 'The sight of your most gracious letter written with your own blessed hand, before I had deciphered it, raised me up in such a height of comfort, that, after I perceived the sense thereof, my fall was greater into the deep dungeon of sorrow than ever I thought any letter of your Majesty's should have thrown me.'[6] The treaty was agreed as it stood. Yet despite his best efforts, Elizabeth believed Cecil could have done better. Together with the Duke of Norfolk, he was summoned home and, as he wrote to Sir Nicholas Throckmorton in Paris, was 'not thanked and not rewarded' but instead was 'sent home with no allowance either in credit or promise'.

Cecil returned to the court at the end of July utterly dejected. He had been away for sixty-three days, during which time he had been forced to pay for his own meals, board and lodging, unlike when he was at court and such expenses were free as part of the 'bouche of court' (from the French *avoir bouche à cour* meaning 'to have mouth at court'). In total, he had incurred unpaid expenses of £383, a huge sum for a man of his meagre living.[7] 'Consider the burden,' he pleaded to the court official William Petre, 'and put your finger to ease us.'[8]

The Marquis of Winchester wrote to the Secretary, attempting to raise his spirits. He consoled him that though 'all good councilors shall have labour and dolor without reward', Cecil's 'charge and pains' were 'far above all other mens, and your thanks, and rewards lest, and worse considered'. He recognised that Cecil was now deeply in debt, 'which must needs discomfort you'. Winchester had also detected that there had been a falling out between the Secretary and the queen, leaving Cecil in 'weak credit' with Elizabeth. The marquis could not help but feel that in Cecil's absence, certain men had worked against him, using 'back councells', secretly briefing the queen to undermine his authority. 'And so long as that manner shall continue,' Winchester warned, 'it must needs be dangerous service and unthankful.'[9]

Cecil would have known exactly to whom Winchester was referring. When he returned, he had found that 'the Court is as I left it'. While Cecil had been absent from court toiling away, Dudley had worked to obtain Elizabeth's total confidence. It was Dudley and his adherents who had persuaded her that she should press for the surrender of Calais. Norfolk called them 'blind men', reassuring Cecil that 'they that make most of their painted sheath will never do such service to the realm as you have done in concluding this peace'.[10] In contrast, Dudley's reaction to his peace treaty had been lukewarm at best, describing it somewhat sarcastically to the Earl of Sussex as 'a perfect peace concluded forever' adding, 'if it will last.'[11]

Without the steady hand of her most trusted adviser present, Elizabeth had allowed her emotions free rein. Her subjects looked on in despair. 'So great is the common dissatisfaction with the Queen and her mode of life that it is quite marvellous that so much delay should occur without some disaster happening to her, and it will not be from any fault of the French if it be not attempted,' de la Quadra reported. The sense of dissatisfaction with Elizabeth's reign was summed up by a contemporary as nothing but 'disunion, disfurniture, miscontentment of the old sort for change, of the new for want of liberty, the grudge of our nobles and gentlemen to see someone in such special favour, the little regard the Queen hath to marriage'.[12]

On that topic there was little chance that Elizabeth would be moved. While in Edinburgh, Cecil had written to her, making his 'continual prayer, that God would direct your heart to procure a father for your children, and so shall the children of all your realm bless your seed. Neither peace or war without this will profit us long'.[13] Elizabeth did not even bother to reply.

The Secretary was close to breaking point. Believing he had lost all influence over the queen, there was no choice, he considered, but to resign his position and 'leave it as I have too much cause, if I durst write all'. As soon as he could get Sir Nicholas Throckmorton 'placed' in his position as Secretary of State, he wrote to the Earl of Bedford, he intended to withdraw from public life, 'which if I cannot do with ease I will rather adventure some small displeasure for so have I cause rather to do than to continue with a perpetual displeasure to myself and my foolish conscience'.[14]

At the same time, Cecil continued to be pressed for an answer on the matter from various suitors. Thomas Randolph wrote to him on behalf of the Earl of Arran, still hoping for 'some token or sign' of Elizabeth's favour, though Randolph admitted that the earl 'did ... despair of himself' that anything would come of his proposal. 'The worst that may ensue is either honourable repulse, or a happy succession so notable an enterprise'. The appearance of the Duke of Holstein, who arrived at court staying from late March until the end of June, upon the scene had not helped matters. During his stay, Holstein had even been created a Knight of the Garter and was well entertained by Dudley, who dined with him on one occasion sharing a whole sturgeon worth 14 shillings.[15] 'This is the man that hath given many a sharp alarm in our camp!' Randolph confessed, 'This is he that breaketh our sleeps and hath oft our tongue.' As for Eric of Sweden's continued proposals, however, few seemed worried that his challenge posed any kind of threat whatsoever. 'Neither doth his tongue agree with any language the Queen's Majesty speaketh, nor his personage such as greatly excelleth, his people neither of such civility or nature ... his religion far from that ours professeth, his support and aid far off when need shall be, a prince evil obeyed at home, and worse beloved of his neighbours!' Randolph exclaimed, confidently predicting that 'of him we have no such fear'.[16] Nevertheless, news had reached England in June 1560 that Eric was planning one final assault for the queen's hand, and intended to set sail from Sweden with 10,000 men and huge quantities of gold. By the summer, rumours were buzzing of his imminent arrival and possible marriage to the queen.[17] Even Elizabeth decided not to travel far from the capital during her summer progress, since she could not be sure whether Prince Eric would be arriving shortly. 'Advertisements of a great prince's coming,' Dudley wrote to the Countess of Sussex, 'very shortly causeth her to make ... almost a posting journey rather than a progress.'[18]

The court had begun its summer progress at Richmond with a banquet hosted by Dudley at Kew, for which he prepared assiduously, ordering sturgeon and quails to be laid on as part of the feast, as well as filberts, walnuts and pears.[19] It was typical of the attention to detail that he would go to in order to impress the queen; similarly, while on progress, Dudley's own chamber was to be decked out with 'roses and other flowers' for twenty-seven consecutive days, costing 13s 6d.[20]

The organisation of the progress tested Dudley's patience to the limit. When one of his officers, Mr Sheldon, had failed to estimate the number of horses that needed to be mustered, he wrote back in a rage. 'I am sorry to see that the Queen's Majesty is more scantly served under me than any other in England, and specially that where I put so great trust there should be so many respects and considerations had for the ease of the country, as yet were that I myself were without regard thereof.' In particular he was concerned about the effect the miscalculation might have upon the queen's reputation, since she would now have to procure even more resources from the surrounding countryside, which might be seen as 'her majesty rather went about a spoil of her people than a safeguard of her realm'.[21]

Dudley's brief soon came to involve more than merely ordering the queen's horses. Through his extensive network of contacts on the Continent, he quickly found himself acting as Elizabeth's personal shopper, ordering dresses and other items of clothing of the latest fashion. One such letter of his survives from 1565, written to Tommaso Baroncelli, an Antwerp merchant who provided him with horses, clothes, paintings, armour and even gunpowder. 'The patterns of bodices which you have sent me for the Queen are beautiful,' Dudley wrote, 'but not what she wants, having several of that make. She wants the kind used in Spain and Italy, worked with gold and silver. I desire you to make every effort that I may have the two white mares, in good condition. About the powder I am unable to give you a definite answer. I will send the pattern and measure of the armour.'[22]

Dudley was also tasked with ensuring that Elizabeth be stocked with her favourite silk stockings; after the queen was presented with a pair during the first year of her reign, she had expressed her delight at their quality and feel, and stated that she would never wear anything else. They were, however, a rare and expensive commodity. At the end of March, Dudley had bought silk hose and pearls for £7 10s, and there are further references to Dudley purchasing silk hose in April and May that year, costing 120 shillings.[23] On 29 July, during the progress, Dudley had also managed to purchase a pair of black silk hose for 53s 4d that he had perhaps given her as a small gift at the banquet at Kew, and another pair two weeks later. Away from the capital, however, it proved difficult to keep the queen in supply. Dudley requested Sir Thomas Gresham to search for some. 'I have made due search for silk hose for the Queen's majesty,' Gresham replied on 18 August, 'but here is none to be gotten. Therefore I have sent her Highness' measure into Spain and thereby to make 20 pairs.'[24]

# With as much speed as you can

Edney, with my hearty commendations this shall be to desire you to take the pains for me as to make this gown of velvet which I send you with such a collar as you made my russet taffeta gown you sent me last, & I will see you discharged for all. I pray you let it be done with as much speed as you can & sent by this bearer Frewen the carrier of Oxford, & thus I bid you most heartily farewell from Cumnor this 24th of August.

Your assured friend,

Amy Dudley[1]

The letter may be but a few lines long, and expresses only a simple instruction to make an alteration to one of her dresses, yet once more it gives us the chance to glimpse briefly into Amy's life.

It was written from Cumnor on 24 August 1560 and is addressed to William Edney, Amy's tailor in London. Edney designed most of Amy's dresses; a bill of his survives for several dresses he had made for Amy, including a 'loose gown of satin ... with lace all over the guard' costing 20 shillings to make; another loose gown 'of Damask, laced all thick overthwart the guard' again costing 20 shillings, kirtles made of satin and russet velvet. Some dresses were relatively simple and cheap, such as a scarlet petticoat 'with a broad guard of velvet, stitched with viii stitches' that cost 4 shillings; others were highly intricate and expensive gowns, such as a 'Spanish gown of russet damask' (most likely a cone-shaped Spanish farthingdale dress that had been introduced into England by Catherine of Aragon) which cost 16 shillings, only to be further decorated with six ounces of lace worth 28 shillings and silk worth 4 shillings. Other items on the list include a bodice and stockings made from crimson velvet; an apron decorated with thin lace and pearls, ribbon and silk; a pair of 'white satin sleeves' decorated in silk and ¾ of an ounce of silver lace worth 5 shillings, and a loose gown of satin 'with lace all over the guard', together with separate payments for yards of silks and ribbon. In total, the bill came to £23 10s 7d.[2]

With her taste for satins and silks, damask and taffeta, Amy was not unlike any other wealthy gentlewoman of her day. Philip Stubbes, in his *Anatomy of Abuses,* described in detail their typical dress, which seems similar to the brief descriptions of Amy's own dresses that Edney's bill presents us with:

> [Women's] gowns be no less famous than the rest, for some are of silk, some of velvet, some of grograin [coarse woollen fabric mixed with silk], some of taffeta, some of scarlet, and some of fine cloth ... If the whole gown be not silk or velvet, then the same shall be laid with lace, two or three fingers broad, all over the gown, or the most part; or guarded [trimmed] with great gardes of velvet, every gard four or six fingers broad at the least, and edged with costly lace ... some [have] sleeves hanging down to their skirts, trailing on the ground, and cast over their shoulders like cow tails. Some have sleeves much shorter, cut up the arm, and pointed with silk ribbons very gallantly, tied with true love knots ... Then have

they petticoats of the best cloth that can be bought, and of the fairest dye that can be made ... they have kirtles [gowns] ... either of silk, velvet, grograin ... taffeta, satin or scarlet, bordered with gardes, lace, fringe, and I can not tell what besides. So that, when they have all these goodly robes upon them, women seem to be the smallest part of themselves, not ... women of flesh and blood, but rather puppets ... consisting of rags and clouts [patches] compact together.[3]

While she lived at Cumnor, Amy was well provided for, even if her husband had become a mostly absent figure in her life. Edney's bill and Dudley's household accounts prove that he still cared for his wife, financially at least. Aside from the looking glass and two yards of blue 'sowing silk' he had sent her through Anthony Forster,[4] Dudley spent 51 shillings on 'linen cloth for my lady' and another 60 shillings 'for apparel sent to my lady' and the charges of William Huggins, 'her man lying in London for the same'[5]. In June 1560, he sent 'a velvet hat embroidered with gold for my lady' costing £3 6s 8d, and no less than ten pairs of velvet shoes at a cost of £3.

When Amy's letter was discovered in the nineteenth century, folded inside Edney's bill for her dresses, it helped to re-evaluate our understanding of Amy and the time she spent at Cumnor Place. Compared to her previous letter to John Flowerdew in August 1557, in which she was in her own words 'not altogether in quiet' upon her husband's sudden departing and somewhat pathetic in tone ('thus I end always troubling you'), this letter seems both confident and positive, giving her 'hearty commendations' to Edney and bidding him 'most heartily farewell'. Rather than expressing any sense of desperation or anxiety, Amy seems decisive and in control of her own affairs, sending her own bearer, one Frewen of Oxford, to Edney, rather than relying on any of her husband's household officers as she had done at Throcking. Earlier dresses had been made by Edney after receiving parcels of the materials he needed from Dudley's financial officer William Grice 'to make, and delivered from me to Mr Grice again, made'.[6]

Amy also had precise ideas of how she wanted the velvet gown she had sent William Edney to look. He had recently sent her a 'russet taffeta gown', with a collar that had evidently impressed her; she now wished for the gown of velvet to be altered to look the same – 'make this gown of velvet which I send you with such a collar as you made my russet taffeta gown you sent me last, & I will see you discharged for all. I pray you let it be done with as much speed as you can.'

The gown that Edney had previously sent Amy, along with the date that it was sent, 6 July 1560, can be also traced from his bill:

> For making a lose gowne of rosset taffeta, the vith of July with 3 gards and
> 6 thin stripes the gard, cut and stript and truste with sarsnet   18 shillings
> For silk to the same                                                5 shillings.[7]

If her previous dress sent six weeks earlier on 6 July was typical of the regularity with which Amy had new dresses made, she would have had around a dozen new dresses made each year; the bill reveals that he had worked on fourteen. Edney immediately got on with the work as requested. In the final bill is a fee of 2s 6d for 'new translating of the coller of your velvet gowne with gold fringe'.

What is intriguing is the sense of urgency in Amy's letter. She needed the gown made as soon as possible: 'I pray you let it be done with as much speed as you can.' Why did she need the alterations to her gown made so soon? Was she expecting someone, or preparing for a specific event on which she might wear her newly altered gown with its new collar fringed with gold? Or, most likely, was she expecting to be reunited with her husband for the first time in over a year, having heard that he would soon be travelling to Windsor, just thirty miles away from Cumnor – barely half a day's journey on horseback – on the final stage of the queen's summer progress?

# I dare not write that I might speak

It had been a cold and wet summer. Contemporaries agreed that the weather had been 'foul', with the temperatures cold enough that men might consider seeking the warmth of the kitchen rather than the lofty and cold dining halls of the country estates that the queen visited on her journey.[1] Elizabeth was not deterred. For the rest of the month, having left Farnham on 8 August, the queen's household passed first through Portsmouth, Southampton and Winchester before stopping at the country residence of William Paulet, Marquis of Winchester, at Basing.

At 85 years old, William Paulet was certainly the elder statesman of Tudor politics. One of the few men to have been born in the previous century who was still active at court, he had begun his career as an MP in the 1520s, and had accompanied Henry VIII to France in 1532, sat as a judge at the trial of Sir Thomas More four years later, before going on to become Lord Steward and eventually Lord High Treasurer in Edward VI's reign, an office he continued to hold through Mary's reign and beyond. He had even sat as the Speaker in the House of Lords in 1559, and would do so again in 1566, though by then his age had begun to severely impair his ability to control debate. Despite the vicissitudes of the Reformation and its ensuing changes at court, he had managed to remain at the centre of power, a fact he put down to his nature being pliable like a willow rather than an oak. Elizabeth was deeply fond of him, and as she departed after her stay, remarked to the gathered crowd that she 'liked so well my Lord Treasurer's house, and his great cheer' before 'openly and merrily' complaining that she wished he was not so old. 'For else, by my troth,' she ended mischievously, 'if my Lord Treasurer were a young man, I could find it in my heart to have him to my husband before any man in England.'[2]

By 1 September Elizabeth had reached Windsor, where the court was 'every hour in a continual expectation of the King of Sweden's coming'. With last-minute repairs being conducted for the possible royal visit, workers toiled 'both night and day'. Meanwhile, the queen continued to enjoy her regular day-long hunting sessions, despite signing a warrant a month earlier noting that 'our said parks be greatly diminished and decayed as well by excessive hunting' and banning the sport in Eltham park for two years in order for its stock to replenish.

As always, it was Dudley, as Master of the Horse, whose duty it was to accompany her. On 7 September he wrote to the Earl of Sussex, boasting how the queen was in 'very good health' and had been out riding with him almost constantly, 'and is now become a great huntress and doth follow it daily from morning till night'. Elizabeth had apparently worn out her geldings by galloping them too hard, since 'she spareth not to tire as fast as they can go'; she now requested that 'some hobbies for her own saddle, specially for some strong good gallopers which are much better than her geldings', be sent over from Ireland, where Sussex was stationed. 'I fear them much,' Dudley confessed, 'but yet she will prove them, for your Lordship doth know the manner of ambling gelding galloping both hard.' The effort, he admitted, would be worth it: 'if she may light up a good horse, surely she shall have a great good treasure & I shall think myself happy.'[3]

That same day, the English ambassador in Scotland Thomas Randolph wrote to his close friend William Cecil, urging the Secretary to reconsider his decision to resign. 'Your absence from Court, if it so chance, will be more grievous to some men than the loss of half their lives ... for my own part I know that when you leave that place you occupy many will greatly doubt what will become of their cause.'[4]

But Cecil had seen and heard enough. Observing the festivities and banquets that filled the daily routine of the progress, together with the endless hunting parties, it must have seemed to him that the queen had abandoned her senses. It was her growing intimacy with Dudley that the Secretary feared most. Their bond seemed to be growing ever tighter, excluding Cecil or any other member of the Council from having proper access to the queen. Alarmed, Cecil wrote to Throckmorton that 'I dare not write that I might speak. God send her Majesty understanding what shall be her surety. And so full of melancholy, I wish you were free from it ... God send me hence with words to pray and sue for her Majesty with all the power of mind and body ... I beseech you either return my letter or keep it safe for me. For letters may be misinterpreted and I do not mean to so deserve.' He ended by expressing his utmost hope that Throckmorton might return as soon as he might, to replace him in his office as Secretary as soon as he could: 'God send me fortune to revoke you with speed.'[5]

The court had been at Windsor for several days before the Spanish ambassador de la Quadra, unable to attend the summer progress due to his precarious financial situation, arrived back to observe what had been taking place in his absence.

Five days after he had arrived at Windsor on 6 September, he wrote his first report back. The timings of de la Quadra's meetings are uncertain, recorded as they are in a single continuous dispatch, but at some stage the ambassador was able to have an interview with Elizabeth herself, who now told him that, whereas at their previous meeting on 3 August when she had signalled that she 'certainly intended to marry', she had once again changed her mind. She told him 'very dryly' that it was 'impossible to resolve it and that she did not intend to marry'. Her inconstancy came as no surprise to the ambassador, already weary of her prevarications.

Afterwards, de la Quadra struck up a conversation with Cecil, whom he had ascertained was currently 'in disgrace and that Lord Robert was seeking to exclude him from business'. Cecil had more interesting news to reveal. After pleading with de la Quadra to keep their conversation secret 'after many protestations and requests', he told the ambassador that 'the queen governed herself in such a way as he considered retiring'. He had been considering his situation for months in the light of Elizabeth's infatuation with Dudley. 'It was a bad sailor,' he continued, 'who on seeing a great storm coming did not seek a harbour while he could.' The queen seemed to have abandoned her office to leisure. Cecil was quick to lay the blame: 'the destruction of the queen would manifestly result from the influence of Lord Robert'. Dudley had, he continued, 'made himself lord of all affairs and of the queen's person, to the extreme injury of all the kingdom, intending to marry her and that he led her to spend all day hunting with much danger to her life and health'.

Cecil despaired. He did not know 'how the kingdom could consent to it', but, with things being as they were, he was 'determined to go to his house, although he believed that they would sooner send him to the Tower than allow him to do so. For the love of God warn the queen of these dangers and persuade her not to ruin her affairs as she has done,' he pleaded, asking de la Quadra to tell her directly 'to watch out for herself and her kingdom'. 'Lord Robert would be better in paradise than here,' he ended, repeating the sentence as if in doing so his hope might become a reality.

De la Quadra replied that he was sorry to hear what Cecil had to tell him. He had always hoped and advised that the queen might 'live peacefully and to marry'. He could go on, but he knew he hardly needed to convince the Secretary of his arguments for the queen's marriage. Cecil knew too well, he explained, how 'little attention the queen had paid, although she heard me willingly enough'.

For a while they talked about the French peace and the recent Scottish treaty Cecil had slaved over. It was not long before the Secretary once again struck up a tirade against the queen's recent behaviour. Elizabeth 'had no respect for foreign princes', he told de la Quadra, 'nor did it seem that they had any influence'. The country was racking up a huge debt, 'without considering how to pay it, for he feared she had lost all credit and the ability to draw money from the merchants of London'.

Then Cecil ended with a bombshell that left de la Quadra quite amazed. He told him:

> that they intended to kill the wife of Robert and now published that she was ill, although she was not but on the contrary was very well and protected herself carefully from being poisoned, and that God would never permit that so great an evil nor could a good result come of an evil business.

'I was certain that he spoke truly and was not deceiving me,' an astounded de la Quadra wrote. The news, he believed, 'cannot but produce a great effect because it is awful and I believe he [Cecil] has many companions in discontent'. Foremost, the ambassador noted, was the Duke of Norfolk, 'as one of the injured and capital enemies of Robert'. With that, the meeting broke up. 'I ended the conversation by showing as I have said that I was sad for what had happened,' the ambassador recalled, 'and that I wished that it would improve without entering into something that could prejudice me.'

The following day, the ambassador happened to meet Elizabeth on horseback as she returned from her daily hunt. The news was no less remarkable. 'The Queen,' de la Quadra reported, 'said to me that the wife of Milord Robert was dead or almost so and asked me not to say anything.'

De la Quadra was perplexed; what could this mean? 'Certainly what is occurring in this affair and what they are doing is a matter of great scandal and shame,' the ambassador continued, 'but with all this I do not know if she wishes to marry him at once nor even if she wishes to marry at all, because it seems to me her resolutions are not firm.' As to choosing a husband, Cecil had told him that 'she wishes to do as her father did'. Like her father, she wanted to be free to choose at her will.[6]

After the customary salutations, de la Quadra finished writing his dispatch and laid down his pen. But then, as the ink dried, some sudden news reached him. He quickly added a scrawled postscript: 'After I wrote this the queen has made public the death of M. Robert and has said in Italian – *Que si ha rotto il collo* – that she has broken her neck, she must have fallen down a staircase.'

Amy had been discovered lying dead at the bottom of a set of stairs at Cumnor Place, with her neck broken and yet without any other mark or wound on her body.

# PART FOUR

✦✦✦

Either chance or villainy

# 35

# My wife is dead

9th September 1560

Lord Robert Dudley to Thomas Blount

Cousin Blount, immediately upon your departing from me there came to me Bowes, by whom I do understand that my wife is dead, and, as he saith, by a fall from a pair of stairs. Little other understanding can I have of him. The greatness and the suddenness of the misfortune doth so perplex me, until I do hear from you how the matter standeth, or how this evil should light upon me, considering what the malicious world will bruit, as I can take no rest. And because I have no way to purge myself of the malicious talk that I know the wicked world will use, but one which is the very plain truth to be known, I do pray you, as you have loved me, and do tender me and my quietness, and as now my special trust is in you, that [you] will use all the devises and means you can possible for the learning of the truth; wherein have no respect for any living person. And as by your own travail and diligence, so likewise by order of law, I mean by calling of the Coroner, and charging him to the uttermost from me to have good regard to make choice of no light or slight persons, but the discreetest and substantial men, for the juries, such as for their knowledge may be able to search thoroughly and duly, by all manner of examinations, the bottom of the matter, and for their uprightness will earnestly and sincerely deal therein without respect; and that the body be viewed and searched accordingly by them; and in every respect to proceed by order and law. In the mean time, Cousin Blount, let me be advertised from you by this bearer with all speed how the matter doth stand. For, as the cause and the manner thereof doth marvellously trouble me, considering my case, many ways, so shall I not be at rest till I may be ascertained thereof; praying you, even as my trust is in you, and as I have ever loved you, do not dissemble with me, neither let anything be hid from me, but send me your true conceit and opinion of the matter, whether it happened by evil chance or by villany. And fail not to let me hear continually from you.

And thus fare you well in much haste; from Windsor, this 9th September in the evening.

Your loving friend and kinsman, much perplexed. R.D.

I have sent for my brother Appleyard, because he is her brother, and other of her friends also to be there, that they may be privy and see how all things do proceed.

Matters were far too serious not to act. Dudley's wife lay dead, and unless the truth was uncovered soon, Dudley knew that his reputation would be ruined. His first thoughts were not for Amy's fate. Rather, he needed to know 'how this evil should light upon me, considering what the malicious world will bruit'. Until he knew the exact details of her death, he would be unable to defend himself against the rumours and malicious gossip that he knew his enemies at court would use against him. It was vital that his innocence be proved beyond doubt, 'considering my case'. Dudley knew too well that his continued relationship with the queen depended upon it. The only way to silence his enemies, and to preserve his own position, would be to ensure that the investigation into his wife's death was carried out with as much care as possible.

Dudley's household officer Thomas Blount was already riding out on the road from Windsor when he received Dudley's letter. He wrote back acknowledging its receipt, confirming that his instructions were to 'use all the devises and policies that I can for the true understanding of the matter, as well by mine own travail as by the order of the law'. He intended to summon the coroner, 'giving him charge that he choose a discreet and substantial jury for the view of the body and that no corruption should be used or person respected'. Blount entirely understood Dudley's reasons for summoning the jury and beginning an immediate investigation. 'Your Lordship's great reasons, that maketh you so earnestly search to learn the truth, the same, with your earnest commandment, doth make me to do my best therein.' Those 'great reasons' could only be hinted at, though both Dudley and Blount knew what was at stake.

Riding from Windsor, Blount decided not to travel directly to Cumnor that evening. Instead, he stopped off at an inn nearby in Abingdon for an evening meal and also to listen to any rumours that were circulating about Amy's sudden death. 'I was desirous to hear what news went abroad in the country,' he later wrote to Dudley. At supper, Blount took the opportunity to strike up a conversation with the landlord, concealing his identity by pretending that he was not local to the area, and was merely passing through on a journey to Gloucestershire. He asked the landlord what news there was.

'There is fallen a great misfortune within three or four miles of the town,' the landlord replied, 'my Lord Robert Dudley's wife is dead.'

'How?' Blount enquired.

'By a misfortune,' the landlord had heard. 'By a fall from a pair of stairs.'

'By what chance?'

The landlord did not know. What was his judgment? Blount asked and, getting to the point, what was 'the judgment of the people'?

'Some are disposed to say well, and some evil.'

'What is your judgment?' pressed Blount.

'By my troth, I judge it a misfortune because it chanced in that honest gentleman's house,' the landlord replied, referring to Anthony Forster. 'His great honesty doth much curb the evil thoughts of the people.'

'Methinks that some of her people that waited upon her should somewhat say to this,' Blount ventured.

'No, sir, but little, for it is said that they were all here at the fair, and none left with her.'

'How might that chance?' Blount asked.

'It is said how she rose that day very early, and commanded all her sort to go the fair, and would suffer none to tarry at home; and thereof much is judged.'

Blount was intrigued. There was clearly more to learn about Amy's death than he had perhaps expected. For the moment, until the coroner's jury had been assembled and the details of the case were investigated, he knew that this was all the information he was likely to obtain. He wrote back to Dudley, who was waiting anxiously at Windsor for further news: 'The present advertisement I can give to your Lordship at this time is, too true it is that my Lady is dead, and, as it seemeth, with a fall; but yet how or which way I cannot learn.'

In fact, long before he had received Dudley's letter, Blount had already learned many of the circumstances in the lead-up to Amy's sudden death from Bowes, a retainer of Dudley's (he had once been given a hat by his master costing 8 shillings) who was still in his service wearing Dudley's livery in 1567.[1] It was Bowes who had been present at Cumnor when the discovery of Amy's body was made.

Bowes had been galloping at pace down from Cumnor on the road to Windsor to inform Dudley of his wife's sudden death, when he had crossed paths with Blount. There he revealed all he knew, prompting Blount to make his own journey to the tavern in Abingdon. Rather than travel direct to Cumnor, he had his own mission: to discover what news of Amy's death had already leaked out. By the time Dudley had written to him, Blount already knew from Bowes every detail of the tragic events that had taken place at Cumnor Place.

While it was still fresh in people's memories, Bowes had already begun his own separate investigation, interviewing members of the household in order to get closer to the truth. He had discovered that on the day of her death Amy wanted to be alone. She would not 'suffer one of her own sort to tarry at home' and insisted that the whole household leave Cumnor Place for the day. A fair was taking place at Abingdon to celebrate the feast of Our Lady, and Amy was 'so earnest to have them gone to the fair' that she grew 'very angry' with those who, preferring to remain with her, made their excuses.

One of the ladies who had refused to depart for the fair was the widow Mrs Odingsells. She told Amy that 'it was no day for gentlewomen to go in'. The following day would be better for gentlewomen to attend, 'and then she would go'.

Amy had grown 'very angry with her also', before replying that 'she might choose to go at her pleasure, but all hers should go'. Asked who should keep her company at dinner if they departed, Amy replied that Mrs Owen should stay behind with her.

By the time Blount reached Cumnor Place, he was able to confirm Bowes' initial investigations. In his conversation with Amy's maid, Picto, whom he noted 'doth dearly love her', he asked 'what she might think of this matter', whether it was 'either chance or villany'. Picto replied that she believed Amy's death was entirely accidental. 'By her faith she doth judge very chance, and neither done by man nor by herself.' Amy was, she said, 'a good virtuous gentlewoman', who had been seen to pray on her knees daily; sometimes she had even been overheard asking God 'to deliver her from desperation'.

Those last words were too important to go unnoticed. 'Then she might have an evil toy in her mind?' Blount asked.

'No, good Mr Blount,' Picto replied, evidently rattled. 'Do not judge so of my words. If you should so gather, I am sorry I said so much.'

Blount was not convinced. 'Certainly, my Lord,' he wrote back to Dudley, 'as little while as I have been here, I have heard divers tales of her that maketh me to judge her to be a strange woman of mind.' He had begun to form his own conclusions on the matter, though he understood that the circumstances of Amy's death remained highly unusual. 'My Lord, it is most strange that this chance should fall upon you. It passeth the judgment of any man to say how it is; truly the tales I do hear of her maketh me think that she had a strange mind in her.' What these other tales were, Blount did not feel he could disclose in his letter. He would write no more of the details, but promised Dudley that 'I will tell you at my coming'.

# 36

# Well-chosen men

In his first letter on hearing of his wife's death, Dudley had ordered Blount to summon the coroner so that an inquest might be held. Before a jury was assembled as part of the inquest, he wanted Blount, by his 'own travail and diligence, so likewise by order of law', to speak first with the coroner, 'charging him to the uttermost from me' to ensure that the members of the jury for the inquest were chosen from 'no light or slight persons, but the discreetest and substantial men' whose 'uprightness will earnestly and sincerely deal therein without respect'. They were to investigate the scene of Amy's death, and 'search thoroughly and duly, by all manner of examinations, the bottom of the matter'. Amy's body should be 'viewed and searched accordingly by them; and in every respect to proceed by order and law'.

When Blount arrived at Cumnor Place, however, it was too late. The inquest had already begun and 'most' of the jury had already been chosen, 'part of them at the house'. According to official legal procedures, when the coroner was informed of a death, frequently by the 'first finder' of the body, he had to go to the body immediately. The interval between a death and the inquest was never more than three days. In Oxford, the coroner normally inspected the body on the day it was discovered.[1] Before examining the body, the coroner ordered the local bailiff to summon a jury for a certain day. Twelve men were gathered from the surrounding area; the law books stated that the jury for the inquest had to comprise twelve males over the age of 12, recruited from the immediate neighbourhood. It was the coroner who had the final choice of jurors.[2] As the jury assembled, the coroner viewed the body alone. In Oxford, the coroner often held the inquest several days later, when he would deliver his personal verdict on the cause of death.

The jurors would then be sworn in by the coroner. They had to swear on the Gospels that they would speak nothing but the truth on any points on which that he might question them. Both the coroner and the jurors then viewed the body, which would have been stripped naked, as was legally required, as the coroner looked for any sign of wounds or bruising. If there were wounds on the body, their length, depth and breadth was recorded, and a thorough examination of the corpse took place. In 1342, the coroners at Oxford held an inquest into the death of an old woman who had died of natural causes. There were suspicions, however, of foul play: 'there was much talk that her husband beat her unduly,' the inquest recorded, so her body was 'rolled over and over before the eyes of the coroners'.[3] She was found not to be injured and a verdict of natural causes was delivered. Unlike on the Continent (in Italy autopsies had been practised since the fourteenth century), a post mortem was not performed.

During the inquest, the jury had to answer several questions put to it by the coroner, under oath. The first was whether the death had been caused feloniously, by misadventure or naturally; if by felony, they were to express a view whether the deceased had been killed by suicide or murder. If they were unsure, the jury might request extra time to make further enquiries. Other questions were aimed at discovering the details of the case. Importantly, the jurors were always asked where the death had occurred, whether inside a house or outside: if the death had occurred inside a house, the owner was requested to be present at the County Assizes, along with the 'first finder' of the body, when the case was presented to the justices.

Blount wrote to Dudley to reassure him about the make-up of the jury. 'To the inquest you would have so very circumspectly chosen by the Coroner for the understanding of the truth, your Lordship needeth not to doubt of their well choosing.' By his own judgment, they were 'as wise and as able men to be chosen upon such a matter as any men, being but countrymen, as I ever saw'. He was sure that they would be 'well able to answer to their doing before whosoever they shall be called'. Blount had, in any case, done as Dudley had asked him, and had spoken to the members of the jury who were present, passing on his master's message that they should proceed with their investigations 'without respect of person'. 'I have good hope they will conceal no fault,' he wrote back, 'if any be.' He had also heard that some of the men were 'very enemies to Anthony Forster'; if there was evidence of foul play at Cumnor Place, they could be trusted not to keep it hidden. 'God give them, with their wisdom, indifferency,' Blount prayed, 'and then be they well chosen men.'

A study of the men who made up the jury that sat at the coroner's inquest into Amy's death reveals that it was indeed made up of local men who lived either in Cumnor or in surrounding villages nearby. It is possible to trace the identities of most of the jurors, whose names feature in a Lay Subsidy taxation record drawn up in February 1560. Most were clearly either gentlemen or yeomen farmers. John Kene, Thomas Spene and Henry Langley all lived in the village. Compared to the two wealthiest men in the village, Forster and William Owen, who were both assessed as having lands worth £20, Kene, Spene and Langley were each assessed as owning £9 in goods. Langley's will still survives, indicating that he left an estate valued at £59 4s 6d. Other wills of jurors resident in Cumnor survive also: these include those of William Cantwell, who owned two mares, five colts and twenty-three sheep, and William Noble, whose material possessions included four coats, four doublets, three pairs of hose and two cloaks, and who wrote in his will that 'every church going cottager' in Cumnor should receive two pence upon his death. Those jurors living in the village seem to have been a tight-knit group, who knew each other well: for instance William Cantwell proved Thomas Spene's will in 1562.[4]

Other members of the jury, while not residing in Cumnor, came from the surrounding local towns and villages. The coroner, John Pudsey, lived at the nearby village of Slipton at the time, where he claimed an annuity of 26s 8d for his service.[5] It is probably his will that was proved in 1563, in which he is described as 'John Puse of the parish of Denchworth', leaving amongst his possessions worth £15 8s 4d three acres of land, three horses, two bullocks, 30 sheep and two pigs.[6] Sir Richard Smythe, the foreman of the jury, is mentioned in the tax return as a 'burgess of Abingdon', assessed as having £10 in goods. Richard Howse is also described as a burgess and was assessed as owning 20 shillings in lands.[7] It is possible that he had family connections with the village at Cumnor, since a John Howse lived in Cumnor, assessed as having £6 in goods. Other members of the jury came from nearby Hinckley; John Syre lived in South Hinckley, where he was assessed as owning 100 shillings worth of goods, while Hugh Lewys and William Ruffyn both lived in North Hinckley; Ruffyn may have had other connections with Cumnor, since he is found taking the inventory and proving the will of a resident of the village, Thomas Buckner, several years later.[8] Edward and John Stevenson, probably brothers, both lived in nearby Southwell, and were also assessed as both owning £9 in goods.

The queen and her favourite:
Elizabeth and Robert Dudley,
drawn from life by Federico
Zuccaro.

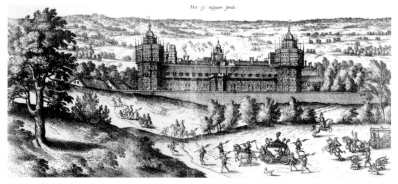

One of Elizabeth's summer progresses to Nonsuch, the Earl of Arundel's residence. In 1559, the earl's lavish entertaining of the queen astounded everyone.

Sir William Cecil, Elizabeth's private secretary, who dominated political life at court.

A copy of a now-lost portrait of Elizabeth in her coronation robes, her long flowing hair a sign of her virginity.

A sketch of Elizabeth's coronation procession: Robert Dudley rides close behind the queen.

Robert Dudley, the queen's Master of the Horse, proudly displaying his garter chain.

A miniature of an unknown lady by Lavinia Teerlinc.
Does the age of the sitter, 18, and the oak spray suggest that
this might be Amy Dudley, painted on the occasion of her marriage?

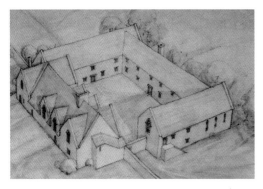

LEFT: A modern reconstruction of Cumnor Place, where Amy was to spend her final days.

A drawing of the ruins of Cumnor Place by Samuel Lysons shortly before it was demolished. Amy's lodgings are supposed to have looked out from the top left-hand window.

ABOVE: An eighteenth-century sketch by Samuel Lysons of the 'pair of stairs' that Amy is reported to have fallen down. The stairs descend from the left before reaching a landing and twisting to the left again.

The long-lost coroner's report into Amy's death, newly discovered in the National Archives.

ABOVE: 'A great resort of wooers': Elizabeth receiving foreign dignitaries. Her hand in marriage was the most highly prized in Christendom.

The 'she-wolf': Lettice Knollys, who earned Elizabeth's unbridled jealousy after she married Robert Dudley in 1578.

OPPOSITE: The young queen: while she was still able to have children few believed that Elizabeth would remain the Virgin Queen.

A later picture reputed to be of Elizabeth and Dudley dancing at court. They were both energetic dancers.

Blount had one more matter to add. In his letter to him, Dudley had further requested that 'my brother Appleyard' be sent for, 'because he is her brother', as well as 'other of her friends also to be there, that they may be privy and see how all things do proceed'. John Appleyard was Amy's half-brother, the eldest son of her mother's first marriage. He had married the sister of William Huggins, one of Dudley's retainers. Like Huggins, Appleyard was closely associated with Dudley, owing his appointment as Sheriff of Norfolk and Suffolk in 1559 to Dudley's favour with the queen, and the two had remained in fairly regular contact: Appleyard had previously sent Dudley a gift of a hawk and, it seems, lent him money on occasion.[9] Having received Dudley's request to oversee the investigations into Amy's death, Appleyard had now arrived at Cumnor Place. 'Your Lordship hath done very well in sending for Mr Appleyard,' Blount told Dudley. It was an astute move, helping to calm any fears of those that might have believed that Dudley would move to cover up or hinder investigations into Amy's death.

Blount promised to write as soon as he knew more. For now, he ended by wishing for Dudley to 'put away sorrow, and rejoice, whatsoever fall out, of your own innocency; by the which time, doubt not but that malicious reports shall turn upon their backs that can be glad to wish or say against you.'

Dudley wrote back impatiently. He remained unsettled, desperate for further news. 'Until I hear from you again how the matter falleth out in very truth, I cannot be in quiet,' he wrote, though he was comforted by the fact that Blount had described the jury as 'discreet' men. He asked Blount to pass another message on to them. 'I pray you say from me, that I require them, as ever I shall think good of them, that they will, according to their duties, earnestly, carefully, and truly deal in this matter, and find it as they shall see it fall out.'

In private, the cause of his wife's death had been preying on Dudley's mind. Could his wife really have been murdered? At first it had seemed obvious that an accident must have taken place, but now he was not so sure. Dudley ordered Blount to tell the jury to reveal in full the results of their enquiries. 'If it fall out a chance or misfortune, then so to say', but if Amy's death did 'appear a villany (as God forbid so mischievous or wicked a body should live) then to find it so'. Dudley was sure that he had nothing to fear, whatever the outcome of the investigation and 'what person soever it may appear any way to touch'. He was determined to ensure that if his wife had indeed been murdered, as he had begun to fear, he would seek 'the just punishment of the act as for mine own true justification'. 'I would be sorry in my heart [if] any such evil should be committed,' he told Blount. Once again it was the protection of his reputation that concerned him most. Whatever the cause of his wife's death, he was determined to prove that he was not guilty of any crime. 'So shall it well appear to the world my innocency by my dealing in the matter, if it shall so fall out.'

'Cousin Blount,' Dudley ended his letter, 'I seek chiefly truth in this case, which I pray you still to have regard unto, without any favour to be showed either one way or other ... I require you not to stay to search thoroughly yourself all the ways that I may be satisfied. And that with such convenient speed as you may.'[10]

Shortly afterwards, Dudley left the court and travelled to his house at Kew, 30 miles away. Preparations for mourning would need to be made. He had already ordered his mourning blacks, made from 'fine black sowing silke'; a servant named Jennings rowed over by boat to Kew especially, 'to take measure of your lordship'.[11] There were also the expenses of the preparations for Amy's funeral: a 'Paris hood' was ordered for the chief mourner at a cost of £2 10s 2d and 'Jasper the joiner' was paid £11 10s 6d to make the coffin, while cloth was sent up from London to make the shroud, along with £100 in gold 'for the charge of the burial'.[12]

At court, news of Amy's death spread rapidly. As soon as she was informed, Elizabeth announced that everyone present was to observe an official period of mourning. One courtier recorded how the place was 'stuffed with mourners, yea, many of the better sort in degree, for the Lord Robert's wife'.[13] Another anonymous eyewitness reported how Dudley and 'all his friends, many of the lords and gentlemen, and his family all be in black, and weep dolorishly'; but he did not believe the display of grief was at all genuine, noting in the margin, 'great hypocrisy used'.[14]

# 37

# It doth plainly appear

It was not long before the gossip Dudley feared began to circulate. Hearing news of Amy's death, the Protestant preacher Thomas Lever wrote to Cecil from Coventry that 'here in these parts seemeth unto me to be a grievous and dangerous suspicion and muttering on the death of her which was the wife of my Lord Robert Dudley'. Not realising that the coroner's inquest into Amy's death had already begun its work, he urged that the case be dealt with as soon as possible with 'earnest searching and trying out of the truth with due punishment'. If Amy's death was found to be the result of foul play, he insisted, 'if any be found guilty in this matter', it should be 'openly known'. 'For if no search nor inquiry be made and known', he remonstrated with Cecil, 'the displeasure of God, the dishonour of the Queen, and the danger of the whole realm is to be feared. And by due inquiry and justice openly known surely God shall be well pleased and served, the Queen's Majesty worthily commended, and her loving subjects comfortably quieted.'[1]

Dudley was frantic to prove his innocence. He had received another letter from Blount, who wrote to confirm that he had passed his latest message to the jury. Perhaps sensing Dudley's nervousness, he reassured his master, 'You need not bid them to be careful: whether equity of the cause or malice to Forster do forbid it, I know not, they take great pains to learn the truth.' He intended to journey to Kew the following day, but not without stopping off first at Abingdon to meet with 'one or two of the jury' to discuss the inquest over dinner: 'What I can I will bring.' But, for the moment, there was little more that Blount could add. 'They be very secret,' he noted, 'yet do I hear a whispering that they can find no presumptions of evil ... I think some of them may be sorry for it,' he admitted, adding, 'God forgive me.' Having considered the details of the case himself, he had come to the same conclusion:

If I judge aright, mine own opinion is much quieted; the more I search of it, the more free it doth appear unto me. I have almost nothing that can make me so much to think that any man should be the doer thereof as, when I think your Lordship's wife before all other women should have such a chance, the circumstances and as many things as I can learn doth persuade me that only misfortune hath done it, and nothing else.[2]

It was welcome news. Dudley, however, was one step ahead, for he had received a letter from 'one Smith, one that seemeth to be the foreman of the jury', undoubtedly Sir Richard Smith (or Smythe) of Abingdon.

'I perceive by his letters,' Dudley wrote to Blount, 'that he and the rest have and do travail very diligently and circumspectly for the trial of the matter which they have charge of.' They had conducted a thorough search and examination, Sir Richard Smith observed; he wanted to let Dudley know that 'it doth plainly appear . . . a very misfortune'. Reading Smith's letter, Dudley must have breathed a private sigh of relief. His reputation was intact. 'Which for mine own part, Cousin Blount,' he wrote of the news, 'doth much satisfy and quiet me.'

Yet Dudley was not yet fully satisfied. He hoped that the investigations would continue 'to the uttermost, as long as they lawfully may'. Even once the verdict had been reached he intended to assemble yet another 'substantial company of honest men [who] might try again for the more knowledge of truth'. He had been in contact with Sir Richard Blount, possibly a relation of Sir Thomas, whom Dudley considered 'a perfect honest gentleman', to try and arrange a second inquiry, which he hoped might include Amy's half-brothers, John Appleyard and Arthur Robsart. He needed to be seen to be doing something. 'If any more of her friends had been to be had,' Dudley added, 'I would also have caused them to have seen and been privy to all the dealing there.'[3]

His wife was dead, but thankfully at least he had been proved innocent of her death. The jury had acquitted him or anyone else of blame, and found that it had all been a tragic accident. Life, Dudley must have considered, might now begin to return to normal. It was with a sense of cautious optimism that he ended his letter:

Well, Cousin, God's will be done; and I wish he had made me the poorest that creepeth on the ground, so this mischance had not happened to me. But, good Cousin, according to my trust have care about all things, that there are plain, sincere, and direct dealing for the full trial of this matter. Touching Smith and the rest, I mean no more to deal with them, but let them proceed in the name of God accordingly:

and I am right glad they be all strangers to me. Thus fare you well, in much haste; from Windsor.

Your loving friend and kinsman, R.D.[4]

Of course, life could never return to normal. Despite Dudley's protestations of innocence, there would always be those who refused to believe him, assuming that the circumstances surrounding Amy's death were far too suspicious for her fall to have been merely an accident.

# 38

# So pitifully slain?

After the coroner's jury had finally finished its investigations, on Sunday 22 September, Amy was buried at the Church of Our Lady in Oxford. Her body had been embalmed, 'safely cered' and placed in a coffin that was taken secretly to Gloucester College (on the site of Worcester College). For several days her body lay in state, beneath hangings of black cloth and escutcheons of both Dudley's and Amy's family arms. Mourners gathered to pay their respects, and a dinner was held in the Great Hall of the college, the walls of which had been draped in black cloth.

Meanwhile, Amy's most treasured and valuable possessions, including her jewellery, were returned to her husband. There was one item that Dudley was especially keen to have back. The household accounts record the substantial payment of £25 6 shillings and 8 pence to Richard Whetell, 'for the redeeming of a diamond of my Lady's'.[1] Jewels, Dudley must have considered, would be wasted on the dead.

On the day of the funeral, two conductors carrying black staves led the procession to the church. It was to be a traditional aristocratic funeral, following the set pattern of mourning devised by the royal heralds, who later fastidiously noted every detail of the event in their records at the College of Arms. Behind the conductors followed eighty poor men and women wearing black gowns, then the university professors and doctors, walking in pairs, according to the degree of their colleges. The choir came next, dressed in their surplices and singing, followed by the minister. In between the two royal heralds, summoned specially and paid the princely sum of £66 16 shillings 8 pence from Dudley's accounts 'for their pains-taking at my Ladies burial', followed Amy's half-brother, John Appleyard, wearing a 'long gown, his hood on his head'. He walked in front of Amy's coffin, carrying the banner of arms, the largest and most prominent of all the funeral insignia.

Amy's coffin was carried by eight tall yeomen. The journey was a long one, and they were attended by four assistants to take turns bearing the load. Two assistants wearing long gowns and with hoods on their heads walked at the front and back of the coffin, and at each corner of the coffin four more hooded gentlemen walked carrying banners. Next came the gentlewomen mourners, some being those with whom Amy had spent her days at Cumnor: Mrs Wayneman, Lady Pollard, Mrs Doylly, Mrs Butler the elder, Mrs Blunt and her neighbour Elizabeth Mutlowe. These were the official mourners, and though many followed behind, including the Mayor of Oxford 'and his brethren', three yeomen in black coats had been appointed to separate out this carefully assembled scene of ritual mourning from the crowds of onlookers and hangers-on.

The procession arrived at the church, entering through the west door. The inside of the church had been draped in black cloth, and a hearse, an elaborate wooden frame constructed over where the coffin would lie, 10 feet long by 7½ feet wide and 14 feet high at the highest point, had been constructed at the upper end of the nave. It had been assembled on floorboards and decorated with escutcheons of arms and badges, with a valance of black sarcenet 'written with letters of gold and fringed with a fringe of black silk'. From the top of each of its four posts hung 'a great escutcheon of arms on paste paper' and from the rails of the hearse black cloth was draped, embellished with more escutcheons. A wooden rail had been constructed 4 feet away from the hearse, draped in black cloth. Seven mourning stools, covered with cushions and black cloth, were set out along the rail. And at the upper end of the church, near the choir, a 'vault of brick' had been built in preparation for the body. It was an impressive display, and news soon reached the court that no expense had been spared. There were rumours that Dudley had spent more than £2,000 on the ceremony.[2]

The coffin was placed inside the hearse. Two gentlemen with banners stood on either side, whilst at its foot, in prominent display, was the great banner held by Amy's half-brother John Appleyard. The mourners quickly fell into their place, according to their degrees, and the service began, 'first certain prayers, then the x commandments, the choir answering in pricksong'. After readings from the gospel came the offerings led by the chief mourner. After each mourner had walked up to the hearse and made their obeisance to the departed, Dr Babington, the Doctor of Divinity, gave the sermon 'whose anthem was *Beati mortui qui in Domino moriuntur* [Blessed are they who die in the Lord]'.[3] Some thirty years later, it would be alleged that Babington, while giving the sermon accidentally spoke out loud to the congregation, 'recommending to their memories that virtuous lady so pitifully murdered, instead of so pitifully slain'. Amy's body may have been laid to rest, but the controversy surrounding her death had only just begun.

# 39

# An evil toy in her mind

We have so far witnessed the events and first reactions to Amy's death: Dudley's immediate concerns that his own reputation first be saved; the scandal that arose as news of the tragedy broke; Dudley's return to court after the coroner's jury returned a verdict of accidental death. Yet none of this explains exactly how – or why – Amy died.

The details of the scene of her death are difficult to place. No record of the exact position of her body, where it lay or in what condition it was found, survives. We know that she was discovered at the bottom of a staircase in Cumnor Place. If later accounts are to be believed, she was found with her neck broken, yet with no other mark or wound to her body. Her headdress, too, supposedly lay intact upon her head while the stairs, at the bottom of which she had been found dead, were 'by report ... but eight steps'.[1]

The first details of how Amy died come from Dudley's own letter to Thomas Blount. 'I do understand that my wife is dead, and, as he saith, by a fall from a pair of stairs.' This is backed up by the landlord's conversation with Blount at the inn at Abingdon. Amy had died 'by a misfortune'; he had heard that this was 'by a fall from a pair of stairs.' Blount later told Dudley that 'my Lady is dead, and, as it seemeth, with a fall; but yet how or which way I cannot learn.'

Could Amy really have broken her neck and died by falling down a 'pair of stairs' only eight steps high? The term 'pair' itself indicates that the stairs leading up to the first floor must have been on two tiers, in the fashion of a dog-leg staircase, pivoting around a corner. If there were two tiers of steps leading up to the first floor, perhaps with a landing separating the two flights, it was probably one of the two tiers that was in fact eight steps high.

After centuries of standing desolate and in ruin, Cumnor Place was demolished in the early nineteenth century, and the staircase on which Amy was supposed to have fallen was pulled down. However, using new documentary evidence, it is possible to recreate what this staircase might have looked like. There is a brief record of how it appeared in a descriptive account of Cumnor Place, recorded in the antiquarian journal, *The Gentleman's Magazine*, before the building was demolished. This describes a 'circular newel stone staircase' in the north-west corner of the building, leading up to a doorway at the western side of the long gallery, on the first floor of the northern side of the quadrangle.[2] Such a basic description gives us some sense as to the character of the stairs; they were probably from the fourteenth century, essentially medieval in fashion, the carved and no doubt worn stone steps winding around the newel, an upright post which supported the staircase.

Yet more evidence has emerged, making it possible to envisage how the staircase appeared. There is a drawing of what must have been the staircase, made before its demolition, in a book of sketches by Samuel Lysons, the author of the *Magna Britannica*, which now survives in the British Library.[3] Lysons' drawing might only be a basic outline of the stairs, but it provides enough information to make a fairly accurate reconstruction of how the staircase might have looked.

Lysons' sketch reveals that the stairs in the north-west corner of Cumnor Place had twelve to thirteen steps in total, broken up by a landing around which the stairs turned on a 180-degree angle. It is not clear from the drawing, however, where the stairs begin and end. It has been argued that 'it would be natural to assume that its foot was at the north end' of the western side of the building, and certainly the account in *The Gentleman's Magazine* suggests that the circular newel stone staircase led to a doorway at the western end of the Long Gallery. If this was indeed the case, the staircase was accessed from the ground floor of the western range of the building, in a room adjoining the Great Hall, described as 'a large room that projected a short distance beyond the line of the other buildings', which was connected to the Great Hall by a 'double arched entrance' and was probably designed as a buttery. The stairs, accessed from this room, would then have led up four stairs to a landing; turning right at an angle of 90 degrees, another flight of stairs, according to Lysons' drawing what seems eight steps in total, at first angled around the turn then leading straight up into the Long Gallery on the north side of the building. The dog-leg design of these stairs in the north-west corner of the building, giving access to the upper rooms, is entirely consistent with the repeated comment of a 'pair of stairs', suggesting that these were indeed the stairs, at the bottom of which Amy's body was discovered one September afternoon. With a picture of the stairs that Amy is supposed to have fallen down in our minds, we can now turn to the likelihood of Amy's death being a simple accident or 'misfortune'.

Most incidents on stairs are nothing more than a stumble, an occasional trip or loss of balance that is quickly rectified. It has been estimated that such missteps occur once every 2,222 stair uses; for a stumble or a slip to result in a fall has been estimated to occur once in every 63,000 stair uses; for that fall to be fatal, the accident would occur roughly once in every 514 million stair uses.[4]

The statistics quickly translate themselves into a human cost. Falls are the second largest case of accidental deaths each year in the United States, behind motor vehicle accidents. They cause more than twice as many deaths annually as drowning or fires and burns. In 1986, for instance, over 1.46 million people were treated in hospital emergency rooms after being injured in falls, 6,200 of whom died. Falls specifically from stairs resulted in nearly 46,000 hospitalisations, with approximately 4,000 fatal falls from stair accidents.[5]

The fact that Amy was found at the bottom of a staircase only eight steps high led many to query whether it would have been possible for her to break her neck falling down so few stairs. Compared to a straight flight of stairs, dog-leg stairs (stairs curved around a landing) are also often seen as a safer design, limiting the distance that a victim can tumble as a result of their angles breaking a fall. Research conducted in Scandinavia and Japan in the 1970s on serious falls from staircases has shown that whereas dog-leg stairs accounted for 63 per cent of all stairs in the study, only 37 per cent of all accidents occurred on them. A quarter of falls on dog-leg staircases that wind around a turn proved to be 'severe', compared to 57 per cent on straight-flight stairs.[6]

We now know from Lysons' sketch that the staircase at Cumnor Place was certainly of a dog-leg fashion, forming the 'pair of stairs' that was soon mentioned after Amy's death. In total, there were probably twelve to thirteen steps on the staircase, though the initial steps leading down from the Long Gallery do seem to be eight steps high. It may have been that Amy was found on the landing, having fallen down these initial steps. If this was the case, it would accord with studies of staircase accidents which have revealed that one third of stair accidents take place on the first step, another 25 per cent on the second step, with an additional 12 per cent on the third step. With 70 per cent of falls occurring on the first three steps, it seems likely that if Amy did fall, she did so possibly tripping at the top of the stairs.[7]

A fatal fall from such a short flight of stairs also need not seem so surprising, especially given that the majority of falls begin at the top three stairs. Research has shown that the highest-risk stairs are those with fewer than ten steps, with examples of 'remarkable injuries which may be caused by short, unexpected falls ... the injuries caused by such falls do not only depend on how far one falls'.[8] One possible reason for this is that the victim might be paying less attention when descending a shorter staircase, believing that they are relatively safe and giving them a false sense of security; another might be that it is at this point that a person's gait must be adjusted to descending the stairs from the flat landing.

Let us imagine the scene. Amy is in the Long Gallery, on the first floor in the north wing of Cumnor Place. As she begins to descend the stairs, of which there are four straight steps before the stairs begin to curve on an angle to Amy's left-hand side, she loses her footing as she attempts to place her foot upon the first stair, misses and stumbles. Perhaps the steps, already two hundred years old, were worn and uneven; perhaps beneath her heavy dresses of damask and her petticoats she could not see her feet to place them accurately on the step. As she attempts to correct her balance, already she is falling too fast and too far forward, clipping another stair and sending her body flying down the rest of the descent, landing upon her head, breaking her neck instantly. If later accounts are to be believed, she was found dead 'without hurting of her hood that stood upon her head', nor any other wound. Medical evidence suggests that this might have been perfectly possible: one study of patients involved in falls and who sustained an acute cervical spine fracture revealed that 46 per cent suffered no facial or head injuries.[9]

Perhaps we might be forgiven in thinking that Amy's death was indeed a simple accident. The circumstances leading up to her death, however, suggest otherwise. On the day of her death, as we know, Amy had been acting strangely. She had awoken 'very early', and had insisted on being alone in the house. She had ordered her household to depart to the fair at Abingdon, and 'would not that day suffer one of her own sort to tarry at home'. She was 'so earnest' that she grew angry with anyone who tried to give their excuses. When her gentlewoman Mrs Odingsells refused, preferring to attend the fair the following day, she grew 'very angry', insisting once more that 'all hers should go'.

This was not the first time that Amy had shown signs of such behaviour. Blount was convinced that something was not right. 'Certainly, my Lord,' he wrote to Dudley, 'as little while as I have been here, I have heard divers tales of her that maketh me to judge her to be a strange woman of mind.'

While at Cumnor, he had interviewed Amy's maid, Mrs Picto. 'What might you think of this matter?' Blount asked. Had Amy died by 'either chance or villany'?

Mrs Picto seemed anxious and defensive, nervous even. She replied that 'by her faith she doth judge very chance, and neither done by man *nor by herself*.'

This was not the question Blount had asked; clearly Picto had considered that Amy may have committed suicide – or at least assumed that others would be thinking along these lines – before dispelling such thoughts from her mind. Her mistress, she said, convincing herself, 'was a good virtuous gentlewoman'; she had even seen her praying daily upon her knees, she stated, letting slip that 'divers times ... she hath heard her pray to God to deliver her from desperation.'

Blount pounced. 'Then she might have an evil toy in her mind?'

'No, good Mr Blount, do not judge so of my words, if you should so gather,' Picto stuttered back, before making her excuses to leave: 'I am sorry I said so much.'

Blount was not so sure. 'My Lord,' he wrote back to Dudley, 'it is most strange that this chance should fall upon you. It passeth the judgment of any man to say how it is; but truly the tales I do hear of her maketh me think that she had a strange mind in her.' What that mind was, Blount would only divulge to Dudley in person, 'as I will tell you at my coming'.

Blount was not the only one willing to consider that Amy might have taken her own life at Cumnor. A letter of Sir Nicholas Throckmorton's written at the French court to Sir Thomas Chamberlain six weeks after Amy's death lamented the rumours that were being spread about Dudley's involvement in his wife's demise. Throckmorton probably did not believe that Dudley could have ordered his wife's death, though he was willing to entertain other, equally sinister, thoughts. 'My friends advise me from home that Lord Robert's wife is dead,' he wrote, 'and hath by mischance broken her neck *herself*.' The gravity of what he had just written seems to have struck him. With his pen paused over the line, Throckmorton suddenly thought better of it. It was a dangerous accusation to be spreading, one that might land him in serious trouble. He crossed out 'herself' and inserted the word 'own', adapting the sentence to read 'hath by mischance broken *her own neck*'. The corrections, however, could hardly go unnoticed. Reading through his letter, Throckmorton must have considered, Chamberlain would be able to draw his own conclusions on that matter.[10]

Could Amy's death have been suicide? Had she decided to end her own life, and deliver herself from the 'desperation' that she had prayed on her knees to be rid of? The suggestion is worth considering, not least because of Amy's strange behaviour on the day of her death. If Amy did intend to kill herself, this might explain her expressed desire to be alone.

The date of Amy's death also possessed some significance: it was the day after Elizabeth's twenty-seventh birthday. Perhaps Amy awoke early with painful thoughts of her husband's absence in her mind. What had he been up to during the banqueting and celebrations to mark the queen's birthday the night before? She had not seen her husband for over a year now, as he waited dutifully upon the queen. Perhaps she had even heard some of the rumours that had been circulating at court; that her husband was courting the queen, spending day and night in her chamber.

There are also other questions to consider. Amy's letter to her tailor William Edney, written fifteen days before her death, suggests that she was in a hurry to have her gown mended with a new collar. What could have been her reason, and why was her demand so pressing? Had she hoped or been told that Dudley might visit her while he was staying at Windsor, only thirty miles away? There is some evidence to suggest that Dudley was planning to make a trip into Leicestershire, when he could have stopped off at Cumnor on his way. In mid-June he seems to have planned to visit his brother-in-law, the 3rd Earl of Huntingdon, at Ashby de La Zouche.[11] This visit must have been cancelled, but perhaps Amy's expectations that she might see her husband for the first time in over a year had been raised.

Amy might also be forgiven if she was having doubts about the future of her own relationship with her husband. Having married young, their union had not produced the heirs that Dudley would have so dearly wished for, and after eleven years of marriage, it was unlikely that any children would be forthcoming. Alone at Cumnor Place, and without fear of being witnessed, Amy might plan a death that would cover up all possible traces of her suicide. By throwing herself down the stairs and making her death look accidental, Amy might receive a decent and Christian burial. Meanwhile, freed from the constraints of her existence, her husband would be free to seek a new wife of his own choosing.

None of this, however, really convinces. Even though the stairs at Cumnor Place were likely to have been the steep and spiralling stone-clad stairs of the original medieval building, from which a fall certainly might prove deadly, there was no guarantee that the attempt would succeed. If she had leapt to her death, there is also the question of why no other mark or wound was found on her body, and why her body had been discovered with her neck broken, 'yet without hurting of her hood that stood upon her head'.

Other questions remain too. Amy had been seen praying daily upon her knees. It was clear that she was a religious woman, who probably stuck devoutly to her faith; though there is little evidence to make any clear case, we know that she had come from a family with strong reforming connections, while her earlier letter to Flowerdew ends with the pious flourish 'and so to God I leave you'. It was through prayer that Amy sought to end her desperation. She would have known that to do otherwise, to end her own life herself, was anathema and a sin in the eyes of God. The Church viewed suicide as equal to murder, a blasphemous decision that went against the will of the Lord. 'For the heinousness thereof,' observed the cleric Michael Dalton, 'it is an offence against God, against the king, and against Nature.' In addition, suicide was believed to be driven by despair and self-destruction which was commonly held to be the work of the devil, hence Blount's question about whether Amy had 'an evil toy' in her mind.

Not only would Amy's soul be in danger of eternal damnation, her suicide would cause significant problems for her husband. Suicide victims were guilty of the criminal offence of *felonia de seipso*, in its shortened version, *felo de se* – a vile crime against oneself. Suicides were tried posthumously by the coroner's jury, and if convicted the punishment was harsh. Any movable goods, household items, money and land in their possession was forfeited to the Crown. This would include Amy's inheritance from the Robsart estate.

The treatment of the body of a suicide victim was macabre. Denied a Christian burial, there was no service, no burial rites, and the minister did not attend. Instead, as William Harrison recalled in his *Description of England*, 'Such as kill themselves are buried in the field with a stake driven through their bodies.' It was a specific ritual, laden with popular custom. The night following the coroner's inquest, officials of the parish, the churchwardens and their helpers carried the naked corpse to a crossroads where they threw it into a pit, and hammered a wooden stake through the body, pinning it to the ground. Since the soul of the dead was said to be possessed by the devil, the stake was meant to hold the body in place so that its spirit might not escape. If it did, then placing it at a crossroads might ensure that it became confused when wandering around. The custom had shown no sign of dying out: for example, in 1573 Thomas Maule was buried at midnight at the 'nighest' crossroads with a stake through his heart since he had hanged himself from a tree after a drunken fit.[12]

The cost of taking one's life, both spiritually and financially, was simply far too high a price to pay. Amy must have known this: if she was genuinely hoping to end her own life, she would continue to pray to God to do so for her, because she was not about to carry out the act herself. If Amy was contemplating suicide, it seems unusual to have written to her tailor William Edney on 24 August, two weeks before her death, requesting that a new velvet gown be made for her, requiring him to 'let it be done with as much speed as you can'.

Amy never did get to wear the gown. Edney nevertheless still sent the bill for his payment, by which time other items included 6s 8d spent on 'making a cloth for the chief mourner'.

If suicide seems more than unlikely, what then was the 'desperation' that Amy had prayed to be delivered from? Was it her despair at the situation that had been developing between her husband and Elizabeth? Or was it something entirely different?

Here, the evidence of the ambassadors' reports should be recalled. They suggest that, over the past two years since Elizabeth's accession, Amy may have instead been suffering from some kind of physical illness. In 1559, the Venetian ambassador had written how 'many persons believe that if his wife, who has been ailing for some time, were perchance to die, the Queen might easily take him for her husband'.[13] Cecil too, in his conversations with de la Quadra days before Amy's body was discovered, inferred that it had been 'published that she was ill'. The most detailed description comes from de la Quadra's report in April 1559 that already referred, seventeen months before Amy's death, to 'a malady in one of her breasts – in the original Spanish, '*esta muy mala de un pecho*', implying that Amy's illness was slowly killing her – 'the queen is only waiting her death to marry Lord Robert'.[14]

If Amy had been suffering from an illness, perhaps it might indeed have been terminal – and the cause of the desperation from which she prayed to be delivered. Perhaps the disease might also have had a role to play in her fatal fall down the stairs at Cumnor. In particular, could some kind of ailment or physical weakness have been responsible for Amy having broken her neck from such a short fall, and still been found lying with her headdress intact upon her head?

For centuries the mystery puzzled historians, until fifty years ago when a novel theory was put forward by Dr Ian Aird. Aird suggested that Amy might have died from the consequences of a spontaneous fracture of her neck bone, which would have caused her to fall down the stairs and appear to have broken her neck without any impairment to her headdress. Aird considered that

> Spontaneous fracture of the spine, or of any bone, occurs when the bone, weakened and softened by disease or age, collapses or breaks under the strain of normal muscular effort ... Diseased or aged bones in the spine may collapse from the slight strain imposed upon them by the normal act of stepping, for example. If that part of the spine which lies in the neck (cervical spine) suffers in this way, the affected person gets spontaneously 'a broken neck', and may collapse then, totally paralysed from the neck down or suddenly dead. Such a fracture is more likely to occur in stepping downstairs than in walking on the level.[15]

Aird recognised that this diagnosis alone would not explain Amy's accidental death. She was, after all, only 28 years old; hardly a candidate for the kind of osteoporosis of the bones that might cause a sudden broken neck. But, as Aird noted, another significant cause of spontaneous bone fractures was 'a cancerous deposit or cancerous deposits in the bones of the skeleton'.

'In a woman of Amy's age,' Aird argued, 'the likeliest cause of a spontaneous fracture of the spine would be a cancer of the breast, and any doctor called now to a patient suffering from the effects of a broken neck without external evidence of severe violence, would automatically proceed to examine the breasts for cancer.'[16]

These cancerous deposits are formed when cancer cells are carried through the blood from the original site of the tumour, spreading especially into the bones of the spine. Here the malignant cells multiply, destroying the bone through decalcification, softening it to the point that it may fracture upon the slightest strain. In the case of breast cancer, secondary deposits are present in the bones before death in 50 per cent of all fatal cases, and in 60 per cent where the bones suffer from cancerous deposits, the spine is affected.[17]

The strength of Aird's case, that Amy had cancer, rests on the Spanish ambassador de la Quadra's words about 'the malady in one of her breasts'. If indeed this 'malady' was breast cancer, then perhaps Amy, in the later stages of the disease, had developed secondary deposits in her neck or the spine, causing them to soften and eventually to spontaneously fracture as she descended the stairs at Cumnor Place.

Aird's theory has gained common ground amongst historians willing to ascribe accidental circumstances to Amy's death. It is certainly plausible, though the argument as a whole seems unconvincing. If her bones were really in such a fragile condition, Amy would have been barely able to walk, let alone climb stairs. That the sudden snapping of her neck as she stepped down the stairs could go unnoticed, without Amy making a final cry of pain, also seems unlikely. But if we accept the ambassador's report, and believe that Amy might have indeed had breast cancer, this could explain an alternative version of her death that has previously been unexplored.

Rather than her neck spontaneously crumbling as she made her way down the stairs, the existence of secondary deposits and malignant cancer cells in Amy's spine or bones elsewhere in her body points to another, different, cause of death. As the secondary deposits spread, the process of decalcification that takes place as the malignant cells multiply would have leached calcium from her bones, which would have been released into her blood. Normally, the kidneys would eliminate excess calcium from the blood, but as more calcium is released, they become unable to cope with the elimination process, and patients develop a condition called hypercalcaemia.

Hypercalcaemia occurs in 10 to 20 per cent of cancer patients, though it is particularly common in breast-cancer patients. Unless treated, the high levels of calcium soon become life-threatening. The first physical symptoms of hypercalcaemia include tiredness and confusion, but as the calcium levels in the blood continue to rise, patients can become agitated and begin to lose their balance, feel faint and collapse. In these circumstances, Amy's strange behaviour, her flares of anger on the day of her death, and perhaps even her sudden fall down the stairs at Cumnor, brought on by her fainting or a sudden loss of consciousness as she descended the steps, all now become understandable. Once she had collapsed, Amy's neck might easily have been broken upon hitting the stone steps as she tumbled to her death.[18]

If Amy had been dying of cancer, her death should have come as little surprise to those close to her. One possible hint of this comes in a letter of Henry Hastings, Earl of Huntingdon, written to Dudley on 17 September enclosing a gift of 'half a dozen pies of a stag'. As he finished his letter, news reached Hastings of Amy's death. He wrote:

> As I ended my letter I understood by letters the death of my lady your wife. I doubt not but long before this time you have considered what a happy hour it is which bringeth man from sorrow to joy, from mortality to immortality, from care and trouble to rest and quietness, and that the Lord above worketh all for the best to them that love him.[19]

Was Amy's 'care and trouble' already known to the outside world? Not only do both the Venetian and Spanish ambassadors seem to have understood that she was unwell, Dudley was expectant that his own situation would soon change; he was reported by de la Quadra to have said in March 1560 that 'if he live another year he will be in a very different position from now'.[20]

Once again there are problems with this theory. If Dudley was waiting for his wife to die, he gave the appearance at least of being genuinely shocked when the final moment came. 'The greatness and the suddenness of the misfortune doth so perplex me,' he wrote upon hearing the news of her death. He was determined, almost fanatically so, that a proper investigation should be carried out by the coroner's jury to discover the truth behind his wife's death, a death that had clearly stunned him.

# The coroner's report

It is to the coroner's inquest and the findings of the jury that we must now turn. It was they who viewed Amy's body and the available evidence; who at first hand would have been able to judge whether Amy had met her death by accident, suicide or by more sinister means. Eventually their findings ruled that Amy's death had been an accident. For centuries, this is all we have known. The report of the coroner's inquest has long been presumed missing, and with it, the knowledge of how exactly Amy died. As one historian has written recently, 'More than four hundred years after the event, there is no possibility of determining the precise cause of Amy Dudley's death.'[1]

But the coroner's report does survive. Buried among the legal records of the National Archives in Kew, the coroner's report into Amy's death has survived undetected for 450 years. It has been filed away among the records of the King's Bench, in classmark KB9, a series of indictment files that are arranged by each legal term, three in each year. The reason it has lain undiscovered for so long may be because the findings of the jury were not actually submitted to the King's Bench to be registered until 22 October 1561, a full year after the incident. As a result, it has been placed in the Michaelmas Term 1561 files.

According to the report, the inquest into Amy's death had opened at Cumnor on 9 September, the day after her death, but would then be eventually postponed until 1 August 1561. The verdict was finally given at the local Assizes in August 1561. The report lists the names of the jury and the coroner, John Pudsey, who had gathered on 9 September for the 'inspection of the body of Lady Amy Dudley, late wife of Robert Dudley, knight of the most noble order of the garter, there lying dead', and goes on to describe how from 9 September they met 'day by day very often'. When it seemed that a verdict was forthcoming, the jury was given 'various several days' by the coroner John Pudsey 'to appear both before the justices ... at the assizes assigned to be held in the aforesaid county and before the same coroner in order there to return their verdict truthfully and speedily'. It would not be until August 1561 that they finally appeared at the local Berkshire Assizes, probably held at Reading. Under oath, the jurors testified that

> the aforesaid Lady Amy on 8 September in the aforesaid second year of the reign of the said lady queen [Elizabeth], being alone in a certain chamber within the home of a certain Anthony Forster, Esq., in the aforesaid Cumnor, and intending to descend the aforesaid chamber by way of certain steps (in English called 'steyres') of the aforesaid chamber there and then accidentally fell precipitously down the aforesaid steps to the very bottom of the same steps, through which the same Lady Amy there and then sustained not only two injuries to her head (in English called 'dyntes') – one of which was a quarter of an inch deep and the other two inches deep – but truly also, by reason of the accidental injury or of that fall and of Lady Amy's own body weight falling down the aforesaid stairs, the same Lady Amy there and then broke her own neck, on account of which certain fracture of the neck the same Lady Amy there and then died instantly; and the aforesaid Lady Amy was found there and then without any other mark or wound on her body; and thus the jurors say on their oath that the aforesaid Lady Amy in the manner and form aforesaid by misfortune came to her death and not otherwise, in so far as it is possible at present for them to agree; in testimony of which fact for this inquest both the aforesaid coroner and also the aforesaid jurors have in turn affixed their seals on the day.

For the first time we can now accurately predict Amy's last movements on the day of her death. According to the jury's findings, upstairs and alone, she fell as she was descending the stairs at Cumnor Place, falling 'precipitously' to the bottom. She had indeed broken her neck, sustained by the falling weight of her body. At the same time, the jury found no evidence of 'any other mark or wound on her body'. To sustain a broken neck from a fall without any other injury to the body might seem unusual, but research into injuries caused by falls from staircases has shown that this is perfectly possible. It was this injury, the jury believed, which had killed her: 'on account of which certain fracture of the neck the same Lady Amy there and then died instantly'.

But the coroner's report also reveals that Amy suffered injuries that transform our understanding of the nature of her death. Previously it had been understood that Amy had no other wounds on her body, which the report confirms, but also that she had suffered no other injuries apart from a broken neck. Amy did, however, suffer two severe wounds to her head, exploding the popular myth upon which Aird's argument is based, that she had died from a broken neck alone, with no other sign of trauma to her body. According to the jury who viewed her body, she sustained two deep cuts to her head, termed 'lesiones' in the Latin of the coroner's report.[2] One was a quarter of an inch deep (approximately 5 mm), the other an extremely deep gash of two inches in depth (5 cm). The approximation for an inch was measured by the length of a thumb, and would have involved the coroner measuring the depths of the wounds in Amy's skull by placing his thumb inside the wounds. In the original Latin text of the coroner's report, the first wound is described as '*profunditatis quarterii unius policis*', literally, 'of the depth of a quarter of one thumb' while the second, '*profunditatis duorum policum*', meaning 'of the depth of two thumbs'. In order for a head wound to be of this depth, Amy's skull would have to have fractured upon impact, causing a deep split in the bone and massive damage to the underlying brain tissue.

Once more it is perfectly possible that a relatively short fall from stairs might cause such injuries, especially if Amy had hit her head upon the stone stairs. As one expert on staircase falls argues, 'The surface of some of the steps may, in fact, have been as welcoming as a cheese grater and just as effective for tearing flesh from bone'; in terms of what injuries a victim might suffer, this has been described as 'comparable to falling into a hole with jagged rocks at the bottom'.[3] According to a separate study, the single largest category of injuries caused by falling down staircases is head injuries, comprising 36 per cent of all injuries. A separate study also showed that 52 per cent of patients who had serious injuries from falling down stairs had also suffered an acute subdural haematoma of the brain, a form of traumatic brain injury in which blood gathers within the outer protective covering of the brain as the result of tears in the veins of the brain, that can often have fatal conclusions.[4]

It is clear that Amy's head injuries were far more severe than this. The coroner's report does not detail where the lacerations to her skull were located, but the fact that there are two wounds might possibly suggest that her head might have landed hard on the edges of two stair treads, causing the skull fracture and the deep brain laceration, especially if Amy had struck the back of her head, which is more vulnerable to fracture. In one study, the edges of steps themselves were shown to be responsible for half of all head injuries, yet causing no injuries at all to the trunk of the body itself, an interesting phenomenon in light of Amy's own specific injuries to her head and neck, yet with no other mark or wound on her body.[5]

Yet the very fact that the coroner's report particularly describes Amy's head wounds in English as 'dyntes' seems revealing in itself. The use of the word was traditionally reserved for describing a blow sustained in violence or battle, usually by a sword. The Tudor poet John Skelton used the word in his poem 'The Auncient Acquaintance, Madam, Between Us Twayn', to describe a battle scene:

> So fersly he fytyth, his mynde is so fell,
> That he dryuyth them doune with dyntes on ther day wach;
> He bresyth theyr braynpannys and makyth them to swell ...

Had Amy therefore died from some sort of blow or puncture to her head, perhaps caused by falling against a sharp object? The edge of the stone stairs still seems most likely, though a study by the Swedish academic Svanstrom demonstrated that in 10 per cent of falls, the victim fell sideways, falling against handrails, balustrades or sidewalls. Possibly Amy fell against a sharp point or edge sticking out that caused the severe nature of her injuries, with the full force of the impact of her fall being concentrated in a small area.

If the depth of the 'dyntes' in Amy's skull seems remarkable, so too does the fact that she died 'without any other mark or wound', in the original Latin '*sine aliqua alia macula siue vulnere*', on her body. That there were no injuries to her arms or wrists, that one might expect to be held out to try and prevent or cushion a fall, nor any sign of bruising or cuts to her body or legs that would have also been affected by the impact of the fall, seems unusual. It is possible that the jury thought so too. While a verdict of death by misfortune 'and not otherwise' was finally reached by the jury, for whatever reason nearly a year after Amy's death, there was some qualification in their decision, which had only been reached '*in so far as it is possible at present for them to agree*' (in the Latin, '*prout eis ad presens constare potest*'). The jury's verdict of accidental death was not without reservation and uncertainty. It was an uncertainty shared by many at court.

There were still too many questions that had been left unanswered. What about the rumours stretching as far back as the previous November, that Amy was being poisoned? And how could William Cecil possibly have known that Amy's death was planned, telling the Spanish ambassador in what seemed like only days beforehand, that 'they intended to kill the wife of Robert'? For the first time in centuries, we now know the nature of Amy's wounds, but we must dig somewhat deeper if the circumstances surrounding her tragic end are to be uncovered.

# PART FIVE

✦

He is infamed
by the death of his wife

Sr I thank yo'u more for yo'r being hear. And the
great frendshipp yo'u haue shewed towardes
me I shall not forgett. I am very
lothe to wyshe yo'u hear againe, but I wold be very
glade to be at the theas. I pray yo'u lett me
hear fro' yo'r what yo'u thinck best for me to
do, yf yo'u dowbt I pray yo'u aske the question
for I hoap yo'u ... ... may aduyse
me together, the more I shall thanck
yo'u. I am sorey so soddonly a chaunge
shuld breede me so great a chaunge, for I
thinck I am hear all this nighte as yt wer
in a dreame. And to far to farre fro' the
place I ... be. under my thinck also this
long foler tyme doo not ego'uste me, for the
deathe I hear to dyscharge all my das. I
pray yo'u helpe this ther selves to be at lybarty
owt off so great bondage. fforgett me
not the yf yo'u be me not, and I will rem'ber
yo'u and fayll yo'u not. And so wyshe
yo'u well to doe. in hast this morning

yo'r very assured
R Dudley

I be ... yo'u S'r forgett not to
offer up my humble servyces
yo'r poor ... ...

# Forget me not

Sir, I thank you very much for your being here, and the great friendship you have shown towards me I shall not forget. I am very loath to wish you here again but I would be very glad to be with you there. I pray you let me hear from you, what you think best for me to do. If you doubt, I pray you ask the question for the sooner you can advise me [to come] thither, the more I shall thank you. I am sorry so sudden a chance should breed me so great a change, for methinks I am here all the while as it were in a dream, and too far, too far from the place I am bound to be, where, methinks also, this long, idle time cannot excuse me for the duty I have to discharge elsewhere. I pray you help him that sues to be at liberty out of so great a bondage. Forget me not, though you see me not and I will remember you and fail you not, and so wish you well to do. In haste this morning.

I beseech you, Sir, forget me not to offer up the humble sacrifice you promised me.

Your very assured,

R. Dudley[1]

While he resided at Kew, Robert Dudley rarely had the chance to be alone as he came to terms with the death of his wife. According to observers, several members of the nobility and councillors 'immediately paid' him homage, and came 'to comfort him'.[2]

One such visitor was William Cecil, who perhaps came alone late one evening, shortly after Dudley had been exiled from the court while the jury of the coroner's inquest into Amy's death considered their verdict. It seems that Dudley had requested the Secretary's visit himself, as he was desperate to learn of his treatment at court and when the queen might be persuaded to let him return. We do not know what conversation passed between the two men, but the following morning Dudley hastily penned a letter to the Secretary thanking him for his visit. It was clear that Dudley remained in shock over the circumstances of his wife's death. He was, he wrote, 'sorry so sudden a chance should breed me so great a change, for methinks I am here all the while as it were in a dream, and too far, too far from the place I am bound to be'. His writing appears rushed, with mistakes scribbled through it. These errors in themselves give some insight into Dudley's state of mind. He was desperate for Cecil's help to return him to his place beside the queen, where he believed he 'should' be, though on second thoughts, he changed this to 'am bound to' be – a more suitable assertion. He had also, at first, written to Cecil, 'the sooner you help me thither', but on reflection thought this might have seemed too much like a plea for help and altered it to 'you can advise me thither'.

There can be little doubt that Dudley found himself in extremely desperate circumstances, which he considered 'so great a bondage'. He urged the Secretary in his letter to 'forget me not, though you see me not' and he promised that in return he would 'remember you and fail you not, and so wish you well to do'. It appears that the two men had reached some kind of agreement at Kew. If Cecil was in any doubt what this was, as Dudley finished his letter, almost as an afterthought, he added in the bottom left-hand corner of the letter the words: 'I beseech you, Sir, forget me not to offer up the humble sacrifice you promised me'.

The balance of power between the two men had shifted entirely. Just weeks before, Cecil had despaired of his diminishing influence with the queen and had talked of retiring from political life altogether. Now he found the queen's favourite dependent on him. It was at times like these that rivals suddenly became friends. But what was the 'humble sacrifice' that Cecil had promised? Cecil knew that he held Dudley's future in his hands. If he wished, he had the power to destroy him. This certainly seems to have been his intention when he spoke to de la Quadra and informed him that Amy's life was at risk, only days before her actual death. In fact, when de la Quadra's dispatch is looked at closely, Cecil's dramatic revelations are not what they at first seem.

The time period over which the events described in de la Quadra's letter took place is uncertain at best. We know that the dispatch was written from Windsor on 11 September, the same day that Elizabeth announced publicly the news of Amy's death to the court. The ambassador writes how he arrived at Windsor five days beforehand, therefore on 6 September, but he does not reveal the date of his audience with the queen and, immediately afterwards, his fateful conversation with Cecil. But we can attempt some basic form of reconstruction. The day after de la Quadra spoke to the queen, he met her again out hunting, when she admitted that Amy was dead, 'or almost so', and asked him not to repeat anything she had mentioned. This meeting, the day before the public announcement of Amy's death, must have taken place on 10 September, making the most probable date for the ambassador's audience with the queen the 9th – a day after Amy's body had been discovered. We know from Dudley's letter to Blount that he first heard of his wife's death on 9 September while he was at Windsor. It seems plausible that this was the date that Cecil also discovered the news.

All this begs the question of whether the Secretary knew that Amy was already dead when he spoke with the ambassador that same day, telling him that 'they intended to kill the wife of Robert'. If he knew that Amy already lay dead, he was quick to realise how he might manipulate the situation to his advantage. While the queen was yet to announce the news to the court, he devised a plan to smear Robert Dudley with the accusations that his wife's death might be imminent, linking it to earlier rumours that Amy was being poisoned. Cecil had calculated what the effect of such revelations would be, as Dudley would immediately be placed in the frame for his wife's murder when the news became public.

It was a plan that required the utmost cunning and duplicity from the Secretary, and Cecil proved more than adept at spinning his story. It was with utter sincerity that, knowing that Amy's body was already cold, Cecil told de la Quadra that although he understood there were plans for Amy to be killed, he hoped that 'God would never permit that so great an evil nor could a good result come of an evil business'.

Two days later, as news broke across the court of Amy's sudden and unexpected death, Cecil continued to spread his rumours. He wrote a letter, dated 11 September, to the English ambassador in Scotland, his friend Thomas Randolph. The letter does not survive, though Randolph's reply suggests that it must have contained information about Amy's death. 'The first word that I read in yours of the XI of this present conferring it with such bruits and slanderous reports as have been maliciously reported by the French and their faction,' Randolph wrote in amazement, 'so passioneth my heart, that no grief ever I felt was like unto it! I neither had word to comfort myself nor advice to give my friend, we measured our affections both for your country and friends, as though we had seen that sorrowful heart that you wrote with your pen.'

At this moment Cecil must have known that he had it within his power to destroy Robert Dudley. But he did not. Elizabeth's favourite remained exiled and absent from his place next to the queen, where he believed that he 'should' be; it was enough for Cecil to be reinstalled as the queen's chief adviser. With a new sense of authority, he returned to the business of state, which of course included the vexing question of Elizabeth's marriage.

A few days later, on 17 September, the Secretary wrote a letter to the Duke of Holstein, one of the many candidates for Elizabeth's hand, but one for whom Cecil had shown some preference. Holstein had written to the Secretary on 23 August, asking for his advice. Now that the war in Scotland had been concluded, he hoped that the queen might be able to consider his suit.[3] Cecil wrote back in agreement:

> Now that those stormy Scottish negotiations have finished I do not see why my lady queen's majesty by regard may not learn of accepting a present marriage with the proposals which she may have, such and so many men indeed I can see brought for many reasons to her, although these are not lacking with us who now have introduced the lord Robert Dudley a widower, his wife being dead, to that position ...[4]

Urged on by Cecil, Holstein wrote to the queen on 20 December, requesting a definite answer. She replied a month later, her formal style barely masking her disappointing news: 'In answer to his request that she would let him know what he had to hope as to the issue of his suit, she assures him that no change whatever has taken place in her sentiments in this matter. In whatever way he may receive her declaration, she cannot say otherwise than this. She must still sing the same song.'[5]

Cecil was determined that whatever the impact of his wife's death might be, Robert Dudley should not be allowed to marry the queen. He encouraged Holstein partly in the hope of finding a strong rival candidate to block Dudley's chances. He also looked to renew Archduke Charles's suit through the Spanish ambassador. 'The Queen has decided not to marry the Lord Robert,' Cecil insisted to de la Quadra in October. He had, he told the ambassador, learned this directly from the queen; 'he thought that the Archduke's matter might be proposed' instead.[6]

It was clear that Cecil was determined to act as fast as he could. When queried about Elizabeth's promise to the Imperial ambassador Helfenstein that when she had finally resolved to marry she would inform the emperor personally, the Secretary grew agitated. 'Cecil was in a hurry to do it,' de la Quadra observed, somewhat bemused, 'and that did not serve his turn.' The ambassador reasoned that once again the Secretary was attempting to play him off against the French. Cecil, he believed, was determined to arouse their 'suspicion and jealousy', especially since the Cardinal of Lorraine had apparently boasted to Throckmorton that Elizabeth was running out of available suitors and 'that if the Queen did not marry an Englishman the best match for her would be the prince of Sweden'.

For the moment, Dudley had pledged that he was in the Secretary's debt. But Cecil understood that this could easily change. For the rest of his career, he remained resolutely opposed to any idea of Dudley marrying Elizabeth, an occurrence which he knew would almost certainly spell the end of his own influence at court. But Cecil was also aware that Amy's death had probably done enough to discredit the queen's favourite. Five years later, when weighing up Dudley's prospects of marrying the queen, the Secretary drew up a table listing his virtues, or as he considered in Dudley's case, his lack thereof. Under 'reputation' he wrote simply, 'Hated of many. His wife's death.' And under the section, 'In likelihood to love his wife,' he wrote his celebrated words giving his pronouncement of Dudley's fated marriage: '*Nuptii carnales a laetitia incipiunt et in luctu terminantur*' – 'carnal marriages begin in joy and end in weeping'. Not finished with his reasoning, on another sheet of paper the Secretary also compiled a separate list entitled 'Reasons against the Earl of Leicester'*.[7]

Nothing is increased by marriage to him either in riches, estimation, power.

It will be thought that the slanderous speeches of the Queen with the Earl have been true.

He shall study nothing but to enhance his own particular friends: to wealth, to offices, to lands and to offend others.

He is infamed by the death of his wife.

* Elizabeth awarded Dudley the title of Earl of Leicester in 1564

He is far in debt.

He is like to prove unkind or jealous of the Queen's majesty.[8]

It was a comprehensive indictment against the man from whom Cecil was determined to protect his mistress.

# 42

# My ears glow to hear

News of Amy's death soon reached the Continent. From the French court, the English ambassador Sir Nicholas Throckmorton wrote to Dudley on 10 October, consoling him on his loss. 'My very good Lord, I understand of the cruel mischance late happened to my lady your late bedfellow, to your discomfort.' A month after Amy's death, he hoped that 'the greatest of your grief' had been overcome, 'and the remembrance thereof presently worn out'. He would be brief, for fear of renewing Dudley's grief, 'but only say that as we be all mortal, subject to many hazards (experience daily showeth) and have no sure abiding in this unequal world, so she is gone before whither we must all follow to a place of more assurance and more quiet than can be found in this vale'.[1]

Politeness hid the ambassador's deep concerns. Throckmorton suspected that far more lay behind Amy's death at Cumnor Place. Rumours were already circulating at the French court that Amy had been murdered; rumours that, if found to be true, Throckmorton believed, would bring down the queen. That same day, he penned a desperate letter to the Marquis of Northampton. 'My Lord, I wish I were either dead, or that I were hence, that I might not hear the dishonorable and naughty reports that are here made of ye Queen's Majesty my gracious sovereign lady' that made 'every hair of my head' stand on end, 'and my ears glow to hear'. He continued:

> I am almost at my wits end and know not what to say: one laugheth at us, another threateneth, another revileth her Majesty and some let not to say what religion is this that a subject shall kill his wife, and ye Prince not only bear withal but marry with him, not sticking to rehearse the father and the grandfather and more than all. Alas that I ever lived to see this day. All the estimation we had got clean is gone and the infamy passeth the same so far, as my heart bleedeth to think upon the slanderous bruits I hear, which if they be not slaked or that they prove true, our reputation is gone forever, war followeth and utter subversion of our green and

country. Help my Lord to slake these rumours, and let honour remain where it ought to be . . .²

Desperate to find out what exactly had happened to Amy and whether the rumours about Dudley's marriage to Elizabeth might be true, Throck-morton wrote other letters to his friends at court, including Henry Killigrew.

'I cannot imagine what rumours they be you hear there, as you write so strange,' Killigrew replied, attempting to calm his friend. 'Unless such as were here of the death of my Lady Dudley; for that she brake her neck down a pair of stairs, which I protest unto you was only done by the hand of God, to my knowledge. But who can let men to speak and think in such cases?'³

And yet the gossip about Amy's suspicious death persisted. By 17 October, Killigrew had changed his mind, writing back to Throckmorton that 'rumours . . . have been very rife, but the Queen says she will make them false'. Indicating that he could not write down on paper the stories he had heard, he said he would send messengers to let Throckmorton know 'what account he wished him to make of my Lord R'.⁴

The following day, Throckmorton continued his frenetic pleas. 'My friends advise me from home that Lord Robert's wife is dead and hath by mischance broken her neck,' he wrote to another friend, Thomas Chamberlain, but it was open gossip at the French court 'that her neck was broken, with such other appendances I am withal brought to be weary of my life.' Without wishing to divulge anything further, 'so evil be the reports as I am ashamed to write them,' he wrote that they both knew 'how much it importeth the Queen's majesty's honour and her realm to have them ceased . . . For though there be wise men at home who know what is meet to be done in such cases, yet the advertisement thereof from ministers abroad hath a great deal more force. I write unto you because then we be both in one ship and then the tempest must touch us both alike.'⁵ The mysterious nature of Amy's death left too many questions unanswered, and the scandal that was escalating abroad threatened to implicate not only Dudley, but also the queen. Action, Throckmorton believed, would need to be taken if Elizabeth was to save her reputation and, ultimately, even her throne.

# 43

# All the resort is to him

Dudley was absent from the queen's side for only a matter of weeks. By 1 October, he was purchasing a new pair of shoes 'for Best at Hampton Court'. It seems he continued to wear black in mourning for his wife – he bought two pairs of black silk hose on 27 November – at least until April when his household accounts record him purchasing white hose once more. His return to court was greeted with fanfare, though two courtiers were reported to the queen for showing Dudley disrespect by not removing their caps as he passed.[1] It was as if nothing had changed. Except that Dudley, with the obstacle of his wife now removed, was free to marry.

For Elizabeth, it seemed as if Amy's death had never taken place. Her feelings for her favourite were undiminished. She was even overheard in a private discussion, 'in commendation of my Lord Robert upon questions moved [to] say that he was of a very good disposition and nature, not given by any means to seek revenge of former matters past, wherein she seemed much to allow him.'[2] Elizabeth was of course referring to Dudley's chequered family history. Many amongst the nobility feared that if Dudley were to marry the queen, he might take revenge for his father's death. In particular, the Earls of Arundel and Pembroke, reflecting on their key roles in deserting Northumberland during Jane's brief reign, would have had good reason to fear that a renewed Dudley ascendancy might seek to punish them for their past deeds. Assured in her own mind that he would not, Elizabeth perhaps began to think seriously about marrying the man who, until now, had always remained unavailable.

Elizabeth's affectionate welcome certainly gave Dudley cause for optimism. 'The Lord Rob in great hope to marry the queen,' one observer at court noted, 'for she maketh such appearance of good will to him.' It was the start of a concerted campaign for the queen's hand in marriage, in which Dudley sought as much support as he could muster. 'He giveth her many goodly presents,' the observer continued. 'His men bruit it for truth. The L[ord Robert] follow him much. All the resort is to him.'[3] People were quick to seek favour with the man they soon expected to be the queen's consort. The Scottish ambassador Thomas Randolph wrote to Dudley sending his commendations. The letter was a clear attempt to ingratiate himself with the royal favourite; perhaps realising Dudley's own Protestant leanings, he also sought to build up a better relationship between Mary Queen of Scots and Dudley. Both queens, he wrote, shared the same 'tenderness of blood', so that 'the one of them do so much in all things resemble the other'. By necessity, therefore, it was obvious that 'whosoever loveth the one of their two majesties, he must also of necessity love the other'.[4]

Dudley was even beginning to persuade those who had been hostile to his affections for the queen in the past. Stationed in Ireland, and far away from having any influence at court, the Earl of Sussex seems to have resigned himself to the inevitable. 'My Lord Robert seemeth to stand greatly in grace and favour,' his man at court wrote to the earl, 'whose exaltation to higher degree is thought to be deferred till after Christmas. At which time it is thought he expecteth a higher place.'[5] A promotion to the ranks of the nobility could only be taken to mean one thing; a promotion to the queen's side as her consort.

Hearing this news, Sussex wrote to Cecil. The most important thing, he believed, was for the queen to produce an heir; if this meant marrying Dudley, then so be it:

> I wish not her Majesty to linger this matter of so great importance, but to choose speedily; and therein to follow so much her own affection as [that], by the looking upon him whom she should choose, omnes ejus sensus titillarentur (all the senses being excited); which shall be the readiest way, with the help of God, to bring us a blessed prince which shall redeem us out of thraldom. If I knew that England had other rightful inheritors I would then advise otherwise, and seek to serve the time by a husband's choice. But seeing that she is ultimum refugium, and that no riches, friendship, foreign alliance, or any other present commodity that might come by a husband, can serve our turn, without issue of her body, if the Queen will love anybody, let her love where and whom she lists, so much thirst I to see her love. And whomsoever she shall love and choose, him will I love, honour, and serve to the uttermost.[6]

Other members of the nobility and their retinues do not seem to have shared Sussex's opinion. Shortly after Amy's death, a retainer of the Earl of Arundel, Arthur Guntor, heard a story from a friend that Elizabeth had recently dined at Dudley's house. While travelling home by torch-light, the queen 'fell in talk with them that carried the torches, and said, that her Grace would make their Lord the best that ever was of his name ... the report is, that her highness should marry him'.

'It is in a number of heads that the Queen will marry him,' Guntor replied furiously, 'I think him to be the cause that my Lord my master [Arundel] might not marry the Queen's highness. Wherefore I would that he had been put to death with his father, or that some ruffian would have dispatched him by the way as he hath gone, with some dagger or gun.'

If the queen decided to marry Dudley, Guntor predicted that there would be trouble, possibly even civil war. 'It may fortune that there will rise trouble among the noblemen, which God forbid.' Arundel for one would not tolerate his rival Dudley marrying the queen; Guntor believed he was already building a coalition of support against him, which included the Earl of Pembroke, the Marquis of Northampton and Lord Rich. As one of Elizabeth's disappointed suitors, Arundel's motivation to wreck Dudley's chances was perhaps obvious. 'With the putting up of his finger', Guntor believed, 'then you shall see the White Horse [the heraldic badge of the Earl of Arundel] bestir himself, for my Lord is of great power'. Guntor hoped nothing would come of the threat; it would be far better, he insisted, if 'a man shall have a ruffian with a dag to dispatch him [Dudley] out of a shop'.[7]

After witnessing Dudley's enthusiastic reception at court, William Cecil decided to act. He wrote to Throckmorton on 25 October, advising him to write to the queen, 'to move the same for order to be taken in the better dispatch of her affairs', which Cecil himself had admitted, 'are too much neglected'. Although Cecil's letter does not survive, the subject of Dudley's marriage to Elizabeth clearly came up, if anything can be deduced from the tone of Throckmorton's horrified reply:

> I know not where to begin: I looked by your last to be somewhat satisfied and resolved, touching the greatest matter of all, I mean the Queen's marriage. I know not what to think, nor how to understand your letter in that point. And the bruits be so brim, and so maliciously reported here, touching the marriage of the Lord Robert, and the death of his wife, as I know not where to turn me, nor what countenance to bear. Sir, I thank

God I had rather perish and quail with honesty, than live and beguile a little time with shame.

There was little point in offering any advice, Throckmorton wrote, if the queen's marriage to Dudley went ahead. He liked Dudley, he admitted; 'I say to you in private that albeit I do like him for some respects well, and esteem him for many good parts and gifts of nature, that be in him, and do wish him well to do,' but he would always place the 'love, duty, and affection, that I bear to the Queen's Majesty' above any friendship.

> And therefore I say, if that marriage take place, I know not to what purpose any advice or counsel should be given; for as I see into the matter, none would serve. If you think, that I have any small skill or judgment in things at home, or on this side, or can conjecture sequels, I do assure you, the matter succeeding, our state is in great danger of utter ruin and destruction. And so far methinketh I see into the matter, as I wish myself already dead, because I would not live in that time.

He begged Cecil 'to signify plainly unto me, not only what is done in that matter, but what you think will be the end':

> And if the matter be not already determined, and so far past ... I require you, as you bear a true and faithful heart to her Majesty and the realm, and do desire to keep them from utter desolation ... I conjure you to do all your endeavour to hinder that marriage. For, if it take place, there is no counsel or advice, that can help. Who would be either patron or mariner, when there is no remedy to keep the ship from sinking? As we begin already to be in derision and hatred, for the bruit only, and nothing taken here on this side more assured than our destruction.

The prospect of Elizabeth marrying Dudley had to be stopped. The consequences of such a match were simply too dire: 'The Queen our Sovereign discredited, condemned, and neglected; our country ruined, undone, and made prey.' With a final plea, 'with tears and fights, as one being already almost confounded,' Throckmorton urged Cecil to redouble his efforts to prevent Dudley getting his way: 'I beseech you again and again, set to your wits, and all your help to stay the commonwealth, which lieth now in great hazard.'[8]

As Throckmorton drew his letter to a close, another thought crossed his mind. Letters such as these, falling into the wrong hands, could be extremely dangerous. He ended by reassuring Cecil that 'for your letters, they be as safe in my hand as your own, and more safe in mine than any messenger's. Think it assuredly, I am as jealous of your safety and well doing, as yourself; and so conceive of me.'

Throckmorton had already decided that something would need to be done. He had begun to write to members of the nobility such as Northampton, urging them not to support any prospect of Dudley's marriage to Elizabeth and 'not to begin to wrestle in a matter so beset with dangers, and to esteem the marriage matter the most beset with great hazards'. He asked Northampton not to get involved and 'be only a looker on', and hinted that 'if you be so happy as to mind it, or so zealous as to hinder it, you may think yourself wise for your judgment'.[9]

By mid-November, malicious gossip from the French court about the nature of Amy's death – and Elizabeth and Dudley's relationship – continued unabated. 'The bruits lately risen from England are marvelous and marvelously talked of,' Throckmorton wrote to the Marquis of Northampton on 17 November. 'They are accompanied with much spite and set so full with great horror. They are no mean persons that give in these parts these rumours.' Throckmorton for one had 'never heard or read' such 'scandalous discourse'.[10] 'They take it for truth,' he implored Cecil on the same day, 'and certain she will marry Lord Robert Dudley, whereby they assure themselves that all foreign alliance and aid is shaken off, and do expect more discontention thereby amongst yourselves. Thus you see your sore, God grant it do not with rankling fester too far and too dangerously.'[11]

Throckmorton decided to take direct action himself, and sent his secretary Robert Jones on a mission to the English court in order to inform the queen of the ruinous situation abroad. That was not Jones's only mission. He had been given another, more specific job: he was to dissuade Elizabeth by whatever means he could from marrying Dudley.

# 44

# Neither touching his honesty nor her honour

Around mid-November the court began a brief winter progress and moved from Hampton Court to Whitehall. During her journey, Elizabeth visited her palaces at Greenwich and Eltham, where she indulged in a final round of hunting trips before Christmas. It was at Eltham that, on the evening of Wednesday 27 November, Dudley decided to hold a 'great banquet' for the queen.[1] He was determined to make an impressive show to woo her. His household accounts record the luxurious purchases made for the occasion, including a 'brick of marmalade' costing 2s 4d and a 'marchpayne' worth 10s. Marchpane was an expensive type of marzipan, which could be moulded into edible shapes and designs to form the centrepiece of Elizabethan dinner parties and banquets. Elizabeth was known to be especially fond of this delicacy. She was given a model of St Paul's Cathedral built out of marchpane, and for New Year's Day 1562, her master cook, George Webster, presented her with a 'faire marchpane being a chessboard'. Dudley also ordered a box of 'collingale', better known as galingale, an aromatic root imported from Italy used to flavour cooking, and two pounds' worth of quinces costing 5s 16d, while other 'kinds of banqueting stuff' cost £4.

Dudley was convinced that this kind of attention to detail would help win favour with the queen. At the banquet, he also presented Elizabeth with a gift, a pair of her favourite silk stockings. His accounts show that on 27 November, he 'paid for ii pair of black silk' at 53s 4d each – some twenty times the price of normal stockings. On the same day, no doubt for the banquet, he bought a new outfit for himself: 'one pair of netherstocks of russet' and a pair of velvet breeches, 'pulled out with cloth of silver', worth 53s 4d.[2] On this occasion at least, Dudley seemed willing to break his period of mourning.

Two days before the banquet, on 25 November, Throckmorton's secretary Robert Jones arrived at court. His first visit was to William Cecil. Jones had some highly sensitive news to pass on to the Secretary. Throckmorton had told him to report, he informed Cecil, how at the French court Mary Queen of Scots had listened to the details of the scandal surrounding Dudley's wife's death and exclaimed that 'the Queen's Majesty would marry the master of her horses'. Cecil realised that the gossip was getting out of hand, threatening even to ridicule the queen on the international stage. It had to be stopped. He asked Jones to put the accusation in writing so that he could show Elizabeth.

The following evening the Council dined at the Scottish ambassador's residence, to which Jones was invited. Halfway through the meal, Dudley excused himself and returned to the court. Minutes later, a gentleman appeared at the dining table requesting to speak to Jones. Once outside, he informed him that Dudley wished to meet with him in secret later that evening. After the meal had finished, Jones made his way to Dudley's chambers at court. He found Dudley in such a rage that he was struggling to contain it. Dudley was quick to explain his anger. Jones's reports had reached the queen herself. Elizabeth had apparently told Dudley about Mary's remarks that she 'would marry her horse-keeper'. Smarting from the insult of being named as Elizabeth's mere 'horse-keeper', Dudley wanted answers. Jones later recalled: 'He asked me, whether the French Queen had said that the Queen's Majesty would marry her horse-keeper'. Dudley had, he admitted, already viewed 'all the discourse of your Lordship's [Throckmorton's] proceedings, together with the intelligence'. In any case, Dudley confronted Jones, 'Mr Secretary told him, that the French Queen had said so.'

'I answered that I had said no such matter,' Jones told Throckmorton. But Dudley did not believe him, and continued his interrogation. 'He laid the matter upon me so strong, as the author thereof being avowed.' Jones refused to admit that he had used those exact words – that Dudley was but the queen's 'horse-keeper', though he confessed, 'I would not deny that the French Queen had said that the Queen would marry the Master of her horses.'

Dudley finally let Jones go, but not before he 'willed me that I should in no case let it be known to Mr Secretary that he had told me thus much'. Jones had no intention of becoming a pawn in whatever game Cecil and Dudley were playing. He decided to take Dudley's advice and not tell the Secretary of their conversation. 'I have not indeed, nor mean not to do.' Musing on the incident, Jones wrote back to Throckmorton that he was sure Elizabeth must also have been involved, given that 'Mr Secretary did declare it only to the Queen, at whose hands My Lord Robert had it'.

It seems that when Cecil briefed Elizabeth on Jones's report, he changed one important detail. 'Master of her horses' was certainly Dudley's official title – plain 'horse-keeper' he was not. The change in wording was only slight, but the change in meaning could not be understated. An expert in the game of diplomatic Chinese whispers, Cecil knew the power of words and the effect they might have upon Elizabeth – especially if he could claim they were spoken by her rival and greatest threat to her throne, her cousin Mary.

As Dudley prepared for his banquet, the expectation remained that he might soon marry the queen. That same night, Jones delivered to Henry Killigrew, one of Throckmorton's allies, a dispatch from his master. Killigrew took it and, with a sorrowful countenance, said, 'I think verily that my Lord Robert will run away with the hare and have the Queen.'

It was on the day of Dudley's banquet that Robert Jones managed to secure an interview with Elizabeth after she had returned from hunting. He duly sent Throckmorton a full description of the interview. Written partly in cipher, a form of letters and symbols understood by both men, Throckmorton annotated its pages with his own transcription of the secret passages, intended for his reading alone.

At 6 o'clock in the evening Jones was finally granted his audience. He told the queen that the Spanish and Venetian ambassadors were spreading the rumour that she was to marry Dudley. Elizabeth wondered why Jones had made the journey at all. 'By my troth,' she replied, 'I thought it was such a matter, and he need not have sent you hither, for it had been more meet to keep you still.' It was this kind of complacency that Jones had come to warn the queen against. He decided to persist, revealing more details of the accusations concerning her relationship with her favourite and the sudden death of his wife. As, in his own words, Jones 'came to touch nearer the quick', Elizabeth flared up and, growing impatient with Jones's pleading, retorted once more: 'I have heard all this before, and he need not to have sent you withal.'

Still Jones refused to give up. His master's care was so great, he insisted, that he felt duty bound to inform her 'of such things as might touch her' in person, rather than risk them becoming further public knowledge. He then proceeded to launch an attack on Dudley and his lineage – 'which I set forth in as vehement terms as the case required,' he assured

Throckmorton. When he claimed that during her brother's reign Dudley's father had hated her more than her sister Mary, Elizabeth suddenly broke into laughter, turning 'herself to the one side and to the other, and set her hand upon her face'.

According to Jones, Elizabeth then said: 'The matter had been tried in the country, and found to be contrary to that which was reported saying ...'

Fearful his letter might fall into the wrong hands, Jones decided to transcribe the next part of his letter in cipher, so sensitive was the information contained in it that he felt it must be for Throckmorton's eyes only. It read:

*[two lines of cipher text]*

Written, on the original letter above, in a faint and delicate hand, Throckmorton's annotations translating the cipher can still be read: 'that he was then in the court and none of his at the attempt at his wife's house'.

Throckmorton must have been stunned. He no doubt now understood Jones's reasons for disguising his words. What could the queen possibly mean? What could this 'attempt at his wife's house' have been exactly? Everything seemed to confirm Throckmorton's worst fears. But there was more. Moving back into English, Jones continued, relaying Elizabeth's words to him: 'and that it fill so out as should neither', the letter once more reverted to cipher:

*[one line of cipher text]*

'Touch his honesty nor her honour', Throckmorton translated.[3]

According to Elizabeth, Throckmorton was to understand, Robert Dudley was innocent of committing any crime, while the notion that Amy might have committed suicide, thereby destroying her honour, was to be forgotten. And yet, Throckmorton must have reasoned, Elizabeth would admit readily that there had been an 'attempt', whatever that meant, upon Amy's life. Something did not seem quite right. Perhaps

Henry Killigrew's words in an earlier letter would have come to mind: 'rumours . . . have been very rife, but the Queen says she will make them false'.

For the moment, Elizabeth seemed certain that no damage had been done to her reputation, and that Throckmorton was simply exaggerating the extent of the rumours. 'My ambassador knoweth somewhat of my mind in these matters,' she told Jones curtly.[4] As for the rumours that had been spread by the Venetian ambassador, she said that she had spoken to no one, 'and nobody but Mr Secretary knew of these matters'.

But as Jones began to divulge the precise details of the accusations, it was evident that Elizabeth was shocked. New, perhaps more malicious, gossip seems to have emerged, possibly about Dudley, which, relayed by Jones, took her by surprise. 'She caused me to repeat the same twice or thrice, which me thought did move her more than that I said touching the Ambassador of Spain's talk.'

Jones left Elizabeth to prepare for Dudley's banquet, perhaps somewhat more perplexed and less certain of how a marriage to her favourite might be perceived than she had been before.

# 45

# If her Majesty so foully forget herself

Tensions at court continued to escalate. It seemed as if faction and violent conflict might break out amongst the nobility, as distinct parties formed opposed to Dudley's ambitions. Their hatred of Robert Dudley stemmed from the fear that if he married the queen, he would become the most powerful man in the kingdom, a king in all but name, who might seek to dominate and destroy them in years to come. Many had good reasons to fear Dudley's wrath, not only for their opposition to his growing influence over the queen, but also for their roles in the downfall and execution of his father, John Dudley, Duke of Northumberland, seven years previously. As Pope Pius IV assessed, 'the greater part of the nobility of that island take ill the marriage which the said queen designs to enter into with Lord Robert Dudley. His father was beheaded as a rebel and usurper of the crown, and they fear that if he becomes king, he will want to avenge the death of his father, and extirpate the nobility of that kingdom.'[1] Many no doubt still remembered John Dudley's parting words, as he left the capital on horseback to fight Mary's rebel troops: 'If ye mean deceit ... God will revenge the same.'[2]

The member of the nobility with the most to lose was the Earl of Arundel, who had been instrumental in Northumberland's downfall when he had encouraged members of the Council to renounce Jane Grey and proclaim Mary queen. A servant recalled that: 'If it chance my Lord Robert to marry the Queen's Highness ... he would remember any old matter passed heretofore, and so be turned unto my Lord my Master's displeasure and hindrance.' Perhaps Dudley was only waiting until he had married the queen to wreak vengeance upon men he regarded as secret enemies to his family. After all, when imprisoned in the Tower, he had carved into his cell wall a verse translation of Psalm 94: 'O Mightie Lord to whom / all vengeance doth belong.'

Throckmorton did his best to stir these tensions. Robert Jones revealed that during his visit he had also been in contact directly with several noblemen whom Throckmorton had written to from France, pleading that they intervene to prevent any marriage between Elizabeth and

Dudley from going ahead. These included Lord Clinton, the Earl of Bedford, the Marquis of Northampton and the Earl of Pembroke, who had told him that they 'like well your lordship's letters and advertisements at this time, and seem to be careful for the due consideration of them'. He had written to Northampton too, urging him to dissuade the queen from marrying one of her subjects. In one of his letters, he begged the marquis to 'begin to wrestle in a matter so beset with dangers, and to esteem the marriage matter the most beset with great hazards of anything that I was ever acquainted with . . . If you be so happy as not to mind it, or so zealous as to hinder it, think yourself wise for your judgment.'[3] Northampton possibly agreed to raise the issue with Elizabeth, though he seems to have shied away at the final moment from doing so, and when Jones mentioned him to Elizabeth during his interview, he reported back that 'touching her Majesty's discourse with him for the not marrying of any other subjects, she affirmed to me that it was never spoken unto him, touching any such matter'.[4]

Northampton may have backed away from confronting Elizabeth in person, but the Earls of Arundel and Pembroke seem to have continued to press for the match not to take place. If this was the case, their alliance was remarkably similar to the one they adopted in their determination to remove Jane from the throne in July 1553, ultimately thwarting Dudley's father, Northumberland's, plans and leading to his downfall. Both men were understandably nervous at the prospect of his son becoming Elizabeth's husband, and effectively king. Matters came to a head when, on 30 November, St Andrew's Day, an argument broke out between Dudley's supporters and Pembroke's men which, one observer recalled, turned into 'a great fray at the court between my Lord Robert's men and Herbert's [the Earl of Pembroke's] men'.[5] The exact words that were traded among the blows were not recorded.

It was in this climate of uncertainty that Throckmorton began to plead once more with Cecil in ever stronger terms actively to oppose Dudley's marriage plans:

If her majesty to so foully forget herself in her marriage as the bruit runneth here, never think to bring anything to pass, either here or elsewhere. I would you did hear the lamentation, the declamation, and sundry affections which hath course here for that matter. Sir, do not so forget yourself as to think you do enough because you do not further the matter.

Remember your mistress is young and subject to affections. You are her sworn counsellor and in great credit with her. You know there be some of your colleagues which have promoted the matter. There is nobody reputed of judgment and authority that doth to her Majesty disallow it, for such as be so wise as to mislike it be too timorous to show it, so as her majesty's affection doth find rather wind and sail to set it forward than any advice to quench it. My duty to her, my good will to you doth move me to speak plainly.[6]

But even as Throckmorton wrote, Jones had some remarkable news to report back.

For several weeks, there had been a rumour circulating that Elizabeth had been intending to promote Robert Dudley in the ranks of the peerage, possibly to an earl or even a duke. One commentator wrote to the Earl of Sussex in Ireland how Dudley, 'whom for degrees of honour I should have first named', now 'seemeth to stand greatly in grace and favour' at court. His 'exaltation to higher degree is thought to be differed till after Christmas. At which time it is thought he expecteth a higher place.'[7] 'It is said that Lord Robert about Twelvetide shall be created Earl of Leicester, and his brother Earl of Warwick,' Robert Jones reported to Throckmorton.

Such a move would have been the clearest signal yet that Elizabeth was ready to renounce her single life and marry her favourite. Those closest to Dudley, including the groom of his chamber John Tamworth, were confident that matters would proceed as expected. 'Mr Tamworth hath said that all is well,' Jones reported, 'and that some matters shall come to pass, some that were looked for.'[8] Preachers at court were using their sermons to tell the congregation 'that we may have no strangers to rule over us' and promote the idea that a native-born Englishman would make the best candidate for the queen's husband. Dudley himself seems to have been confident that he might soon receive a promotion, and had ordered his household officers to investigate purchasing Dudley Castle, his family's ancient baronial seat, from his cousin Lord Dudley. He evidently hoped to create a landed estate that might support his elevation within the peerage. He also began to spend lavishly once more, and as his period of mourning for the death of his wife drew to an end, if it was not forgotten already, on Christmas Day he rewarded trumpeters and fife players with 43s 4d and another 10s for servants who brought him new hose, possibly for the queen.[9] Another 30 shillings was spent on 'banqueting stuff', and Dudley purchased a new hat made especially for the festivities costing 10 shillings and a pair of 'sweet gloves' worth 31 shillings.[10]

Somewhat strangely, one of Dudley's few supporters was William Cecil. 'Mr Secretary is the only minister for Lord Robert, and he has been a good time,' Jones informed Throckmorton; 'this comes from a good place, and how it is to be credited the circumstances of some doings can well declare. I fear now that your Lordship's friendliness hath at his hands been used thereafter.'[11] Throckmorton was puzzled. What kind of double bluff was the Secretary playing? Had Cecil not told him secretly to urge others at court not to support Dudley's suit? He wrote again to the Secretary with further news of the scandal that Elizabeth's behaviour with Dudley was causing. While he had been at the French court, the Spanish ambassador to France had visited his residence in person. According to Throckmorton, he

> earnestly required me to tell him whether the Queen, my mistress, were not secretly married to the Lord Robert; for, said he, I assure you, Mr Ambassador, this court is full of it, and whatsoever any man doth make your mistress believe, assure yourself there was never Princess so overseen if she do not give order in that matter betimes. The bruits of her doings, said he, be very strange in all courts and countries. He said the Queen, your mistress, doth show that she hath honour but for a few in her realm, for no man will advise her to leave her folly.

This was followed, Throckmorton informed Cecil, with other rumours and gossip 'which were grevious for me to hear'.[12]

Pleading with Cecil was not Throckmorton's only line of attack. In late December he wrote to Dudley himself from Orléans. He took the opportunity to inform Dudley of recent events; the recent death of Francis II, the French king and husband to Mary Queen of Scots, had ensured that those 'most desirous to trouble England' had now tempered their attacks and vitriolic gossip against Elizabeth, and 'shall not have so ready means to execute their malice'. But this did not mean that Elizabeth's attitude should become any 'less considerate, or her Council less provident', he warned; 'assuredly the Queen of Scotland, her cousin, carries herself so honourably, advisedly, and discreetly, that I cannot but fear her progress.' It was to be lamented that both queens were now without a husband. If only one of these two women, he told Dudley, might be 'transformed into the shape of a man, to make so happy a marriage as thereby there might be an unity of the whole isle'. Marriage, he wrote, was the means by which kingdoms might be strengthened and royal dynasties united.

> Whoever is conversant in stories will perceive that estates have by no one thing grown so great, and lasted in their greatness, as by marriages ... The proof is notoriously seen by the house of Austria, in whose hands the half of Europe is at this day, which is come to pass by marriage only. Their first ancestor, not many years ago, was a mean Count of Hapsburg in Switzerland. As they have come to this greatness by this means, so that race retains still that principle to retain and increase their greatness.[13]

Throckmorton may not have said as much directly, but the ambassador's views must have been clear to Dudley. There was little that Dudley himself could offer the queen, certainly not the wealth and gains that Throckmorton was talking about. He had few lands of his own; what he did own was entirely in the queen's gift.

Throckmorton was not the only one worried about the queen's reputation. In December, one of her suitors, the Duke of Holstein, wrote to her, alarmed to hear reports 'that she has not been in good health'.[14] He also had serious questions over her recent conduct and was 'anxious about her honour'. The letter horrified Elizabeth, who finally seemed to have become aware that rumours about herself and Dudley were spreading across the courts of Europe. She wrote back to Holstein in January, urging him not to believe a word that he had heard. 'She will never forget what is done to herself in this respect,' she told him, 'she will consider it a favour if he will believe none of the rumours which he hears, if they are inconsistent with her true honour and royal dignity.'[15]

It was as if the queen had suddenly realised that the situation with Dudley could continue no longer. Jones noticed the definite change in Elizabeth's mood: 'The Queen's Majesty looketh not so hearty and well as she did, by a great deal; and surely the matter of my Lord Robert doth greatly perplex her and is never like to take place, and the talk is somewhat slack, as generally misliked.'[16] It would mean that there could be no promotion for Dudley, regardless of whether or not she thought that he deserved it, as the risk to her reputation was just too great. Everything had apparently been prepared, the patents of parchment announcing Dudley's new title had already been drawn up, when Elizabeth decided to act. Jones described the remarkable scene to Throckmorton:

> The Queen's Majesty stayeth the creation. The bills were made for the purpose, at the day appointed. When they were presented, she with a knife cut them asunder. I can by no means learn, and yet I have talked with such as know much, that my Lord Robert's matters will not go, as was looked for; and yet the favours be great which are showed him at the Queen's Majesty's hands.[17]

Elizabeth had finally begun to understand the magnitude of Amy's death and the consequences of her decision if she chose to marry Dudley. She had hoped that, with what must have seemed the greatest obstacle, his wife, now removed from the scene, she might marry the man she loved. Now she saw all the dangers and complications of marrying a widower so soon after his wife's mysterious and unexplained death. If she chose love over her kingdom and duty to her people, she would, as de la Quadra had predicted, 'one evening lay herself down as Queen of England and rise the next morning as plain Mistress Elizabeth'.

As New Year approached, Cecil could gleefully report back to Throckmorton that 'Whatsoever reports or opinion be I know surely that my Lord Robert hath more fear than hope, and so doth the Queen give him cause'.[18]

Just before Christmas, Thomas Parry, Elizabeth's Treasurer and Master of the Wards, died. His death opened a void at court, not merely because two important positions in Elizabeth's household now lay vacant. Parry had also been one of Elizabeth's most trusted confidants and closest advisers since her teenage years. Cecil was quick to take his place. It was a sign of his renewed authority and favour with Elizabeth that he was appointed to Parry's former position of Master of the Wards, a lucrative post that would more than remunerate him for the heavy debts he had accrued during his mission to Scotland.[19] Parry's death also dealt a further blow to Dudley's hopes. Parry had been known to favour the queen's marriage to Dudley, though after Amy's death he had become disillusioned and was reported to have been 'half ashamed of his doing for the Lord Robert'.

Parry was not the only member of Elizabeth's household to have been embarrassed by his mistress's conduct with Dudley. In January 1561, Catherine Ashley's husband John, the Master of the Jewelhouse, was 'committed to his chamber and put out of the court' for offending Dudley with words of 'displeasure'.[20] There is no record of what was said, though Elizabeth told Catherine that 'she could never forgive [her] husband nor never love him'. Distraught at her loss of favour, Catherine wrote to Dudley pleading for his forgiveness. 'I never see so woeful a man as I found of my husband, for he thinketh as he had good cause that all his service is forgot: for intending nor meaning harm ...'[21] Within six weeks, she was forgiven and back at court.

As Dudley's star seemed to wane, Cecil's only rose further. Yet the Secretary understood the queen's nature too well to capitalise on Dudley's misfortunes; knowing Elizabeth's strong rebellious streak, her anger at realising that she could never marry her favourite might also be easily transferred to those whom she considered had robbed her of her only hope of romance. To start with, the rumours about which Throckmorton had been so concerned needed to be silenced. On New Year's Day Cecil drew up a list of business that needed to be conducted; beneath Throckmorton's name, he scribbled the words, 'req. memoryall'.[22] On 15 January, at 'midnight fall', he wrote to Throckmorton:

> I have professed, and do avow earnest friendship to you. And in respect thereof, I must advise you not to meddle with the matters of this court otherwise than ye may be well advised from hence. What her Majesty will determine to do only God I think knoweth. And in her, his will be fulfilled. Writings remain and coming into adverse hands may be sinisterly interpreted. On ye other part servants or messengers may be reporters to whom they list, and therefore I cannot safely give you so plain counsel as I wish. But in one word I say contend not where victory cannot be had.[23]

This was not the only sensitive correspondence that Throckmorton received. The Secretary's letter arrived shortly after another from his friend Sir Henry Killigrew, who had written only two days before warning Throckmorton that his close association with him had led to his own 'poor credit, which waxeth in decay'. Ever since Robert Jones had arrived, he remarked, 'this change began & hath been augmented ... what I mean I think you know better than I'. Killigrew urged Throckmorton to drop his campaign against Dudley, 'which some hurt doth serve no purpose & by so doing incur the displeasure of the princes and such as be able to

*Death and the Virgin*

do most with her'. He had been told as much himself through an intermediary, 'who was willed of the Council to let you understand that you did but strive against the stream'. Enough was enough:

> I can not dilate this matter unto you ... In few words; whatsoever you do that tendeth to mislike or disallow the great liking that some have of my L[ord] R[obert] is taken but practice of your own hand, rather of ill will than well meaning to the state. I can say no more unto you; but if you write unto me, let it be so as all men may see it, and yet I pray you write to avoid the suspicion that may else be conceived.[24]

Throckmorton did not reply. Nor did he write on the subject of Amy's death and the infamy it had caused ever again. On that matter the case was closed, for the moment at least.

# A proposal

In spite of the whirl of rumour and suspicion that his wife's death had caused, Robert Dudley had not abandoned his hopes; free to marry once more, he was determined that his next bride would be the queen. But his own ambitions and emotions blinded him to the fact that Elizabeth had begun to turn against the idea of marrying him. Yet it was true that more than any other man he still stood the greatest chance of winning her affections, if only he could persuade Elizabeth that marrying him would mean that she would not destroy her reputation as queen. To do so, he would need significant backing, but with little chance of support from either the Council or the nobility, Dudley looked elsewhere for a powerful figure who might back his suit and persuade the queen that she could marry him without forsaking her crown.

Elizabeth's one-time suitor Philip II was an obvious choice. Dudley had worked hard to befriend Philip when he was married to Queen Mary, and ever since Elizabeth's accession he had sought to present himself to the Spanish ambassador as 'the best servant that His Majesty has here'.[1] With Philip's support, Dudley might also hope to win over religious conservatives like Norfolk and Arundel, who, despite having aired their animosity towards him, were long-standing friends of the Spanish king.

It was a daring proposition, but Dudley had nothing to lose. He arranged for the first moves to be made by his brother-in-law, Henry Sidney, who visited de la Quadra in late January to tentatively discuss the plans. 'He began beating about the bush very widely,' the ambassador reported, but Sidney soon revealed his true intentions: if Philip would support a marriage between Dudley and Elizabeth, he told him, Dudley would 'thereafter serve and obey your Majesty like one of your own vassals, and a great deal more to the same effect'.

Sidney decided to counter any obstacles head-on. If de la Quadra was 'satisfied about the death of Robert's wife', there was surely no other reason why the ambassador should not urge Philip in writing to consider the proposal, 'as, after all, although it was a love affair yet the object of it was marriage, and that there was nothing illicit about it'. As for Amy's death, he was 'certain that it was accidental, and he had never been able to learn otherwise, although he had inquired with great care and knew that public opinion held to the contrary'.

De la Quadra was intrigued. 'If what you say is true,' he replied, 'the evil was less, for, if murder had been committed, God would never help nor fail to punish so abominable a crime.' Nevertheless, he understood the difficulty of Dudley's position; whatever he did to try and change the public perception about his wife's death, 'it would be difficult for Lord Robert to make things appear as he represented them'.

'It was quite true that no one believed it,' Sidney responded, 'even preachers in the pulpits discoursed on the matter in a way that was prejudicial to the honour and interests of the Queen.'

As the conversation progressed, Sidney began to hint at a way forward. Religion was to be the bait. Sidney told de la Quadra that the religious situation in England was in disarray, and that the queen wished to restore it by holding a general Council. The ambassador's interest revived. The Council of Trent, the general synod of the Catholic Church, was about to reconvene, and he had been urging England to send a representative in the hope that Elizabeth might one day return to Rome. Sidney pressed de la Quadra to write to Philip, 'so that Lord Robert should receive the boon from your Majesty [Philip]'s hands'. But de la Quadra was hesitant; he had been made to look a fool when he had previously acted on Mary Sidney's advice in the past; there was no reason why trusting her husband should be any different. Sidney replied that Elizabeth would say nothing unless prompted, but that he 'might be sure that she desired nothing more' than Philip's support, perhaps in the form of a written letter, 'to conclude the match'. Sidney also reassured de la Quadra that 'Lord Robert himself would come' and 'assure you of his desire to serve you [Philip] at all times and in all things to the full extent of his means and abilities'.[2]

Sidney was true to his word. On 13 February, de la Quadra met Dudley and Sidney together. Dudley pleaded for the ambassador to write to Philip and 'recommend the queen to marry him, and he would promise to render your Majesty all the service his brother-in-law had told me, and very much more'. De la Quadra answered that he must wait until he had received instructions from his master, yet with diplomatic tact he concluded that he could act under his previous instructions by requesting that Elizabeth 'make up her mind and settle the succession'. If, by any chance, any particular suitors were discussed, he would speak of Dudley 'as favourably as he could wish'. Dudley 'seemed very well satisfied with this,' de la Quadra reported, 'as he must have expected that I should not answer him in this way.' Dudley begged the ambassador to speak with the queen at once.[3]

Two days later at a meeting with the queen, de la Quadra did as he had promised, assuring Elizabeth of Philip's full support in her marriage plans, 'as I now heard that the matter was under discussion'. Elizabeth's reply was intriguing, as once again she resorted to familiar tactics. 'After much circumlocution she said she wished to confess to me and tell me her secret in confession, which was that she was no angel, and did not deny that she had some affection for Lord Robert for the many good qualities he possessed.' But she had certainly never decided to marry him, or anyone else, 'although she daily saw more clearly the necessity for her marriage, and to satisfy the English humour that it was desirable that she should marry an Englishman'.[4] What would the Emperor think, she asked, 'if she married one of her servitors as the duchess of Suffolk and the duchess of Somerset had done?'[5] Without committing himself either way, de la Quadra replied that he believed Philip would be pleased to hear of her marriage to whoever she chose, adding that the emperor would be particularly happy 'to hear of the advancement and aggrand-isement of Lord Robert' as he understood Elizabeth 'had great affection for him and held him in high esteem'. Elizabeth seemed pleased, de la Quadra thought, at least as pleased as 'her position allowed her to be'.

When the news was reported back to Dudley he was overjoyed; it was the moment he had been waiting for. Elizabeth seemed to be suggesting that she might be prepared to marry him, provided he could find the necessary support abroad. He was desparate for further news and requested that de la Quadra bring up the subject again in his next interview, 'as he knew it was only fear and timidity that prevented the Queen from deciding'. Once again Dudley promised that if the match went ahead, he would ensure that a representative was sent to the general Council; alternatively, he would make the journey himself.[6]

The episode is remarkable. Was Dudley really prepared to restore the Catholic religion for the sake of marrying the queen? Moreover, was Elizabeth really prepared to go along with Dudley's scheme? The question has attracted much debate. At the time, the bargain was viewed as evidence of Dudley's ruthless determination to marry the queen at all costs, and earned him universal scorn as soon as the news became public. If he was prepared to abandon his own religion, by all evidence of the reformed faith, to what other levels might he be prepared to stoop to achieve his aim? When Dudley's plans were revealed some were quick to make the connection with his wife's death. 'Hereby the Lord R[obert]'s ambition appeared', one observer at court recorded on hearing the news, 'that to be king he would procure the banishment of the gospel. A great argument to prove his consent to the murdering of his wife, to have the queen, that would betray his country to be king.'[7]

There is certainly no reason to question the truth of de la Quadra's reports. The ambassador wrote to Dudley several weeks later, recalling the conversations he had had with both Dudley and the queen. Specifically he remembered in detail that Elizabeth 'approved of what your Lordship said to me on the matter one morning in your chamber and one evening in the Savoy, and lately again, when we were walking alone in the park, which will be too fresh in the memory to need further reminder. I will only say that, if I mistake not, you told me that if you married the Queen you would go to the Concilio yourself if needful.'[8]

This last sentence is worth considering, for at no point during his negotiations with de la Quadra did Dudley actually promise the restoration of Catholicism, despite any wishful thinking by the ambassador. Instead, he had offered 'to restore religion by way of a general Council'. In the context of the religious debate swirling around in 1561, this had a different meaning entirely. In November 1560, Pope Pius IV had summoned a General Council of the Church to meet in January 1561, and had even extended the invitation to German Lutheran princes. The English were also to be invited, the Pope having appointed Abbot Martinengo as his 'nuncio' or representative to take the invitation to Elizabeth.[9]

Cecil had no intention of admitting Martinengo into the country, let alone allowing England to send a representative to a council convened by the Pope. In order to undermine its authority, the Secretary wanted to organise a carefully coordinated response with German and French Protestants, with the message that they would only attend a free council of the general Church, free from papal constraint.[10] Dudley was therefore offering a clear alternative to what Cecil hoped for: the admission of the papal nuncio resulting in English attendance at the Council of Trent, convened by the Pope. Depending on what the Lutheran princes considered their position on the Council to be, Dudley may have thought his proposal would have shown a conciliatory attitude that could help reform the Christian Church and end schism in Europe. But he was not offering to turn the clock back and restore allegiance to Rome. Still, the deal was enough, Dudley considered, to secure Philip's support and perhaps finally realise his ambition to marry the queen.

# Many things handled of marriage

Elizabeth had given both Dudley and de la Quadra hope. She had certainly expressed greater interest in Dudley than she had in any previous suitor. She seems to have let slip the details of the scheme to her Secretary in mid-March. Cecil's private reaction must have been one of horror, but he knew that he had to play his hand carefully. He realised that to object might drive Elizabeth further into Dudley's arms, so instead he pretended to welcome the idea, even suggesting to de la Quadra that Philip should write a personal letter in support of the marriage, which could be presented in front of a delegation of bishops and peers, 'all of them confidants of Robert and informed of the Queen's wish', so that the match could go ahead 'with the accord of these deputies'.[1]

De la Quadra remained confident that matters were progressing well. In early April, he had been given new lodgings at Greenwich to prepare for Martinengo's arrival, which Dudley and Elizabeth assured him presented no problem provided he titled himself 'ambassador of the Bishop of Rome'.[2] The forthcoming meeting of the Knights of the Garter on St George's Day was even being pencilled in as a possible date to propose a match between Elizabeth and Dudley in front of the nobility of the kingdom; by all reports, Dudley was 'delighted' with the outcome.[3] 'He was', de la Quadra reported to Philip II, 'excessively overjoyed and could not cease saying how much he desired to serve your Majesty.'[4]

Everything seemed to be going to plan. Dudley had even seen his own position at court improve, with new lodgings at court adjoining the queen's, upstairs and away from the stench of the river. But then things began to unravel. A priest was arrested at Gravesend, who was identified as the chaplain of Sir Edward Waldegrave, a former councillor of the late Queen Mary. Under examination, he confessed that he still said mass daily in Waldegrave's chapel, and was travelling to Flanders to distribute money to poor Catholics living in exile. Cecil was quick to act, and two of Mary's ex-councillors, including Waldegrave, were arrested and charged with breaking the recent Act of Uniformity. Further investigation in Waldegrave's house uncovered a letter, mentioning Martinengo's visit and expressing the hope that this would be followed by greater toleration of English Catholics and the release of Marian bishops.[5]

In this climate of fear, Cecil was able to paint a convincing picture of a plot being hatched that would use Martinengo's arrival to pave the way for the return of Catholicism and papal control. The threat seemed a real one, and within days news of its discovery had reached Throckmorton, who wrote back, confused: 'Such intelligence as I have here doth make me afraid ... for fear of change of religion there amongst you, as for fear of incantation which will move you to be partial or affectionate to the Spanish fortune.'[6] Cecil knew otherwise. He wrote back to Throckmorton a month later, boasting of his handiwork:

What the matters be, the writings will declare, howsoever the end is, the way thereto was full of crooks ... And yet was I forced to seek bye-ways, so much was the contrary labour by prevention. The Bishop of Aquila [de la Quadra] had entered into such a practice with a pretence to further the great matter here, meaning principally the church matter and percase, accidentally, the other matter also, that he had taken faster hold to plant his purpose than was my ease shortly to root up. But God, whose cause it is and the Queen's Majesty, whose only surety therein resteth, hath the one by directing, the other by yielding, ended the matter well ...

When I saw this Romish influence towards, about one month past, I thought it necessary to dull the papists' expectations by discovering of certain mass-mongers and punishing of them, as I do not doubt but you have heard of them. I take God to record that I meant no evil to any of them, but only for the rebating of the Papists' humours which, by the Queen's Majesty's lenity, grew too rank. I find it hath done much good.[7]

Cecil had achieved the exact outcome he had intended. The Privy Council refused entry to Martinengo; the Secretary distributed their verdict 'to sundry places', setting out the details of the supposed conspiracy in full.[8] Cecil received further good news from the meeting of the Knights of the Garter on St George's Day. The Earl of Sussex, having travelled back from his post in Ireland and seemingly oblivious to the controversy surrounding Elizabeth's relationship with Dudley, proposed that the Order should petition the queen to marry Dudley. But a delegation comprising Norfolk, Arundel and Lord Montague stepped in to object, and would only allow a petition to be written in more general language, urging Elizabeth to marry but without stating to whom.[9]

De la Quadra was stunned at the pace of change. So, too, was Elizabeth. On 27 May the ambassador met the queen who told him that 'some of the imprisoned bishops and other papists in London went about saying that she had promised to turn Catholic at the instance of Lord Robert', adding that they had heard the news from members of the ambassador's household. De la Quadra protested that this was simply malice on the part of the Protestants themselves. Elizabeth replied that she was convinced of the ambassador's innocence, and hoped that differences in religion would not prevent a 'perfect friendship' with Philip. But she wanted to know 'whether it was true that your Majesty had promised Lord Robert your friendship and support if religion were restored here?'

'His Majesty has promised nothing to the Lord Robert, nor has asked any conditions from him,' the ambassador replied, 'but only that hearing by my letters and of the goodwill that Lord Robert professed to the restoration of religion, his Majesty has ordered me to thank him and praise his good intention, whilst promising a continuation of the favour his Majesty has always shown him.'

'I do not think that Lord Robert has ever promised you that religion should be restored here,' Elizabeth insisted.

'Yes, he has,' retorted de la Quadra, 'by means of the Concilio, and if you would send for him here and then I believe he will confess as much in your presence as you yourself have promised exactly the same thing.'

Elizabeth did not deny the charge, remarking that 'this was only on certain conditions'. De la Quadra replied that he did not remember hearing of any, but 'perhaps my memory was at fault'; in any case, he urged her 'not to miss the opportunity that God gave her to pacify and tranquilise her country for good'.[10]

One man was privately delighted with the outcome. Having worked behind the scenes to frustrate de la Quadra's hopes and ruin Dudley's plans, the Secretary wrote smugly to Throckmorton: 'The Bishop of Aquila [de la Quadra] had won more with former preludes than was easy to overtake; but in the end, thanks be to God, he findeth all his conceptions and practices unjointed, and under foot. What he will do to recover them I cannot tell.' As for Elizabeth's favourite, he added; 'I can see no certain disposition in her Majesty to any marriage, and any other likelihood doth not the principal here find, which causeth him to be perplexed.'[11]

*

Cecil may have succeeded in thwarting Dudley's plan, but throughout the summer of 1561 the rumours that the queen was to marry her favourite continued unabated. Those close to her could not fail to notice how during her summer progress, Elizabeth's 'goodwyll and favour contynwyth styll'. 'The progress hath given great entertainment to my Lord Robert,' wrote one observer; 'there is talk of a parliament and that the succession must be declared.' The rumour was that Elizabeth would place a proposal to marry Dudley before its members. But this was mere tattle, and came to nothing.[12]

Dudley still clung close to the idea that he might one day wed the queen. Yet he remained frustrated by Elizabeth's failure to raise him to the rank of earl, despite the rumours during Christmas 1560 that he would soon be promoted. When he now discovered this 'could be obtained by no means' he decided to confront Elizabeth directly. What reason did she have for preventing him from being elevated to a higher rank, possibly to the earldom of Warwick, a position which his father had enjoyed?

Elizabeth reacted angrily. 'She loved the house too well,' she retorted, 'to lay that offensive name upon them who have been traitors three descendants.' Dudley was crushed. Sensing his disappointment, she patted his cheeks. 'No, no,' she reassured him, 'the bear and ragged staff [the emblem of the Dudley house] is not so soon overthrown.'[13]

Instead Elizabeth decided to promote Dudley's elder brother Ambrose to Earl of Warwick in December 1561, and still no reward for Robert was forthcoming. Elizabeth was fond of Ambrose, though he was no match for his brother; she later admitted that Ambrose had 'the grace and good looks of Lord Robert', yet 'his manner was rather rough and he was not so gentle as Lord Robert'. She retained a special affection for him nevertheless. 'I will rather drink in an ashen cup than that you or yours should not be succoured,' she once wrote to him.[14] Dudley was overjoyed that the title had been restored to his family. It was 'comfortable news', he told the Earl of Shrewsbury, 'that it hath pleased the Queen's Majesty, of her great bounty and goodness, to restore our house to the name of Warwick'.[15] It was a sign that the dynasty had been forgiven for its past treasons, and that the sons of the Duke of Northumberland were now fully returned to royal favour.[16] Indeed, many expected that greater things might still come for Robert. Ambrose's elevation, the Earl of Bedford wrote, 'induces a good expectation for my Lord Robert, of whose case there never was greater hope than is even now'.[17]

Elizabeth, however, was still in no mood to consider marriage to anyone. She had once more refused the Swedish king's suit, despite wagers being taken as far away as Peebles that the royal pair would marry; London booksellers were even confident enough to produce souvenirs with both their faces printed side by side.[18] 'I am most sorry of all that her Majesty is not disposed seriously to marriage,' Cecil lamented, 'for I see likelihood of great evil … God send our Mistress a husband, and by time a son, that we may hope our posterity shall have a masculine succession. This matter is too big for weak folks, and too deep for simple.'[19] But Elizabeth remained 'still far from marriage far ought that I can perceive'.[20] 'The Queen's majesty remayneth still stranger to allow of marriage,' he bemoaned in October 1561, and hoped 'whereof God alter her mind'.[21] 'Some think of the succession if her Majesty should not marry, or lack issue,' Cecil confided to Sir Nicholas Throckmorton two months later, 'This song hath many parts, but for my part I have no skill but in plain song.'[22]

Dudley, meanwhile, judged that he could afford to wait; time was on his side. If only he might gain the support he needed he still might win the queen. He knew her mind, and how quickly she might change it, but his persistence, he believed, would pay off in the end. Early the following year, Dudley decided to capitalise on his chances by arranging for a play, *Gorboduc*, to be staged before Elizabeth at Westminster, 'with great triumph as had been seen'. Its message was that the queen should marry and produce an heir to prevent her realm descending into civil war.[23] 'Many thinges were handled of marriage,' one observer recalled.[24] In the play, the king, Gorboduc, failed to name a single heir, resulting in division, death and strife: 'lo unto the Prince / Whom death or sudden hap of life bereaves / No certain heir remains …' Elizabeth was urged 'to shun the cause of such a fall'.[25] The week before *Gorboduc* was staged, Dudley boasted to the Spanish ambassador that his chances of marriage were 'at a very good point'.[26] He now once again contacted him, requesting that Philip II write to the queen in favour of his suit.[27] More confident of his chances, there were to be no concessions on religion this time.

Elizabeth also seemed to be signalling that she might one day consider marrying Dudley. She had 'quite made up her mind to marry nobody whom she had not seen or known', she told de la Quadra, 'and consequently she might be obliged to marry in England, in which case she thought she could find no person more fitting than Lord Robert'. She too asked for Philip, 'who might take advantage what the world was saying about the marriage', to write advising her to marry Dudley, 'so that if she should feel disposed to it, people might not say that she had married to satisfy her own desires, but rather by the advice of her princely friends and relatives.'[28]

Elizabeth seems to have been playing an intricate game. It was clear that the prospect of marriage to Dudley was in her mind; it had, after all, been over a year and a half since his wife's death, time enough for the scandal to die down. Yet she remained unable to commit herself to any man or openly declare her feelings. She knew that the ambassadors at court would pounce upon any sign of personal affection, that her words would be studied and examined to exhaustion. She fell back to professing this was only 'what Robert wanted'; as for herself, 'she asked for nothing'. De la Quadra was not taken in by her excuses. He joked with her 'not to dilly-dally any longer, but to satisfy Lord Robert at once'.[29]

By April 1562, it seemed to the court that Dudley was now 'in grete hope of the marriage'. There were rumours that he would be made a duke in preparation for a wedding, and even some of his own household had left his employment, 'who being in despair of the thing were departed from his service'.[30] Events reached at head at the annual meeting of the Knights of the Garter on St George's Day, 23 April. It was here that Elizabeth had caused such controversy by appointing Dudley to the Garter in 1559. In 1561, the Earl of Sussex's petition to the queen to accept Dudley's marriage suit had been blocked by the Duke of Norfolk and the Earl of Arundel.[31] Now, a year later, things were different. At the beginning of the meeting, it was agreed that Dudley's crest could be altered to include his family emblem of the bear and ragged staff – perhaps the clearest indication that he might yet be promoted to a higher rank within the nobility. Then, astonishingly, Norfolk rose to petition Elizabeth himself that she should marry, 'first generally, and at length of the L[ord] R[obert]'. He was joined by 'the most part of the knights there present'. Only Arundel and the Marquis of Northampton disagreed, and showed their displeasure by storming out of the meeting.[32]

The dissension of Northampton and Arundel, however, was enough to unnerve Elizabeth, who had perhaps hoped, expected even, that her nobility would have united to present Dudley as their candidate, allowing her to marry without risk of factional strife to come. Although Elizabeth expressed her pleasure and joy in their petition, going so far as to admit that Lord Robert, 'who she believed deserved the rule of the world,' was a worthy choice', nevertheless she insisted that she needed to give the matter of her marriage 'deeper consideration'.[33]

Then came new revelations. A servant of the Spanish ambassador named Borghese Venturini revealed to Cecil that his master had alleged that 'the Queen was secretly married to Lord Robert', with full details of their relationship composed in a sonnet, 'full of dishonour to the Queen and Lord Robert'.[34] The news was too much for the queen to bear. Elizabeth immediately dismissed de la Quadra from court. Once more Dudley's chances had been dashed. Cecil seems to have deliberately timed their exposure to perfection. It is likely that he bribed Venturini to confess.[35] 'There is a matter here likely to be made great,' he boasted to a friend, just days before the news broke.

# Death possessed every part of me

In October 1562, the worst fears of Cecil and the Council appeared to have been confirmed when Elizabeth fell ill with smallpox. The queen slipped into a feverish coma; for two hours as she lay unconscious members of the Council gathered around her bed and argued over who might be considered her successor. 'Great lamentation made,' one observer at court noted, 'no man knoweth the certenty for the succession; every man asketh what parte shall we take.'[1]

When Elizabeth suddenly regained consciousness, to the amazement of all present, her first words were 'to beg her Council to make Lord Robert protector of the kingdom with a title and an income of £20,000'. According to one report, 'The Queen protested at the time that although she loved and always loved Lord Robert dearly, as God was her witness, nothing improper had ever passed between them. She ordered a groom of the Chamber, called Tamworth, who sleeps in Lord Robert's room, to be granted an income of £500 a year.' Elizabeth believed she was dying; there was no reason for her to tell anything but the truth. 'Death possessed every part of me,' she later recalled. And yet her request that the Groom of the Chamber, 'Tamworth', should be given an annuity of £500 has puzzled historians ever since de la Quadra's dispatch was uncovered in the Spanish archives in the nineteenth century. John Tamworth, a close friend of both Dudley and the queen, regularly lent his master money to pay off his gambling debts, 'lost at pley', and had recently been appointed Constable of Windsor Castle.[2] If Tamworth knew things that Elizabeth wished to remain secret, he was certainly well rewarded for his dedication and service. Among Cecil's papers is a payment from May 1561, 'to Mr Tamworthe to be geven in rewarde by the Queen Maries commandment – one hundred pounds'.[3]

Only Dudley was allowed to be in the queen's presence as she made her recovery, 'owing to the disfigurement of her face'. He was clearly both shocked and relieved when he wrote to the Scottish Secretary William Maitland, informing him of the news. 'Doubtless, my Lord, the despair of her recovery was once marvellous great, and being so sudden the more perplexed the whole state, considering all things, for this little storm shook the whole tree so far as it proved the strong and weak branches ... Well this sharp sickness hath been a good lesson.'[4]

Elizabeth's words had renewed Dudley's hope that she might now finally consider marriage. 'The hopes of Lord Robert are higher than ever', one ambassador observed. But Elizabeth recognised that in her feverish delirium she had been rash to reveal her inner thoughts. Evidence of a more careful and considered judgment can be found in her appointment, several days later, of both Dudley and the Duke of Norfolk to the Privy Council, a clear sign that she was not willing to allow her favourite's influence to dominate official government business.

Elizabeth's near-fatal illness had brought the issue of the succession into sharp relief. At a new Parliament, called for the beginning of 1563, it was the main topic of discussion. A petition was drawn up by the Commons, urging Elizabeth to take 'some honourable husband whom it shall please you to join to you in marriage. Whomsoever it be that your majesty shall choose, we protest and promise with all humility and reverence to honour, love and serve.'

From the outset there were rumours that the petition had been staged by Dudley.[5] The Parliament had begun with a sermon by Dr Anthony Nowell, the Dean of St Paul's, who told the queen that while her sister Mary's marriage had been a 'terrible plague' upon England, 'the want of your marriage and issue is like to prove as great a plague'.[6] Nowell was a close contact of Dudley's, who remained in correspondence with him and may have been part of his network.[7] So, too, was the Member of Parliament, Richard Gallys, who initiated the debate.[8] The petition itself was read by Thomas Norton, one of the authors of *Gorboduc*, and a copy of the petition is to be found among Dudley's surviving papers.[9]

The Lords also drew up their own separate petition which encouraged Elizabeth to marry 'where it shall please you, to whom it shall please you, and as soon as it shall please you'. The implication was that she would be free to marry Dudley without recrimination.[10] Elizabeth was furious at their temerity. 'The marks they saw on her face were not wrinkles,' she told them, 'but pits of smallpox, and although she might be ageing, God could still send her children.'[11]

The Commons and the Lords refused to give up. For two months the debates raged. 'The heads of both houses,' Cecil wrote to a friend, 'are fully occupied with the promise of surety to the realm if God should, to our plague, call her Majesty without leaving of children. The matter is so deep I cannot reach into it.'[12] In the end, Elizabeth relented. In her closing speech to Parliament she made a vital concession. If there were any who believed that she had taken a 'vow or determination' never to give up her single life and marry, she remarked, 'put out that heresy, your belief is awry'. The speech revealed her inner turmoil over the very question of marriage. While she admitted that she thought it 'best for a private woman', she confessed that she did 'strive with myself to think it not meet for a prince'. But she would, she told them, try her best to overcome her hesitations, 'and if I can bend my liking to your need I will not resist such a mind'.[13] She had given no direct answer or firm commitment, but for the Commons and nobility, exhausted by the lengthy sessions and desperate to return home, that was commitment enough. For Dudley, however, the outcome could not have come as more of a disappointment.

Elizabeth knew that Dudley must have been behind Parliament's attempts to force her to marry. She would not forget it. Several months later, Elizabeth took her revenge. In her clearest signal that she had decided never to marry her favourite, instead she came up with the idea of marrying Dudley to her cousin, Mary Queen of Scots. It was a bizarre plan, yet Elizabeth's reasoning was simple. Mary would no longer seek to usurp her position if married to a man she considered 'her brother and best friend' whom she knew 'was so loving and trusty'. The arrangement, she stated, would 'best remove out of her mind all fear and superstition'. If Mary wished to marry 'safely and happily', she considered, 'she would give her a husband who would ensure both, and this was Lord Robert'. Mary's Secretary, William Maitland, was astonished when he heard of the proposal. The gesture was, he admitted, 'great proof of the love she bore to his Queen, as she was willing to give her a thing so dearly prized by herself', but he knew that Mary would refuse to marry him and attempted to make excuses: 'even if she loved Lord Robert as dearly as she did', she would not want to deprive Elizabeth 'of all the joy and solace she received from his companionship'. Privately, others recognised that Mary's 'noble stomach' would never 'imbase itself so low as to marry in place inferior to herself'.[14] They were right. When Mary discovered her cousin's plans she was furious: 'Do you think it may stand with my honour to marry my sister's subject?'[15]

As part of her plans to make Dudley a palatable husband for Mary, Elizabeth decided to finally give Dudley his long-awaited promotion, and made him Earl of Leicester on 29 September 1564. During the ceremony, as Dudley knelt before her, Elizabeth could not help but show her delight, 'putting her hand in his neck to tickle him smilingly'.

'I see the Queen's Majesty very desirous to have my Lord of Leicester placed in this high degree to be the Scottish Queen's husband,' Cecil wrote to a friend, 'but when it cometh to the conditions which are demanded, I see her then remiss of her earnestness.'[16] He was right. Elizabeth soon thought better of allowing her favourite to leave her side. She even began to talk of a bizarre idea that Mary and Dudley might live with her at court, in a *ménage à trois* that would allow Elizabeth to see Dudley daily, while she would 'gladly bear the charges of the family' of the couple, 'as shall be mete for one sister to do for another'.[17]

Dudley was aghast; marriage to Mary Queen of Scots was the last thing he wanted. 'I cannot get the man to take her,' the Scottish ambassador Thomas Randolph complained.[18] Even Elizabeth admitted that her plans were coming unstuck simply because Dudley 'had not consented' to them.[19] According to William Camden, writing years later, Dudley did all he could to sabotage Elizabeth's scheme. The day after he had been created an earl, he took the visiting Scottish ambassador William Melville aside to inform him that the entire plan was the invention of 'Mr Cecil, his secret enemy'. He had little choice: if he refused the match, he would seem to upset both Mary and Elizabeth, but if he accepted and 'appeared desirous of that marriage' he 'should have offended both Queens and lost their favour'. Dudley begged Melville to tell Mary that 'she would not impute that matter to him, but to the malice of his enemies'. In secret, he also let Mary know that the queen's proposal was only intended to prevent her marrying elsewhere.[20]

It was not long before a new suitor for Mary's hand appeared on the scene. The 18-year-old Lord Henry Darnley had a claim to the English throne through his mother, Margaret Lennox, Henry VII's grand-daughter. Darnley had previously been kept under house arrest, but was mysteriously allowed passport to travel to Scotland where he wooed Mary with his elegant dancing and poetry. Soon she was determined to 'have' him.[21] Cecil believed that some 'device' had been used to arrange his journey, while the Spanish ambassador considered that Darnley's match had been arranged 'with the concurrence of some of the great people there'.[22] It was easy to guess who had been behind Darnley's journey. One of the first letters he wrote after arriving in Scotland was to Dudley himself, thanking him 'assuredly as your own brother' for his 'accustomed friendliness'. 'Though I am far from you ... I shall not be forgetful of your great goodness and good nature showed sundry ways to me.'[23]

When Mary did eventually marry Darnley, Elizabeth, who had found the match 'very strange and unlikely', was both angry and perplexed.[24] Yet for Dudley, hope still seemed to remain. Mary's marriage to Darnley had saved him from losing Elizabeth: it would not only encourage the queen to address her own single status, but an important precedent had also been created. In marrying Darnley, Mary had wed someone of lower rank than herself – and an Englishman at that. Whereas Dudley had previously believed that one of the reasons for Elizabeth's 'delay in accepting my advances' was 'principally caused by the Queen having been told that the Queen of Scotland was going to marry a powerful Prince, and this alarmed her', with Mary having made the opposite choice, he contemplated, 'my business will be more easily arranged'.[25]

# The inward, suspicious mind

Elizabeth continued to tease her favourite, promising Dudley that if she ever chose to marry, he would be the one. She had told him herself, he boasted to the French ambassador, 'quite openly on more than one occasion, and furthermore he enjoyed as much of her favour now as he had ever done'. During the Christmas festivities of 1565, she was reported to have told him he should 'only wait till Candlemas, then she would satisfy him'. Dudley remained hopeful; but Elizabeth's promises were meaningless. 'If she thinks fit to disengage herself,' the French ambassador considered, 'no one will call her to account or give testimony against her.'[1] Indeed, Candlemas came and went without a word.

'I have never said hitherto to anybody that I would not marry the earl of Leicester,' Elizabeth retorted to the Imperial envoy Bruener, who argued that she had done exactly that several years earlier. 'But Lord Robert was married then,' Elizabeth shot back, 'and there was no possibility of treating such a thing at the time.'[2] Elizabeth knew that the death of Dudley's wife had changed everything. Yet it was marriage itself that she was not willing to agree to. 'They said of me that I did not marry because I was fond of the Earl of Leicester, and that I would not marry him because he had a wife already,' she told the Spanish ambassador; 'although he has no wife alive now, I still do not marry him.'[3]

Dudley became a useful shield to protect the queen from the unwelcome suits for her hand that would continue throughout the rest of the 1560s. Whenever it seemed as if ambassadors and envoys were pressing her for an answer or decision, she suddenly revived her interest in her Master of the Horse, paying him just enough attention as to unnerve foreign dignitaries from pursuing their cause too closely. After hearing what she had to say about Dudley, one envoy who was attempting to promote Archduke Charles's suit stormed off: 'if she were to marry she would take no one but the Earl of Leicester,' he complained; any claim otherwise was but a 'subterfuge'. The Earl of Sussex, the main supporter of the archduke's suit, disagreed. Elizabeth had promised him in person, he told the envoy, that 'firstly she would marry, and secondly that she would not marry the Earl of Leicester or any other of her countrymen'. 'He had not been able to believe it until she told him herself,' Sussex insisted.[4]

Through the confusion and division, Elizabeth was able to retain a commanding position. 'She deals with them in a way that deceives them all!' the Spanish ambassador observed astutely. 'When she speaks to the Duke of Norfolk she says one thing, and when she speaks to the Lord Robert, quite the contrary.' Even Dudley felt that 'She is so nimble in her dealing and threads in and out of this business in such a way that her most intimate favourites fail to understand her, and her intentions are variously interpreted.'[5]

And so the charade continued. The court was her playground, and Elizabeth would choose with whom she wished to play. 'The Queen did fish for men's souls', the courtier Sir Christopher Hatton would later reflect, 'and had so sweet a bait that no one could escape her network'. At the heart of Elizabeth's behaviour lay her incessant desire and need to be the centre of men's attention, for which the buzz of the various marriage suits and negotiations suited her perfectly. 'The Queen would like everyone to be in love with her,' the Spanish ambassador de Silva remarked astutely, 'but I doubt whether she will ever be in love with anyone, enough to marry him.'[6]

The games of courtship, the thrill of the chase, provided Elizabeth with more than enough excitement. 'I do not think anything is more enjoyable to this Queen than treating of marriage, though she herself assured me that nothing annoys her more,' the Spanish ambassador commented, 'she is vain and would like the whole world to be running after her.' He knew exactly where Elizabeth's behaviour was leading: 'it will probably end by her remaining as she is,' he added, though he ended with an afterthought: 'unless she marries Lord Robert who is still doing his best to win her'.[7]

The fact remained, however, that although he may not have been her husband, Dudley owed everything he had to the queen's generosity. Without it, he would be quickly undone. Elizabeth took care to remind him that he was her creature and was dependent upon her alone. 'If by her favour he had become insolent,' she told him on one occasion, 'she would lower him just as she had, at first, raised him.'[8] She would continue to humiliate and embarrass him whenever she liked. When Dudley requested leave from court to travel to France as part of an embassy, Elizabeth replied that she could not send 'a mere horse-keeper' to wait upon so great a monarch as the French king. Besides, she added in a kinder tone, 'I cannot live without seeing you every day.' Yet she crushed his hopes just as sharply with her words that followed. 'You are like my little dog. As soon as he is seen anywhere, people know that I am coming, and when you are seen, they say I am not far off.'[9] On a separate occasion, in front of the Spanish ambassador Guzman de Silva, who had been sent to replace the disgraced de la Quadra, she took to deliberately humiliating Dudley. At first she called him over, 'showing him favour as usual,' before turning to the ambassador: 'Do you know this gentleman?' she asked. 'It was so long since I saw him,' de Silva responded, playing the game, 'I might well have forgotten him.' 'What!' cried Elizabeth, 'is he so presumptuous that he fails to wait upon you every day?'[10] Dudley's reaction is not recorded, though it seems likely he bore Elizabeth's stinging remark with patient silence. He understood that he was nothing else but her subject. It was a gulf that would always remain between them, a social and political divide that Elizabeth was unwilling to cross. 'I have always loved his virtues,' the queen told the French ambassador, 'but the aspiration of greatness and honour which is in me could not suffer him as a companion.' 'It is true she has shown an inclination towards him,' the Spanish ambassador admitted, 'but [she] has said that she would not marry a subject, but only an equal.'

Above all, Elizabeth understood that marriage and motherhood, whether with Dudley or any other suitor, would remove from her the power to rule, and the authority over her subjects. The simple truth was that Elizabeth refused to be a mere woman; it is unlikely that she would become a mere wife. When she expressed her desire to remain single to the Scottish ambassador, Sir James Melville, he replied: 'I know the truth of that, Madam, you need not tell it me. Your Majesty thinks if you were married you would be but Queen of England; and now you are both King and Queen.'[11] Elizabeth steadfastly refused to allow any other man to rule over her, let alone Dudley. 'Is my Lord of Leicester King, or is Her Majesty Queen?' one of her guards once implored her when he had been rebuked by Dudley. The question was enough to touch a nerve and send Elizabeth into a blind fury. 'By God's death, my Lord,' she exploded at Dudley, 'I have wished you well, but my favour is not so locked up in you that others shall not participate thereof, for I have many servants unto whom I have, and will at my pleasure, confer my favour . . . if you think to rule here, I will take a course to see you forthcoming. I will have here but one mistress and no master.'

In response, Dudley's moods alternated between unbounded optimism and crushing despair. 'The Queen will never decide to marry me,' he lamented to the Spanish ambassador in 1565, 'she has made up her mind to wed some great Prince, or at all events no subject of her own.' By the autumn of that year, it seemed to observers that Elizabeth was displaying a 'certain coolness' towards him. 'The Queen's Majesty is fallen into some misliking of my Lord of Leicester,' Cecil wrote, 'and he therewith much dismayed.' Elizabeth had apparently voiced her opinion in 'many overt speeches' against him. 'She is sorry for her loss of time,' the Secretary observed, adding 'and so is every good subject.'[12]

Their estrangement followed an episode which had resulted in Dudley storming off to his chamber in 'deep melancholy', where he remained for four days 'showing by his despair he could no longer live'. Elizabeth had recently 'begun to smile' on another courtier, a 'young man of pleasant wit and bearing' named Sir Thomas Heneage. Cecil believed it was the Queen's display of favour to Heneage that had been 'so misliked by my Lord of Leicester, with such infinite toys'. Dudley soon confronted the queen directly. 'She was apparently much annoyed at the conversation,' the Spanish ambassador reported back in late August 1565.[13] Dudley retaliated by spending an unusual amount of time with the 24-year-old Laetitia Knollys, the wife of the Viscount of Hereford. Laetitia, better known as Lettice, was related to Elizabeth through her grandmother Mary Boleyn, Anne Boleyn's sister. She was also well known for being 'one of the best looking ladies of the court'.

It was enough to send Elizabeth into a jealous rage of her own, and she flew into 'a great temper'. According to the Spanish ambassador, she 'upbraided' Dudley 'with what had taken place ... in very bitter words'. 'The Queen's Majesty seemed to be much offended with the Earl of Leicester,' William Cecil noted in his diary, 'and so she wrote an obscure sentence in a book at Windsor.'[14] The book still survives, having been discovered in the early twentieth century. The inscription reads:

> No crooked leg, no bleared eye,
> No part deformed out of kind,
> Nor yet so ugly half can be
> As is the inward, suspicious mind.
>
> Your loving mistress, Elizabeth R.[15]

Reading the dispatches sent to him from London by his ambassador, Philip II was fascinated. 'The whole affair and its sequel,' he wrote back with enthusiasm, 'clearly show that the Queen is in love with Robert, and for this reason, and in case at last she may take him for her husband, it will be very expedient to keep him in hand.'[16] Even Cecil refused to rule anything out. 'To tell you truly,' he reported to a friend, 'I do not think that the Queen's Majesty's favour to my Lord of Leicester be so manifest as it was, to move men to think that she will marry with him. And yet his Lordship hath favour sufficient, as I hear him say, to his good satisfaction.'[17]

By the autumn of 1565, Elizabeth seemed to be once again treating Dudley better, though the Spanish ambassador had noticed a change: 'many people say that he no longer occupies the place he used to, and the show of favour is to conceal the change.'[18] Early the following year, after a series of rows with the queen, Dudley attempted to break free, asking Elizabeth's permission to leave the court 'as other men did', under the appearance of visiting his sister Lady Huntingdon, who had fallen ill. It was the first time in years that he had been away from Elizabeth's side.

Remarkably, Elizabeth was initially glad to see him go, telling her cousin Lord Hunsdon that 'it hath often been said that you should be my Master of the Horse, but it is now likely to come true'. [19] It seemed as if relations between Elizabeth and Dudley had broken down entirely. As Dudley's absence lengthened, gossip began to spread. 'Of my Lord of Leicester's absence, and of his return of favour to others here,' Cecil wrote to Sir Thomas Smith, 'if your man tell you the tales of court or city, they be fond and many untrue. Briefly I affirm, that the Queen's Majesty may be, by malicious tongues, not well reported, but in truth she herself is blameless, and hath no spot of evil intent.'[20]

But Elizabeth soon changed her mind. By the middle of March 1566, the Spanish ambassador was reporting that Elizabeth 'is so thin that a doctor who has seen her tells me that her bones may be counted'. Dudley was advised by a friend to hurry back as soon as he could, if he wanted to save his career: 'Touching your coming here, I hear divers opinions; some say tarry, others, come with speed. I say, if you come not hastily, no good will grow, as I find Her Majesty so mislikes your absence that she is not disposed to hear of anything that may do you good.'[21]

Dudley returned, only to leave under a cloud once more just a few weeks later. Once again, it was not long before Elizabeth needed him back at her side, with it being reported to the earl by the queen's own gentlewomen that he should make a 'hasty repair' on account of 'Her Majesty's unkindness taken with your long absence'.[22] In early May, Dudley received a letter from Sir Nicholas Throckmorton insisting that he return, accompanied by a stinging letter from Elizabeth, a copy of which does not survive. Dudley replied in despair. He was amazed at the queen's unkindness towards him, especially after his years of dedicated service and the favour she had previously shown him. 'If many days' service and not a few years' proof have made trial of unremovable fidelity enough without notable offences,' he wrote, 'what shall I think of all that past favour which in some unspeakable sort remained towards me [?]'

'In times past,' Dudley admitted, it would have been of great comfort to him to receive a letter from the Queen, but the situation had 'so changed as I dare scarce now think what I have been told before to say and write'. Instead of writing, he requested that Throckmorton 'give humble thanks' to Elizabeth, 'for the pain taken with their own hands, although I could wish it had been of any other's report or writings; then I might yet have remained in some hope of mistaking'. As for himself, he admitted that the contents of the queen's letter had so upset him that 'it makes me another man, but towards them ever faithful and best wishing, whilst my life shall last'. He would nevertheless remain loyal to his royal mistress to the end, no matter what treatment he might receive:

> Well, I know with whom I have to do. I will always submit to their good will. I can justly confess much from them, and acknowledge very little of myself, but I will endeavour to my uttermost, whatsoever they do with me, to serve, honour, and obey them. No small grief it is to me to find them thus now, that so far otherwise have seen them not long ago; and my grief the greater because I see that remediless which I thought should never have needed help. Thus I will leave troubling you, knowing it is no pleasure to my friends to hear what is unpleasant to myself.

And in a postscript, as if to underline his own feelings of despair, he added bluntly, 'I see I need not to make so great haste home, when no good opinion is conceived of me; either a cave or in a corner of oblivion, or a sepulchre for perpetual rest, were best homes I could wish to return to.'[23]

Much of this was simple posturing, designed for dramatic effect. Of course Dudley knew that the queen would wish him to return, no matter how foul her moods might become. And despite his initial refusal to do so, he found himself able to pen a personal letter to Elizabeth, ending it with a new cipher, a black heart representing his grief. After reading it three times over, Elizabeth 'showed sundry affections, some merry, some sorrowful, some betwixt both'. Within days her favourite was once again back at court.[24]

# Sparks of dissention

Robert Dudley's closeness with Elizabeth remained a source of hostility between himself and the rest of the nobility, especially those who wished to see the queen marry and secure her succession as soon as possible. During 1565, the Earl of Sussex, with the support of the Duke of Norfolk and the tacit backing of Cecil, had sought to reopen marriage negotiations with Archduke Charles. Dudley naturally opposed the match for his own sake, preferring instead to attempt to sabotage the negotiations by supporting a rival French candidate, the 14-year-old Charles IX. It was a preposterous match, but it was one which Dudley saw as his only chance of keeping his own ambitions alive. Unsurprisingly, Dudley's actions made him highly unpopular with the supporters of the archduke's suit. 'There are sundry rumours that the Lords here do not accord together,' Cecil wrote to his friend Sir Thomas Smith in October 1565, 'that my Lord of Leicester should not have so great favour as he had; that my Lord of Sussex and he should be in strange terms.'[1]

Rivalry soon developed into mutual antipathy. Sussex, who immediately after Dudley's wife's death had seen no harm in allowing Elizabeth to marry whom she liked, even if that meant Dudley himself, now became his enemy. 'They grew into a direct forwardness, and were in continual opposition,' the seventeenth-century historian Robert Naunton judged, 'the one setting the watch, the other the centinel, each on the other's actions and motions.'[2] The pair fell out spectacularly in the summer of 1566 after Dudley sharply criticised Sussex's handling of Irish affairs as Lord Deputy there. 'Hard words and challenges to fight were exchanged,' while Sussex lashed out, telling him that 'neither he nor anyone of his family had ever been traitors to their sovereign'.[3]

Sussex was joined in his opposition to the Queen's favourite by his cousin the Duke of Norfolk, whose hatred of Dudley was long-standing. Matters had not been helped by one particular incident in May 1565, when in the middle of a tennis match between Norfolk and Dudley, 'my Lord Robert being hot and sweating', Elizabeth took a napkin out of her sleeve and wiped the sweat off Dudley's face. Incensed by such a blatant show of affection, Norfolk burst out that Dudley was 'too saucy' and swore that 'he would lay his racket upon his face'. 'Whereup rose a great trouble and the Queen sore offended with the Duke', one observer recalled.[4] A delegation of noblemen led by Norfolk later approached Dudley, ordering that he refrain from touching the queen, or visiting her private apartments without permission early in the morning, often while Elizabeth remained in a state of undress. 'The Queen would not marry him,' Norfolk later told Dudley during a fraught meeting designed to force him into supporting Archduke Charles's marriage suit. 'Only trouble could come from him attempting to bring it about,' he warned, 'since all those who wished to see the Queen married, the whole nation in short, blamed him alone for the delay that had taken place.' So great would the hatred aroused against him be if he did not support Elizabeth's marriage to the archduke, 'evil could not fail to befall him'.[5]

The threat of violence was strong enough for both sides to arm themselves, as the court began to take on the appearance of a military tattoo. After their confrontation, Dudley's supporters took to wearing blue, Norfolk's dressed in yellow, while both began to parade their armed retinues through the streets in their hundreds.[6] Sussex complained to the queen, 'there be drawn to him great bands of men with swords & bucklers . . . he and all his be in that sort armed'.[7] Cecil, too, was worried: 'I wish that God would direct the hearts of those two earls to behold the harm that ensueth of small sparks of dissention betwixt noble houses, especially such as have alliances and followers.'[8] There were several attempts at reconciliation over the spring and summer, but the Spanish ambassador for once considered it to be just 'dissembling in the English way'; both parties remained 'of the same opinion as before'. The Venetian ambassador could see the situation deteriorating even further. 'They are nevertheless not reconciled, and each of them walks with a large company of armed men to secure himself.'[9]

Behind the threats of violence and the outbreaks of factionalism lay the united concern that, nearly eight years since the queen had acceded to the throne, Elizabeth remained without a husband and without an heir. She had just turned 33; it was evident that she would soon be beyond an age at which she might reasonably be expected to have children. Elizabeth's poor health, moreover, was the source of constant anxiety and speculation. In March, a doctor told de Silva 'that a stone is forming in her kidneys. He thinks that she is going into a consumption.'[10] Two months later, she had been struck down by a fever; the Scottish ambassador Sir James Melville recalled how 'no man believed any other but death to be the end of it, all England being the overthrow in a great perplexity'. Elizabeth did recover, but throughout her summer progress she was also troubled with 'her indisposition, which is an issue on the shoulder' and prevented her from going on the hunt.[11]

Renewed calls for Elizabeth to marry or settle her succession came at the same time as Parliament was to be recalled in the autumn of 1566. Elizabeth had little choice but to call for it; she was desperate for money and needed Parliament to grant her a new subsidy. Yet Elizabeth had merely prorogued the Commons since its last sitting three years before; the MPs who returned to Westminster in 1566 were the same members who had petitioned the queen to marry in the previous Parliament. To their satisfaction, Elizabeth had promised to do just that. But that was three years ago.

Behind the scenes, in the run-up to Parliament, a campaign had begun for Elizabeth finally to resolve the questions of both her marriage and the succession. An anonymous petition which was circulated began with the words: 'We may despair of your marriage, we may despair of your issue.'[12] In his diary entry for 6 October 1566 Cecil wrote that 'Certain lewd bills thrown abroad against the Queen's Majesty for not assenting to have the matter of succession proceed in Parliament and bills also to charge Sir William Cecil, the Secretary, with occasion thereof.'[13]

One of these 'lewd bills' was probably a document that has been preserved, entitled *The common cry of Englishmen made to the most noble lady, Queen Elizabeth, and the High Court of Parliament*. It set out its case clearly from the beginning: 'If you O Queen do die ... void of issue and wanting a known successor and ordered succession, as the case now standeth, what good can continue? What evil shall not come? ... This lack is that rack whereon England rubbeth, the sand where it sticketh and sinketh daily to destruction.' Turning to Elizabeth's promises made during her last Parliament, the document claimed that her delay in marrying 'did daunt and grieve the hearts of you and thousands which loved you for your good attempt'. It was even bold enough to inform her that now, at the forthcoming Parliament, was the moment at which Elizabeth must be true to her word: 'it is time to claim the performance ... Show forth again that affection.' Even if Elizabeth chose to marry, however, it warned that she may have left it too late to bear children: 'It is not your marriage, most noble Queen, which can help this mischief for a certain ruin cannot be stayed by an uncertain means. It is uncertain whether ever you shall marry. It is uncertain whether you shall have issue in your marriage. It is uncertain whether your issue shall live to succeed you, if you have one.'[14]

Cecil had not wanted matters to go this far. He had hoped that Elizabeth would have honoured her promise to Parliament three years previously to marry and thereby in time provide the realm with a natural heir. Now the Secretary still hoped that if Elizabeth would commit to marriage, then talk of her succession would become irrelevant. In a note he composed before the opening of Parliament, he made his thoughts perfectly clear: 'To require marriage is most natural, most easy, and most plausible to the Queen's Majesty', whereas 'To require the succession is hardest to be obtained, both for the difficulty to discuss the right and for the loathsomeness in the Queen's Majesty to consent thereto ... The mean betwixt these,' Cecil concluded, 'is to determine effectually to marry, and if it succeed not, then proceed to discussion of the right of the succession.'[15]

Unless some solution was found, there was bound to be trouble when Parliament met. The Council decided to broach the subject of marriage with Elizabeth. At a meeting on Saturday 12 October, Norfolk, as the most senior member of the nobility, came forward to address the queen. 'Madam, you know that I have taken an oath to your Majesty as a Councillor,' he began, 'by which I am obliged to have regard to your well being and that of your subjects. Pardon me, therefore, if I take the liberty of putting this matter before you.' Reminding her of the petitions that both houses had presented before her in the last Parliament, he told her that they had taken no action as they still were waiting for her answer. He begged her to allow this session of Parliament to discuss both the succession and her marriage.

Elizabeth's response was sharp and pierced with anger. The succession was her own business, and she had no wish for their counsel either. She had no desire to be buried alive, she remarked, as she felt her dying sister Mary had been when during the last days of her reign people had flocked to Elizabeth's side at her residence at Hatfield. Elizabeth wanted no such journeys during her reign. As to her marriage, 'they knew quite well that it was not far off'. She trusted that when it came to parliamentary matters, each of them would do their duty. And with that, she took her leave and left the chamber.[16]

The Council had failed to get the queen to appreciate the seriousness of the debate; when the House of Commons did meet, sure enough there were urgent calls for Elizabeth to either marry or settle the succession before any subsidy might be granted. Elizabeth was angry and frustrated. She confided to de Silva 'that she did not know what these devils wanted'.[17] Elizabeth was confident, however, that her nobility would not join with the Commons in echoing their demand for the succession to be settled. Her confidence was misplaced.

The Lords sent their own deputation to the queen to convince her of the need to marry. Finding her in her Presence Chamber, a spokesman presented the Lords' case clearly to Elizabeth. It was the custom of kings, her ancestors, to provide for the succession and 'preserve the peace of the kingdom'; now necessity 'compelled them to urge this point, that they might provide against the dangers which might happen to the kingdom if they continued without the security they asked'. The Commons, they told her, were 'so resolved to settle the succession before they would speak about a subsidy, or any other matter whatever; that, hitherto, nothing but the most trivial discussion had passed in Parliament, and so great an assembly was only wasting their time.' If Elizabeth would only declare her will on this one point, or else put an end to the Parliament, 'every one might retire to his home'. After the spokesman had finished, each nobleman in turn – beginning with the Duke of Norfolk – added their case.

Elizabeth would not listen. The Commons had already been 'very rebellious'; surely they would never have dared attempt 'such things during the life of her father', she told them. As for themselves, as subjects they had no right to 'impede her affairs' and 'what they asked was nothing less than wishing her to dig her grave before she was dead': 'My Lords, do what you will; as for myself, I shall do nothing but according to my pleasure. All the resolutions which you may make have no force without my consent and authority; besides, what you desire is an affair of much too great importance to be declared to a knot of harebrains.' 'On this she dismissed them in great anger,' the French ambassador reported.[18]

But the dramas that would beset the Parliament had only just begun. The following day, 23 October, the Commons sent a committee to the Lords to discuss what next steps should be taken. Two days later they received word that the Lords had agreed to join with the Commons, 'in the suit to the Queen's Majesty, viz., for marriage and succession'.[19] With Norfolk as their spokesman, the Lords and Commons made a joint petition to the queen.

This was too much for Elizabeth. She lashed out – 'so angry' that she exploded in fury at Norfolk, calling him a traitor. In Norfolk's defence, the Earl of Pembroke interrupted, telling her that 'it was not right to treat the Duke badly, since he and others were only doing what was fitting for the country, and advising her what was best for her, and if she did not think fit to adopt the advice, it was still their duty to offer it'.

Astonished, Elizabeth turned her anger upon him; 'he talked like a swaggering soldier,' she exclaimed.

Then the queen looked over to Dudley, standing in the corner of the room. She could not believe that he would have the temerity to be part of the delegation now forcing her to declare her successor; 'she had thought if all the world would have abandoned her he would not have done so.'

Dudley was taken aback. 'I would die at your feet,' he protested.

'That has nothing to do with the matter,' screamed Elizabeth.

'With this she left them,' the Spanish ambassador de Silva recorded, 'and had resolved to order them to be considered under arrest in their houses. This she has not done, but she has commanded them [Dudley and Pembroke] not to appear before her.'[20]

Elizabeth remained furious with Dudley, suspecting that he had been one of the guiding hands behind the attempt to press her into marriage. She had good reason to be suspicious. Trouble had begun in Parliament after one 'master Molyneux' made a 'mocion' for the 'reviving of the suit for Succession and to proceed with the subsidy'. Molyneux's motivation in doing so has been shrouded in mystery however Molyneux's brother was secretary to Sir Henry Sidney, Dudley's brother-in-law. And in Cecil's own memorandum against Dudley written in the previous year, listing his 'owne particular frends' whom he considered Dudley might lavish with patronage if he became Elizabeth's consort, he named one 'Mollynex'.[21] It seems plausible that Molyneux might just have been acting on Dudley's behalf.

Elizabeth herself was sure enough. As Cecil later recorded in his diary, 'Pembroke and Leicester were excluded the Presence Chamber for furthering the proposition of the succession to be declared by Parliament without the Queen's allowance.'[22] Later, in the privacy of her own chamber, Elizabeth confided in de Silva, complaining 'greatly of all of them, and particularly of Leicester'. 'She asked me what I thought of such ingratitude from him,' he recalled, 'after she had shown him so much kindness and favour, that even her honour had suffered for the sake of honouring him. She was glad, however, of so good an opportunity of sending him away.'[23]

It was not to last. Dudley returned to his familiar trick of conveniently falling ill, and Elizabeth's fury soon abated. Enquiring of the Spanish ambassador if he had seen Dudley, 'and what he had said about these affairs', she told him that already she had been approached by her councillors in person; 'many of them had asked pardon, saying they had no intention of offending her, but rather of serving her'.[24] By early December, Elizabeth was still complaining about Dudley's behaviour, though her tone had softened. She was now under the impression that Dudley was blameless in the affair, and told de Silva that 'she thinks he acted for the best, and that he was deceived. She is quite certain that he would sacrifice his life for hers, and that if one of them had to die, he would willingly be the one.'[25] If there was one man that she could forgive no matter what his fault, it was Dudley.

Elizabeth might have vented her anger in private, but she could no longer avoid a confrontation with her Members of Parliament, who were still demanding that she make some form of statement about her marriage and the succession. On 5 November Elizabeth eventually agreed to receive a deputation of thirty representatives from the Commons and the Lords. Before them she delivered one of her most celebrated speeches:

> As for my own part, I care not for death; for all men are mortal. And though I be a woman, yet I have as good a courage, answerable to my place, as ever my father had. I am your anointed Queen. I will never be by violence constrained to do anything. I thank God I am endued with such qualities that if I were turned out of the realm in my petticoat, I were able to live in any place in Christendom.[26]

Her words were filled with scorn and fury. Only she would decide when she would marry or name her heir. She would never be forced into doing so, as the Commons were now attempting. 'It is monstrous,' she told them, 'that the feet should direct the head.' She believed that she had already made her own position on her marriage perfectly clear.

She had told them at the previous Parliament that she hoped to marry and have children, but that under no circumstances would she name her successor. Her own situation during her sister's reign, when men had flocked to her as heir to the throne, had taught her that lesson. 'I stood in danger of my life, my sister was so incensed against me: I did differ from her in religion, and I was sought for divers ways. And so shall never be my successor.' As for her marriage:

> I will never break the word of a Prince, spoken in a public place, for my honour's sake. And therefore I say again, I will marry as soon as I can conveniently, if God take not him away with whom I mind to marry, or myself, or else some other great let happen. I can say no more, except the party were present. And I hope to have children, otherwise I would never marry.[27]

Elizabeth ordered Cecil to report her words to the Commons. It took the Secretary three drafts to re-word her speech before he was able to repeat it. As for Elizabeth's original words, in the margin of his transcript, Cecil wrote: 'This was not reported.' Cecil's sanitised version of the speech, read out to the Commons the following day, toned down her words.[28] When he had finished reading out his speech, the Commons merely sat silently in disbelief.

Elizabeth was back in control: having made plain that she would not tolerate any further agitation, she had set out the terms of the future debate. Marriage and the succession were to be her choice, and hers only. When Elizabeth told both houses that she would forgo one part of the subsidy, their bargaining power was reduced, pre-empting any further moves they might attempt. The Commons did try one final time, but it was to little avail. When the subsidy bill was drawn up, they inserted into its preamble Elizabeth's promise to marry, thereby proclaiming to the nation at large the queen's undertaking. When she came to read through the draft, Elizabeth spotted their intentions immediately. 'I know no reason why,' she scribbled in the margin, 'any of my private answers to the realm should serve as a prologue to a subsidy book, neither yet do I understand why such audacity should be used to make without my licence an act of my words.' The text of the preamble was quickly dropped: in its place, was merely a reference to 'the great hope and comfort' that the members had displayed upon hearing that Elizabeth had promised to get married when convenient.[29]

The entire session of Parliament had been a disappointment; for the Commons, the Council, but most of all for Dudley. He had gambled on settling the succession to force Elizabeth to name her heir – leaving him with one final chance of marrying her. Yet Elizabeth had given no indication that she would consider his suit. She had promised to marry 'as soon as I can conveniently', but not to him. Dudley's heart must have sunk when he heard the words: 'I can say no more, except the party were present' – 'except' in this context meaning 'unless'. But Dudley was there, ready to take her hand in marriage. Instead Elizabeth had signalled that she was prepared to re-engage with proposals for a match with Archduke Charles, who was obviously the person whom she had hinted at in her speech, so long as 'God take not him away . . . or myself, or else some other great let happen'.

Dudley had to face the truth. His chances of marriage to Elizabeth were over. He spent the New Year brooding, coming to terms with his loss. His relations with the queen had cooled since his attempt to pressurise her into naming her successor, but the queen was quick to restore him to his former favour; in January she called the Spanish ambassador de Silva over to her side, telling him that 'she should be glad if I would show some love and friendship to Lord Robert as I used to do'.[30]

In contrast, Elizabeth's concession to Parliament that she would marry had delighted supporters of the archduke's suit such as Sussex and Norfolk. Dudley was determined to fight them all the way. Although he had finally come to realise that his own suit to marry the queen stood no chance, he was resolved that neither would the archduke's. Perhaps he considered that if he was not able to have the queen, no one else would either. His decision to oppose Archduke Charles's suit was in reality both a religious and a political one: having reinvented himself as a committed Protestant, Dudley was keen to prevent the spread of Hapsburg influence and the threat of England becoming a Catholic nation under the thumb of its vast empire. Amid the politics of faction, there was also his own future at court to consider: the thought of Sussex and Norfolk being victorious in their quest to place the archduke on the throne as Elizabeth's consort was hardly one upon which the earl would have wished to dwell.

Dudley's opposition would not come without cost. It earned him no friends among the Council, who were by now desperate to see Elizabeth married to any husband she might find. It would also reopen the divisions and old animosities between himself and Sussex, the consequence of having enemies in high places.

# PART SIX

---

We all be flesh and blood

# The murder of his sister

By the spring of 1567, it was over six years since Amy Dudley had been discovered dead. Yet the scandal was far from forgotten. Almost a year after Amy's death, probably around the time that the coroner's jury submitted its findings to the local Assizes, the facts of the case were once again the subject of debate. This time, another of Dudley's rivals, the Earl of Arundel, had decided to look into the case. Unconvinced that the findings of the jury in the coroner's report were entirely accurate, the Spanish ambassador reported in September 1561 how Arundel was even seeking to reopen the case. Dudley confronted him about his behaviour and 'had such words' with him. This only drove Arundel on further. According to the Spanish ambassador, 'the Earl [of Arundel] went home and he and others are drawing up copies of the testimony given in the inquiry respecting the death of Lord Robert's wife'. Dudley was 'now doing his best to repair matters as it appears that more is being discovered in that affair than he wished'.[1]

Arundel was not the only one who had his suspicions that something was not quite right about the nature of Amy's death and the coroner's investigation that had followed. Among those who had begun to doubt that things were not as they seemed was one of Amy's few surviving relations, her elder half-brother, John Appleyard.

One of Dudley's first actions upon learning of his wife's death was to send for her relatives, including Appleyard, 'that they may be privy and see how all things do proceed'. It was a wise move, helping to limit any immediate damage to his reputation. 'Your Lordship hath done very well in sending for Mr Appleyard,' his servant Thomas Blount had admitted, and Dudley seemed satisfied that Appleyard 'hath been there, as I appointed'. There is no doubt that the presence of Amy's closest family members at the inquest would have done much to clear Dudley's name and reassure those who might have assumed he would have attempted to pick the jury in order to obtain the verdict he wanted.

There is no mention of Appleyard's feelings at the time or thoughts concerning his sister's sudden death, and his silence might well have been taken as a sign of his acceptance that Amy had died accidentally. But as time passed, Appleyard became less convinced. According to his later testimony, during the intervening years 'he had oftentimes moved the earl [Dudley] to give him leave to countenance him in the prosecuting of the trial of the murder of his sister'. He always believed that Dudley himself was innocent, 'but yet he thought it an easy matter to find out the offenders, affirming therewith, and showing certain circumstances, which moved him to think surely that she was murdered'.[2]

Dudley wanted nothing more to do with the case. The jury's verdict was final; nothing useful would come of raking over the details of her death, which would merely reopen old wounds. He replied that he 'thought it not fit to doubt any further in the matter, considering that by order of the law it was already found otherwise, and that it was so presented by a jury'. But Appleyard had apparently refused to give up, convinced that there was some crucial evidence missing. The jury's findings, he argued, were incomplete: 'the jury had not yet given up their verdict.'[3]

Now, nearly seven years later, Appleyard's suspicions about Dudley's own involvement in Amy's death had begun to emerge. When Dudley wrote telling him that he was unable to help with his requests, Appleyard grew angry, 'and said amongst other things that he had for the earl's sake the murder of his sister'.[4] These were dangerous enough accusations, but there was worse to come. Dudley discovered that Appleyard had been 'practised with by court persons to join with them' against him, and had been 'moved to search the manner of his sister's death'.

Alarmed, Dudley called for Thomas Blount to once again investigate the matter. Blount recalled how Dudley had told him 'that there was villany meant towards … and practiced against' him by 'certain persons' unknown, but he was determined to find out who his enemies were. As Blount remembered during their conversation, Dudley replied how he 'should not be in quiet until you knew who they were and what they had to say against you'. Dudley urged Blount to visit Appleyard immediately to find out 'who the parties were and what matters they had to say'.

Blount's investigations led him to uncover that Appleyard had been approached several weeks before by a mysterious boatman, who met him on the bank of the Thames.

'Sir, I am not acquainted with you,' the unnamed boatman had told Appleyard, 'nor you with me, but I have matters of great weight and secrecy to impart with you, the which if you will promise me, as you are a gentleman, to keep secret I will impart them with you; if not I will say nothing.' He added: 'They shall be for your great advantage both with money and good friends.'

Hesitating, Appleyard replied that he would only do so 'if they were matters meet to be kept without peril'.

'They might,' the boatman replied.

'Then say on – I will keep them secret; but what is your name?' Appleyard queried.

But the boatman would not reveal his identity until Appleyard swore an oath on a book, 'that whatsoever fall out you shall never betray my name'. After Appleyard agreed and swore an oath, the boatman revealed himself and continued his conversation, explaining that he was a messenger from 'such persons' – Appleyard would not be drawn on his oath – 'in this sort'.

'They say they know you are ungently handled at my Lord of Leicester's hands,' said the boatman, 'and have spent under him all you have. If you will join with them who do mind to charge him with certain things, and do as they will do, you shall lack neither gold nor silver.' Above all, the boatman continued, they knew that Appleyard, as Amy's half-brother, was 'the meetest man to prosecute, that is, the death of your sister. One other is that my lord of Leicester is the only hinderer of the queen's marriage.'

To prove the truth of his words, the boatman promised to take Appleyard to a house where he would find £1,000, 'whereof to take so much as you list, and shall have from time to time so much as you shall require, with the assured friendship of those I have named'.

'I have heard what you have said,' Appleyard told the boatman, 'and this I say. According to my promise, whatsoever you have said I will never utter, your name I am sworn to keep.' But he was not interested in the money, nor in betraying Dudley to them. 'To answer you this, I say my lord of Leicester is better my good lord than he is reported to be.' He continued to pledge his loyalty to Dudley: 'if I would be hired with money and friends, I would have both, but I will never whilst I live forsake him.'

When Blount heard the story from Appleyard he was amazed. 'Then you will come to my lord according to your promise,' Blount retorted, 'and tell him who they be, and what they would charge him with, and name unto him this merchant.'

'I will tell him as much as I have said to you and who they be,' Appleyard replied, 'but I am sworn not to name the person unto whom I am sworn.'

How could his master know the truth, unless he knew the names of his accusers? Blount asked. Appleyard had a simple solution. 'I am sworn not to name him; but this much I will do. I will show the person and point with my finger and say "This is he" and then let my lord do what he list.'

But Appleyard did not live up to his promise, and with Dudley growing frustrated and demanding to know who his unnamed adversaries were, Blount visited Appleyard's chamber once more, where he found Appleyard's half-brother, William Huggins.

It was the opportunity Blount had been looking for. He managed to tease out of Huggins the full story of the episode, how he had seen Appleyard meet with the boatman in his nightgown, and how he had seen men in 'tawny coats' standing nearby. Blount wanted to know more. He needed to know the names of the men who sought to prosecute Dudley for the death of his wife. Who were they?

'Did he tell you their names?'

'Yes.'

'Who were they?' Blount demanded.

'By God, very great,' William replied.

'Who, I pray thee?'

'My Lord of Norfolk, my Lord of Sussex, Thomas Heneage, and others.'

Blount was taken aback. 'Well, William, these are somewhat great persons. I judge it may be untrue, for if my Lord of Norfolk should go about such a practice, my lord is marvelously deceived in him, for my lord doth take him for his great friend.'

Suspecting that a plot was being formed against him, Dudley arranged to meet Appleyard between London and Greenwich, where Blount remembered how he 'fell far out with him, and so far angry as I never see him before'. In his own judgment, he recalled, 'if they had been alone, my lord would have drawn his sword upon him'. Instead, after 'great words of defiance', Dudley bade him to depart, before turning to

Blount, telling him that Appleyard 'was a very villain, and with knavery went . . .'[5]

There Blount's testimony ends, for any remaining pages of the surviving document are missing or have been destroyed. Soon after, however, Appleyard was arrested and thrown in the Fleet prison, to await further investigation by the Council. As the investigations progressed, Dudley was kept informed by Sir Nicholas Throckmorton, who, having grown closer to Dudley in recent years, now reported on the details of the case in Dudley's defence. Throckmorton wrote of Blount's testimony:

> By Mr Blount's writing, you shall understand what hath been proceeding touching Appleyard. Huggins is sent for, after whose examination I think the matter shall suspend until you return. Lord Arundel remains here about that business. Lord Pembroke has shewed himself in this and in the handling of it your assured friend. Your well-willers would have you go through now with this matter . . .

The letter ends with the cryptic sentence, 'This night as fair lady lodges in your bed.'[6]

In late May 1567, Appleyard appeared before the Council to testify what had occurred. Suddenly he was quick to change his story. 'He denieth that ever he made any report or mention of the duke of Norfolk or earl of Sussex to be named by the said party.' Aside from a small attack on Dudley's generosity in which he claimed 'he had received many fair promises of good turns, but he never had the fruits thereof' ('And yet being remembered of those pleasures following,' the Council memoranda recorded, Dudley 'could not deny them'), Appleyard seems to have taken the blame. On 31 May he fully admitted to his guilt:

> Most honourable, when I consider the greatness of my faults most heinously committed, I both blush and fear to write. I blush, as ashamed of my facts, and fear, as one condemning myself unworthy of grace at your hands. But the noble clemency I yesterday received doth somewhat abandon from me despair, although shame doth still remain, for it cannot be covered, my faults being truly confessed by my own mouth in so honourable a presence; so that where before I stood in hope (by your honourable means to her majesty) to have happened of somewhat in my relief, I now wish rather a mountain to overwhelm me, and hide me from your sights, than once to dare show my spotted face in your honourable

presences, for (unworthy of it) I have heretofore had place and countenance of credit, and better liked of by all your honours than I could deserve, which now is so justly blemished, as I see in myself no possibility, as hereby I can have comfort in my life, ever to recover your good opinions ... methinks I see in myself, what inquiry and what whisperings are, in judging mine offences, which (once known) when it shall please god to move in your honours my deliverance, then I shall stand in worse case; for even as one ashamed of light, shall either wish all absence of day, or else, for fear of wonderment, must, like the black bat, afraid to be seen of the birds, shroud myself in some desert; for I shall see no man look towards me, whom I shall not fear doth behold me, to gaze of my shames committed. So the more I consider of myself, the deeper causes I find to sink in despair.[7]

Yet Appleyard was still not convinced that the nature of his sister's death had been properly investigated. 'For the matter of my sister,' he told the Council, he wished to undertake an 'examination of all such persons as I shall give in name to your honours, laying reasonable or likely cause why I present them.' Unfortunately, no such list of names survives, though Appleyard also requested that he be able to view a copy of the coroner's report into Amy's death, 'whereby I may see ... trial of the cause'. His wish was granted. The coroner's report on Amy's death that had been filed away was unearthed from the archives, and a copy was sent to Appleyard to read for himself. At the same time, Cecil sent him a list of questions to which the Council wanted answers, this time in writing:

First how and wherefore you devised the tales that were reported from you to my Lord of Leicester, or certain persons that should solicit you in the name of my Lord of Norfolk's grace, the Earl of Sussex and others, to stir up matter against my Lord of Leicester for the death of his wife ... Secondly, to declare plainly what moved you to use any speeches to cause the death of the Earl of Leicester's wife to be taken as procured by any person; and what you think thereof by the sight of the presentment made by the jury charged by the coroner and now returned into the King's Bench. To these matters the Lords would have you answer as plainly in writing at length as you have already done by speech.[8]

Five days later, Appleyard again changed his mind. He wrote to the Council from his cell in the Fleet prison. Confessing that his offences had been 'heinous and such as deserveth far greater punishments than yet I have tasted,' he called for mercy. He was already desperate. He had previously written of the harsh conditions he was living in: 'as my health, my good lords, is very evil, so are my charges great, for I have nothing to feed on but that I send ready money for into the town; and surely, my lords, I have very little, and I may not speak with any friends to help me, so that I must very shortly take what of alms the house will give me'. Soon he was desperate to be released. Besides his imprisonment in the squalid surroundings of the Fleet, 'which I have endured close a full month this night,' he had become 'afflicted with sickness, and most miserable poverty ... I have not money left to find me two meals'. Meanwhile the Council had sent him a copy of the coroner's report, which he had been given the opportunity to read through. Whether desperation or rational argument swayed him, he was now finally ready to let the matter of his sister's death be put to rest:

> With remembrance of my most bounden duty, my singular good lords, I received from your honours, by Mr Warden of the Fleet, the copy of the verdict, which in my other letter I humbly sued for, by whom I yesterday returned the same to your lordships again; in which verdict I do find, not only such proofs testified under the oaths of fifteen persons, how my late sister by misfortune happened of death, but also such manifest and plain demonstration thereof, as hath fully and clearly satisfied and persuaded me; and therefore, my lords, commending her soul to God, I have not further to say of that cause. For I have of your honours required nothing that might bring trial of her unhappy case to light, but I have in all justice received the same, yea, even with the offer of your noble assistances.[9]

Whether or not Appleyard truly believed his words, the supplication worked. Two days later, on 6 June 1567, he appeared before the court of Star Chamber to have judgment passed upon his case:

> Appleyard ... showed himself a malicious beast, for he did confess he accused my Lord of Leicester only of malice: & that he hath been about it these 3 years & now, because he could not go through with his business to promote, he fell in this rage against my lord & would have accused him of 3 things: 1. of killing his wife. 2. of sending the lord Derby in to Scotland. 3. for letting the queen from marriage. He craved pardon for all these things ... My lord keeper answered that ... in King Henry 7th days,

there was one that lost his ears for slandering the Chief Justice: so as I think his end will be the pillory.

John Appleyard was released and soon faded from the spotlight, only to spectacularly reappear when he raised a rebellion in Norwich in the spring of 1570. He was sentenced to life imprisonment and for the next four years languished in Norwich Castle. In the spring of 1574 Appleyard fell suddenly ill, and in May an order was granted in the queen's name for his removal, to be placed in the house of the Dean of Norwich under house arrest, where he would remain until his death.[10]

It was not long before Amy's death once again began to fade from men's memories.

# Rather yet never had wife than lose them

Although there is no firm evidence that Dudley had any physical relationships with other women in the years following his wife's death, this did not prevent the usual gossip from circulating. The historian William Camden wrote later how Dudley was 'given awhile to women and in his latter days doting above measure on wiving' while other rumours hinted that Dudley paid up to £300 to ladies at court whom he had seduced to keep their silence.

It seemed inconceivable that the most eligible man at court should live a life of celibacy, though for at least a decade after Amy's death, Dudley does not seem to have been interested in seriously pursuing any other woman apart from the queen. Even when his own wife was alive, he had spurned her for the chance to be by Elizabeth's side. As long as he believed that he stood a chance of marrying the queen, Dudley focused solely on winning her hand. The prize was simply too great to allow his desires to wander.

Yet, as his hopes of marriage faded, Dudley began to reassess his situation. Though his devotion and love remained with the queen, it had been over twelve years since his wife Amy had passed away. After numerous failed attempts to further his suit with Elizabeth, he recognised that he would now have to look elsewhere if he was to father his own heir.

Gilbert Talbot, the young son of the Earl of Shrewsbury, had not been at court for long when in May 1573 he wrote to his father and informed him that Dudley 'is very much with her Majesty, and she shows the same great good affection to him that she was wont; of late he has endeavoured to please her more than heretofore'. But Gilbert was shrewd enough to have already picked up some of the court's finer subtleties. In particular, he noticed Dudley's reputation with the other ladies of the court: 'There are two sisters now in the Court that are very far in love with him, as they have been long ... they (of like striving who shall love him better) are at great wars together, and the queen thinketh not well of them, and not the better of him; by this means there are spies over him.'[1]

The two sisters in question were Douglas, aged 29, and Frances, aged

20, the daughters of William Howard, Baron Howard of Effingham.[2] Douglas was the eldest and considered the more beautiful of the two sisters. At the time of Elizabeth's accession, she had been a maid of honour in Elizabeth's court, though she soon left to marry John, Lord Sheffield, in October 1560. Douglas had two children by him, before John died in December 1568. Without any regular source of income, she was forced to return to court as one of the gentlewomen of the Privy Chamber.

It was some time after her husband's death that she began her affair with Dudley, an affair that came to dominate the rest of her life. For years it remained a secret. The only clue to the exact nature of Dudley's relationship with Douglas comes from an undated letter from one 'R.L' to a lady, discovered in the early twentieth century. Its contents reveal how their relationship had begun 'after your widowhood began, upon the first occasion of my coming to you'. Dudley claimed that he had been clear about the terms of their relationship from the start. They might enjoy each other's company, he insisted, but their affair must remain a secret. At first Douglas was content with this arrangement; she was no doubt flattered by the attention that the queen's favourite was paying her, a widow, and seemed happy to slip into the role of mistress, keeping their indiscretions hidden from Elizabeth's eye. She told Dudley that she wanted nothing else from their liaison, 'without any further expectation or hope of other dealing'.

But if Dudley believed that he could continue to enjoy both his position alongside the queen and carry on his illicit relations with one of her gentlewomen, he was mistaken. Douglas soon wanted more: she wanted to marry him. Dudley recoiled in horror, and when Douglas pressed him for an answer, 'a greater strangeness fell out'. Reconciliation followed, before Douglas grew discontented with her situation once more and wrote to Dudley begging him to set out his intentions. In a letter that seems to have been written in response to one of her entreaties, Dudley insisted, 'I have, as you well know, long both loved and liked you and found always that faithful and earnest affection at your hand again that bound me greatly to you. This good will of mine, whatsoever you have thought, hath not changed from that it was at the beginning towards you.'

It was all he could offer, however. Having 'thoroughly weighed and considered both your own and mine estate', Dudley did not believe he could 'proceed to some further degree than is possible for me, without mine utter overthrow'. They both knew the obstacle standing in the way of their union. Nevertheless, Dudley felt the need to spell it out:

> You must think it some marvellous cause, and toucheth my present state very near, that forceth me thus to be cause almost of the ruin of my own house; for there is no likelihood that any of our bodies of mankind like to have heirs; my brother you see long married and not like to have children, it resteth so now in myself; and yet such occasions is there, as partly I have told you or now, as if I should marry I am sure never to have the favour of them that I had rather yet never had wife than lose them, yet is there nothing in the world next that favour that I would not give to be in hope of leaving some children behind me, being now the last of our house.[3]

Dudley's situation was desperate; he wanted a wife and children to continue the house of Dudley, yet he knew Elizabeth would never allow him to marry without forcing him to lose all he had. His greatest concern, he once told the Duke of Norfolk, was that the queen's affection might one day turn 'into anger and enmity against him, which might cause her, womanlike, to undo him'. It was that fear which drove him to remain single all these years, Elizabeth's loyal servant, devoted in body and soul to her service. And yet one line in Dudley's letter to Douglas stands out above the rest: 'I had rather yet never had wife than lose them'. Just as Dudley might ignore Douglas's pleas for marriage, so he had chosen to forget his other marriage, acting as if it had never taken place in order to please his royal mistress. Amy, it seems, had always come second in Dudley's mind. His favour and companionship with Elizabeth was simply too precious to lose.

Instead, Dudley urged Douglas to marry another. Apparently there was a candidate he had in mind, though 'it is not my part to bid you take them,' he told her. 'Only this I will say, that for my sake you have and do refuse as good remedies as are presently in our time to be had. The choice falls not oft[en], and yet I know you may have now of the best.' Dudley's position was final: 'I must this conclude, that the same I was at the beginning the same I am still toward you, and to no other or further end can it be looked for.'

Douglas had one, particularly urgent, reason for getting married so soon. On 7 August 1574, she gave birth to a baby boy, named Robert. The baby could hardly be kept secret and Dudley readily admitted to being the father; he also ensured that the child would brought up in the custody of his cousin John Dudley of Stoke Newington and then in the household of his friend Lord North where he apparently had 'leave to see the said ladie [Douglas]'.[4]

Elizabeth's silence over her favourite's relationship with Douglas is curious. Did she know of Dudley's liaison with Douglas and the pregnancy before the news became public? In May 1574, when Douglas would have been almost six months pregnant, Elizabeth gave Douglas a gown for her elder daughter Elizabeth, which suggests that she was still at court. Whatever the case, Dudley's honesty saved him from the queen's fury. Quick to describe the child as 'the badge of my sin', he made clear that his liaison with Douglas had been a purely physical one, an error of judgment. Perhaps Elizabeth's silence was a sign that she might permit her favourite's lapse this once. She would not be so forgiving a second time.

After the birth of their son, Dudley and Douglas seemed happy to share custody of their boy, though Dudley soon lost interest in Douglas and they drifted apart. This was not to be the end of the story. Years later, during a court case brought by her now adult son Robert, claiming a share of the Dudley inheritance, Douglas swore on oath that Dudley had contracted to marry her in 1571, and later, in 1573, when she discovered that she was pregnant, married her in a secret ceremony, insisting that their marriage be kept a secret: 'For if the Queen should know of it,' Dudley had told her, 'I were undone and disgraced, and cast out of favour for ever.'[5] She testified that she had been married by a clergyman who produced a marriage licence; that Sir Edward Horsey (who by now was conveniently dead) had given her away and that there were seven witnesses to the marriage, including Dudley's Italian doctor Julio Borgarucci. No witnesses, however, were alive thirty years after the event.

Douglas also had new details to reveal about the end of her relationship with Dudley. She recalled how she was visited by Dudley 'in the close arbour of the Queen's garden at Greenwich'. He promised her £700 a year for life, she recalled, if she would renounce and disclaim their marriage. Dudley also offered her £1,000 to deliver their son to Sir Edward Horsey, the captain of the Isle of Wight, 'there to be brought up by him'. When Douglas refused, Dudley flew into a rage and stormed off, 'with protestation not to come any more to her'.[6] It was then, she insisted, that Dudley had attempted to have her poisoned, and 'had some ill potions given her, so that with the loss of her hair and nails, she hardly escaped death'.

Such accusations seem remarkable, coming as they did decades after the events were supposed to have taken place. Could Douglas's story have been correct? Her son Robert was born in August 1574. This would indicate that her pregnancy began in December 1573. Douglas claimed that it was then, 'in the wintertime at night', some time between mid-November and Christmas Day, after she had told Dudley of the news and reminded him of his promise to marry her, that a secret marriage ceremony was performed in her chamber at her family home in Esher.[7] 'The ring, wherewith they were so married,' Douglas later confessed, 'was set with five pointed diamonds, and a table diamond, which had been given to him the said earl [Dudley] by the then Earl of Pembroke's grandfather, upon condition that he should not bestow it upon any but whom he did make his wife.' The Duke of Norfolk, she claimed, had been 'the principal mover of the said marriage', suggesting that the match had been arranged before the duke's execution in 1572. Dudley, 'pretending a fear of the Queen's indignation, in case it should come to her knowledge, made her vow not to reveal it till he gave leave; whereupon all her servants were commanded secrecy therein'.

Douglas's testimony was startling, somewhat fantastical even; by now, giving evidence in front of the court, she was an old woman whose memory could not be fully relied upon. If she were to be believed, there would need to be further proof. Douglas's case was not helped by the fact that she insisted that Dudley's servants had stolen all corroborating evidence of their marriage. The only witnesses Douglas could produce were two women, one Mrs Erisa, who had stayed with her two weeks after she had given birth, and a servant, Magdalen Frodsham. Both testimonies quickly unravelled. Magdalen stated that she had been tracked down by a man named Drury, who offered to write her testimony for her which he 'made her' subscribe to. When she had been first approached, she apparently said 'What would they have me do? I was very young and cannot remember anything.' Her two statements that followed were hardly more encouraging. In the first, Magdalen stated that she had been 19 at the time and had been invited by Douglas to the ceremony; in the second, she now claimed that she had been a small child who had merely wandered into the room at the time of the service.

Mrs Erisa was clearer in her recollection of events. According to her testimony, Magdalen had not even entered Douglas's service until after her child had been born. She had not been present at the supposed ceremony, but Douglas hoped that she would confirm a crucial piece of supporting evidence – that upon hearing of his son's birth, Dudley, while attending the queen's progress in Gloucester, had sent her a letter of congratulations signed, 'Your very loving husband'. Mrs Erisa agreed that she had seen the letter, but could not remember those exact words. She did, however, recall that a month after the boy was born she had travelled down to Cornwall; during the journey she met Dudley at Salisbury by arrangement, where he greeted her saying, 'How do my Lady and my boy?'

None of this was enough to prove anything. The case collapsed and it was ruled that there was no evidence that Dudley had ever married or been betrothed to Douglas. His illegitimate son Robert had no claim of inheritance to his estate. Perhaps the most revealing part of Mrs Erisa's testimony was her recollection of Douglas's 'tears and bitter complaints that Lord Leicester was false to her'. There had been no wedding; only the promise of one, which was something entirely different.[8]

Dudley had never wanted to marry Douglas. Now, with Douglas revealed as his mistress and a bastard son whom he would never be able to claim as his legitimate heir, Dudley would have to abandon her altogether. If he wanted to produce a male heir who might inherit his title and estate, he would have to look elsewhere.

# I may fall many ways

The truth was that Robert Dudley had already set his sights upon another. She was Lettice Knollys, by all reports one of the most beautiful women of Elizabeth's Privy Chamber. Lettice was the eldest daughter of Sir Francis Knollys and his wife Catherine and a distant cousin of the queen. Between 1544 and 1546, her father was Master of the Horse to the young Prince Edward. It is likely that during these years Lettice formed a close relationship with Elizabeth, and may even have remained with her at Hatfield during Mary's reign, when the rest of her family, ardent Protestants, fled into exile at Frankfurt. Upon Elizabeth's accession, Sir Francis was appointed vice-chamberlain of Elizabeth's household, and Catherine made one of the four ladies of the bedchamber. Lettice herself was paid a salary as a gentlewoman of the Privy Chamber.

By 1560, Lettice had left the Privy Chamber to marry Walter Devereux, Viscount Hereford and later Earl of Essex, with whom she had five children. She remained at court, however, where she was linked to Dudley back in 1565, but perhaps too much should not be read into their supposed flirtation, as Lettice would have been heavily pregnant with her son Robert at the time.

Essex was sent to Ireland as commander of the garrison there in the autumn of 1573, and did not return until November 1575. In his absence, rumours began to abound that Lettice and Dudley had grown close. There is some evidence for this. By 1572, Dudley was sending her deer from the chase at Kenilworth as a present, and she is known to have hunted there with her sister in 1574 while her husband was away. She accompanied the queen on her visit to Kenilworth the following year, and once again spent time hunting there on a separate occasion. By this time Lettice may have been estranged from her husband. She had decided not to follow him to Ireland, preferring instead to remain at her home in Chartley. Later, when the earl was on his deathbed, he wrote to Elizabeth begging her to look after his children, but made no mention of Lettice.[1]

It is easy to guess why the earl had fallen out with his wife. Near the end of 1575, the Spanish ambassador reported that it was 'publicly talked about in the streets' that there was a 'great enmity which exists between the Earl of Leicester and the Earl of Essex in consequence, it is said, of the fact that while Essex was in Ireland his wife had two children by Leicester.'[2] The ambassador may not have believed such wild rumours, though he would admit that, 'it being well known that Dudley had seduced his wife,' the pair had certainly fallen out.[3] 'Great discord is expected in consequence'.

Rumours about Dudley's private life continued to circulate, though few were recorded; people were far too cautious for that. The preacher Thomas Wood wrote to Dudley's brother Ambrose in August 1576, warning him of the stories about Dudley's behaviour: 'Many verie ill and dishonourable bruits are spread abroad of my Lord your brother, which I do often hear to my great grief,' he wrote, adding that 'if the rest touching his ungodly life (as the common report goeth) be as true as that before mentioned, God's judgment in the opinion of all godly men without speedy repentence is not far off'.[4]

Ambrose replied that he hoped that whatever the allegation was, it would prove false, though he admitted, 'I must needs confess we be all flesh and blood and frail of nature, therefore to be reformed.'[5] No sooner had he sent his letter than Dudley himself had decided to write to Wood, explaining himself. His letter leaves little doubt that the rumours were true. Whether they concerned his relationship with Lettice or his failed affair with Douglas, Dudley seemed unrepentant. 'I will not justify myself for being a sinner and flesh and blood as others be,' he wrote back:

And beside, I stand on the top of a hill, where I know the smallest slip seemeth a fall. But I will not escuse myself; I may fall many ways and have more witnesses thereof than many others who perhaps be no saints neither, yet their faults less noted though some ways greater than mine. But let not them triumph in that theirs is more covered or that they are not so greatly touched.

As for himself, he recognised that he had his failings, admitting that:

For my faults, I must fly to the merciful God, who I know can and will forgive mine, though they were greater than any earthly man is able to charge me with, as soon as they that think they are most clean in his sight. And for my faults, I say, they lye before him who I have no doubt but will cancel them as I have been and shall be most heartily sorry for them.

Nevertheless, he was sure that many of the rumours charged against him had been stoked up by his enemies. It was only natural, he guessed, given the exclusive position of favour he held with the queen. 'I have many ill willers, and I am none of those that seek hypocritically to make myself popular. I use no indirect instruments nor dealings (I thank God) and thereby lye the more open to all mens' judgments. And he had need be a perfect saint that should escape in any place slanderous tongues.'[6] Yet the 'slanderous tongues' continued to wag. It would soon become difficult for them not to.

Lettice's husband, Essex, returned to court in November, where he remained until summer 1576, returning to Ireland once more. It was widely believed that Dudley had a hand in sending him there. Within weeks he was dead, having succumbed to a mysterious illness, probably dysentery, in Dublin on 22 September. The timing of his death, so soon after his departure for Ireland and amid rumours that Dudley had been courting his wife, was bound to raise suspicions. Letters from Essex written a week before his death did nothing to allay these. It seems he had come down with some form of gastric complaint, which had also affected two other members of his household. 'A disease took me and Hunninges my boy and a third person to whom I drank,' he wrote to a friend, informing him of his deteriorating condition, 'which makes me suspect of some evil received in my drink, for ever since I have been greatly troubled with a flux and vomits, and my page extremely ill also till now of late he is recovered, and I from ill to worse.'

According to another of his servants, the earl was soon passing '20 or 30 stools every day, and is already many times bloody and the rest of his stools burnt black colour'. The medicines of the day had not been of much help; the powdered unicorn's horn he had taken a week after falling ill had only 'made him vomit many times' and despite the advice of the best doctors in Ireland, his only hope was to return home. Essex urged his doctor to meet him on the Welsh shore as soon as he was able to land, with 'all things necessary for this disease', and his servant had been given specific orders to inform the doctor of the earl's fears that he had been poisoned. 'He asks me to say that he doth the more mistrust himself because he is in extreme weakness, and the page that waited on his cup and a third person to whom he drank were all taken after one manner.'[7]

Essex never made the trip to the mainland. An inquiry was held into the circumstances of his death, but it found no evidence of foul play.

The inquiry had, however, been instituted by Sir Henry Sidney, Dudley's brother-in-law, who remained assiduously loyal to Dudley. If, as Essex suspected, he had been poisoned, it would be unsurprising if there were little evidence to show for it.

Almost two years to the date of her husband's death, on 21 September 1578, Dudley married Lettice in secret at Wanstead House in Essex. Marriage had certainly been on Dudley's mind for some time. His friend Lord North, who was present at the marriage ceremony, later recalled how he and Dudley had been 'very conversant ... by the space of this ten or twelve years last past'; on many occasions Dudley had confided in him that 'there was nothing in this life which he more desired than to be joined in marriage with some godly gentlewoman, with whom he might lead his life to the glory of God, the comfort of his soul, and to the faithful service of her Majesty, for whose sake he had hitherto forborne marriage, which long held him doubtful'. When asked which lady he had in mind, Dudley told North about Lettice; North agreed, and 'comforted his lordship therein and heartened him thereto'.[8]

At the time of their wedding, Lettice had recently fulfilled the expected period of mourning for her husband, which she had followed dutifully; there was a portrait of the countess 'in mourning weeds' at Leicester House.[9] She would not contemplate marrying Dudley until this mourning period was over. Lettice's caution was understandable. Her husband had died in suspicious circumstances, and she could have guessed Elizabeth's likely reaction when she eventually found out about the marriage. Lettice therefore continued to lead her former life, living discreetly at her father's home and continuing to style herself the Countess of Essex.

With his marriage to Lettice, Robert Dudley had crossed a breach. He was 46, and, conscious of his ageing years, was determined to start a family and hopefully provide a male heir for his noble house. There was one significant problem still to overcome, but for the moment, Dudley preferred not to dwell upon that. Knowing the queen's likely reaction if she were to discover the truth, he understandably requested his chaplain Humphrey Tyndall keep his marriage secret for now.

Three days later, Elizabeth arrived at Wanstead, the scene of Dudley's marriage ceremony, where she would end her summer progress. Lettice, meanwhile, had managed to slip away quietly, returning to her father's house.[10] A month later, Dudley sat up all night with the queen when she had a particularly painful toothache.[11] There is no indication that she suspected anything.

There could be no turning back. Dudley had taken another wife, and in doing so had forsaken any hope of marrying the queen. This much was certain; what was not, however, was Elizabeth's reaction when she discovered that her favourite had married without her permission.

Dudley must have calculated that there was little point asking. He had already had enough trouble with the queen's capricious nature that year. In the spring he left court to travel to the hot baths at Buxton, a treatment for what seems to have been the early onset of rheumatism. Just weeks into his visit, Dudley received a mysterious letter from Sir Christopher Hatton, urging him to return to court as soon as he could:

> Since your Lordship's departure the Queen is found in continual great melancholy. The cause thereof I can but guess at, notwithstanding that I bear and suffer the whole brunt of her mislike in generality. She dreameth of marriage that might seem injurious to her, making myself to be either the man or a pattern of him. I defend that no man can tie himself or be tied to such inconvenience as not to marry by law of God or man, except by mutual consents, as both parties, the man and woman, vow to marry each to other, which I know she hath not done to any man and therefore by any man's marriage she can receive no wrong, with many more arguments of the best weight I could gather. But, my Lord, I am not the man that should thus suddenly marry, for God knoweth I never meant it. By my next [letter] I think you shall hear more of this matter; I fear it will be found some evil practice ...[12]

Without Dudley by her side, Hatton admitted, the court had become an empty, dull place. 'This court wanteth your presence,' he pleaded. 'Her majesty is unaccompanied and, I assure you, the chambers are almost empty.'[13]

Ten days later, after Dudley had decided to write his own letter to the queen, Hatton replied with more favourable news. Elizabeth had been delighted with Dudley's words, which she had read twice over, 'because they chiefly recorded the testimony of your most loyal disposition from the beginning to this present time ... The Queen rejoiced much in the matter and was pleased to protest that she full well believed it, whatever the malice of the world make of the contrary.'[14] Elizabeth now wished for Dudley to return immediately, since she 'thinketh your absence much drawn in too [great] length', adding that if Dudley's treatment at the spa did not work 'a full, good effect' she would 'never consent that you cumber yourself and her with such long journey again'.

What marriage could Elizabeth possibly have been thinking of? Hatton's words to Dudley, 'I am not the man that should thus suddenly marry' certainly infer that perhaps Elizabeth suspected that Dudley might soon wed. Yet Dudley showed no sign that he believed his relationship with Lettice had been uncovered by the queen. He wrote to Walsingham from his baths at Buxton in June: 'I find great good in this bath already for the swelling you felt in my leg, not by drinking but by going into the bath ... I would fain write to Lord Cobham, but I am pulled away from this, being forbidden to write much, as this day I have to her Majesty and others.'[15] Dudley's reply to Hatton in July also suggests that he too had felt the pains of his absence from Elizabeth. 'I hope now, ere long, to be with you, to enjoy that blessed sight which I have been so long kept from. A few of these days seem many years, and I think I shall feel a worse grief ere I seek so far a remedy again.'

If not Dudley's marriage to Lettice, there was another marriage Elizabeth could have been dreaming of – the prospect of her own.

# No man can tell

'If I were a milkmaid with a pail on my arm, whereby my private person would be little set by,' Elizabeth told Parliament in 1576, 'I would not forsake that poor and single state to match with a monarch.' As the years went by, she had become increasingly content with her single status, and began to draw on her virginity as a source of pride. The cult of 'the Virgin Queen' was born, fuelled by the works of the poet Edmund Spenser who celebrated her as 'the flower of Virgins' who 'no mortal blemish may her blot'.[1]

As perceptions of the queen changed, so too did the ways in which she was portrayed. In a series of pictures of Elizabeth, known as the 'Sieve' portraits, painted between 1579 and 1583, Elizabeth is depicted holding a sieve, a symbol of her virginity. This referred to the story of Tuccia, a Vestal Virgin at Rome, who when she was accused of breaking her vow of virginity, proved herself by filling a sieve from the waters of the River Tiber and carrying it back to the temple of Vesta without spilling a drop. In the portraits, the sieve was also a symbol representing the state: the queen's chastity made her state impenetrable to foreign influence and domination. Once a hindrance, Elizabeth's virginity was now the pride of her nation.

Suitors had come and gone during the intervening years. Much to the Earl of Sussex's annoyance and frustration, Elizabeth finally decided to dismiss Archduke Charles's marriage proposal on the grounds of religion. As far as Sussex was concerned, the dangers that England would face if the queen did not marry far outweighed the imaginary concerns of those who protested against the archduke's Catholicism and who 'put on spectacles to search a scruple under collar of religion to hinder this most godly marriage'.[2] Sussex mentioned no names, but it was obvious that he was referring to Dudley. According to the Spanish ambassador, upon his return Sussex approached Dudley and demanded his support for the archduke's marriage, threatening that 'if he did not fulfil his word and the queen would not agree, in consequence of the views of certain persons, he was determined to publish the names of those who had stood in the way of the match, so that the country might know how he and others had striven to bring it about for the public good and who had prevented it'.[3] Dejected, Sussex had to face the fact that this 'godly marriage' was now unlikely to ever take place. 'When I remember who work in this vineyard,' he complained in a letter to William Cecil, 'I can hardly hope of a good wine year, and then see the more I go on credit the greater is my loss.'[4] Among those toiling in the vineyard, Sussex must have considered, was Dudley himself.

As Elizabeth approached her forties and seemed unlikely ever to have children and produce an heir, fewer suitors came forward. At the same time, Elizabeth could not help but realise that she was becoming dangerously isolated on the international stage. The Pope had issued a papal bull of excommunication against her, *Regnans in Excelsis*, which also encouraged Catholic dissidents to forcibly remove her from her throne by whatever means, even assassination. Several plots against her life would follow. During the early 1570s, after the issuing of the papal bull and the deterioration in relations between England and Spain in the aftermath of the Ridolphi Plot, a serious international conspiracy which had seen the Duke of Norfolk executed for his part in the plot, Elizabeth had been keen to seek an alliance with France. The then Duke of Anjou, shortly to become Henri III of France, had proposed marriage, but the match had broken down once a familiar stalemate ensued over the question of religion, since Elizabeth refused to allow Anjou 'the free exercise' of his Catholic faith.

After the collapse of talks with Henri, attention had turned to the possible marriage of Elizabeth to his brother Francis, Duke of Alençon – whom Elizabeth's new secretary Francis Walsingham had heard was less of a staunch Catholic – with hope that he might 'easily ... be reduced to the knowledge of the truth'. But Alençon was still in his teens, nearly half Elizabeth's age; added to this, he was considerably shorter than Elizabeth, with an incredibly large nose and, as Elizabeth had discovered, had 'great blemish in his face' – scarring from the result of smallpox.

The match seemed doomed from the start; Elizabeth was quick to dismiss it. 'Considering the youngness of the years of the duke of Alençon compared to ours,' she wrote to Walsingham, she could barely take the proposal seriously. She had, however, sent Lord Clinton to France to inspect the duke in person, 'such was the importancy of our own subjects of all estates to have us marry'. Clinton's verdict was not good. He had been impressed with his character, but his appearance was an altogether different matter. 'As to his visage and favour everybody doth declare the same to be far inferior and that specially for the blemishes that the smallpox hath wrought therein so as his young years considered ... we cannot indeed bring our mind to like this offer.'[5] Elizabeth informed Walsingham in July 1572 that, 'specially finding no other great commodity offered to us with him, whereby the absurdity that in general opinion of the world might grow to commend this our choice after so many refusals of others of great worthiness might be counterprised.'[6]

Six years later, in 1578, the marriage negotiations were reopened. Once again, considerations of foreign policy were the driving force behind Elizabeth's overtures, intending to distract Alençon from his military adventures in the Netherlands. Elizabeth was now 45; Alençon was still half her age, yet had matured to a more respectable 22. Predictably, one man stood above all others in his opposition to the match. Robert Dudley had become increasingly concerned about the physical damage that Elizabeth might sustain in attempting to conceive an heir. It was in his mind a danger too great to risk. He was determined to speak to the queen about the dangers of the match: 'I mean not to leave as long as I may have leave and opportunity to put her Majesty in better remembrance of this manner of course which maketh me afraid.' 'The more I love her,' he added in a letter to Francis Walsingham, 'the more fearful am I to see such dangerous ways taken. God of his mercy help all.'[7]

For William Cecil, whose long wait for the queen's marriage had now stretched twenty years, it was a risk worth taking. He admitted that her age, past the menopause for most women, might 'yield occasion to doubt either her conception or her good delivery'. Yet the queen's own doctors had told him otherwise. Despite her age, she had, he wrote, 'no lack of natural functions in those things that properly belong to the procreation of children, but contrariwise by judgment of physicians that know her estate in those things, and by the opinion of women, being most acquainted with her Majesty's body in such things as properly appertain to show probability of her aptness to have children even at this day.' Many women, he added, 'have had and have still, children when they are past the years her Majesty hath'. Perhaps now, with Alençon, the queen might finally marry. The peace of the realm had always relied on Elizabeth marrying 'some person meet for her contentation'; though the choice of husband should, of course, be Elizabeth's own, despite many offers, he recounted wistfully, 'yet none hath taken effect. The very true causes thereof are to be referred to God's will without imputation to any certain known cause.'[8]

Initially, Dudley had been sceptical that the marriage would ever happen. 'For my own opinion,' he told a friend, 'if I should speak according to former disposition, I should hardly believe it will take place.'[9] Yet the marriage negotiations continued throughout late 1578, and on 5 January 1579, Anjou's friend and envoy, Jean de Simier, Baron de St Marc, arrived in England to negotiate the terms for Elizabeth's marriage and pave the way for a visit by Alençon himself. He came armed with 12,000 crowns' worth of jewels as presents for the queen and her advisers. Described by Camden as 'a man of wit and parts, and one thoroughly versed in love-fancies, pleasant conceits and other gallantries', Elizabeth was instantly delighted with the company of this small, chattering man, whom she nicknamed her 'Monkey', from the French word for the animal, *singe*, a pun on the allusion to his name.

Simier brought a form of sophistication to wooing that Elizabeth had not seen before. He stole love trophies from her to send back to his master; on one occasion her handkerchief, on another her nightcap. Opponents of the match condemned this 'unmanlike, unprincelike, French kind of wooing', but Elizabeth was convinced that Simier was genuine. 'He had shown himself faithful to his master, is safe and discreet beyond his years,' she wrote to Walsingham, adding somewhat pointedly, 'we wish we had such a servant of whom we could make such good use.'[10]

Elizabeth seems to have spared little thought for Dudley's feelings. When one of her gentlewomen gently reproached Elizabeth for making Dudley's life a misery with her enthusiasm for a union with Alençon, Elizabeth exploded with rage. 'Dost thou think me so unlike myself and unmindful of my own royal majesty that I would prefer my servant, who I, myself, have raised, before the great Prince of Christendom, in the honour of a husband?' she snapped back.

As Simier's wooing of the queen continued apace, Dudley seems to have been willing to support the negotiations in public, being appointed one of the commissioners to negotiate with Simier. He told the French ambassador Mauvissière in February that he believed that Elizabeth would need to have an interview with Alençon before she could commit to marriage, and expressed a desire for an alliance with France. Otherwise, Dudley's thoughts on the matter are curiously silent. He knew too well not to tempt fate by letting his emotions show. To reveal an opinion on the matter either way might push the volatile queen in precisely the opposite direction. He wrote to Walsingham, advising him:

> You know her disposition as well as I, and yet can I not use but frankness with you ... I would have you, as much as you may, avoid the suspicion of her majesty that you doubt Monsieur's love to her too much, or that you lack devotion enough in you to further her marriage, albeit I promise I think she hath little enough herself to it. But yet, what she would others think and do therein you partly have cause to know ... You have as much as I can learn, for our conference with her majesty about affairs is but seldom and slender ... For this matter in hand for her marriage, there is no man can tell what to say. As yet she hath imparted with no man, at least not with me, nor, for ought I can learn, with any other.[11]

Behind the scenes, Dudley did all he could to frustrate the progress of Alençon's suit. According to the Spanish ambassador, Dudley had even gone so far as to prostrate himself at the queen's feet, begging her not to allow the Frenchman to visit. Alençon's passport to England was granted against Dudley's wishes. 'He is so much offended that he has retired to a house of his five miles away where the Queen has been to see him and where she remained two days because he feigned illness.'[12] The emotional strain upon Elizabeth was plain for all to see. 'She hath deferred three whole days with an extreme regret and many tears before she would subscribe the passport,' one observer wrote, and was only 'induced thereunto and almost forced' by those keen for the marriage to take place and who wished to spite Dudley.[13]

Among those urging Elizabeth to marry was Sussex, whom the Spanish ambassador remarked 'led the dance in order to upset Leicester and deprive him of French support'.[14] Dudley was once again furious with the earl. A 'close friend' of his apparently told the Spanish ambassador that he cursed 'the French and is greatly incensed against Sussex, as are all of Leicester's dependants'.[15]

The marriage proposals had split the Council, and caused the traditional rivalries to erupt once more. Sussex had been quick to favour the match; along with Cecil he saw the marriage as the ideal opportunity to maintain a balance of power against Spain. Dudley and Walsingham, on the other hand, remained distrustful of the Catholic French monarchy, and set on launching a campaign against Spain, wishing for England to stand alone as a Protestant nation against Europe's Catholic powers. Soon the debate over the Anjou marriage had become drawn along religious lines. Catholics, hoping that the marriage would 'result in their being allowed freedom for their faith', had been approached by the French ambassador with a mind to strengthening the match.[16] They included a significant group of covert Catholics and members of the extended Howard family, Lord Henry Howard, Sussex's second cousin, and Sir Edward Stafford, who both wrote tracts in favour of the marriage.[17]

Alençon arrived at Greenwich early in the morning of 17 August and stayed at the court for twelve days. The visit was kept secret from the public, in case of any unwanted hostility, though the evidence was everywhere to be seen at court. Elizabeth's own councillors seemed to have been in denial about it, with many absenting themselves from court in order to avoid meeting the duke.

A week later there was a ball at court. As Elizabeth danced, Alençon stood watching, hidden from behind a tapestry. As the other guests pretended not to notice this courtly game taking place, Elizabeth made playful gestures in his direction. It made a change from her previous courtships where her exchanges had been conducted behind a screen of diplomacy and the bargaining of ambassadors. Elizabeth was enchanted by the duke; his manners and wit quickly made up for any disappointment she might have felt over his appearance, and, if the miniature of him painted by Nicholas Hilliard is to be believed, his supposed pock marks had not disfigured his face. Elizabeth was more than happy to be wooed by her 23-year-old suitor, whom she nicknamed her 'Frog'. 'The Queen is delighted with Alençon and he with her', the Spanish ambassador Mendoza reported back to Philip II, 'she had let out to some of her courtiers, saying that she was pleased to have known him, was much taken with his good parts, and admired him more than any man. She says that for her part she will not stand in the way of his being her husband.' The French ambassador Mauvissière was thrilled and wrote to Catherine de' Medici about her son's visit: 'These loving conferences have lasted eight days.' Elizabeth was 'overcome with love ... she told me she had never found a man whose nature and actions so suited her.'[18]

Dudley was not present for Alençon's visit, having departed the court in late July in protest. The Spanish ambassador Mendoza reported that he was 'in great grief' and 'much put out'. Despite having married Lettice almost a year before, he was determined that if he could not have the queen, no one else would. He instigated a campaign against the match from a distance, and on his return to the Council displayed the full force of his opposition towards the marriage. At an emergency session of the Council to discuss the matter in early October, he stated that he no longer believed that the marriage was the right way forward, and had decided to oppose it owing to 'new reasons'.[19] It seems that Dudley had grown nervous that the marriage had raised the hopes of Catholics that Elizabeth would return to the old faith. Two weeks later, having journeyed to Kenilworth, he wrote to Cecil explaining his fears that 'I do assure your lordship since Queen Mary's time the papists were never in that jollity they be at present in this country.'[20]

It was around this time that Alençon's envoy Simier, about to return to France, realised that Dudley still had the power to destroy his master's chances with Elizabeth. He decided to hit back in a final attempt to save the match. On the eve of his departure from court to return home, he informed the queen of the news that seemed to be open knowledge to everyone except her. Her favourite was married; indeed, he was wed to her cousin and gentlewoman Lettice Knollys.

According to William Camden, Elizabeth was at first incredulous, then furious, growing into 'such a chafe that she commanded Leicester not to stir out of the Palace of Greenwich, and intended to have committed him to the Tower of London'. It was only after the intervention of the Earl of Sussex, 'his greatest and deadliest adversary', that Elizabeth calmed down, the earl reasoning with her that 'no man was to be troubled for lawful marriage, which estate amongst all men hath ever been held in honour and esteem.'[21] In Elizabeth's eyes Dudley had been unfaithful to her. Not only that, but he had married Lettice without her permission. Elizabeth may have had her suspicions, but on hearing the news confirmed, whispered to her by Simier, it must have seemed as if she was the last person at court to be let into the secret.

After facing Elizabeth's wrath, Dudley was immediately banished from court. In a letter to Sir Christopher Hatton, he excused his absence: 'I am not, God knows, to serve her Majesty wherein I may, to the uttermost of my life, but [am] most unfit at this time to make repair to that place where so many eyes are witnesses of my open and great disgraces delivered from her majesty's mouth.'[22] He further wrote to Cecil, excusing his absence from the Council table that day. 'I perceive by my brother Warwick your Lordship hath found the like bitterness in her Majesty towards me in that others (too many) have lately acquainted me withal.' He reflected how Elizabeth had 'grown into a very strange humour, all things considered, towards me, howsoever it were true or false as she is informed, the state whereof I will not dispute'.

Dudley knew that he had been cornered; there was little that he could do to repair the damage. He remained resolved against the French marriage, he wrote, but did not want to 'be suspected a hinderer of that matter which all the world desired and were suitors for'. He had offered to go into exile, 'for avoiding such blame as I have, generally, in the realm', a statement reminiscent of a later pledge, written from Antwerp in 1582, in which Dudley recognised there could be no place for him in England if the Anjou marriage went ahead, so he had 'procured a place in Germany, to dwell there, should the marriage take place'. He ended with words filled with frustration and despair, perhaps the most heartfelt he ever wrote:

> I carried myself almost more than a bondman many a year together, so long as one drop of comfort was left of any hope, as you yourself, my Lord, do know. So being acquitted and delivered of that hope, by both open and private protestation and declaration discharged, methinks it is more than hard to take such an occasion, to bear so great displeasure for ... So may I say, I have lost both youth, liberty, and all my time reposed in her, and, my Lord, by the time I have made an even reckoning with the world, your Lordship will not give me much for my 20 years' service; but I trust she that hath been so gracious to all, will not only be gracious to me ... [23]

Dudley had been genuinely taken aback by the ferocity of the queen's reaction to his marriage, yet Elizabeth's scorn extended beyond words. She caused Dudley serious financial problems by recalling a loan of £5,000 she had made to him three years earlier. Between December and January he drew up a list of lands that he planned to assign to friends and family as a way of raising money. [24]

Dudley's problems were to continue for months. The Spanish ambassador wrote in February 1580 how Elizabeth was still 'not showing so much favour as formerly to the Earl of Leicester': 'The French ambassador had high words with Leicester the other day about his trying to persuade him to confess to the Queen that he was married, as Simier and the ambassador had assured her.'[25] And as late as July 1580, Dudley wrote to Cecil apologising for his absence at court, which he put down to the removal of 'her majesty's wonted favour'.[26]

# Your old patient

Elizabeth's anger towards Dudley flared up again only a few months after she heard the news of his marriage to Lettice. For in February 1580 she discovered that Douglas Sheffield had again secretly married, this time to Edward Stafford, on the eve of his departure on a mission to France.

Somehow, Elizabeth was convinced that Dudley and Douglas had already married, thereby annulling not only Dudley's recent marriage to Lettice, but also making Douglas's marriage to Edward Stafford a bigamous one. Stafford was summoned back from France for an urgent interview with the queen. It soon became obvious why he had been called back. Forcing him to admit that he had married Douglas in secret, Elizabeth then stunned Stafford by claiming that she had evidence that Douglas was already married to Dudley. She promised him that if he renounced his bride 'she would better the estate of the Staffords', but Stafford defended his wife and assured the queen that he would find out the truth from her in person.

Elizabeth remained determined that there should be an investigation into whether Dudley had indeed married Douglas. If there was evidence of a binding contract then 'he should make up her honour with a marriage, or rot in the Tower!' she exclaimed. Sussex took the role of examiner, interrogating Douglas in detail over the exact nature of her relationship with Dudley. Yet there was nothing, for no documentary proof could be found that any such union had ever taken place. Under pressure, Douglas broke out weeping, exclaiming that she had trusted Dudley 'too much to have anything to show, to constrain him to marry her'.[1]

Douglas's confession seems to have drawn a line under this particular crisis for Dudley, yet it did not stop Elizabeth throwing herself into her own marriage proposals with abandon. 'The affair of Monsieur takes greater foot than was looked for and receiveth no small furtherance,' Walsingham wrote, disheartened.[2] Other members of the Council were also having doubts about the marriage. Sir Ralph Sadler believed that

Elizabeth was too old to bear a child; she would suffer from her husband's neglect as a result, when Alençon would be 'in his best lust and flourishing age'.[3] In the end, only four councillors approved the match. Fearful of confronting the queen with the result of their deliberations, they simply wrote to Elizabeth with the ambiguous formula: 'if she will show to us any inclination of her mind, we will so proceed as all her honour shall be preserved, and whatsoever may seem burdensome, we will bear it with common consent'.[4] This was not what Elizabeth had wanted to hear. She had expected to have their undivided support; anything less might risk future faction and division if she went ahead with the match.

Elizabeth eventually resigned herself to ending the match altogether. Not long after she wrote to Alençon, informing him of her decision. It would be better, she said, if they were to remain 'faithful friends'.

> You realise, my dearest, that the greatest difficulties lie in making our people rejoice and approve. The public practice of the Roman Religion so sticks in their hearts. I beg you to consider this deeply, as a matter which is so hard for Englishmen to bear that it passes all imagination. For my part I confess there is no prince in the world to whom I think myself more bound, nor with whom I would rather pass the years of my life, both for your rare virtues and sweet nature.

She ended: 'with my commendations to my dearest Frog.'[5]

The Anjou marriage continued to dominate Elizabeth's foreign affairs until Anjou's death in June 1584, mainly since marriage, as usual, was crucial for strengthening a French alliance over Spain. But as the queen grew older, it was clear that she was simply buying time, using the prospect of marriage as bait for the French. Alençon remained her 'Frog'; Elizabeth seems to have been genuinely fond of him and they continued their correspondence. He came to visit again in 1581, staying for three months. Elizabeth gave further promises that she would marry, going so far as to kiss her prince on the lips and place a ring on his finger declaring that Alençon 'will be my husband'. When the news leaked out, Hatton pleaded with tears in his eyes that her people would never forgive her if she did marry. Dudley, too, was horrified. 'So great appearance of mislike is there in her majesty's heart,' he wrote to the Earl of Huntingdon when the final negotiations were taking place in the spring of 1581, 'as assuredly I can neither account him loving nor loyal that will indirectly seek to press her to it.'[6] In a moment of fear, he went so far as to ask Elizabeth whether she was still a virgin; was she a woman or a maid? Elizabeth answered calmly. Nothing she had said could not be unsaid. The following day she broke everything off.

When Alençon departed, Elizabeth told him that she would easily give a million pounds to see her 'Frog' swimming in the Thames again. Privately, she knew that the affair had run its course. She also knew that her final chance to marry had slipped away. She would face the rest of her reign alone. As Alençon prepared to sail, she sat at her desk to write a sonnet 'On Monsieur's Departure', expressing her sorrow:

> I grieve and dare not show my discontent;
> I love, and yet am forced to seem to hate;
> I do, yet dare not say I ever meant;
> I seem stark mute, but inwardly do prate.
> > I am, and not; I freeze and yet am burned,
> > Since from myself another self I turned.
>
> My care is like my shadow in the sun –
> Follows me flying, flies when I pursue it,
> Stands, and lies by me, doth what I have done;
> His too familiar care doth make me rue it.
> > No means I find to rid him from my breast,
> > Till by the end of things it be supprest.
>
> Some gentler passion slide into my mind,
> For I am soft, and made of melting snow;
> Or be more cruel, Love, and so be kind.
> Let me or float or sink, be high or low;
> > Or let me live with some more sweet content,
> > Or die, and so forget what love e'er meant.[7]

Two years later Alençon was dead from fever. Elizabeth was inconsolable; wiping away her tears, she wrote to his mother, Catherine de' Medici, giving expression to her grief:

Although you were his mother, you have several other children, but for myself I find no consolation, if it be not death in which I hope we shall be reunited. Madame, if you could see the image of my heart you would see there the picture of a body without a soul, but I will not trouble you with sorrows for you have too many of your own. I will turn a great part

of my love for him to the King my good brother and you, assuring you
that you will find me the most faithful daughter and sister that ever Princes
had.[8]

Robert Dudley knew that his marriage to Lettice would permanently
change his relationship with Elizabeth. They had become mutually
dependent on each other, with none of the affectionate displays that had
so scandalised the court in previous years gone by. Youth had deserted
them both; they were now both approaching their fifties, and there was
no longer any chance that Elizabeth might bear a child. Cecil still clung
to the forlorn hope that a Protestant succession might be secured and
that the queen might yet be fertile enough to produce an heir. The royal
doctors promised him that it would still be possible from a medical point
of view. But the danger of childbirth to the queen's own life suggested
otherwise.

Dudley's presents to the queen at New Year began to lose their usual
personal touch; though they still remained the most costly on the list of
presents given to Elizabeth, they were far less ostentatious – by 1578 only
a clock set in gold. Dudley's letters to the queen, while still frequent,
never regained their earlier intimacy. Those that survive are full of
devotion, and though Dudley remained her 'OO', the letters seem more
formal and somewhat more stilted than before:

> Your poor OO has no other way but prayer to offer for recompense, and
> that is that God will long, safely, healthfully, and most happily preserve
> you here among us, and as He hath begun, so to continue in discovering
> and overthrowing all unloyal hearts towards you ... I will never doubt His
> defending you, and overthrowing all mischievous devices against you.
> I have too boldly troubled you thus far, but your wonted goodness, to
> your OO only joy and comfort, makes them keep the old manner.[9]

In another, he wrote how his heart was 'bound to remain more desirous
than able to serve you'. He had written from 'your old lodging in the
Castle of Kenilworth, where you are daily prayed for and most often
wished to be', but to which Elizabeth would never return.

Dudley continued to be a beneficiary of the queen's favour, financially
at least. In June 1580 he was made Keeper of the New Forest, and by 1584
he had been made Lord Steward, one of the most prestigious offices of
the household that Elizabeth had refused to fill after the death of the

previous incumbent, the Earl of Pembroke. Dudley was, he acknowledged to Elizabeth, 'your old patient ... ready to yield sacrifice for your service, as it has from you received all good things'.

He remained by Elizabeth's side, but more as a close friend and trusted adviser. On occasion, in moments of weakness or of panic, often surfacing during a bout of illness, Elizabeth demanded the pressence of her old favourite. He was her lifelong companion whom she could not do without. 'I find her Majesty very desirous to stay me,' Dudley wrote to Walsingham in September 1585. 'She makes the case only the doubtfulness of her own self, by reason of her often disease taking her of late, and this night worst of all. She used very pitiful words to me of her fear she shall not live and would not have me from her. You can consider what manner of persuasion this must be to me from her.'[10]

Despite the many letters of Dudley's to the queen that still exist, only one of Elizabeth's to him is known to have survived. Written in 1586, it gives a sense of the relaxed, chatty style that must have pervaded their conversation:

> Rob: I am afraid you will suppose by my wandering writings that a midsummer moon hath taken large possession of my brains this month, but you must needs take things as they come in my head, though order be left behind me ... I will end that do imagine I talk still with you and therefore loathly say farewell OO though ever I pray God bless you from all harm and save you from all foes with my million and legion of thanks for all your pains and cares. As you know, ever the same, E. R.[11]

There were new favourites at court to flatter the queen. Dudley might grow old (his receding hairline, greying temples and beard a sign of his age – he turned 52 in 1584), but Elizabeth was determined to remain young for ever. No matter that her hair had long fallen out and was now replaced by a red wig or that her teeth were rotted and black; she would continue her dalliances with fresher, younger men, whose strong physique caught her eye, just as Dudley's had done twenty-five years before.

When her godson, Sir John Harington – upon whom the queen had long cast an indulgent eye – visited her at court, she complimented him upon his tight clothing: 'The Queen loveth to see me in my last frieze jerkin,' he reported, 'and saith "'Tis well cut".' Another particular teenager whom she noticed was Robert Devereux, the 2nd Earl of Essex, Lettice's eldest child with her first husband and now Dudley's stepson.

Eighteen years old, he was tall and powerfully built, with a high forehead and large eyes, a straight nose and a shock of russet hair. Dudley knew that Elizabeth would be enchanted with him, and seems to have brought the boy to court in an effort to counter the influence of another popular favourite of the queen's, Sir Walter Raleigh. Slightly bemused by Elizabeth's attention, Essex wrote to Dudley, who had temporarily left the court, informing him that 'Since your Lordship's departure her majesty hath been earnest with me to lie in the court and this morning she sent to me that I might lie in your Lordship's lodging, which I will forebear till I know your Lordship's pleasure, except the Queen force me to it.'[12]

Elizabeth may have been taken with the young Earl of Essex, but she could never forgive his mother Lettice, reviling her as a 'she wolf' who had taken her Robert away from her.[13] One story recounts how, when Lettice returned to court wearing fine robes, Elizabeth stormed up to her, boxed her ears and screamed that 'as but one sun lights the East, so I shall have but one queen in England'. The countess slowly came to play an important part in Dudley's life, especially after the birth of their son and heir, Robert Dudley, Baron Denbigh, in June 1581. Elizabeth resented Lettice's influence over her favourite, particularly when she came to live openly and in permanent residence with him at Leicester House, an affront to the queen who, according to one report, revealed her anger to Dudley 'about his marriage, for he opened the same more plainly than ever before'.[14]

Three years later, tragedy struck the couple. In July 1584, after a few days' sickness, their son died. Dudley was devastated, a broken man. His 'Noble Imp', as he called him, was gone. 'The afflictions I have suffered may satisfy such as are offended,' he wrote to Sir Christopher Hatton, 'at least appease their long hard conceits ... I beseech ... God to grant me patience in all these worldly things, and to forgive the negligences of my former time, that have not been more careful to please Him, but have run the race of the world.'[15] Even Elizabeth was able to feel some sense of sorrow at Dudley's loss. 'I have told her Majesty of this unfortunate and untimely cause,' Hatton wrote to him, 'whereof I assure your Lordship I find her very sorry, and wisheth your comfort even from the bottom of her heart.'[16]

It was of small consolation. Dudley and Lettice would have no more children. The countess was approaching 44; she was, in the words of the French ambassador, 'fort agee'.[17] Dudley left the court immediately, 'to comfort my sorrowful wife for the loss of my only little son'. He wrote to Cecil from his home at Wanstead, thanking him 'that it pleased you so friendly and honourably to deal in behalf of my poor wife. For truly, my Lord, in all reason, she is hardly dealt with; God only must help it with her Majesty.'

Two months later, Dudley was faced with another, very different, crisis.

# Leicester's Commonwealth

'My very good Lord,' Francis Walsingham wrote to Dudley on 29 September 1584, 'Yesterday I received from the Lord Mayor enclosed in a letter a printed libel against your Lordship, the most malicious-written thing that ever was penned since the beginning of the world.'[1]

The printed work had come straight off a secret press in Paris or Antwerp. Bound in green leather covers, it had been given the lengthy title *The Copy of a Letter Written by a Master of Art of Cambridge to his friend in London, concerning some talk passed of late between two worshipful and grave men about the present state, and some proceedings of the Earl of Leicester and his friends in England*. When it was finally reprinted in 1641, it was given the catchier title of *Leicester's Commonwealth*.

The work had been written in the form of a conversation between a London gentleman, a Catholic lawyer and a Cambridge academic about to embark on a career at the Inns of Court. The fact that all three were presented as being sympathetic to the late Duke of Norfolk, at the same time as favouring the Duke of Alençon's proposed marriage to Elizabeth, might suggest that the tract had Catholic leanings, though the three characters had also been chosen to present a balanced set of opinions, representing the views of educated and loyal subjects who were neither religious extremists nor radicals. Even the Catholic lawyer 'with such moderation and duty towards his prince' rejected any form of resistance to the queen.

As they begin their dialogue, the three figures discuss the nature of treason, blaming both extreme Protestants as well as Catholics for their willingness to serve a higher authority than their monarch. Instead, men of moderation should join together to fight extremism in all its forms, they argue, urging that co-operation and toleration exist on both sides. This much agreed, the conversation takes an entirely different turn. All three are in accord: the greed of Elizabeth's favourites at court, 'great falcons of the field', were determined to prevent religious peace and unity. Chief amongst these, they argue, was Robert Dudley, 'the greatest enemy that the land doth nourish'. Dudley comes under particular attack not only for his influence over the queen, but for his desire to enrich his own power at court:

> What meaneth his so diligent besieging of the prince's person? His taking up the ways and passages about her? His insolency in court? His singularity in Council? His violent preparation of strength abroad? His enriching of his accomplices? The banding [together] of his faction, with the abundance of friends everywhere? What do these signify ... but only his intent and purpose of supremacy? What did the same things portend in times past in his father but even that which now they portend in the son.[2]

The rest of the tract was nothing less than a savage personal libel against Dudley, the nature of which can be detected in the subtitle of the French version that was soon circulating on the Continent: *A Discourse on the abominable life, plots, treasons, murders, falsehoods, poisonings, lusts, incitements and evil stratagems employed by Lord Leicester*. Not only was the familiar territory of Dudley's traitorous ancestors once again raked over (he was 'noble only in two descents, both stained with the block'), its portrait of Dudley as an arch-Machiavellian conspirator, determined to succeed at all costs, was truly shocking.

Among the many accusations that abound within its pages, the most lurid focused upon Dudley's relationships with women and his supposedly voracious sexual appetite. The author of the tract was convinced that 'no man's wife can be free from him whom his fiery lust liketh to abuse ... kinswoman, ally, friend's wife or daughter, or whatsoever female sort besides doth please his eye ... must yield to his desire.' There were not two single noblewomen who attended upon the queen, it was alleged, 'whom he hath not solicited'.[3] Dudley was even accused of paying £300 for sex with one of the queen's gentlewomen, and the death of Dudley's son and heir was held up as a sign of God's vengeance upon him: 'The children of adulterers shall be consumed and the seed of a wicked bed shall be rooted out.'

Dudley's relationships with both Douglas Sheffield and Lettice Knollys, women dubbed in the tract 'his Old and New Testaments', are given extended coverage. It explained how Dudley had gone to extreme lengths to cover up his relationship with Lettice, hiding it from the queen by sending her 'up and down the house, by privy ways, thereby to avoid the sight and knowledge of the Queen's Majesty. And albeit he had not only used her as his good liking before, for the satisfying of his own lust, but also married and remarried her for the contention of his friends'. Lettice was accused of falling pregnant with Dudley's child before her husband had died, 'which she was enforced to make away with, cruelly and unnaturally'.

The whole question of Dudley's supposed marriage to Douglas Sheffield was also brought up. 'Though it was surely done as bed and Bible could make the same,' Dudley had left Douglas for Lettice, having been 'content to assign to the former a thousand pounds with other petty considerations (the pitifullest abused that ever was poor lady) and so betake his limbs to the latter.' Douglas, according to the tract, had been under the false impression that Dudley had given her his word that he would one day marry her, and had been deceived by his wiles. 'And for this cause he hath his terms and pretences, I warrant you, of contracts, precontracts, postcontracts, protracts and retracts.'[4]

Even more serious accusations followed. After establishing Dudley as a serial adulterer, he was then portrayed as a murderer, bent on removing anyone who happened to cross his path. 'His Lordship has a special fortune that when he desireth any woman's favour, then what person so ever standeth in his way, hath the luck to die quickly for the finishing of his desire.' In the mind of the tract's author, Dudley's part in the deaths of the husbands of both Douglas and Lettice, Lord Sheffield and the Earl of Essex, was beyond doubt. A number of recent deaths, including the Earl of Sussex and Sir Nicholas Throckmorton, who had been taken ill at Dudley's home after eating a salad, were also blamed upon Dudley, who was portrayed as a 'great poisoner' who employed 'cunning men' who supplied him with 'secret poisons' that he had used to end their lives.

Of course there was one death that the author of *Leicester's Commonwealth* could hardly ignore. Twenty-four years had passed since Amy's suspicious death at Cumnor Place. If Amy had lived, she would have been 52. William Cecil had been proved right. Robert Dudley did indeed remain 'infamed' by his wife's death, the memory of which seemed determined never to fade. Now, in the pages of *Leicester's Commonwealth*, were new details and accusations about how Amy had met her death that fateful afternoon in September 1560. And, for the first time, a direct charge was made against Dudley, naming him as a conspirator in his wife's death – or rather her murder.

'His Lordship changeth wives and minions, by killing the one,' the tract alleged. When Dudley 'was in full hope to marry her Majesty, and his own wife stood in his light, as he supposed ... he did but send her aside to the house of his servant Forster of Cumnor by Oxford.' It was here that Amy 'had the chance to fall from a pair of stairs, and so to break her neck, but yet without hurting of her hood that stood upon her head'.

But, according to *Leicester's Commonwealth*, Amy's death was no accident. Dudley's friend and associate Sir Richard Verney had been commanded to remain with Amy 'that day alone, with one man only'. It was Verney who had 'sent away perforce all her servants from her, to a market two miles off'. The author of the tract was certain that if one person knew how Amy had met her death, Verney did. 'He (I say) with his man can tell how she died.' Sir Richard Verney's servant, who had been with him on the day of Amy's death, was another, but he was no longer alive to tell his story. A few years later he had apparently been arrested 'for a felony in the marches of Wales' where he had offered 'to publish the manner of the said murder'. It was to cost him his life. Before he had the chance to make his confession, he 'was made away privily in the prison'. Not long afterwards, Verney was on his deathbed in London where, crying out 'piteously, and blasphemed God', he turned to the attendant priest and told him everything. 'All the Devils in Hell did tear him in pieces,' he said, racked with guilt over his part in Amy's death. In addition, there was another person, a lady who had been part of Amy's household at Cumnor, 'the wife also of Bald Butler, kinsman to my Lord' who knew what had taken place, and 'gave out the whole fact a little before her death'.

According to the tract, it was Dudley who had instructed Verney to 'first attempt to kill her by poison, and if that took not place then by any other way to dispatch her, howsoever'. The tract's author claimed to have proof backing his accusations, from the highest possible authorities. Indeed, it was alleged that no less than the then current Professor of Physic at Oxford, Dr Walter Bayly of New College, would be able to back up these assertions.

As a young man, Bayly had apparently attended on Amy during her illness. When Dudley's men saw that Amy was 'sad and heavy', they began to persuade her that she was suffering from an 'abundance of Melancholy and other humours', which might be cured, if only she would 'take some potion'. This Amy absolutely refused to do. She had grown nervous that her death was being planned, as she 'well knew by her other handling'. There was little chance that she was going to take any medicines given to her by her husband's men, 'suspecting still the worst'. Dudley's men, however, had devised a means of getting around her hesitation. Making contact with Walter Bayly without Amy's knowledge, it was arranged for the doctor to visit Amy to diagnose her condition, when he might desire her 'to take some little potion at his hands'. Once the prescription had been given, Dudley's men would 'send to fetch the same at Oxford'.

Born in 1529, when Walter Bayly would have been in his early thirties. He had been educated at Winchester before attending New College, Oxford, in 1548 to read medicine. He excelled as a student, and was quickly made a fellow of the college two years later in 1550, taking his BA in 1552. This was followed by an MA in 1556, and he was admitted as a doctor to practise medicine on 21 February 1559. At the time he came to be involved in Amy's case, Walter Bayly would have only just begun working as a doctor a few months beforehand. Perhaps whoever approached Bayly considered that, as an ambitious young man starting out his career in medicine, he might be impressionable enough to comply with their demands.

They were to be mistaken. After he paid a visit to Amy, Bayly began to grow suspicious. By his own diagnosis, Amy had 'small need' of 'physic', and yet Dudley's men seemed unusually keen to make sure that she was provided with medicine – too keen in fact. 'Seeing their great importunity', Bayly suspected that something was not right. He flatly refused their requests for any medication or potions, 'misdoubting (as he after reported) least if they had poisoned her under the name of his Potion: he might after have been hanged for a cover of their sin'.

That same year, Bayly resigned his fellowship of New College. The coincidence of the timing, in the months before or after Amy's death, should not be viewed too suspiciously however. He had recently married, which might explain his decision to leave his post. It was certainly not accompanied by any mark of disgrace; a promotion soon followed in 1561, and Bayly was elevated to the position of the Queen's Professor of Medicine at the university.

It was in this capacity that, five years later, when Elizabeth visited Oxford in person in September 1566, Bayly took part in a mock disputation in the university church – the same church where Amy's body had been interred back in October 1560. There, sitting in the front pews alongside Dudley, Elizabeth listened to the arguments set out intently and 'gave very attent care unto them', remaining in her seat 'until the full end thereof' – no less than five hours, from 2 o'clock until 7 o'clock in the evening. It must have been on this occasion also that the author of *Leicester's Commonwealth* was present to hear Bayly speak, as a passage in the tract reveals:

> For I heard him once myself in a public act in Oxford (and that in the presence of Leicester, if I be not deceived) maintain that poison might be so tempered and given as it should not appear presently, and yet should kill the party afterward at which time it should be appointed.[5]

By the time *Leicester's Commonwealth* was published, Walter Bayly was a respected figure at court, whose friends included the Countess of Hertford and Lady Dacre, to both of whom he sent copies of his books. He also sent a copy of his treatise on eyesight to Francis Walsingham, who may have been another patient of his. Bayly was certainly very familiar with Robert Dudley, having been his doctor for several years previously. He had entered Dudley's service in the 1570s, if not before. His medical advice was increasingly required to treat Dudley's health complaints, probably rheumatism, which was alleviated by taking the waters at the hot spa at Buxton in the Peak District. Bayly accompanied Dudley there for three consecutive summers, with Dudley writing back to Sir Christopher Hatton on one occasion in May 1578 to inform him that Bayly had been keeping him in hand and had advised him to stay longer 'because the late hot weather had returned again'.

When later that year Elizabeth was found to be suffering from an extreme bout of toothache, it was Dudley who recommended Bayly to her. His advice was well received, and he was sent along with Dr John Dee to Frankfurt to consult with German physicians on the Queen's condition. When Elizabeth's toothache eventually did clear up, Bayly was rewarded with a twenty-one-year lease on land in Stanfield, worth £21 per annum, and three years later in December 1581, Elizabeth appointed Bayly as 'one of her physicians in ordinary', one of her personal attendant doctors.

The appointment provided Bayly with the recognition and prestige he had long sought. The same year he was made a fellow of the prestigious College of Physicians. He quickly moved up through the ranks of the institution. His growing influence was matched by a professional confidence that witnessed him publish three books in three years, in 1586, 1587 and 1588, including 'A Brief Treatise on the Eyesight' and 'A Short Discourse on the Three Kinds of Pepper'. Bayly's treatment for curing bad eyesight included 'the washing of the eyes with the urine of a childe and sometimes a drop the same into the eyes'; if this was not sufficient, patients might wish to try 'the liquor of the liver of a goat'. One of his recipes survives in a manuscript at the British Library. Intending to cure one 'who had an inveterate consumption of the lungs', the ingredients included a camomile ointment for the breast, 'an electuarie' to help digestion 'and break the wynd' and a form of linctus for 'flegme and shortnesse of breath.' 'It shall be good that you boil in water or small ale these herbs', Bayly recommended, listing hyssop, liquorice and aniseed, 'a handful of great raisins', six figs and husked barley. 'Boil these in water or small ale ... and at the end put a little cinnamon to it & sweeten it with sugar; or if you boil it in water draw almonds with it, & you may drink hereof in the morning fasting.'[6]

Medical success eventually made Bayly a wealthy man. By 1590, aged 61, he finally felt able to purchase a significant landed estate, paying £715 9s 4½d for lands from the queen. He died in March 1592. He was buried in the antechapel of New College, Oxford, where his monumental brass still survives. It records how 'his fame soon brought him to the fore; and then the Queen Elizabeth, she called him to her court that there, to her physicians she might add him too'.[7] Yet the date of his death also reminds us that Walter Bayly was still very much alive at the time of the publication of *Leicester's Commonwealth* and its accusations naming him and his, albeit entirely innocent, role in the months leading up to Amy's death. If he so chose, he could have easily denied them. As far as we can tell, he did not.

# The scar remains

On its publication *Leicester's Commonwealth* was immediately denounced. By October 1584, in a highly unusual move, Elizabeth herself went out of her way to defend her favourite and issued a proclamation against the work, ordering all copies to be surrendered. Amnesty was offered to anyone who instantly submitted their copies to the authorities; otherwise they risked imprisonment.

It made little difference. Despite these strict measures, the tract became something of a clandestine bestseller, shifting more copies in manuscript – harder to detect than the printed works – than the thousand copies of the first edition that were swiftly impounded. By April 1585, it became the topic of jokes at court, while a copy of the tract was even able to be smuggled without detection into the Tower for a prisoner to read.[1]

In June, Elizabeth issued another proclamation dealing specifically with *Leicester's Commonwealth*, in a further attempt to suppress the work. She blamed the 'great negligence and remissness' of the authorities in London, 'where it was likely these books would be chiefly cast abroad,' for not doing enough to enact her initial proclamation.

> The very same and divers other such like most slanderous, shameful, and devilish books and libels have been continually spread abroad and kept by disobedient persons, to the manifest contempt of her Majesty's regal and sovereign authority, and namely, among the rest, one most infamous containing slanderous and hateful matter against our very good Lord the Earl of Leicester, one of her principal noblemen and Chief Counsellor of State, of which most malicious and wicked imputations, her Majesty in her own clear knowledge doth declare and testify his innocence to all the world.

She added that, before God, she knew in her conscience 'in assured certainty, the libels and books against the said Earl, to be most malicious, false and slanderous, and such as none but the devil himself could deem to be true'. She judged that the accusations were not merely an attack on Dudley, but on her own 'princely government', 'as though her Majesty should have failed in good judgment and discretion in the choice of so principal a counselor about her, or be without taste or case of all justice and conscience in suffering such heinous and monstrous crimes (as by the said libels and books be infamously imputed) to have passed unpunished'.[2]

Despite its outrageous and highly damaging contents, in public Dudley seems to have kept silent about the publication of the work. Privately, he was furious and sought to punish the author of the tract as quickly as he possibly could. Soon, however, he resigned himself to the fact that such libels were to be expected, given his prominent position at court. 'In these dangerous days,' he wrote in August 1584 to a friend, 'who can escape lewd or lying tongues? For my part I trust the Lord will give me His grace to live in His fear, and to behave myself faithfully to my sovereign and honestly to the world. And so shall I pass over these calumniations.' It was perhaps for this reason that Thomas Lupton wrote a short tract entitled *Of Virtuous Life* in praise of his patron Dudley, to whom he sent the work asking for the queen's permission for publication, 'thereby your kindled flame will give such a light that many shall see themselves much deceived, your enemies amazed and so ashamed, your lovers and friends thereby much rejoiced, and slanderers' reports ... be clean banished'.[3]

Instead it was left to his loyal nephew Sir Philip Sidney, the son of his sister Mary, to defend his uncle and the family name. Sidney was proud of his ancestry, and though his surname was that of his father Sir Henry Sidney, he believed that 'my chiefest honour is to be a Dudley'. There had been no more faithful servant to the queen than his uncle Robert: 'The Earl's mind hath ever been to serve only and truly, setting aside all hopes, all fears, his Mistress ... having restored his overthrown house, and brought him to this case.' The tract was, he believed, 'so full of horrible villainies as no good heart will think possible to enter into any creature, much less to be likely in so noble and well known a man as he is'.

As for the allegations contained within it, Sidney dismissed them as mere tittle-tattle. 'What is it else, but such a bundle of railings, as if it came from the mouth of some half-drunken scold in a tavern, not regarding while evil were spoken ... dissimulation, hypocrisy, adultery, falsehood, treachery, poison, rebellion, treason, cowardice, atheism.'

There was no proof to back up any of the charges, he insisted; perhaps referring to the mention of Dr Bayly's testimony concerning the events leading up to Amy's death, he believed the author of the work had been foolish in 'bringing persons yet alive to speak things which, they are ready to depose upon their salvation, never came into their thought'. Of course he knew that in these circumstances, the truth was irrelevant. The writer's purpose had been to 'backbite boldly so that, though the bite were healed, yet the scar would remain'.

Sidney was ready to defend his uncle against any charge. He issued a challenge that, if the author would come forward and name himself in the next three months, he would travel across the Continent to meet him to defend Dudley's honour. 'Thou therein liest in thy throat, which I will be ready to justify upon thee, in any place of Europe.'[4] No one came forward. Who could the anonymous writer of *Leicester's Commonwealth* have been? And where had he gained his information, especially the revelations that Robert Dudley had ordered the murder of his wife?

Sir Francis Walsingham was at first convinced that the writer must have been 'Morgan the Queen of Scots' agent in France'. Dudley, too, was quick to believe that Mary had been behind the work, telling a friend that he intended to 'persecute' her 'to the uttermost, for that he supposeth your Majesty to be privy to the setting forth of the book against him'.[5] This was an easy conclusion to reach. Hot off a secret press based at Paris or Antwerp, we know that the book was promoted by the Jesuit Robert Parsons (the book itself, with its green bindings and cover, quickly became known as 'Father Parsons' Greencoat'), as part of a Catholic propaganda attack to vilify Elizabeth, countering the hundreds of Protestant tracts that had already castigated the crimes and sins of Mary Stuart.

But Parsons had been involved merely in distributing and organising the printing of the work. When, fifteen years later, he was accused of having written *Leicester's Commonwealth* himself he denied it. In his defence, Parsons stated that the book 'is believed to have been due to a combined effort, a number of Catholics having had a part in it, but chiefly Charles Arundell, a nobleman who had recently come to Paris from England and who was extremely hostile to the Earl.'[6] Parsons was right, as Walsingham's investigations were to prove. His finest agent, Thomas Rogers, had tracked down the location of a thousand copies of the tract at a printer's in Rouen. The crucial breakthough came when, having won the confidence of the circle of Catholic conspirators in Paris who had fled England to live in exile, he was offered the use of a town house as a residence. This happened also to be 'the lodging of Charles Arundell when he is at Paris,' he informed Walsingham, with the telling remark: 'If I must lodge there, I must lodge amongst a great number of the libels in French that were written against the Earl of Leicester.'[7] It was not long before it was rumoured in Paris that 'an Englishman is here newly arrived, by the practice of Leicester, to kill Charles Arundell and others'.[8]

There was good reason to suspect that Charles Arundell was the author of *Leicester's Commonwealth*. He had long held a bitter hatred against the Dudleys. His father, Sir Thomas Arundell, had been executed in Edward VI's reign when Charles was still a boy. Arundell never forgave Dudley's father, the Duke of Northumberland, for pressing for his death. Arundell had then been taken in by his mother's family, the Howards, the dynasty of the Duke of Norfolk, his second cousin, who brought him up as a committed Catholic. It was here that he formed an impressive group of friends and patrons including the Earl of Oxford and the Earl of Sussex, his first cousin once removed.

It was Arundell's connection with Sussex which had seen him join a group of Catholic dissidents determined to support Elizabeth's marriage to the Duke of Alençon, in the hope that this would lead to the restoration of the Catholic faith in England. Led by Oxford, they sought to undermine and destroy their chief opponent, Robert Dudley. Oxford was convinced that there was still mileage to be had in attacking Dudley over his wife's death. Arundell later remembered how Oxford had offered him £500, 'first to begin with my Lord of Leicester about his wife making all the strength he could under collar of pretending request of justice'.[9] What this meant exactly is not clear; most likely it was a statement concerning his first wife's death, though Oxford was keen to accuse Dudley of being complicit in the Earl of Essex's death also.[10] The earl was convinced that Dudley's doctor, Dr Julio Borgarucci, was an accomplished poisoner who had been able to dispatch his victims secretly. According to Arundell, Oxford had already been 'sekeinge for poison of Ceasare [Julio] that was with my Lord of Lester'.[11] Oxford was determined to destroy Dudley, confident that he could do so by proving that the accusations that had circulated about Dudley's involvement in the deaths of his wife and the Earl of Essex were true. Eventually, he sought the support of the authorities and informed Francis Walsingham 'of a certain practice which himself forsooth had found out against him', but when he could find no witnesses to corroborate his accusations, his charges were 'put to bed for want of proof'.[12]

Oxford decided to go even further. He proposed an attack on Dudley at the 'garden stayre' at Whitehall, 'as he landed from my Lord of Essex'; when Dudley was forewarned in advance, he planned a second ambush near Wanstead. When this and Oxford's other intrigues were discovered, the earl was 'commandid to kepe his chamber abowte the libellinge between him and my Lord of Lester'.[13]

Charles Arundell had been privy to Oxford's accusations, and may have even been the original author of them, hence Oxford's offer of £500 to elaborate his story. In the end, however, Arundell uncovered some new, more sensational, information which might better suit their cause. He had discovered, he believed, that Dudley had been married in secret to Douglas Sheffield, who happened to be Arundell's own cousin through his Howard family relations. It is likely that it was Arundell who passed this information on to Alençon's agent, Simier, who whispered it into Elizabeth's own ear. How Simier precisely received his information is unknown, though Alençon, thoroughly embarrassed by the affair, blamed his legal adviser, Combelles, for causing Dudley's problems. One of Walsingham's agents, William Herle, told Dudley that Combelles had 'the worst humours and dispositions towards your lordship that might be'. Combelles had apparently put together a 'secret cabala . . . to undermine your estate'.[14] It is easy to guess the membership of this secret group: Arundell was a known ally of Combelles, and it was Arundell who had escorted Simier on his return to Dover in November 1579.

In revenge for Arundell's revelations, Dudley was determined to smash the group of Catholic dissidents that had gathered around the Earl of Sussex. In 1582, Dr William Tresham, a Catholic exile in Paris, wrote to Sussex explaining that he had fled 'contrary to my duty' because of 'only the extreme fear of the cruelty of the Earl of Leicester'.[15] Indeed, in the wake of several plots on Elizabeth's life, Dudley believed that any Catholic had become a danger to the queen's own safety: 'There is no right papists in England that wisheth Queen Elizabeth to live long,' he wrote, 'and to suffer any such in her court cannot be but dangerous.'[16]

Dudley had worked from within to undermine Sussex and his allies.

Whether through bribery or coercion, he had somehow managed spec-tacularly to win over the Earl of Oxford, who confessed that he, together with other Catholics such as Charles Arundell and Henry Howard, another conspirator, had been working with the French. When Dudley presented Oxford's charges against him to the queen, the group collapsed. Arundell fled, together with Howard, to the sanctity of the Spanish ambassador's residence. Both eventually gave themselves up and were imprisoned; the ambassador reported how Dudley was looking to pin extra charges upon them and 'their close friend' Sussex, spreading rumours that they had been 'plotting a massacre of the Protestants, beginning with the Queen'.[17] Oxford followed their arrest with a further testimony against Arundell and Howard, alleging that they had held conspiratorial meetings concerning the Queen of Scots at the Earl of Northumberland's estate at Petworth in Sussex.[18]

Charles Arundell was not a man to accept such accusations quietly, much less from his former friend whom he now detested as a turncoat and traitor to his religious cause. He retaliated with lurid accusations over Oxford's personal life, insisting that Oxford was a closet homosexual whom he had caught in a compromising position with his servant boy, 'all in a sweat'.[19] Arundell further disclosed how Oxford had apparently hired assassins to murder various men, including the Protestant John Cheke, which he had found out 'by the discovery of a gentleman that serves this monster and would not consent to such a villainy'. It all sounds suspiciously similar to many of the stories and devices used in *Leicester's Commonwealth*.[20]

Arundell was eventually restored to his position, but two years later revelations that he had been implicated in a Catholic conspiracy to kill Elizabeth, known as the Throckmorton Plot, forced him to flee the realm. It was in December 1583 that Arundell arrived as an exile in Paris. One of the first visits he made was to another distant relation of his through his Howard connections: his cousin Douglas Sheffield. It is at this point that the story takes a very interesting turn indeed.

Douglas Sheffield had left the country when her husband Sir Edward Stafford became resident English ambassador in France. For the previous few years Douglas had been living in Paris, where she was regularly in attendance at the French court and had become a close confidante of Catherine de' Medici. She had even advised on a new set of household ordinances that would ensure greater privacy for the French King Henri III, modelled on her own experiences within Elizabeth's household.

As soon as he discovered that Charles Arundell had arrived in Paris, Francis Walsingham went on the alert. He warned Stafford not to come into contact with him, nor allow his wife's close alliance with Arundell to affect his duty. Stafford was furious and protested his innocence, complaining to Cecil that 'there is an evil meaning in the writer'.[21]

Despite Walsingham's warnings, Douglas and Stafford repeatedly entertained Arundell at their home apparently unaware, so they later claimed, of the reasons for his sudden departure from England. During their dinner-party conversations in Paris, could Douglas and Stafford have passed on details of Dudley's private life, including his own relationship with Douglas, together with details of their secret marriage, to Arundell? It seems likely. Arundell bragged to a Spanish agent residing in Paris that Stafford could be easily bribed, while the pair remained in close contact over the coming years.

The motive was also quite clear: both Douglas and Stafford, for obvious reasons, remained hostile to Dudley, and would have wished for his reputation to be damaged, if not destroyed. Both had also become close to the Catholic Church. Dudley sensed that the pair might turn against him, and if Stafford's letter to William Cecil, written at the beginning of May 1584, is correct, relations between them had grown frosty: 'I have written to my Lord of Leicester, but more because it was your advice than for anything else; for at my going away, he sent for me and assured me he would be as good a friend to me as any I left behind, and yet I have found the contrary. I am but a poor gentleman, but I love plain dealing.'[22]

Could Stafford and Douglas have been involved with the preparation of *Leicester's Commonwealth*? Walsingham certainly thought so. Nothing could be proved, but in late 1585, Stafford's servant, named Lilly, was detained and examined by Walsingham, who then wrote to Stafford complaining that the ambassador had not done enough to prevent the distribution of *Leicester's Commonwealth*. Walsingham advised Stafford that, in his opinion, Lilly had been involved in the affair. Stafford's reply was unconvincing. He had been curiously reluctant to send a copy of the tract to the court, confessing to Cecil that 'the Earl of Leicester is ever subject to take not well that which cometh from me'.[23] Excusing his inaction, he explained that he had not thought it fitting to get involved, as a public official, in the private affairs of an individual. Nevertheless, he had still managed to confiscate thirty-five copies of the work, indeed whenever he had discovered them, until he found that he could no longer keep up with the number being produced. 'And for Lilly,' he wrote, 'if he perchance saw or read a book, surely that were in reason no such criminal cause; but sure I had rather cause to think that my Lord of Leicester should be so incensed against him for the love the poor fellow bare to me than for any cause else.'[24]

Whatever Douglas told Arundell over their conversations at supper in Paris seems to have formed a significant portion of the tract, for among the many accusations contained within the work, the intimate details of Douglas's affair with Dudley feature the most prominently. With the necessary information gathered, during the spring of 1584 Arundell and his Catholic circle of friends worked to compile *Leicester's Commonwealth*. Arundell now decided to include the details he knew about Amy's death, the accusations against Sir Richard Verney and the involvement of Walter Bayly. It was this information that Oxford had probably wished to solicit from him earlier. Now, Arundell felt, was the right time to collect all the intelligence he could gather against Dudley his enemy; if enough mud was thrown, some would surely stick. For Arundell it was sweet revenge, part of the Catholic fightback from exile. 'Instead therefore of the sword, which we cannot obtain, we must fight with paper and pens, which cannot be taken from us,' wrote Sir Francis Englefield, Mary I's former Secretary and now a leading spokesman for English Catholics at the Spanish court.[25]

If Douglas had provided her cousin with the vital, most intimate, knowledge he needed to write *Leicester's Commonwealth*, she soon came to regret it. At the time, sitting around the dinner table bitterly recalling her appalling treatment, she had probably thought that the disclosure would have been the best means of revenge. Perhaps Douglas had been unaware of how Arundell intended to tell her story. When she discovered what had been written about her and her affair with Dudley she was horrified, with the result that she was 'laid up' with 'the melancholy of the fear of the misinterpretation'. Her 'sickness' on learning of the tract's publication, Stafford later recalled, 'was so long and almost of life, as in truth I was a good while greatly afraid of'.[26]

The story refused to die. In spring 1585, a French translation of *Leicester's Commonwealth* appeared, entitled *Discours de la vie abominable*

*... le my Lorde de Leicestre.* Essentially reprinting most of its original contents, it also included what Stafford termed a 'villanous addition' that gave details of how Dudley had seduced a lady at court through the use of a potion containing his own semen. Though the lady was not identified, the very fact that she was described as being still alive narrowed down the options.

No doubt embarrassed by the scandal, Douglas's husband Stafford informed Walsingham of the publication of this French version in March. Interestingly, Stafford decided not to tell Dudley of the new edition, since he 'would be loath to do anything subject to bad interpretation'. At the end of his dispatch, it also appears that Stafford knew far more than he was letting on. It seems that he had known about the publication for some time, yet had never reported it.[27] Stafford recommended that he should not be ordered to suppress it, since his 'nearest have a touch in it'. 'I am in a peck of troubles what to do in it, for to complain of it were to have the matter more to be divulged abroad and to [be] more looked into.' If he was honest, he argued that if it was 'between God and Leicester's conscience' and also 'in the opinion of most Englishmen', his wife's conscience was 'no farther touched than an honorable intent and a weak woman deceived'.[28]

*Leicester's Commonwealth* spawned a whole raft of new anti-Dudley attacks, each adding their own slant on the question of how Amy had met her death. Another tract, a 'Letter of Estate', written shortly afterwards in 1585, soon found itself it the hands of the Privy Council. It reiterated the accusations in *Leicester's Commonwealth*, giving further details of how two of Amy's servants had been in the parlour playing cards when her death occurred, but as they 'plain hearing someth[ing falls] down the stairs,' one maid joked to the other, 'down for a shilling, the other lik[ewi]se merely answering up for another'. They continued playing, 'little suspecting what was fal[len].' After their game had ended, the tract continued, 'and hearing no body make any [move to] take up what was fallen, one of them steppe[d to the] stairs foot to see what it should be. W[hat to their] appalled spirits there appeared unto them, the corpse of that noble lady without breath, se[eming to have] her neck bone broke in sunder'.[29] The findings of the coroner's jury had reported that Amy's death had been an accident: 'Most falsely and slanderously it [is] given forth that she fell by chance down the stairs and brake h[er neck]'. For the writer of the tract, and doubtless many others, this seemed scarcely believable. 'A likely matter, a lady to fall down [the stair]es and never heard cry, her neck to [be broken but with no] blood spilt.' Few were willing to argue against the verdict, the pamphlet insisted, since those that considered otherwise were bound to find themselves in dangerous territory. 'His Lordship said [so, and then] who durst say the contr[ary.] Much mutte[ring] there was about this sudden death of hers, but [no] man durst say a word for his life.'

A few months later, in March 1586, an anti-Protestant pamphlet written by the Catholic Julius Briegerus entitled *Flores Calvinistici* added to the growing rumours that Amy had been murdered. Devoting a third of its length to a similarly blistering attack upon Dudley, this time the work claimed that Amy had been 'destroyed by a small nail thrust gradually into her head'.[30]

In the end, however, the suppression of *Leicester's Commonwealth* was so effective that its impact was slight. It seems that almost all printed versions of the work were destroyed. It would not be until 1641 that the book was once again reprinted, this time to draw parallels with the leading figure at court at the time, Thomas Wentworth, Earl of Strafford, and close friend of Charles I, who was standing trial on charges of treason. Then, *Leicester's Commonwealth* provided a useful moral warning against the dangers of an over-mighty courtier. Its re-publication was a popular success, and further editions soon followed. Its tales now became the accepted version of events, with writers and historians alike taking it as the standard source on Dudley's life. A new legend of Robert Dudley, poisoner, adulterer, murderer, had been created. It was a legend that would be reinforced throughout the generations, reaching its apogee in Sir Walter Scott's *Kenilworth*. Never again would Robert Dudley's name be free from the taint that he had arranged the murder of his wife Amy.

# The Journal

The accusations concerning Amy's death contained in *Leicester's Commonwealth* are remarkable, as is their detail. Specific names of those involved in the supposed covering up of her murder had been revealed: Sir Richard Verney; the wife of 'Bald Butler'. Yet these details in themselves prove nothing. We have little idea how Charles Arundell obtained them and, coming twenty-five years after the event and in the context of the rash of lurid and exaggerated accusations that fill the tract, it has proved impossible to take the charges seriously, let alone substantiate them. For centuries, *Leicester's Commonwealth* has provided the only account of Verney's involvement in Amy's death and the sole suggestion that Robert Dudley had arranged for his wife's murder.

But more evidence does survive. In the British Library there exists a remarkable document, found among the papers of Robert Beale, the Secretary to the Privy Council during Elizabeth's later years, and now in the library's Yelverton collection (Additional manuscripts 48000–48196) deposited there in the 1950s. Catalogued under Additional Manuscript 48023 is a large volume measuring 31½ inches by 20½ inches, still bound in its original sixteenth-century calf leather. It is titled 'A Journall of Matters of State happened from time to time as well within and without the realme from and before the death of King Edw. the 6th untill the yere 1562', and is a diary written by an unknown author detailing political events in and around the court at the time. It was first noticed by the Victorian editors of the Historical Manuscripts Commission in 1871, who failed to realise its significance, listing it as a 'brief chronology of occurrences in England, 1559 to 1562'.[1] For years it went unnoticed until 1978, when the historian George Bernard, following up the reference, unearthed the journal in the British Library.

The journal provides a wealth of first-hand information about the early years of Elizabeth's reign. It reads as if it were the working notes of a history book in the making, perhaps even a dictated text. Its pages are littered with instructions from the narrator to the copyist on points to follow up: 'Enquire for the conclusions of peace between England and

France for the matters of Scotland. I think Mr Raylton had them. Enquire for the league between England and Scotland.'[2] The text is virulently anti-Dudley, portraying Dudley's father, the Duke of Northumberland, as a Machiavellian schemer who worked to bring down the Duke of Somerset and his brother Sir Thomas Seymour: 'He procured and maintained hatred between the brethren, so that he might the rather dispatch one and at length the other, and in the end rule alone himself.'[3] Dudley himself is constantly portrayed in a bad light, with frequent asides commenting negatively on his behaviour. His attempt to secure Philip II's support for his marriage to Elizabeth in early 1561, for example, was regarded by the author of the journal as 'a great argument to prove his consent to the murdering of his wife, to have the Queen, that would betray his country to be king'.[4] Despite this professed loathing, it seems a bizarre, but nonetheless important, fact that the author had never met Dudley until he saw him return to court after his period of mourning for his wife's death: 'for myself I knew him not, for I never saw him before, nor knew not that it was he till he was past.'[5]

The journal is clearly a contemporary document, written down at the time the events occurred. From September 1561, it is recorded in monthly entries and there is a marked shift in tense, from the past to the present and even the future tense, suggesting the writer was compiling his text from the autumn of 1561 at the earliest, and certainly by September 1562, referring to 'the xth of this present' month.[6]

We cannot be sure precisely who the author of the journal was. He was on friendly terms with both Sir Ralph Sadler and Roger Ascham, and also held strongly Protestant views. But there is one key sentence in the journal which allows us to have an educated guess at whom its author might be. In the summer of 1560, the author writes: 'Remember how Mr Askam [Roger Ascham] being at Tuttenham [Tottenham] I began an oration on this matter.'[7] The key here is the location: Tottenham was the residence of none other than John Hales, the Clerk of the Hanaper. In two separate commissions that year, Hales is described as living at Tottenham High Cross.[8] John Hales was also a good friend of Ralph Sadler's, whom he served as deputy Master of the Wardrobe during Edward VI's reign.[9] Both John Hales and his brother Stephen were also trustees for Sadler's son in February 1560.[10]

John Hales was a Protestant firebrand and a close ally and friend of the Duke of Somerset, who had acted as his patron during the reign of

Edward VI. This was perhaps reason enough to detest Robert Dudley, the son of a man who had plotted and arranged for his patron's execution back in 1552. After Somerset's downfall, Hales departed for the Continent in self-imposed exile, not to return until mid-1559. This might explain why Hales only met Robert Dudley for the first time a month after his wife's death. The perplexing fact that the journal ends abruptly in 1562 might plausibly be explained by what we know of Hales' later career, when he became embroiled in a fresh dispute over the succession, championing the cause of Lady Catherine Grey in a tract that would earn Elizabeth's scorn and Hales' subsequent imprisonment.[11] Hales' arrest in 1562 also accords with the abrupt ending of the journal at the end of that year. It would also explain how the journal came to be in other hands.

It seems that after Hales' arrest, the journal, together with Hales' other books, came into the possession of Thomas Norton. Though Norton had previously shown a strong interest in the issue of the succession, co-authoring *Gordobuc*, it seems that he was not involved in promoting Catherine Grey's cause. Instead, Norton was employed to assist with the investigation of Hales by the Privy Council, which would explain how the journal ended up in his hands.[12]

When Norton died in March 1584, the Privy Council sent Thomas Wilkes, Clerk of the Council since 1576, to seize the papers in his study, and a full inventory of its contents was produced. That inventory still survives. Labelled 'A catalogue of all the books, papers and matters of state founde in Tho: Nortons studie and commited by Her Majestie to the charge of Thomas Wilkes, Clarke of the Counsell', it lists seventy-three manuscripts in Norton's possession. One is recorded as a 'Journall of matters of state happened from time to time as well within and without the realme from and before the death of King Edw. the 6th until the yere 1562'. It can be none other than the journal itself.[13]

Wilkes kept Norton's papers, including the journal, in his custody for at least three years: eventually they were transferred over to Robert Beale, Wilkes' colleague as Secretary of the Privy Council and also a friend of Norton's, some time after 1586. Fortunately, it was this that probably saved them from being destroyed along with the rest of the archives of the Privy Council in the great fire of Whitehall Palace in 1619.

Yet the survival of the journal provides us with one remarkable new piece of evidence which enables us to understand more about Amy's death. There is a passage in an entry for 1560 which stands out above the rest:

> How the Lord Robert's wife brake her neck at Foster's house in Oxfordshire
> ... her gentlewomen being gone forth to a fair. Howbeit it was thought
> she was slain, for Sir ... Verney was there that day and whilst the deed
> was doing was going over the fair and tarried there for his man, who at
> length came, and he said, thou knave, why tarriest thou? He answered,
> should I come before I had done? Hast thou done? quoth Verney. Yea,
> quoth the man, I have made it sure. So Verney came to the court.[14]

The similarity to the account in *Leicester's Commonwealth* is fascinating, almost unbelievable. Here, for the first time, is separate evidence corroborating the fact that Sir Richard Verney had ordered Amy's death. Yet over twenty years separate the two documents. And, unlike *Leicester's Commonwealth*, the journal is a contemporary document, written around the time of Amy's death.

For centuries, historians have been under the impression that the story told in *Leicester's Commonwealth* was most likely a fabrication on the part of its author, intertwined with its other fantastical charges ascribed to Robert Dudley. The discovery of the passage in the journal changes this. The fact that the accusations against Sir Richard Verney were circulating immediately after Amy's death, and over twenty years before the publication of *Leicester's Commonwealth*, suggests either that the rumour was common knowledge at court at the time, or that something more sinister had in fact taken place. But there is still more.

The journal also provides us with fresh revelations concerning Amy's movements before her death:

> The people say she was killed by reason he [Dudley] forsook her company
> without cause and left her first at Hyde's house in Hertfordshire, where
> she said she was poisoned, and for that cause he desired, she might no
> longer tarry in his house. From thence she was removed to Verney's house
> in Warwickshire, and so at length to Foster's house.

The chronology of Amy's movements described here is startlingly accurate. We know this from the surviving records in Dudley's household accounts. Having been in Lincolnshire at the time of Elizabeth's accession, Amy travelled to William Hyde's house in Throcking,

Hertfordshire, in early 1559. Dudley came to visit her at Hyde's during the Easter recess of 1559, when the accounts record that 'Mr Hide ... lent your lordship at pley at his own house' forty shillings.[15] Amy also wrote one of her two surviving letters from 'Mr Heydes'. After June 1559, Amy's movements become more difficult to trace. She made an unspecified journey into Suffolk, accompanied by Picto and Thomas Blount, taking with her a purse filled with 40 pistoles, worth £25.[16] Yet after travelling to London to visit her mother's family at Camberwell, there is no indication that she returned to Hyde's.

The accounts then suggest that Amy was certainly at Sir Richard Verney's house in Compton Verney in Warwickshire by September 1559. The remainder of the entries then refer to Amy's presence at Anthony Forster's house at Cumnor Place, where she may have arrived in December 1559, with various presents, including a looking glass and two yards of blue sewing silk, being sent 'to my ladie by Mr Forster'.[17] There can be little doubt, as the journal suggests, that Amy did indeed move from Hyde's house to Verney's and eventually to Forster's at Cumnor, where she was to spend her last days.

Just as intriguing is the suggestion that Amy had decided to leave Hyde's for fear that she was being poisoned. Suddenly the accusation in *Leicester's Commonwealth* that Dudley had instructed Verney to 'first attempt to kill her by poison', and that Amy 'absolutely' refused to take the medicines given to her, 'as suspecting still the worst', do not seem so far-fetched.

We already know that rumours were circulating even before Amy's death that she was being poisoned. Over the eighteen months before her death, time and again the ambassadors' reports all make mention of Dudley's intention to poison his wife. Nearly a year before Amy died, the Imperial ambassador Bruener had considered that although Dudley was 'married to a beautiful wife he is not living with her, and, as I have been told by many persons, is trying to do away with her by poison ... It is just like him to protract this marriage until he has sent his wife into Eternity.'[18] And on 18 November 1559, de la Quadra had written to Philip how 'a certain person who is accustomed to give me veracious news' had reported 'that Lord Robert has sent to poison his wife ... All the Queen has done ... in the matter of her marriage is only keeping Lord Robert's enemies and the country engaged with words until this wicked deed of killing his wife is consummated.' This 'certain person' was likely to have been Bruener, with whom he shared his London residence. In January 1560, de la Quadra wrote with further gossip; Bruener was going to tell him 'what he knows of the poison for the wife of Milort Robert,' he recalled, 'an important story and necessary to be known'.[19]

Aside from *Leicester's Commonwealth*, two other sources also confirm the fact that, as the journal suggests, Amy herself suspected she was being poisoned. The first comes from the pen of the Spanish ambassador, de la Quadra. In his dispatches, he stated that it had been reported that Amy had been ill in 1559. Later, in June, he suggested that Amy had made a recovery from whatever her 'malady' might have been. De la Quadra confirmed that 'the wife of the Lord Robert is already better, and it is said that she has been warned not to eat anything that is not very safe'.[20]

The common theory that Amy was suffering from some form of terminal illness, perhaps breast cancer, is based on de la Quadra's earlier statement in April 1559 that she was suffering from a 'malady' in her breast, yet ignores this later report. In addition, Amy's energetic movements in the spring of 1559, travelling down from William Hyde's in Throcking to London on the occasion of her husband's instalment as a Knight of the Garter, visiting her own family home at the same time before perhaps travelling into Suffolk, do not point to the actions of a terminally ill woman. Equally, the surviving bills for dresses and silks, together with Amy's letter to her tailor Edney in the final weeks before her death, do not suggest the behaviour of an invalid, but instead someone who remained active, looking forward to the future.

The second piece of evidence indicating that Amy believed that she was being poisoned comes from William Cecil, in his conversation with de la Quadra several days before Amy was discovered dead. 'They intended to kill the wife of Robert and now published that she was ill, though she was not but on the contrary was very well and protected herself carefully from being poisoned ...'

We now know that Cecil's conversation with de la Quadra most likely took place *after* Amy's death but before the news had been publicly announced, allowing the Secretary to make maximum political capital out of her death. Yet it seems unlikely that Cecil had anything to do with Amy's death; despite their tense relationship, together with Cecil's fears that if Dudley did marry Elizabeth, his position would be destroyed, Cecil and Dudley remained close friends at a distance. 'I will never desire towards him but well,' Cecil admitted to Sir Nicholas Throckmorton in July 1561.[21] In any case, Cecil had nothing to gain and everything to lose from Amy's death, especially since it gave Dudley the opportunity to marry the queen.

In this case, who were 'they' who, in Cecil's words, intended to kill Amy? On this question, the journal has more to say about Sir Richard Verney. 'This Verney and divers others his servants used before her death, to wish her death, which made the people to suspect the worse.' In the months before Amy's death, 'Many times before it was bruited by the L. Rob. his men that she was dead.'

We know little about Sir Richard Verney except that he was from Compton Verney in Warwickshire, where he sat as Dudley's deputy lieutenant for the county. Ambrose Cave, who recommended Verney into Dudley's service, clearly thought him 'a gentleman meet to serve' who 'would willingly endeavor himself'.[22] By the time *Leicester's Commonwealth* was published, he had been dead for sixteen years; no will of his survives, though a document dated February 1568 mentions a George Verney, naming him as the son of 'late' Sir Richard Verney.[23] After Verney's death, we know that Dudley took care of his estate, left in disrepair by Verney's son George; 'the unthrift,' Dudley wrote to Cecil, 'that your Lordship and I had so much to do withal'.[24]

Sir Richard Verney was close to Dudley, certainly close enough to be considered a dependant. There survives among Dudley's papers a letter from him, dated 20 April 1560, four months before Amy's death. In it, Verney explains why he was unable to visit Dudley at court, as requested:

> I am very sorry that I can not, according to your Lordship's expectation and my duty, make my repair presently towards you for two principal causes. The one health, which I possess not as I could wish. The other wealth, which doth not abound in me as perhaps is thought. But as it is both I and all things else mine are and always shall be to my best power advanced in any your affair or commandment when opportunity offreth.

Verney's letter continues, apologising for the death of a pair of Dudley's hawks that were being looked after on his estate: 'but like as I know your lordship can best consider, that casual things may have many times such casual end, so I have good hope you will please let them pass'.[25]

Aside from Verney, the journal also mentions the involvement of 'the L. Rob. his men'. This must refer to Dudley's household servants and his retinue, known as 'retainers'. The practice of employing a retinue of personal servants, a kind of private bodyguard, although a throwback of feudal society, was still common in the sixteenth century. During the reigns of Henry VII and Henry VIII, legislation had been passed to outlaw the practice, though it had slowly crept in again during the minority rule of Edward VI, when licences were granted to noblemen to employ an armed band of followers ranging from 50 to 200 men. Each 'retainer' would be paid a wage and would wear their master's 'livery', a coat decorated in the colour and heraldic symbol of his noble house.

Many of these retainers were unflinchingly loyal to their master and absolutely dedicated in their service, ready to make whatever sacrifice was needed. As Sir Richard Verney himself emphasised to Dudley, 'both I and all things else mine are and always shall be to my best power advanced in any your affair or commandment when opportunity offreth'. Sir Thomas Lucy, for instance, wrote to Dudley offering to 'do your lordship any service or pleasure' even if he might be 'one of the least of your lordship's friends in power or ability ... although as willing as the greatest in heart and good will as your lordship shall well understand when occasion shall serve'.[26] Dudley's retinue even swore an oath of allegiance to him, promising their devotion, but also their committed secrecy. The text of the oath is preserved in his archives:

> I do swear to be true, faithful and loyal to his Excellency, my Lord and Master Robert, Earl of Leicester etc. And namely that I shall faithfully keep secret all such things as secretly by word or writing from time to time by his Excellency or others in his name committed to me, and shall not reveal the same to any person but with the assent and good liking of his Excellency, nor hold any intelligence by speech, writing or message with any to the contrary.[27]

There was, however, a darker side to a nobleman's retinue. It was an age when every man carried a dagger or sword under his cloak, and was not afraid to use it. None more so than those men employed in the personal service of their lord, to whom they felt especial loyalty and would defend his interests as if they were their own. Frequently this would extend to violence: the legal files are filled with examples of retainers and servants threatening, injuring, maiming and sometimes even killing enemies or opponents of their masters. In the capital, armed bands of followers walked the streets, occasionally crossing paths. Many saw it as their duty to do their master's bidding. For example, in 1578 twenty-five retainers of Lord Rich attacked Edward Windham in broad daylight in Fleet Street, urged on by their master who ordered them with cries of 'Drawe, villens, drawe', 'Cutt off his legges' and 'Kyll him'. Windham only escaped by firing a pistol at Rich before fleeing into the shelter of the French ambassador's residence.[28]

Robert Dudley was no exception to this kind of behaviour, and was as likely as many other noblemen to employ men of shady backgrounds and suspicious pasts. Just the year before Amy's death, he was warned by the Earl of Derby, who wrote to him about a man named Richard Warwick who had recently entered Dudley's service. 'I assure your lord considering his evil behaviour it is much against your honour to keep such one as he.' Richard Warwick had apparently been an accomplice in a violent robbery committed on All Saints' Day.[29] There is little sign that Dudley took any notice.

There is also evidence that Dudley too made full use of his own retinue for whatever purposes he wished, including violence. Behind his charm and serene behaviour lay an altogether more ruthless side. While later historians would remark how he was able to put his passions 'in his pocket', occasionally there are glimpses of his almost cut-throat behaviour, especially when it came to his suit to marry the queen. Those he considered his enemies would feel the force of his temper, or worse.

Often the threat of force was implicit. When King Eric of Sweden renewed his suit with Elizabeth, he sent Robert Keyle, an attaché to the Swedish embassy, to the English court. Dudley was quick to make Keyle feel an unwelcome visitor. 'Lord Robert at my coming made a great search for me to some of my friends, that he might speak with me ere I dealt with the Queen and Council,' Keyle reported, 'but when he saw he might not, he wrought marvellously to have me in prison; but he troubled himself in vain, wherefore he is very angry.' Keyle did not take the threat lightly. He knew that Dudley's men, known better as 'cutters', were armed with swords and knives, ready to do damage. He had been warned to 'take heed'; 'they look as though they would do some hurt', he admitted.[30]

A London merchant, John Dymock, also had dealings with the Swedish king. Acting as an agent for Elizabeth's mistress Catherine Ashley, who had taken such a dislike to Dudley that she was determined to destroy any chance he might have of marrying the queen, Dymock travelled to the Swedish court with letters from Ashley letting it be known that Elizabeth was privately 'well minded' towards Eric.[31] When Dudley discovered what had been going on he was enraged, and determined to see Dymock punished. One evening, two large men knocked on the door of Dymock's apartment. Dymock's servant was inside, but decided to remain silent and hide. When they had departed, he followed the pair and overheard them saying that 'they would watch all night for him; for if they did not bring him they would lose Lord Robert's favour forever'.[32]

The news soon got back to the queen, no doubt through Catherine Ashley. Elizabeth was furious, taking the extreme measure of rebuking Dudley in front of the entire nobility. 'She would never marry him, nor none so mean as he,' she blistered, 'with a great rage and great checks and taunts.' Above all, it was the behaviour of his household officers and retinue, 'such as travailed for him', that appalled her, 'seeing they went about to dishonour her'.

It was not the only occasion when Dudley's friends and retinue would interfere on their master's behalf. When Elizabeth began to flirt with the courtier Sir Thomas Heneage, paying him more attention than Dudley would have liked, the Spanish ambassador reported how one of Dudley's friends approached Heneage with threatening words, 'saying that if he did not moderate himself in his talk of affairs he would get a cudgeling'.[33] A year later, the Earl of Sussex wrote to the queen complaining of the nature of Dudley's menacing retinue. 'There be drawn to him great bands of men with swords & bucklers as well from the Inns of Court as from other places, whereby he and all his be in that sort armed.'[34] Sussex urged Elizabeth to order 'all his to unarm and all gathered by bands to depart,' or else that he might be permitted to depart from court 'into my barge, where I may after shift myself as I can'.

It would be entirely understandable that members of Dudley's own household might wish to interfere in their master's affairs. The prize, many must have considered, was too great. In the years following Amy's death they were keen to spread rumours to foreign ambassadors desperate for news to send back to their countries, in an attempt to promote their master's suit. In December 1561, there was 'greater boasting thereof by the Lord Robert's men than there is likelihood in his mind'.[35] One observer knew better than to trust the reports that were being spread around. 'There is foolish talk in the Court of the Queen and the Lord

Robert, which for my obedience I will neither write nor speak.'[36] In the same fashion it was Dudley's men together with Sir Richard Verney, according to the journal, who spread rumours about his wife's health, that she was dying or 'that she was dead' and used 'to wish her death, which made the people to suspect the worse'. Could they really have gone further than this?

If Dudley's men had planned to murder his wife Amy, they had reasons for wishing to do so. Despite their marriage of ten years, Amy had failed to provide Dudley with an heir. Perhaps they believed she was barren. Besides, it seemed as if an altogether more attractive alternative was open to their master if he chose. If Amy was dying of breast cancer, then perhaps they were simply hoping to hurry her death. Inspired by their master's words that 'if he live another year he will be in a very different position from now', and in the expectation that he would marry the queen once Amy had passed away, they perhaps waited anxiously.

But Amy was taking too long to die naturally. Perhaps the 'malady in her breast' – by no means confirmed as cancer – had disappeared, as both the Spanish ambassador and Cecil had suggested; perhaps Dudley's men had therefore arranged for her to be slowly poisoned, at the same time playing tricks on her mind in the hope that she would take an overdose of medicines prescribed for her 'melancholy'. But this, too, failed. Amy, suspecting that she was being poisoned, continued to move residences before finally going to stay at Anthony Forster's – a reputable gentleman whose 'great honesty' maybe convinced her that she would be safe in his house. At Cumnor Place, did they approach Dr Bayly to provide a convincing cover for professionally administering further 'medicines' to treat her bouts of desperation? And, when Bayly became suspicious and refused to co-operate, did they find themselves with only one option remaining?

This, of course, is pure conjecture. Amy's assertion that she was being poisoned could have been the product of a paranoid mind. According to *Leicester's Commonwealth*, Amy had been 'sad and heavy' and was persuaded that 'her disease was abundance of Melancholy and other humours'. This fits with her servant Picto's testimony to Thomas Blount that Amy would 'pray to God to deliver her from desperation'. If Amy was receiving treatment for some kind of depression, it might have been possible that in an unstable and fragile mental state – she had certainly the capability for irrational moods and bursts of anger, as her behaviour on the day of her death showed – she believed that she was being slowly poisoned.

Perhaps. Yet Amy's desperation could have equally been formed out of a fear that she was being stalked down by Dudley's servants, willing her death. It was to her husband whom she turned for help. Once Amy had reported to Dudley that she thought she was being poisoned, he took swift action and 'desired, she might no longer tarry' at William Hyde's house. This does not seem like the behaviour of a man complicit in his wife's poisoning, just as his initial letters of shock at the news of Amy's death read as genuine expressions of confusion and concern, albeit chiefly for his own reputation. It seems from this evidence that Dudley, away at court and attending on matters of state that he considered altogether more important, might not even have known what exactly was taking place at Throcking, of Amy's treatment, or of Sir Richard Verney's involvement in the possible mental abuse and attempted poisoning of his wife. Equally, Amy's half-brother John Appleyard, who had 'oftentimes moved the earl to give him leave to countenance him in the prosecuting of the trial of the murder of his sister', also believed that Dudley himself was innocent, 'but yet he thought it an easy matter to find out the offenders, affirming therewith, and showing certain circumstances, which moved him to think surely that she was murdered'.[37] What those circumstances were, or whom he considered 'all such persons' he wished to examine, 'laying reasonable or likely cause why I present them', Appleyard unfortunately never divulged.[38]

There is other evidence that Dudley's servants seem to have kept information from him. Why, for instance, had Thomas Blount departed from Windsor to Cumnor before Dudley had found out about Amy's death? And why did Dudley's servant Bowes, returning from Cumnor on the road to Windsor, tell Blount a full story of what had gone on at Cumnor Place when he met him in passing, but only relate to his master the bare facts that 'my wife is dead, and, as he saith, by a fall from a pair of stairs', leaving Dudley to comment, 'Little other understanding can I have of him'?

When Robert Dudley first learned of his wife's death, his first impressions were that something much more sinister must have taken place. 'If it appear a villany (as God forbid so mischievous or wicked a body should live),' he wrote upon hearing the news. He hoped the truth would out and seems to have gone to the utmost lengths to ensure that the necessary investigations into Amy's death were carried out by the coroner, if anything to save his reputation. Others were of the same opinion; the cause of Amy's death was open gossip at the French court, with many convinced that she had been murdered: 'that her neck was broken, with such other appendances I am withal brought to be weary of my life'. Sir Nicholas Throckmorton was horrified at the tales being told. 'So evil be the reports as I am ashamed to write them,' he wrote, knowing full well 'how much it importeth the Queen's majesty's honour and her realm to have them ceased'.[39]

Elizabeth for one was convinced that Dudley was free from any blame for his wife's death. The coroner's inquest had reported a verdict of accidental death, though her defence of her favourite to Robert Jones in her interview with him in November 1560 only raises further questions. Dudley was innocent of any crime, she insisted, since he was not present at Cumnor Place when Amy had died; in addition, 'none of his', she also said, had been 'at the attempt at his wife's house'. What attempt could this possibly have been? Though the coroner's jury had reported a verdict of accidental death, the very word 'an attempt' hardly describes an accident.[40]

Elizabeth's choice of words might have been a slip of the tongue, or Jones might also have taken liberties to report back to Throckmorton a sense that Elizabeth knew more about Amy's death than she was willing to let on. It should also be remembered that Elizabeth's understanding of the details of the case was not always entirely accurate; at the time of hearing of Amy's death, she believed that Amy was dead 'or nearly so', when the coroner's report makes clear that Amy must have died instantaneously from her injuries.

It is to the newly discovered coroner's report we must once again turn. As has been discussed previously, it provides us with new details about how Amy met her death and the nature of her injuries. Were Amy's injuries merely the result of an accident? The alternative case, especially in light of the revelations contained in *Leicester's Commonwealth* and now reiterated in the journal, is worth considering. The coroner's report confirms the widely held view that Amy had broken her neck, yet, unusually, without any other mark or wound to her body, giving rise to the suspicion that Amy's neck could have been broken beforehand and her body laid at the foot of the staircase at Cumnor Place. Amy had also suffered severe head injuries, in particular, two 'dyntes', lacerations to her skull, one half a thumb-length deep, the other two thumb-lengths in depth.

As has been argued, these injuries could have been plausibly caused through the simple accident of a fall, especially if Amy had hit her head on the stone steps as she fell. And yet the depth of the second wound, around two inches (5 cm) deep gives cause for query. The word used in the coroner's report to describe her head injuries, 'dyntes', was a common term to describe wounds inflicted by a blow, and though no mention is made in *Leicester's Commonwealth* or the journal (which does not discuss Amy's injuries beyond her broken neck), two other, much later accounts, written in the mid-seventeenth and early-eighteenth centuries, make use of the villagers' own stories, and both suggest that Amy suffered wounds to her head.

According to the antiquarian Anthony Wood, who visited Cumnor Place in October 1658 and recorded the experience in his diary, 'the inhabitants will tell you there that she was conveyed from her usual chamber where she lay, to another where the bed's head of the chamber stood close to a privy postern door, where they in the night came and stifled her in her bed, bruised her head very much, broke her neck, and at length flung her down stairs, thereby believing the world would have thought it a mischance, and so have blinded their villany.'[41]

Wood's comments were followed up by Elias Ashmole in his *Antiquities of Berkshire*, published in 1719, where, borrowing heavily from *Leicester's Commonwealth*, he made several additions of his own, including how Dudley himself had 'laid a plot with ... Forster, his tenant, to make away his wife ... the plot being laid, and the night appointed, they make advantage to convey her to another chamber, where her bed's head should stand just against a door which she did not know of: in the middle of the night came a man with a spit in his hand, open the privy door, run the spit into her head, and tumbled her down the stairs, to make the people believe she had killed herself'.[42]

While both accounts, written too long after Amy's death to claim much historical veracity, are widely acknowledged to be inaccurate in their detail (Amy was found dead in the afternoon, having spoken with Mrs Odingsells in the morning before her death, rather than being discovered dead in the 'middle of the night'), it is interesting to note how there was a widespread belief in the oral tradition among the villagers at Cumnor that Amy had suffered the head injuries we now know she did.

If one is to place a sinister interpretation on the nature of Amy's fatal injuries set down in the coroner's report, combined with the accusations in *Leicester's Commonwealth* and the journal, one might just possibly envisage a scenario where she might have been ambushed either in the Long Gallery on the first floor or at the top of the stairs, struck across the head twice and had her neck forcibly broken. The murderer would then have been able to lay Amy's body at the bottom of the stairs, making her death seem as if an accident.

One significant problem remains: if Amy was killed on the order of Sir Richard Verney, how could his man, after committing the crime, have escaped the scene unnoticed? To explain this we must return to the detail of the staircase at Cumnor Place. Intriguingly, it seems that there was another separate entrance to the staircase, which allowed access from the outside of the building through a 'pointed arched doorway, situated in the outer court'. This must have been the outer courtyard on the north side, several metres from the main entrance to the courtyard from the road. This arched doorway led through to an outer staircase, which in the *Gentleman's Magazine* account of Cumnor Place is described as 'communicating with a circular newel stone staircase', the staircase that Amy is supposed to have fallen down. This is backed up by the sketch of the staircase drawn by Samuel Lysons, which indicates that there was an additional doorway accessing the staircase on its landing, hidden behind a small passageway, between the two flights of stairs. An intruder, entering the building from the main road through this arched doorway and outer staircase, would therefore have had immediate access to the staircase where Amy was discovered and to the Long Gallery on the first floor. It would have been perfectly possible for him to escape just as fast into the outer courtyard, without anyone noticing.

Once more, all this remains but conjecture. There is one final surprise, however, that the journal has to offer us.

# The queen's man

Robert Dudley's initial reaction to his wife's death had been explicit from the outset that the coroner's jury investigating Amy's death should 'seek chiefly truth in this case ... without any favour to be showed either one way or other'. In fear of his reputation dissolving amid rumours of foul play, he had gone out of his way to make sure that this was the case. He had instructed Thomas Blount to call for the coroner, 'charging him to the uttermost from me to have good regard to make choice of no light or slight persons, but the discreetest and substantial men, for the juries', and he was pleased with Blount's reply, stating that 'you do well satisfy me with the discreet jury you say are chosen already'. He had further asked Blount to send the jury a message 'that I require them, as ever I shall think good of them that they will, according to their duties, earnestly, carefully, and truly deal in this matter, and find it as they shall out'.

Reading Dudley's letters to Blount, his determination that the jury should be 'discreet' seems almost obsessive, taking up most of his correspondence with his servant. Yet what did these words actually mean?

There is an interesting parallel to be found in a separate trial involving one of Dudley's men, Edward Dekesone, which had taken place at the Assizes at Stafford, six months before Amy's death. Dekesone was acquitted of any crime. A friend, Sir Ralph Bagnall, reported back to Dudley in a letter, describing the trial and the jury. 'For the satisfying of the world there was nothing omitted or left undone,' he wrote, before reassuring Dudley: 'My good lord, as the Justices of the Assizes are known to be learned and most discreet men, so have I thought it my part and duty to advertise your lordship that I do find by divers reasons and arguments that they be the men that doth most honour and love you.'[1]

It might be suggested that the 'discreet men' on the jury, therefore, were to be equated with those who might also 'most honour and love'. Dudley's influence and power were certainly able to sway the processes of justice, something of which Dudley was well aware. In December

1559, he had written a personal letter to a sheriff, urging that a servant of his, Edward Langham, should be offered bail. Langham, who had attended upon his wife Amy for two days while she resided at Christchurch in June 1559, had now been indicted of 'an article of felony'. Dudley believed that there was 'small proof like to be' of Langham's guilt, and was prepared to argue with the sheriff that Langham was 'a gentleman and one that I would be loath should suffer such reproach of slander'. 'For the example I would gladly give in showing little favour towards any of mine that accordingly would commit so great an offence,' Dudley wrote to the sheriff, 'as in this matter I would be glad there should be due examination had, and sufficient trial made. But be assured as much as the accused yet is but of one man and the charges will be great for him to lie in prison long. I do pray so much favour at your hands as that he may be bailed.'[2]

Dudley's behaviour towards the coroner's jury at Amy's inquest seems just as intrusive. Not only had he looked to influence its composition, he had wanted to pass on his own message to them, in what might be seen as an attempt to pressurise its members to make what Dudley at least considered to be the right decision. Yet Thomas Blount reassured him that 'you need not bid them [the jury] to be careful ... they take great pains to learn the truth', saying that they went about their business 'very secret'.

The jury's actions were clearly not secret enough. Just days later Blount had arranged to meet one or two members of the jury in Abingdon, in order to gather information; he informed Dudley that 'what I can I will bring'. Nor did it prevent the foreman, Sir Richard Smith, writing to Dudley personally informing him of their verdict in advance, that Amy's death 'doth plainly appear ... a very misfortune'. 'Touching Smith and the rest,' Dudley wrote back to Blount, satisfied, 'I mean no more to deal with them ... I am right glad they be all strangers to me.'

Was this really true? Were Sir Richard Smith and the jury really 'all strangers' to Dudley? It seems strange that Smith should have decided to write to Dudley during the investigation, informing him of the jury's verdict before it had been reached. Until now it has been impossible to draw any connection between Dudley and the foreman Smith. For the first time the journal provides us with clues to his identity. Discussing the investigation into Amy's death, it states:

> This woman was viewed by the coroner's [in]quest whereof one Smith was foreman who was the queen's man being Lady Eliz. and was put out of the house for his lewd behaviour. It was found by this inquest that she was the cause of her own death, falling down a pair of stairs, which by report was but eight steps.[3]

If true, and Smith was indeed 'the queen's man', this places an entirely new slant upon the independence and veracity of the jury's findings. Who, then, exactly was the foreman, Sir Richard Smith, 'the queen's man'?

An important clue lies buried in the surviving papers of Elizabeth's 'jaoler', Sir Henry Bedingfield, who had kept her under house arrest at his residence during the early, turbulent, years of the reign of her sister Mary, at the height of suspicions of Elizabeth's complicity with Wyatt's rebellion in 1554. In a letter to his brother Edmund, describing the princess's various ailments, including severe bouts of swelling to her face, Bedingfield also discussed the most recent changes to Elizabeth's own private household: 'As touching Cornwallis to be removed from hence, and one Richard Smith to be placed in his room, I do hear credibly that the same Richard hath been long sick and not so recovered as he is able to serve as yet ...'[4]

Sir Richard Smith had local links to the area, and in 1564 would become Mayor of Abingdon. Further to the evidence of the journal, the coroner's inquest into Amy's death confirms that Sir Richard Smith was indeed the foreman. Among the other jurors' names, most of whom have been shown to be local gentlemen or yeomen from the surrounding area, only John Stevenson can possibly be found to have any direct links with Dudley, with his name appearing in Dudley's livery bill for the previous year. According to a book of wages, his yearly salary was £4, in addition to his board and bedding, also paid for by Dudley, which came to £16 10s.[5] As Dudley's retainer, he would have shown particular loyalty and dedication to his lord, much as Sir Richard Verney had professed.[6]

Yet John Stevenson was not the only name connected with Dudley. Six years later, hidden in his household accounts for May 1566, there is the following entry: 'I pray you deliver to this bearer four ells of black taffeta for a short gown and three yards of black velvet to guard the same, which my Lord doth give to Mr Smith, the Queen's man.'[7] Here then is the evidence that, contrary to his protestations, Dudley did indeed remain in contact with the foreman of the jury at his wife's inquest, Sir Richard Smith, 'the queen's man'. The household accounts also reveal further information that has yet to be fully explained. Perhaps it is mere coincidence, but on 26 September, eighteen days after Amy's death, Robert Dudley made a payment to Anthony Forster of £140. This was followed by another payment of £170 on 25 October, totalling a sum of £310.[8] The payment might have been a repayment for a loan of £300 that Forster had made to Dudley on 2 May 1559, but the timing of the payments seems more than coincidental.[9] In addition to the payment made to Forster, there appear on the same page of the accounts two other payments:

> Paid unto Francis Barthewe stranger for money due unto him by your lordship for the which Anthonny Forster stoode bownd      VIICxix li
> Paid unto Anthonny Butteler the xvi daye of November for the discharge of a bounde in the which Thomas Blunt esquier stoode bounde unto the said Anthonny Butteler      C li[10]

The sums of money involved here are staggering, even by Robert Dudley's accounts. Dudley had authorised a payment of £719 to Francis Barthewe, 'stranger', most likely a Flemish merchant named Francis Bartie, who supplied Dudley with expensive commodities and had previously loaned him money – just one of the many creditors that Dudley would rack up debts to during his lifetime. The other payment, made later in November 1560, is to Anthony Butler, for £100. Once again the reason for this payment is not known, aside from the fact that Thomas Blount stood bound as part of the legal agreement. Who, in any case, was Anthony Butler? At this point, it is worth recalling a sentence in *Leicester's Commonwealth*: 'the wife also of Bald Butler, kinsman to my Lord, gave out the whole fact a little before her death.'

There is also another vital clue in the description of Amy's funeral procession recorded by the heralds who were present:

> Then the chief mourner, Mrs Norrys, daughter and heir of the lord
>    Williams of Thame, her train borne by Mrs Buteller the younger, she
>    being assisted by Sir Richard Blunte, knight.
> Then Mrs Wayneman and my lady Pollard.
> Then Mrs Doylly and Mrs Buteller thelder.
> Then Mrs Blunte and Mrs Mutlowe ...

Could 'Mrs Buteller the younger' or 'Mrs Buteller thelder' have been the Mrs Butler, the wife of 'Bald Butler' mentioned in *Leicester's Commonwealth*, who revealed the truth of Amy's death on her own deathbed? 'Bald Butler' remains unidentified; we know that Dudley was related distantly to the Butlers of Ashton-in-the-Walls, and two Butlers are mentioned in his will.[11] Perhaps there is a case for suggesting that this Anthony Butler might be a candidate for being 'Bald Butler', her husband. If so, why was he being paid £100 at this particular time, so soon after Amy's death?

What intentions lay behind those transactions, now just lines in a ledger book, will perhaps always remain a mystery. Equally mysterious is the possibility of Elizabeth's own involvement in the inquest into Amy's death. If Sir Richard Smith was indeed her 'man', could he have been influenced by Elizabeth to ensure that the jury reported back the verdict that she wished to hear? Perhaps this is what Sir Henry Killigrew meant when he wrote to Sir Nicholas Throckmorton shortly after Amy's death that 'rumours ... have been very rife, but the Queen says that she will make them false'. The queen herself talked of an 'attempt at his wife's house', though she herself was certain that 'none of his' – meaning Dudley's men – were present at the time. Information contained in the journal, condemning Sir Richard Verney and Dudley's men as authors of the crime, suggests otherwise. The coroner's report, presented here for the first time, also provides significant evidence to cast doubt on whether Amy's death was truly an accident. This book has attempted to explore all possible clues, opening up new avenues of investigation and providing fresh evidence to the case; yet 450 years on from Amy's mysterious death, clues they must remain. For the historian, unlike the detective, the dead can only reveal so much.

There is one certainty, however. Amy's death marked a fundamental change in Elizabeth's relationship with her favourite. Perhaps, if his wife was indeed suffering from a terminal illness and had died from natural causes, Elizabeth might have one day considered marrying Dudley. Amy's sudden and violent death at the bottom of a set of stairs at Cumnor, and the rumours and scandal that went with it, soon extinguished that hope. Elizabeth, unable to marry the only man she perhaps truly loved, was to remain single the rest of her life; it was the making of the Virgin Queen.

Elizabeth must have known that Amy's death had been the sad culmination, directly or not, of her dalliances with Robert Dudley. It was she who had kept him at court; it was her decision to keep him at court away from his wife. On this the journal has the final and intriguing word: its author had heard from his friend 'P', who remains unidentified, that when Dudley 'went to his wife, he went all in black, and how he was commanded to say that he did nothing with her, when he came to her, as he seldom did'.

'*He was commanded to say that he did nothing with her, when he came to her.*' It was none other than Elizabeth who lay firmly in the background, instructing her favourite, obtaining what she wanted. It paints a scene of Dudley travelling to visit Amy dressed in black, as if he was already mourning her expected passing. The tragedy was that even if she had lived, in both Dudley's and the queen's eyes, Amy was already dead.

## → Finis ←

Four years after the publication of *Leicester's Commonwealth*, Dudley was dead. He had written to Elizabeth just days before:

> I most humbly beseech your Majesty to pardon your poor old servant to be thus bold in sending to know how my gracious lady doth, and what ease of her late pain she finds, being the chiefest thing in the world I do pray for, for her to have good health and long life. For my own poor case, I continue still your medicine and find that [it] amends much better than any other thing that hath been given me. Thus hoping to find perfect cure at the bath, with the continuance of my wonted prayer for your Majesty's most happy preservation, I humbly kiss your foot. From your old lodging at Rycote, this Thursday morning, ready to take on my journey, by Your Majesty's most faithful and obedient servant.

> R. Leicester

In a postscript he added: 'Even as I had writ this much, I received Your Majesty's token by Young Tracey.' They were the last words he ever wrote.

At 4 o'clock in the morning of 4 September 1588, Dudley passed away. He was 56 years old. According to the Spanish ambassador, Elizabeth locked herself away in her Privy Chamber and refused to come out 'for some days'. Eventually Cecil ordered the doors to be broken down. It was impossible to conduct any business with her, Walsingham wrote, by 'reason that she will not suffer anybody to access unto her, being very much grieved with the death of the Lord Steward'.[1] Two months later, it was reported that the queen was 'much aged and spent, and very melancholy'; those close to her knew that Dudley's death was to blame.[2] The Earl of Shrewsbury, writing to congratulate her on her defeat of the Spanish Armada, added his own expression of sorrow for Dudley's death. Elizabeth thanked him for his letter, but did not wish to ever discuss the loss of her favourite again. 'As for the other matter contained in your said letters,' she wrote, 'although we do therein accept and acknowledge your careful mind and good will, yet we desire rather to forebear the remembrance thereof as a thing whereof we can admit no comfort, otherwise by submitting our will to God's inevitable appointment, who, notwithstanding his goodness by the former prosperous news, hath nevertheless been pleased to keep us in exercise by the loss of a personage so dear unto us'.[3]

Others, privately rejoicing at the news, thought differently. One fierce critic of Dudley's composed what he believed to be a fitting epitaph of the man many detested:

> Here lies the valiant soldier
> that never drew his sword.
> Here lies the loyal courtier
> that never kept his word.
> Here lies the noble lecher
> that used art to provoke.
> Here lies the constant husband
> whose love was firm as smoke.
> Here lies the politician
> and nut worm of the state.
> Here lies the Earl of Leicester
> that God and man did hate.[4]

Elizabeth always rejected the idea that she had ever been in love. 'I am too much burdened with cares to turn my attention to marriage,' she later admitted, 'for Love is usually the offspring of leisure, and as I am so beset by duties, I have not been able to think of Love. As therefore, nothing has yet urged me to marry, I have not been able to mediate on this man or that man.' Small things perhaps revealed otherwise. Years later, after Elizabeth's own death in March 1603, a small silver-gilt casket was discovered next to her bed. Inside, folded neatly and bound in silk ribbon, was Dudley's final letter, upon the back of which Elizabeth had written in her own hand, 'his last letter.'[5]

When Elizabeth died, the Tudor line ran into the sand. It had lasted for over a century, since Henry VII had won the crown on the battlefield at Bosworth in 1485; it ended, just as William Cecil had always feared, with the queen childless, without an heir.

Amy Robsart's suspicious death at the bottom of the stairs at Cumnor Place over forty years earlier continued to fascinate long after the event. 'The surest way to charm a woman's tongue', an early-seventeenth-century play explained, 'is to break her neck; a politician did it'. The playwright John Webster seemed convinced of Dudley's guilt, as the conversation between two characters in *The White Devil*, written in 1612, demonstrates:

LODOVICO:    You that were held the famous politician,
             Whose art was poison.
GASPARO:     And whose conscience, murder.
LODOVICO:    That would have broke your wife's neck down the stairs,
             Ere she was poison'd.

The legend of Amy Robsart would gather apace, and though Cumnor Place had fallen into ruin by the seventeenth century, it became a popular attraction for Victorians, inspired by Sir Walter Scott's *Kenilworth*, with its wholly inaccurate – as Scott would have readily admitted – and anachronistic tale of Amy's murder. The ruined and deserted buildings became known as 'Dudley Castle', as local residents took to believing that the place had become haunted by Amy's ghost. According to Alfred Bartlett in his *Historical ... Account of Cumnor Place*, written in 1850:

> The apparition was said to appear chiefly in the form of a beautiful woman, superbly attired, and was mostly to be seen at the foot of a stone staircase, in the north-western angle of the building, where the remains of her Ladyship are said to have been discovered. At length the panic became so general, and the building so dreaded, that the fear-stricken superstitious villagers had recourse to exorcism to expel the spirit; and the tradition yet remaining is, that the ceremony was performed by nine Parsons from Oxford, who laid the ghost in a pond in the adjoining close, and it is said that the water never afterwards froze over the spot. The story exists in the neighbourhood to the present day, and the pond is still pointed out as the receptacle of Madame Dudley's spirit.[6]

Over time, Amy Robsart's tomb in the chancel at St Mary the Virgin Church in Oxford was dismantled and forgotten, and the location of her body eventually lost. In October 1947, after a fire the previous year had destroyed the chancel roof and damaged its floor, the opportunity was taken to excavate beneath the floor in the hope of finding Amy's grave. It soon became clear that further vaults of brick had been built in the eighteenth and nineteenth centuries, obscuring any hope of finding Amy's tomb. After two days of brief excavation, the report concludes, 'it was agreed that no traces of Amy Robsart's interment had been located and the conclusion arrived at was that the whole floor area had, at some time subsequent to the date of her death and burial, been completely disturbed. That being so, there was no point investigating further, and instructions were given for the human remains which had been discovered to be re-interred in the voids exposed, the whole filled in, consolidated and covered with hardcore.'[7]

All that remains today of any sign of Amy's grave is a small marble tile, easily missed in the floor of the chancel:

In a Vault of brick
At the upper end of this Quire
Was buried
AMY ROBSART
Wife of
LORD ROBERT DUDLEY K.G.
On Sunday 22nd September
A.D.1560

Reading the white marble inscription, one would hardly imagine the controversy that Amy's death one September afternoon 450 years ago had caused.

# →→ Appendices ←←

## Appendix I

### The Coroner's Report into Amy Robsart's Death
National Archives, KB 9/1073 (Part 1) mm.80

Inquisicio indentata capta apud Cumner in comitatu predicto nono die Septembris anno regni metuendissime domine Elizabeth dei gracia Anglie, Francie, et Hibernie regine fidei defensoris &c. secundo coram Johanne Pudsey, generoso, uno coronatore dicte domine regine in comitatu predicto super visum corporis domine Amee Dudley, nuper uxoris Roberti Dudley, prenoblis ordinis garterii militis, ibidem iacentis mortue: per sacrum Richardi Smythe, gent., Humpris Lewys, gent., Thome Moulder, gent., Ricardi Knyghte, Thome Spyre, Edwardi Stevenson, Johannis Stevenson, Ricardi Hewse, Willemi Cantrell, Willemi Noble, Johannis Buck, Johannis Kene, Henrici Langley, Stephani Ruffyn, & John Syre: qui quidem juratores, pro veritate inde dicenda ad requisicionem nostrorum jurati, a predicto nono die de die in diem sepius adiournabantur; et ulterius ex parte ipsius coronatoris diversi dies seperales dati sunt eis ad comparendos tam coram justiciariis dicte domine regine ad assias in comitatu predicto capiendas assignatas quam coram eodem coronatore pro veredictione suo veraciter et festinantius inde reddendo usque ad primum diem Augustii anno regni dicte domine regine tercio; ad quem diem iidem juratores dicunt super sacrum suum quod predicta domina Amea octavo die Septembris anno regni dicte domine regine secundo supradicto sola existens in quadam camera infra domum cuiusdam Antonii Forster, armigeri, apud Cumner predicto, ac intendens discendere cameram predictam per quosdam gradus anglice vocatos 'steyres' camere predicte ad tunc et ibidem casualiter cecidit precipiter desuper gradus predictos usque ad imum eorundem graduum per quod eidem domine Amee non solum ad tunc et ibidem acciderunt in capite suo due lesiones anglice vocate 'dyntes', una earum profunditatis quarterii unius policis et alter profunditatis duorum policum, verum etiam raccione casualis laesus sive ocasus illius et ponderis corporis ipsius domine Amee cadentis de gradibus predictis, eadem domina Amea collum suum proprium ad tunc et ibidem fregit, de qua quadam fraccione colli eadem domina Amea ad tunc et ibidem instanter obiit; et predicta domina Amea sine aliqua alia macula sive vulnere super corpus

377

ipsius Amee ad tunc et ibidem inventa fuit; et sic juratores predicti dicunt super
sacrum suum quod predicta domina Amea modo et forma supradictis per
infortunam ad mortem suam devenit et non aliter, prout eis ad presens constare
potest; in cuius rei testimonio huic inquisicioni tam predictus coronator quam
juratores predicti sigilla sua alternatim apposuerunt die et . . .

Inquisition as indenture held at Cumnor in the aforesaid county on 9 September
in the second year of the reign of the most dread Lady Elizabeth, by the grace of
God queen of England, France, and Ireland, defender of the faith, etc., before
John Pudsey, gent., a coroner of the said lady queen in the aforesaid county, on
inspection of the body of Lady Amy Dudley, late wife of Robert Dudley, knight
of the most noble order of the garter, there lying dead: by oath of Richard Smith,
gent., Humphrey Lewis, gent., Thomas Moulder, gent., Richard Knight, Thomas
Spyre, Edward Stevenson, John Stevenson, Richard Hughes, William Cantrell,
William Noble, John Buck, John Keene, Henry Langley, Stephen Ruffyn, and
John Sire: which certain jurors, sworn to tell the truth at our request, were adjour-
ned from the aforesaid ninth day onwards day by day very often; and finally
various several days were given to them by the selfsame coroner to appear both
before the justices of the aforesaid lady queen at the assizes assigned to be held in
the aforesaid county and before the same coroner in order there to return their
verdict truthfully and speedily, until 1 August in the third year of the reign of the
said lady queen; on which day the same jurors say under oath that the aforesaid
Lady Amy on 8 September in the aforesaid second year of the reign of the said
lady queen, being alone in a certain chamber within the home of a certain
Anthony Forster, esq., in the aforesaid Cumnor, and intending to descend the
aforesaid chamber by way of certain steps (in English called 'steyres') of the aforesaid chamber there and then accidentally fell precipitously down the aforesaid
steps to the very bottom of the same steps, through which the same Lady Amy
there and then sustained not only two injuries to her head (in English called
'dyntes') – one of which was a quarter of an inch deep and the other two inches
deep – but truly also, by reason of the accidental injury or of that fall and of Lady
Amy's own body weight falling down the aforesaid stairs, the same Lady Amy
there and then broke her own neck, on account of which certain fracture of the
neck the same Lady Amy there and then died instantly; and the aforesaid Lady
Amy was found there and then without any other mark or wound on her body;
and thus the jurors say on their oath that the aforesaid Lady Amy in the manner
and form aforesaid by misfortune came to her death and not otherwise, in so far
as it is possible at present for them to agree; in testimony of which fact for this

inquest both the aforesaid coroner and also the aforesaid jurors have in turn affixed
their seals on the day and . . .

## Appendix II

### The Dudley–Blount Letters

These contemporary copies of the five letters between Robert Dudley
and Thomas Blount were made sometime after Amy's death, perhaps
on the occasion of John Appleyard's accusations that Amy had been
murdered. The originals no longer survive. The letters, first discovered
by Lord Braybrooke during his investigations into the Pepys Collection
in the 1830s, are presented here for the first time exactly as the copyist
transcribed them. This accounts the unusual markings that occasionally
occur between the words – marks made by the copyist's pen. We cannot
be absolutely sure whether any material has been altered or excluded
altogether.

**Robert Dudley to Thomas Blount, 9 September 1560**
Magdalen College, Cambridge, Pepys MS 2503 (Letters of State II) fo. 703r

Cosin Blount. Imediatlie upon yoʳ departinge from me, there
cam to me Bowes, by whom I do understand that my wife is dead,
and as he saithe by a fall from a paire of stayres, little other understandinge
can I have of him, the greatnes and the suddenness of the
mysfortune : dothe so perplix me, until I do heare from yoᵘ howe the
matter standethe, or howe this evill shuld light upon me, considering
what the malicious worlde will bruyte: as I can take no reste:
And because I have no waie to purge my selfe of the malicious talke
that I knowe the wicked worlde will use, but one, which is the verie
plaine trothe to be knowen: I do praie yoᵘ as yoᵘ have loved me and
do tender me and my quietnes . and as nowe my speciall trust is in
yoᵘ. That will use all the devises and meanes you can possible for the
learning of the trothe wherein have no respect to any leving person
And as by yoʳ owne travel and diligence, so likewise by order of

lawe, I mean by calling of the coroner and charging him to the _
uttermost from me, to have good regarde to make choyse of no light or
sleight persons : But the discretest and substanciall men for the Juries
suche as for there knowledge may be able to serche thorowlie & duelie
by almaner of examynacons the bottom of the matter: and for there
uprightness will earnestlie and seacretlie deale therein without
respect: And that the bodie be viewed and serched accordinglie by them:
and in everie respect to procead by ordre and lawe. In the meane
tyme cosin Blounte let me be advertised from yoᵘ by this berer wᵗ all
spede howe the matter dothe stande: ffor as the cause and the man
thereof dothe mvelouslie trouble me considering my case many waies,
so shall I not be at rest till I may be ascertained thereof, praying
yoᵘ even as my trust is in yoᵘ, and as I have ever loved l yoᵘ, do not
dissemble wᵗ me, nether let any thing be hidd from me: But sende
me yoʳ trewe conceyte and openion of the matter, whether it happened
by evill chaunce, or by villanye, And faile not to let me heare
contynewallie from you. And thus faire you well in moche
hast ffrom windsore this ixth of September the evening

yoʳ loving frende & kynnysman
moche perplexed
R. D.

I have sent for my brother Appleyarde
bycause he is her brother and other of
her frendes also to be theare that they
maie be previe and se howe all thinges
do proceade.


## Thomas Blount to Robert Dudley, 11 September 1560

Pepys MS 2503 (Letters of State II) fos. 705r–6r (705–707)


Maie it please yoʳ lordship to understand, that I have receyved yoʳ
lres by Brysto, the contentes whereof I do well perceyve : and that yoʳ
lordshipe was advertised by bowes : ymediatlie upon my departing that
my ladie was deade and also yoʳ straite charge geven ~~unto~~ me . that I
shuld use all the devices and policies that I can for the trewe understanding
of the matter : as well by myne owne travel : as by thorder of lawe,

As in calling the coroner, gevinge him charge that he chowse a
discrete and substanciall Jurie : for the viewe of the bodie, And that no
corruption shuld be used or persons respected / yo$^r$ L great reasons
that makethe yo$^u$ so earnestlie searche to learne a trothe : The same
w$^t$ yo$^r$ earnest comandement dothe make me to do my best therein /
The present advertisement I can give to yo$^r$ L at this time is ; to trewe
it is that my ladie is dead: and as it seamethe w$^t$ a fall; But yet
howe or whiche waie I cannot lerne /. yo$^r$ L shall heare the maner
of my proceeding sence I cam from yo$^u$: The same night I cam from
windsore I laie at Abington all that night, and because I was
desirous to heare what newys went abroade in the countrie. At my
supper I called for myne hoste, and asked him what newys was there
aboutes, taking upon me I was going into Gloucestershier, he saide
there was fallen a great misfortune wtin thre or iiii myles of the
towne, he saide my lorde Robert Duddeleys wyfe was dead, and I
axed him what was his Judgment, and the Judgment of the people,
he saide some were disposed to saie well and some evill, what is yo$^r$
iudgement saide I: by my trothe saide he; I iudge it a misfortune, bicause
it chaunced in that honest gentlemans howse, hys great honestie saide
he : dothe moche cut the evill thoughts of the people, my thinke said I
that some of her people that wayted upon her shuld somewhat saie to
this / no sir said he but little, for it was saide that they were all
here at the fayre, and none lefte wt her : . howe might that chaunce
saide I : . Then saide he it is saide here, that she rose that daie very
earelie, and commanded all her sorte to go the faire and wold suffer
none to tarie at home; and thereof is moche iudged /. And trewlie
my lorde I did first learne of Bowes as I met wt him comyinge
towards yo$^r$ L of his owne being that daie : and of all the rest of there
beinges / who affirmed that she wold not that daie suffer one of her
owne sorte to tarye at home, and was so earnest to have them
gone to the faire, that w$^t$ any of her owne sorte that made reason
of taryinge at whome, she was verie angrie : And cam to M$^{rs}$
Odingselles the wedowe, that lieth w$^t$ Anthony Fforster, who refused
that daie to go to the faire . and was verie Angrie w$^t$ her also . /
Bycause she saide it was no daie for gentlewomen to go in But
saide the morowe was moche better / And then wold she goo /
[fo.705v (706)]
Whereunto my ladie answered and saide, that she might chowse and

go at her pleasure : but all hers shuld go : and was verie angrye.
They asked who shulde kepe her companye yf all they went, she saide
M$^{rs}$ Owen shuld kepe her companye at dyner, the same tale dothe
picto who dothe dearelie love her, confirme / Certenly my lorde as
little while as I have bene here : I have harde diverse tales of her /
that maketh me iudge her to be a strange woman of mynde, In axing
of picto what she might thinke of this matter, either chaunce or vilany /
she saide by her faithe she doth iudge it verie chaunce, and nether
done by ~~her~~ man nor by her selfe: / ffor her selfe she saide she was
a good virtuous gentlewoman; and daielie wold praie upon her knees,
and diverse tymes she saithe that she hathe harde her praie
to god to deliver her from disperacone. Then saide I she might have
a evell toye in her mynde /. no good M$^r$ Blount said picto, do not
iudge so of my words / yf you shuld so gether ; I am sorie I said so moche /
My lorde it is most strange that this chaunce shuld fall upon yo$^r$ w ...
it passeth the Judgment of any man to saie howe it is, but trewlie
the tales I do here of her, maketh me to thinke she had a strange mynde
in her: as I will tell yo$^u$ at my comyng /
But to thinquest yo$^u$ wold have so verie circumspectlie chosen by the
coroner for the understanding of the trothe, yo$^r$ L nedeth not to doubt
of there well chosinge / Before my coming the inquest were chosen
and part of theem at the house / yf I be able to iudge of men and of
there ablenes / I iudge them and speciallie some of them, to be as
wise and as able men to be chosen upon suche amatter as any men
being but countrie men, as ever I sawe, And aswell able to answere
to there doings before who so ever they shalbe called, And for
there trewe serche w$^t$out respect of person : I have done yor message
unto you / I have good hope they will conceale no fawte yf any be
ffor as they are wise, so are they as I have parte of them
verie Enemies to Anthony Fforster god give them wt there
wisdom indiferencie, and then be they well chosen men / More
advertisement at this tyme I cannot give yo$^r$ L, but as I can
lerne so will I advertise, wishing yo$^r$ L to putt awaie sorowe
and reioce what so ever fall out of yo$^r$ owne inosency by the
which in tyme doubt not; but that malicious reports shall
turne upon there backes that can be glad to wish or have against
yo$^u$. And thus I humblie tak my leave from cumner the xith of
September

yo<sup>r</sup> Lordships lif and leving
T.B.

Yo<sup>r</sup> L hath done verie well in
Sending for m<sup>r</sup> Appleyarde


## Robert Dudley to Thomas Blount, 12 September 1560
Pepys MS 2503 (Letters of State II) fo. 711r


Cosin Blounte untill I heare from yo<sup>u</sup> againe, howe the matter
Fallethe out in verie trothe I cannot be in quiet, and yet yo<sup>u</sup> do well
Satisfie me w<sup>t</sup> the discrete Jurie you saie are chosen alredie; unto
Whom I praie you saie from me, that I require them as ever I
Shall thinke good of them, that they will accordinge to there dueties
Earnestlie, carefullie, and trewlie deale in this matter to fynde it as
They shall se it fall out; And if it ~~chaunce~~ ffall out a chaunce
Or misfortune; then so saie; and if it appeare a villainye (as
god forbid . so myschevous or wicked bodie shuld lyve) then to finde
it so, And god willing I shall never feare the dire . . . . . . . . . . . . . . . . . .
prosecution accordinglie what person so ever it maie appeare any
meane to touche: aswell for the iust punishment of the act : as
for myne <sup>owne</sup> trewe iustisacione, ffor as I would sorie in my harte
any suche evell should be comytted, so shall it well appeare to the
worlde my innocensie . by my dealing in the matter . if it shall so
fall out / And therefore Cosin Blount I seke cheflie trothe in this
case, whiche I praie yo<sup>u</sup> still to have regarde unto w<sup>t</sup>out any favor
to be shewed either woone waie or other, when yo<sup>u</sup> have done
my message to them: I require yo<sup>u</sup> not to staie to searche .
thorowlie yo<sup>r</sup>self always that I may be satisfied, And that w<sup>t</sup>
suche convenient spede as you maie, thus fare yo<sup>u</sup> well in hast
at Kewe this xiith of September ~~156~~

Yo<sup>rs</sup> assured
R.D.

## Thomas Blount to Robert Dudley, 13 September 1560

Pepys MS 2503 (Letters of State II) fo. 709r

I have done yo<sup>r</sup> lordships message unto the iurye, yo<sup>u</sup> nede
not to byde them to be carefull, whether equitie of the cause
or mallice to forster do forbid it, I knowe not, They take
great paynes to learne a trothe, tomorrow I will wayte upon
yo<sup>r</sup> L and as I come I will break my fast at Abingdon /
and there I shall mete wth one or two of the iurye . and
what I can I will bringe / they be verie secrete, And yet
do I heare a whispering that they can finde no presumptions
of evell / And if I maie saie to yo<sup>r</sup> L. my conscience . / I think
some of them be sorie for it, god forgive me . and yf I iudge
amysse ., myne owne opeinon is moche quieted, the more
I serche of it, the more free it dothe appeare to me ./ I
have almost nothing that can make me so moche to think
that any man shuld be the doer thereof as when I think
yo<sup>r</sup> L wif before all other wemen shuld have suche a chaunce
The circumstances and as many thinges as I can learne doth
perswade me that onlie misfortune hath done it and
nothing els / my self will wayte upon yo<sup>r</sup> L tomorowe
and saie what I knowe in the meane tyme I humblie
tak my leave from Comner the xiiith of September

    Yo<sup>r</sup> L lif & lyving
    T.B.

## Robert Dudley to Thomas Blount, undated.

Pepys MS 2503 (Letters of State II) fo. 707

I have receyved a lre from one Smythe one that seamethe to be
foreman of the iurye. I perceyve by his lres that he and the rest have
and do travell verie diligentlie and circumspectlie for the tyrall
of that matter whiche they have charge of, and for any thing that
he or they by any serche or examynacone can mak in the world hetherto
it dothe plainelie appeare he saithe a verie misfortune, whiche for
myne owne parte Cosin Blount dothe muche satisfie and quiet

me: nevertheless because of my thorowe quietnes and all others –
hereafter .: my desire is that they may contynewe in there enquerye
and examynacone to the uttermost as longe as they lawfullie
maie; yea and when thies have geven there verdyt . thoughe it be
never so plainelie founde, assuredlie I do wishe that an other substanciall
company of honest men might trye againe for the more
knowledge of trothe: I have also requested to Sir Ric Blount
who is a perfite honest gentleman to helpe to the furtheraunce
thereof. I trust he be w$^r$ yo$^u$ or thing long w$^t$ m$^r$ Norris likewise
Appleyarde I heare hath bene there as I appointed & Arthure
Robsert her brothers, yf any more of her frendes had bene to
be hand. I wold also have caused them to have seene and bene
previe to all the dealing there, well cosin godes will be done
and I wishe he had made me the poorest that crepeth on the
grounde, so this myschaunce had not happened to me, But
good cosin according to my trust have care above all thinges
that there be playne sencere and direct dealing ~~full~~ for the
full tryall of this matter: Touching smyth and the rest
I meane no waie to deale w$^t$ them; but let them proceade
In the name of god accordinglie, and I am right glad they be
All strangers to me. Thus fare yo$^u$ well in moche hast
From Windsore

Yo$^r$ loving frend and kinsman
R.D.


# Appendix III

**Passages in *The Copy of a Letter Written by a Master of Art of Cambridge***
(*Leicester's Commonwealth*) covering Amy Robsart's death

1)
For first his Lordship hath a special fortune, that when he desireth any woman's
favor, then what person soever standeth in his way hath the luck to die quickly
for the finishing of his desire. As for example, when his Lordship was in full
hope to marry her Majesty and his own wife stood in his light, as he supposed,
he did but send her aside to the house of his servant Forster of Cumnor by

Oxford, where shortly after she had the chance to fall from a pair of stairs and so to break her neck, but yet without hurting of her hood that stood upon her head. But Sir Richard Varney, who by commandment remained with her that day alone, with one man only, and had sent away perforce all her servants from her to a market two miles off, he (I say) with his man can tell how she died, which man, being taken afterward for a felony in the marches of Wales and offering to publish the manner of the said murder, was made away privily in the prison. And Sir Richard himself, dying about the same time in London, cried piteously and blasphemed God, and said to a gentleman of worship of mine acquaintance not long before his death that all the devils in hell did tear him in pieces. The wife also of Bald Butler, kinsman to my Lord, gave out the whole fact a little before her death. But to return unto my purpose, this was my Lord's good fortune to have his wife die at that time when it was like to turn most to his profit.[1]

2)

*Gentleman:* But yet (quoth the gentleman), I had rather of the two be his wife for the time than his guest, especially if the Italian surgeon or physician be at hand.

*Lawyer:* True it is (said the lawyer), for he doth not poison his wives, whereof I somewhat marvel; especially his first wife, I muse why he chose rather to make her away by open violence than by some Italian confortive.

*Gentleman:* Hereof (said the gentleman) may be divers reasons alleged. First that he was not at that time so skillful in those Italian wares, nor had about him so fit physicians and surgeons for the purpose; nor yet in truth do I think that his mind was so settled then in mischief as it hath been sithence. For you know that men are not desperate the first day, but do enter into wickedness by degrees and with some doubt or staggering of conscience at the beginning. And so he at that time might be desirous to have his wife made away, for that she letted him in his designments, but yet not so stony-hearted as to appoint out the particular manner of her death, but rather to leave that to the discretion of the murderer.

Secondly, it is not also unlikely that he prescribed unto Sir Richard Varney at his going thither that he should first attempt to kill her by poison, and if that took not place, then by any other way to dispatch her howsoever. This I prove by the report of old Doctor Bayley who then lived in Oxford (another manner of man than he who now liveth about my Lord of the same name) and was Professor of the Physic Lecture in the same University. This learned grave man reported for most certain that there was a practice in Cumnor among the conspirators to have poisoned the poor lady a little before she was killed, which was attempted in this order:

They seeing the good lady sad and heavy (as one that well knew by her other handling that her death was not far off) began to persuade her that her disease was abundance of melancholy and other humors, and therefore would needs counsel her to take some potion, which she absolutely refusing to do, as suspecting still the worst, they sent one day (unawares to her) for Doctor Bayley and desired him to persuade her to take some little potion at his hands, and they would send to fetch the same at Oxford upon his prescription, meaning to have added also somewhat of their own for her comfort, as the Doctor upon just causes suspected, seeing their great importunity and the small need which the good lady had of physic; and therefore he flatly denied their request, misdoubting (as he after reported) lest if they had poisoned her under the name of his potion he might after have been hanged for a cover of their sin. Marry, the said Doctor remained well assured that this way taking no place she should not long escape violence, as after ensued. And the thing was so beaten into the heads of the principal men of the University of Oxford, by these and other means – as for that she was found murdered (as all men said) by the crowner's inquest, and for that she being hastily and obscurely buried at Cumnor (which was condemned above as not advisedly done), my good Lord, to make plain to the world the great love he bare to her in her life and what a grief the loss of so virtuous a lady was to his tender heart, would needs have her taken up again and reburied in the University church at Oxford, with great pomp and solemnity – that Doctor Babington, my Lord's chaplain, making the public funeral sermon at her second burial, tript once or twice in his speech by recommending to their memories that virtuous lady so pitifully murdered, instead of so pitifully slain.

A third cause of this manner of the lady's death may be the disposition of my Lord's nature, which is bold and violent where it feareth no resistance (as all cowardly natures are by kind), and where any difficulty or danger appeareth, there more ready to attempt all by art, subtilty, treason, and treachery. And so for that he doubted no great resistance in the poor lady to withstand the hands of them which should offer to break her neck, he durst the bolder attempt the same openly.[2]

## Appendix IV

### The Journall of Matters of State
British Library, Additional MS 48023 fo. 353r

Howe the Lorde Roberte's wife brake her necke at Foster's howse in Oxfordshere in die natiuitatis Marie A° 1560, her gentellwomen being gon forth to a fier. Howebeyt yt was thought she was slayne, for Sir ——— Varnye was there that daie and whyleste the deade was ~~doying~~ doing was goinge over the fier and tarried there for his man, who at length cam, and he saied, thowe knave, whye tarieste thowe? He answered, shoulde I com before I had don? Haste thowe don? quoth Verney. Yea, quoth the man, I have made hytt sure. So Verney cam to the courte. This woman was viewed by the coroner's queste, wherof one Smyth was foreman whoe was the quene's man being Lady Eliz. And was putt owte of the howse for his lewed behavior. It was found by this enqueste that she was cause of her owne death, falling downe a paier of stayers, which by reporte was but eight steppes. But the people saye she was killed by reason he forsocke her company withowte cause and lefte her firste at Hyde's howse in Hertford shere, where she saied she was poisoned, and for that cause he desired, she might no longer tarry in his howse. From thence she was removed to Varney's howse in Warrwickshere, and so at leingth to Foster's howse. Many times before yt was bruted by the L. Rob. his men that she was ded. And P. vsed to saie that when the Lorde Rob. went to his wife he wentt all in blacke, and howe he was commaunded to saye that he did nothing with her, when he cam to her, as seldome he did. This Varney and divers others his servauntes vsed before her death, to wyshe her death, which made the people to suspecte the worse. Ane her death he mourneth, leaveth the courte, lieth at C. Whither the lords resorted to him to comforte him. Himself all his frindes, many of the lords and gentellmen, and his famylie be all in black, and weape doloruslie, greate hypocrysie vsed.

Howe the Lorde Roberte wyfe brak her necke at Foster's
Cours in Oxfordshyre in die nativitatis Mariae A° 1560 her
thoughe she was slayne for ... was there
that dede and in whome the deade was ... was there
her the fayr, and harvnd there sr his man, wee as
lemytte ram, and he sayd there knave whie tarrnesse
there, he answered sayde I rou before I cast don
haste terms don verbym, yea & that man I came male
fytt sere, so verrey raud to the towne, The woman was
Rewed off the Corners ynosse, whereof one Smyth
was foreman, whoe was her kinned man off my Lady Ely
and was putt onte off the Cours for his lewd behavor,
It was founn by thes enqueste, that she was caust off
her owne deathe fallinge downe a payer off stayres,
but by reporte was but eyght steppes but the people
saye she was killed by reasn to forserte her runnyng
from Cumnor house and lesse for forste at Cudel howse in
Hertford shyre, where she said she was poysoned, and
for that cause she desyred, she mygt no longer tarry
in his Cours from thene she was removed to Anthony
Cours in Warwickshyre, and so at lengyth to Foster's
forwse, Many tymes before it was bruted off the —
boo, his men that she was deade dal, And I use
to say that when the Lorde Rob went to his wyfe her
wernt all in blacke, and come she was remannded to saye
that he did nothing wth her, when he cam to Cours at
stowne he did thes Warney and divers others his
servante use before her deathe to wysse her deathe wch
made the people to Foster's the worse. And her
deathe he remembth, leaves the towne, both at C—
whither the Lordes resorted to hm to comforte hm (was) exprest
all his strind, many off the Lorde and gentell men, and
his faumly to all in blacke, and weare dolorrise, greate
Expenryse was

The Trinitie after mrcelmas daye he repayrth to the
Courts, at Cumpton poinct, And mr Dannett and I met
hm, and yt was reported to the Quenes, that he in
dyscryet wold not do hm reverense, but me putt off or caps
And for my selfe I knewe hm not, for I never sawe hm
before, ne ... knewe not yt was he, tyll he was past,
Enquire for the conclusion off peace betweexe Eng: and fr.
for the matters off Skotland. I hm met mr Rayleon will
them. Enquire for the league betwene Engl and Skotland.
The fr I retirneth his blacke till Easter followinge.

# ⤜ List of Abbreviations ⤛

| | |
|---|---|
| AGS | Archivo General de Simincas |
| APC | Acts of the Privy Council |
| BL | British Library |
| BRL | Birmingham Reference Library |
| BRO | Berkshire Record Office |
| CA | College of Arms |
| CKS | Centre for Kentish Studies |
| CLRO | Corporation of London Record Office |
| *CPR* | Calendar of the Patent Rolls |
| *CSP Domestic* | Calendar of State Papers Domestic |
| *CSP Foreign* | Calendar of State Papers Foreign, Elizabeth I |
| *CSP Scottish* | Calendar of State Papers relating to Scotland and Mary, Queen of Scots |
| *CSP Spanish* | Calendar of State Papers Spanish, preserved in the archives at Simincas |
| *CSP Venetian* | Calendar of State Papers Venetian |
| Dudley Papers | Dudley Papers at Longleat House |
| *EHR* | *English Historical Review* |
| *Hardwicke Papers* | *Hardwicke State Papers* (ed. P. Yorke, 2 vols, 1778) |
| Haynes | Haynes, S., *Collection of State Papers . . . Left by William Cecil* (1740) |
| *Household Accounts* | *Household Accounts and Disbursement Books of Robert Dudley, Earl of Leicester, 1558–1561, 1584–1586* (ed. S. Adams, Camden Society, 5th series, vol. 6, 1995) |
| HMC | Historical Manuscripts Commission |
| Journal | 'A journall of Matters of State happened from time to time as well within and without the realme from and before the death of King Edw. the 6th untill the yere 1562', printed in *Religion, Politics, and Society in Sixteenth-Century England* (eds. I.W. Archer, S. Adams, G.W. Bernard, Camden Society, 5th series, vol. 22, 2003), pp. 35–122. |

| | |
|---|---|
| Lettenhove | J.M.B.C. Kervyn de Lettenhove (ed.), *Relations Politiques des Pays-Bas et de l'Angleterre, sous le règne de Philippe II* (11 vols., Brussels, 1882– 1900) |
| Lodge | E. Lodge (ed.), *Illustrations of British History* (1791) |
| Machyn | *The Diary of Henry Machyn*, ed. John Gough Nichols (Camden Society, vol. 42, London, 1848) |
| Melville | *The Memoirs of Sir James Melville of Halhill*, ed. G. Donaldson (1969) |
| Murdin | Murdin, W., *A Collection of State Papers ...* (London, 1759) |
| PRO | Public Record Office (now National Archives) |
| *Sadler Papers* | *The State Papers and Letters of Sir Ralph Sadler* (ed. A. Clifford, 2 vols, Edinburgh, 1809) |
| VCH | Victoria County History |

# ⇥ Notes ⇤

**Prologue**

1 BL Cotton MS Titus B II fo. 419r.
2 Dudley Papers, I, fo. 151r: Arundel to Dudley, 21 July 1560.
3 Camden, *History*, pp. 52–3.
4 *CSP Spanish 1558–67*, p. 182.

**Chapter 1**

1 *CSP Spanish 1547–49*, pp. 19–20.
2 Dudley was born on 24 June 1532: in 1587 he mentioned in a letter to Cecil that this date was his birthday; *CSP Foreign 1587*, p. 129.
3 Tytler, *England in the Reigns of Edward VI and Mary*, II, p. 155.

**Chapter 2**

1 Durham University Library, Bamburgh Select MS 15, p. 4.
2 Norwich Commissary Court MS, Walpoole, fo. 77r.
3 Collinson, 'Letters of Thomas Wood', pp. 13–14.
4 *Holinshed's, Chronicle*, p. 977.

**Chapter 3**

1 *Chronicle of Edward VI*, pp. 32–33.
2 Hatfield House, Cecil Papers, 155, art. 29.
3 A separate argument has been put forward for the identity of the portrait being that of Lady Jane Grey. For several reasons this remains unconvincing. See *Lost Faces: Identity and Discovery in Tudor Royal Portraiture*, pp. 79–83; Ives, *Lady Jane Grey*.

**Chapter 4**

1 Wall (ed.), *Two Elizabethan Women*, pp. xix, 54–5; Williams, *The Later Tudors*, p. 500.
2 Dudley Papers, II, art. 12.
3 PRO E 328/101.
4 BL Additional MS 32091 fo. 172r.
5 PRO C 78/17/10.
6 Wilson, *Sweet Robin*, p. 47.

**Chapter 5**

1 There was no truth in this. Robert Dudley was born on 24 June 1532 while Elizabeth was born on 7 September 1533.
2 Camden, *History*, p. 53.
3 Bibliothèque Nationale de France, MS Français 15970 fo. 14.
4 Nichols (ed.), *Literary Remains*, p. lxxvii.
5 Wilson, *Sweet Robin*, p. 18.
6 Thomas Hatcher, *G. Haddoni Legum Doctoris, S. Reginae Elizabethae a supplicum libellis, lucubrationes passim collectae*, pp. 419–20.
7 Ascham, *Works*, II 101–4.
8 Vives, *On Education*, pp. 204–5; Rosenberg, *Leicester, Patron of Letters*, pp. 30–1; Wilson, *Sweet Robin*, pp. 16–17.
9 Dee, *Compendious Rehearsal*
10 *Letters and Papers* Henry VIII viii pp. 58, 135–9.
11 *Letters and Papers* Henry VIII xviii pt.1 pp. 229, 231–2, 291; BL Sloane MS 2442 fo. 27v; *CSP Foreign 1547–53*, pp. 164, 245; *CSP Spanish 1550–52*, pp. 229, 325.
12 BL Cotton MS Vitellius C XI fo. 334v.
13 PRO SP 10/6/21.
14 BL Hatfield MS M485/39, vol. 150, fo. 85; printed Haynes, *State Papers*, p. 100.
15 PRO SP 10/6/19; SP 10/6/22.
16 BL Hatfield MS M485/39, vol. 150, fo. 80v; printed Haynes, *State Papers*, p. 96.
17 PRO SP 10/6/9; Strype, *Ecclesiastical Memorials*, II, i, p. 188.
18 PRO SP 10/6/7.
19 PRO SP 10/6/12.
20 PRO SP 11/4/2; printed Ellis (ed.), *Original Letters*, II, ii, 256; Leti, *Historia Elizabetta*, I, 201.
21 Haynes, *State Papers*, p. 90.
22 BL Hatfield MS M485/39, vol. 150, fo. 78; printed Haynes, *State Papers*, p. 95.
23 PRO SP 10/6/7.

## Chapter 6

1  *CSP Spanish X*, p. 215.
2  *CSP Spanish 1553*, p. 3.
3  Inner Temple Library, Petyt MS 538, vol. 46, fo. 9.
4  Bindoff, 'A Kingdom at Stake', *History Today*, 3 (1953), p. 647.
5  *Vita Mariae*, pp. 247–8.
6  Nichols (ed.), *Greyfriars Chronicle*, p. 79; *CSP Spanish 1553*, pp. 80, 106.
7  Nichols, *Chronicle of Queen Jane and Mary*, p. 7.
8  Ibid., p. 8.
9  BL Harleian MS 353 fa. 139r.

## Chapter 7

1  Nichols (ed.), *Chronicle of Queen Jane and Mary*, p. 17.
2  BL Harleian MS 353 fa. 142r.
3  *Household Accounts*, pp. 92–3.
4  APC, 10 September 1553.
5  *Le Report de un Judgment done en Banke du Roi* (1571)

## Chapter 8

1  BL Lansdowne MS 94 fo. 21.
2  *CSP Spanish XI*, p. 393; *CSP Venetian VI*, pp. 1058–9.
3  De Lisle, *Sisters Who Would Be Queen*, p. 143.
4  *CSP Spanish XI*, p. 335; *CSP Spanish XII*, pp. 153, 166–7, 200.
5  Collins (ed.), *Letters and Memorials of State*, I, 36.
6  The date of the pardon was 22 January: *CPR Philip and Mary*, II, 150–1.
7  Collins (ed.), *Letters and Memorials of State*, I, 35.
8  McCoy, 'From the Tower to the Tiltyard', pp. 425–426.
9  *CPR Philip and Mary*, II, 121.
10  BRL Hagley Hall MS 351613.
11  APC IV, 323–4; BRL Hagley Hall MS 346501, 346869.
12  Dudley Papers, III, fo. 67.
13  Dudley Papers, III, fo. 66.

## Chapter 9

1  Strype, Sir Thomas Smith, pp. 249–50.
2  *CSP Spanish XIII*, p. 251.
3  BL Lansdowne MS 1236 fo. 37.

4  *CSP Spanish 1553*, pp. 393–5; *CSP Spanish 1554*, pp. 197, 231, 233, 276, 308; *CSP Spanish 1554–8*, pp. 4, 23; BL Cotton MS Titus B II fo. 109v.
5  BL Cotton MS Titus B II fo. 109.
6  BL Harleian MS 444 fo. 29r-v.

## Chapter 10

1  BL Harleian MS 4712 fo. 275.
2  Sir Thomas Smith, *De Republica Anglorum*, 131.
3  Stone, *Family, Sex and Marriage*, p. 198.
4  William Harrington's *Commendations of Matrimony* (1528), op. cit., p. 65.

## Chapter 11

1  Among the portraits included are King Philip II, the Duke of Alva, the Duke of Feria, Charles V and the Duchess of Parma. Adlard, *Amye Robsart and Earl of Leycester*, pp. 263–4.
2  Collins (ed.), *Letters and Memorials of State*, I, p. 34.
3  Machyn, p. 128.
4  Van Meteren, *Nederlandishe Historie* (1575), cited R.E. Pritchard (ed.), *Shakespeare's England: Life in Elizabethan and Jacobean Times*, p. 29.
5  Bartlett, *An Historical Descriptive Account of Cumnor Place*, pp. 34–5.
6  J.E. Cussans, *History of Hertfordshire: Hundred of Odsey* (1873), pp. 150–3; VCH Hertforshire III 274; IV, 112; *Household Accounts*, Appendix I, p. 380.
7  PRO C2/211/27; VCH Hertfordshire, IV, p. 112.
8  VCH Hertfordshire, IV, p. 113.
9  VCH Hertfordshire, IV, p. 114.
10  Dudley Papers, V, art. 3; Dudley MS, XIV, fo. 6v.
11  The manor of Hales Owen: BRL HH MS 351493; 390016.
12  *La Vie d'Elizabeth*, pp. 444–5.
13  Chamberlin, *Elizabeth and Leycester*, pp. 92–3.
14  PRO SP 70/40 fo. 72.
15  *CSP Venetian*, VI, iii, 1059.
16  Until recently it was believed that Lady Elizabeth had died in the winter of 1557–8: a new document conveying chattels from the estate from her

administrator of her will, her son John Appleyard, disproves this since it is dated 27 June 1557; Longleat MS 3188.

17 PRO CP 26(1)94; Norfolk Record Office MS MC5/29.

18 PRO C54/529 mm. 26,31; mm. 32,44; C54/533, mm. 8,20; PRO LC 4/188/287.

19 PRO C54/546 m. 6; Dudley Papers, XX, fo. 58v.

20 BL Stowe MS 571 fos. 101v, 121.

21 Waldman, *Elizabeth and Leicester*, pp. 60–61.

22 Tytler, II, p. 493.

23 4&5 Philip & Mary, c. 12.

24 BRL Hagley Hall MS 351494; PRO C 54/546 m.6; LC 4/188/415, 432.

25 BRL Hagley Hall MS 351621; PRO C/50/120; Society of Antiquaries, MS 139 fos. 129–31

**Chapter 12**

1 Wriothesley, *A Chronicle of England*, ii, p. 95.

2 Strype, *Sir Thomas Smith*, pp. 249–50.

**Chapter 13**

1 Lettenhove, I, p. 277.

2 *CSP Venetian* VI, iii 1285.

**Chapter 14**

1 PRO SP 12/1/7.

2 Machyn, p. 178.

3 BL Royal MS 17 C III fo. 2v.

4 PRO SP 63/1/12.

5 PRO SP 12/1/7 fo. 12r–v.

6 PRO SP 59/2/48 fo. 113r.

7 BL Harleian MS 6991/216.

8 Read, Burghley, p. 520.

9 BL Additional MS 35830 fo. 66v–67r.

10 Harrington, *Nuguae Antiquae*, vol. 11, p. 215; Johnson, *Elizabeth*, p. 199.

11 Printed in Read, *Walsingham*, vol. 1, pp. 423–43.

12 BL Lansdowne MS 102 fo. 69–70v.

13 See comment in BL Landsowne MS 102 fo. 45r.

14 Certain Precepts for the well ordering of a man's life (1584); Folger MS Va. 321 fos. 56v–59, L.B. Wright (ed.), *Advice to a Son* (Ithaca, New York, 1962), p. 11.

15 Strype, *Sir Thomas Smith*, p. 249.

16 Read, *Mr Secretary Cecil*, p. 124.

17 Somerset, *Elizabeth I*, p. 82.

18 PRO SP 12/1 fos. 3–5.

**Chapter 15**

1 BL Stowe MS 571 fo. 37v; PRO E 101/427/8; BL Lansdowne MS 3 fo. 200r.

2 PRO SP 12/24 fos. 104–107.

3 Dudley Papers, II, fo. 6; III fo. 19.

4 Reese, *The Royal Office of Master of the Horse*, pp. 138–9; Wilson, *Sweet Robin*, p. 87.

5 EHR LXV (1950), p. 96.

6 BL Cotton MS Caligula E V fo. 56r; PRO SP 12/1/5.

7 *CSP Spanish 1558–67*, p. 599.

8 *CSP Spanish 1558–67*, p. 313.

9 Ibid.

10 Hatfield House, Cecil Papers, vol. 154, art. 86.

11 *Leicester Correspondence*, p. 176.

12 Melville, p. 98.

13 *CSP Spanish 1558–67*, p. 208.

14 Klarwill, p. 114.

15 *CSP Domestic Addenda*, XVII, 31.

16 BL Cotton MS Titus B VII fo. 12r.

17 PRO SP 15/17/205.

18 *CSP Domestic Addenda*, p. 575.

19 Elizabeth would have probably read the Italian edition as part of her education. Significantly, the preface to the 1561 edition is by Sir John Cheke, Elizabeth's tutor. Perry, *The Word of a Prince*, p. 130.

20 Klarwill (ed.), *Queen Elizabeth and Some Foreigners*, p. 231.

21 Hatfield House, Cecil Papers, vol. 154, art. 86.

22 Melville, *Memoirs*, p. 37.

23 *CSP Spanish 1558–67*, p. 387.

24 *CSP Spanish 1558–67*, p. 57.

**Chapter 16**

1 Kempe (ed.), *The Loseley Manuscripts*, p. 65.

2 BRL HH MS 351493 and 390016.

3 See Cooper, *On Some Tudor Prices in Kent*.

4 *Household Accounts*, pp. 41, 55.

5 Longleat, Thynne Papers, III, fos. 21, 23, 24.

# Notes

## Chapter 17

1 Hayward, *Annals of the First Four Years of the Reign of Queen Elizabeth* (1840), pp. 6–7.
2 Machyn, p. 182.
3 Others sensed a free-for-all. As the funeral ended, it was reported that observers tore down the mourning cloth and coats of arms decorating the Abbey, 'every man a piece that could catch it'; Machyn, p. 183.
4 Strype, *Ecclesiastical Memorials*, III, ii, p. 548.
5 De Maisse, *Journals*, p. 58.
6 Hibbert, *The Virgin Queen*, p. 89.
7 BL Donation MS 4847 fo. 117.
8 Hughes and Larkin, *Tudor Royal Proclamations*, II, pp. 102–3.
9 *CSP Spanish 1558–67*, p. 387.

## Chapter 18

1 Johnson, *Elizabeth*, p. 78.
2 Clapham, *Elizabeth of England*, p. 89.
3 Hentzner, *Journey to England in 1598*, p. 33.
4 Clapham, p. 89.
5 PRO SP 12/6/36 fo. 78.
6 Johnson, *Elizabeth: A Study in Power and Intellect*, p. 201.
7 Wright, *Queen Elizabeth*, I, pp. 308–9; Fénelon, *Correspondance Diplomatique*, I, p. 124; Harrington, pp. 75–7; Birch, *Memoirs*, I, p. 136; HMC Rutland, I, p. 232.
8 BL Additional MS 35185 fo. 23v.
9 R.R. Tighe and J.C. Davis, *Annals of Windsor*, I, (1858), p. 641.
10 Melville, p. 96; Rye, *Murder of Amy Robsart*, p. 12.
11 *CSP Venetian*, VIII, pp. 2, 11.
12 Johnson, *Elizabeth*, p. 214.

## Chapter 19

1 *Household Accounts*, p. 41.
2 *Household Accounts*, pp. 44, 54.
3 *Household Accounts*, p. 86.
4 *Household Accounts*, p. 42; *CPR 1558–60*, p. 60.
5 *Household Accounts*, p. 54.
6 *Household Accounts*, p. 90.
7 'Item to Mr Hides servant carrying your

lordship's letters to his master vs'. *Household Accounts*, p. 48.
8 *Household Accounts*, p. 46.
9 *Household Accounts*, p. 48.
10 *CSP Venetian*, VII, p. 3.
11 Hoak, p. 125; Neville Williams calculated that the court spent £16,742, not including the expenses for the banquet. 'The coronation of Queen Elizabeth I', 401.
12 PRO LC 2/4/3 fo. 4.
13 PRO LC 2/4/3 fo. 19.
14 PRO LC 5/32 fo. 237.
15 PRO LC 2/4/3 fo. 10.
16 *CSP Venetian 1558–80*, pp. 11–12.
17 Elizabeth spoke: 'And I acknowledge that Thou hast dealt as wonderfully and as mercifully with me as Thou didst with Thy true and faithful servant Daniel, Thy prophet, whom Thou deliveredst out of the den from the cruelty of the greedy and raging lions. Even so was I overwhelmed and only by Thee delivered. To Thee therefore only be thanks, honour, and praise forever, Amen.'
   Later, by the seventeeth century, the garbled version of the text had come to end in a more convincing fashion: 'Some have fallen from being princes of this land to be prisoners in this place; I am raised from being a prisoner in this place to be prince of this land'. Hayward, *The Life and Reign of King Edward the Sixth with the Beginning of the Reign of Queen Elizabeth*, p. 458.

## Chapter 20

1 CLRO, Court of Aldermen, Repertories, XIV, 1558–61, fos. 97r–98r, 99r.
2 CLRO, Court of Aldermen, Repertories, XIV, 1558–61, fo. 102r.
3 CLRO, Court of Aldermen, Repertories, XIV, 1558–61, fo. 103v.
4 A mark was a monetary value whose worth was fixed at 13 shillings 4 pence.
5 CLRO, Court of Aldermen, Repertories, XIV, 1558–61, fo. 104r.
6 CLRO, Court of Aldermen, Repertories, XIV, 1558–61, fo. 98v.
7 BL Egerton MS 33320.

8 Printed, A. F. Pollard (ed.), *Tudor Tracts 1532–1588*, pp. 365–95.

9 Mulcaster, Sig Ciii

10 *CSP Venetian VI*, no. 883, pp. 1041–1095.

11 A total of 696 yards, for which Thomas Ackworth was paid £145. PRO LC 2/4/3 fo. 11v.

12 Nor did Elizabeth make too much of a fuss about the religious services, for now at least. Instead, a compromise was found: the coronation ceremony was performed by the Catholic Bishop Oglethorpe, while George Carew, Dean of the Chapel Royal, celebrated mass separately, without raising the host; Williams, *The Later Tudors*, p. 233.

13 *CSP Venetian 1558–80*, p. 17.

14 Dudley does not seem to have taken part in the coronation tournament: he is not mentioned in the surviving records: College of Arms, Tournament Portfolio, it. 4a–f.

**Chapter 21**

1 Klarwill, p. 94.

2 Klarwill, p. 193.

3 Somers Tract, I, p. 175.

4 BL Lansdowne MS 94 fo. 30; Harliean MS 5176 fo. 97.

5 Klarwill, p. 185.

6 Strype, *Sir Thomas Smith*, p. 205.

7 Ibid., pp. 186–7.

8 Ibid., p. 206.

9 *CSP Spanish 1558–67*, p. 63, 180.

10 PRO 31/3/26 fo. 156.

11 Hatfield House, Cecil Papers, vol. 148, art. 25; cited Read, *Burghley*, pp. 210–11.

12 *Hardwicke Papers*, p. 174.

13 J. B. Gabe and C. A. Scham (eds.).

14 J. Bruce (ed.), *Correspondence of Matthew Parker*, pp. 129–32.

15 'The Count of Feria's Dispatch of 14 November 1558' in *Camden Miscellany XXVII* (1987).

16 Klarwill, pp. 37–8, 43.

17 Klarwill pp. 258–9.

18 Strype, *Sir Thomas Smith*, p. 242.

19 Ibid., p. 244.

20 Klarwill, p. 44.

21 PRO SP 63/2 fos.82–83.

22 *CSP Spanish 1558–1567*, p. 3.

**Chapter 22**

1 AGS E 8340/233 fo. 20v; Lettenhove, I, pp. 273, 279, 566.

2 *CSP Spanish 1558–1567*, p. 8.

3 *CSP Spanish 1558–67*, p. 9.

4 *CSP Spanish 1558–67*, p. 16.

5 Lettenhove, I, pp. 398–401; *CSP Spanish 1558–67*, p. 22.

6 C. Martin and G. Parker, *The Spanish Armada* (1988), p. 281.

7 The ambassador had also reported that 'Other persons assert that she will take a very handsome youth, 18 or 20 years of age, robust etc, judging from passion, and because at dances and other public places she prefers him more than anyone else.' Any identification of this young suitor has not been sustained; *CSP Venetian 1558–80*, p. 19

8 *CSP Venetian 1558–80*, p. 28; Strype, *Sir Thomas Smith*, p. 247.

9 Camden, *Annales*, I, p. 26.

10 BL Lansdowne MS 94 fo. 94.

11 Camden, *Annales*, I, p. 27.

12 On this point, see Doran, *Monarchy and Matrimony*, p. 2; C. Levin, *The Heart and Stomach of a King*, pp. 41–2.

13 This was a sentiment shared by Armagil Waad, who wrote to Cecil that 'I wish that you would proceed to the reformation, having respect to quietness at home, the affairs you have in hand with foreign princes, the greatness of the Pope and how dangerous it is to make alteration in religion, especially in the beginning of a prince's reign'. For him, the appropriate metaphor should be observed: 'Glasses with small necks, if you pour into them any liquor suddenly or violently will not be so filled'; Read, *Mr Secretary Cecil*, pp. 127–8.

14 PRO SP 71/28, 15 July 1561.

15 *CSP Spanish 1558–67*, p. 31.

16 Doran, *Monarchy and Matrimony*, p. 24.

17 *CSP Spanish 1558–67*, p. 35.

18 *CSP Spanish 1558–67*, p. 37.

19 The Venetian ambassador later reported how: 'The Queen retired to bed, and after her there entered, by the light of many torches, the King her father in

company with the Duke of Alba. That Duke, having one of his feet bare, lifted the coverlet of the Queen's bed on one side, and, having inserted his foot beneath the sheet, advanced it until it touched the naked flesh of the Queen; and in such manner the marriage was understood to have been consummated in the name of King Philip through the agency of a third person – that which was never afterwards to be understood by anyone.'

20 *CSP Spanish 1558–67* p. 49.
21 Ibid., p. 2.
22 Ibid., p. 54.
23 Klarwill, p. 30.
24 *CSP Spanish 1558–67*, p. 75.
25 *CSP Spanish 1558–67*, p. 72.
26 *CSP Spanish 1558–67*, p. 63.
27 *CSP Venetian 1558–1580*, p. 71.

### Chapter 23

1 *Household Accounts*, p. 62.
2 *Household Accounts*, p. 69.
3 *Household Accounts*, p. 88.
4 *Household Accounts*, p. 52.
5 Ellis (ed.), *Original Letters Illustrative of English History*, 1st series (1824), p. 101.
6 PRO SP 12/6/31, fo. 63r.
7 Dudley Papers, Box I, fo. 14.
8 Dudley Papers, II, fo. 15.
9 Dudley Papers, I, fo. 46r.
10 Dudley Papers, I, fo. 13.
11 Dudley Papers, I, fo. 74r.
12 Dudley Papers, I, fo. 29r.
13 *Household Accounts*, pp. 70, 156.
14 Dudley Papers, I, fo. 207.
15 Dudley Papers, I, fo. 56.
16 Dudley Papers, I, fo. 48r.
17 Dudley Papers, I, fo. 25r.
18 Dudley Papers, I, fo. 40v.
19 PRO SP 12/6/35, fo. 76.
20 Dudley paid Pembroke's servant who delivered the hat 3s 4d in reward; *Household Accounts*, p. 61.
21 *Household Accounts*, p. 63.
22 *CSP Spanish 1558–67*, p. 27.
23 *CSP Spanish 1558–67*, p. 63.
24 *CSP Venetian 1558–1580*, p. 81.

### Chapter 24

1 *Household Accounts*, p. 49.

2 *Household Accounts*, pp. 55, 90: 'Item to Thomas Johns to buy a hoode for my ladye xxxvis'.
3 *Household Accounts*, pp. 60–1.
4 *Household Accounts*, p. 60: 'Item deliveryd to my lady ther by your lordship's commandment Cs'.
5 *Household Accounts*, pp. 61, 94.
6 *Household Accounts*, p. 60.
7 Where supper was somewhat less expensive – 27s 6d for 'all our suppers'; *Household Accounts*, pp. 94–5.
8 *Household Accounts*, p. 99. Also, p. 95: 'Item for spises bought by the cookes when your lordship rode to my ladyes xxiis'.
9 Dudley lost 10s to Fowler and £4 to Bagnall; *Household Accounts*, p. 99.
10 Jackson, 'Amye Robsart', p. 85.
11 Dudley Papers, XIV, fos. 26, 32.
12 *Household Accounts*, p. 59. See also Dudley Papers, I, fos. 59, 100, for their friendship.
13 BL Stowe MS 856 fos. 34v–35r.
14 Jenkins, *Elizabeth and Leicester*, p. 129.

### Chapter 25

1 Lettenhove, II, p. 27.
2 *CSP Spanish 1558–67*, p. 67.
3 Ibid.
4 *Household Accounts*, p. 63.
5 Pickering also wrote to Dudley in 1572 asking for a favour: Dudley Papers, II, fo. 94.
6 Lettenhove, II, p. 26.
7 Klarwill, p. 88.
8 Klarwill, p. 93.
9 Klarwill, p. 51.
10 *CSP Spanish 1558–67*, p. 63.
11 Klarwill, p. 52.
12 Haynes, p. 212.
13 Klarwill, p. 81.
14 Klarwill, p. 76.
15 Klarwill, p. 78.
16 Klarwill, p. 113.
17 *CSP Scotland IV*, p. 396; Murdin, pp. 559–60; *CSP Domestic II*, p. 12.
18 Harington, *Tract on the Succession*, p. 40.
19 *CSP Domestic V*, pp. 136–7.
20 'Historical Memoranda of John Stowe 1564–7' in *Three Fifteenth-Century*

*Chronicles*, J. R. Gardiner (ed.), pp. 128–47.

21 *CSP Spanish 1558–67*, p. 387.

22 See also *CSP Spanish 1558–67*, p. 387.

23 *Anglia Legaten N. Gyldenstenstiernas Bref. Till Kongl. Maj. 1561–62*, p. 18.

24 Mauvissiere, *Memoires* (Paris, 1731), I, p. 62.

25 Klarwill, p. 217.

26 Klarwill, p. 231.

27 Klarwill, pp. 41–2.

28 Klarwill, pp. 114–15.

**Chapter 26**

1 *Household Accounts*, p. 102.

2 *Household Accounts*, p. 65.

3 *Household Accounts*, p. 64.

4 *Household Accounts*, p. 68.

5 *Household Accounts*, p. 68.

6 *Household Accounts*, p. 103.

7 *Household Accounts*, p. 102.

8 Lettenhove, I, 556.

9 *Household Accounts*, p. 68; Lambeth Palace Library MS 3196 fo. 29r.

10 Dudley Papers, I, fos. 14r, 18r.

11 *Household Accounts*, p. 69.

12 *Household Accounts*, p. 69.

13 *Household Accounts*, p. 92.

14 T. Kemp (ed.) *The Black Book of Warwick* (Warwick, 1889), pp. 26–51.

15 Dudley Papers, I, fos. 84r, 171r.

16 Dudley Papers, I, fo. 108r.

17 Dudley Papers, I, fo. 36r.

18 Bodleian Library Additional MS C 94; PRO E328/176.

**Chapter 27**

1 *CSP Spanish 1558–67*, pp. 73–4.

2 Harrison, *Description of England*.

3 Dudley Papers, I, fo. 84r.

4 Dudley Papers, III, fo. 43r; cited Wilson, *Sweet Robin*, pp. 94–5.

5 Dudley Papers, I, fo. 39r.

6 Nichols, *Progress and Public Processions*, II, p. 105.

7 *CSP Spanish 1558–67*, p. 314.

8 Machyn, p. 206.

9 PRO 31/3/24 [Baschet transcripts] fo. 98r; SP 12/6/7 fo. 11r.

10 Journal, p. 81.

11 Klarwill, p. 120.

12 Klarwill, p. 121.

13 Wood, III, p. 227; BL Harleian MS 6986/12.

14 *Holinshed's Chronicle*, III, p. 1153; De Noailles, III, pp. 86–7.

15 Chamberlin, *Private Character of Queen Elizabeth*, pp. 46–8.

16 Somerset, *Elizabeth I*, p. 48.

17 Dudley Papers, I, fo. 20r; printed *Wiltshire Archaeological Magazine*, vol. XVIII (1878), p. 23.

18 Dudley Papers, I, fo. 80r.

19 PRO 31/3/24, fo. 111r.

20 PRO SP 12/6/23, fo. 39r.

21 PRO SP 12/6/30, fo. 67r.

22 Dudley Papers, I, fo. 86r.

23 Klarwill, p. 122.

24 Codoin, xcviii, p. 89.

25 *CSP Spanish 1558–67*, p. 95.

26 Ibid., p. 96.

27 Klarwill, p. 125.

28 *CSP Spanish 1558–67*, p. 99.

29 *CSP Spanish 1558–67*, p. 99.

30 *CSP Spanish 1558–67*, pp. 101–2.

31 BL Additional MS 48023 fo. 352.

32 PRO SP 12/16/1, fo. 5.

33 Dudley Papers, I, fo. 204v–205r.

34 Codoin, lxxxvii, p. 245; Forbes, *A Full View of the Public Transactions in the Reign of Queen Elizabeth*, I, p. 261.

35 AGS E 812 fo. 141.

36 *CSP Spanish 1558–67*, p. 106.

37 *CSP Spanish 1558–67*, p. 114.

38 *CSP Scottish 1547–63*, p. 215; Throckmorton told Cecil that the couple would be a perfect match: 'marriable both and the chief upholders of God's religion'. Forbes, *Public Transactions*, I, p. 147.

39 Forbes, I, pp. 166, 171.

40 *CSP Foreign 1558–59*, p. 508; *Sadler Papers*, I, p. 437, 447.

41 See *CSP Spanish 1558–67*, pp. 80–81, 90; Klarwill, pp. 110–11.

42 *CSP Spanish 1558–67*, p. 115. See also Bruener's comments that 'the Bishop of Aquila was told as a fact that the Queen was not willing to contract the alliance with His Princely Highness, and only wished to keep both us and her realm in dalliance with mere words, until she should marry Mylord Robert or some one else for whom she might have a

fancy. Of the former it is said that he seeks to poison his wife, for he is indeed a great favourite with the Queen.' Klarwill, p. 152.

43 *The Harleian Miscellany*, IV (1809), 478.

44 PRO E 179/69/78; Williams, *A Tudor Tragedy*, p. 50.

45 The manuscript is in the College of Arms, M. 6 fos. 56–62, and is discussed in R. McCoy, 'From the Tower to the Tiltyard', 425–35; 432–5.

46 *CSP Spanish 1558–67*, p. 113.

47 *CSP Spanish 1558–67*, p. 107.

48 *Household Accounts*, p. 151.

49 Klarwill, p. 162.

50 *CSP Spanish 1558–67*, pp. 113–14.

51 Dudley Papers, I, fo. 86r.

52 Dudley Papers, I, fo. 100r.

53 Dudley Papers, I, fos. 94r, 112r, 123r.

## Chapter 28

1 *Sadler Papers*, II, p. 43

2 *CSP Spanish 1558–67*, p. 119.

3 Klarwill, p. 104.

4 *Household Accounts*, p. 78. See also *CSP Foreign 1558–9*, pp. 404, 483, 501.

5 *CSP Foreign 1559–60*, p. 5.

6 *CSP Spanish 1558–67*, p. 74.

7 Robinsons, *Zurich Letters*, I, 46.

8 *CSP Spanish 1558–67*, p. 109.

9 *CSP Spanish 1558–67*, p. 96; AGS E 812 fo. 112. The calendar misprints Arundel in the original manuscript as the Earl of Bedford. In fact, Bedford and Pickering seem to have been good friends, with Pickering giving Bedford a steel saddle in early 1559. *Household Accounts*, p. 46.

10 *CSP Spanish 1558–67*, p. 109.

11 Klarwill, pp. 156–7.

12 Haynes, *State Papers*, I, p. 212

13 Klarwill, pp. 156–8.

14 *CSP Spanish 1558–67*, p. 102.

15 Klarwill, p. 151.

16 *CSP Spanish 1558–67*, p.117

17 *CSP Spanish 1558–67*, p. 117; Froude, *History of England*, VII, pp. 165–7.

18 *CSP Spanish 1558–67*, p. 112.

19 Klarwill, p. 152.

20 Klarwill, p. 157.

21 Klarwill, pp. 156–8.

22 Klarwill, pp. 156–8.

## Chapter 29

1 *A History of the County of Berkshire*, IV (1924), pp. 398–405.

2 Dudley Papers, V, fo. 283.

3 BRO Wills H 285; G 313.

4 BRO Wills D 188; J 292.

## Chapter 30

1 Lettenhove, II, pp. 478–9.

2 BL Royal MS B I fo. 20; *CSP Foreign 1559–60*, p. 190.

3 PRO SP 70/11, fos. 5, 76, 77.

4 *CSP Foreign 1560–61*, pp. 500–1.

5 *CSP Foreign 1560–61*, pp. 119–20, 219, 260.

6 *CSP Foreign 1559–60*, p. 370.

7 PRO SP 70/5, fo. 31r – v; Murdin, p. 749.

8 *Sadler Papers*, I, pp. 380–1.

9 PRO SP 12/7, fos. 185r–190v.

10 PRO SP 12/7/73, fo. 191v; *CSP Foreign 1560–61*, pp. 223–4.

11 *CSP Foreign 1560–61*, pp. 220–24.

12 Haynes, *State Papers*, p. 230.

13 PRO SP 52/1, fo. 318r.

14 BL Lansdowne MS 102 fo. 1r.

15 Haynes, *State Papers*, p. 253.

16 Forbes, I, 395.

17 *CSP Foreign 1560–61*, p. 594.

18 *CSP Spanish 1558–67*, p. 127.

19 Forbes, I, 455.

## Chapter 31

1 *CSP Foreign 1559–60*, pp. 233–7.

2 Adams, 'West Midlands', p. 320; Adams, 'Dudley Clientele', p. 254, n. 108; Dudley Papers, I, fo. 44r; *Household Accounts*, p. 73.

3 *CPR Foreign 1560–63*, p. 321; BL Additional MS 48023 fo. 353v; Journal, p. 67; AGS E 812 fo. 63; *Household Accounts*, p. 116.

4 *Household Accounts*, p. 117.

5 *Household Accounts*, p. 154; Lettenhove, II, p. 304. Dudley also played tennis on 6 April and 11 April; *Household Accounts*, p. 155.

6 PRO C54/584/5; *Household Accounts*, pp. 113, 118, 165.

7 Dudley Papers, III, fo. 28r; *Household Accounts*, p. 113.

8 *Household Accounts*, p. 155; Dudley

Papers, I, fo. 104r.

9  Dudley Papers, I, fo. 92r.
10 BL Additional MS 32091 fo. 172r.
11 Dudley Papers, I, fos. 106, 172.
12 Dudley Papers, I, fo. 131r.
13 Dudley Papers, XIV, fo. 15r; XV, fo.
   24v; Greater London Record Office
   P92/Sav/1957; Dudley Papers, I, fo. 70;
   PRO SP 10/14/144.
14 Collinson, *Letters of Thomas Wood*, pp.
   13–14.
15 *CSP Spanish 1558–67*, p. 133.
16 *CSP Spanish 1558–67*, p. 141.
17 *Household Accounts*, p. 137: 'Item paid
   unto Mr Darcy for money by him
   disbursed for iii staves broken by your
   lordship at Grenwiche vs'; p. 153: 'To the
   armorer of Grenewiche whan your
   lordship shuld have runn at Whit hale
   for the bringing of your armor and
   mending your head peec being broken
   xs.'
18 Dudley Papers, I, fo. 114.
19 Dudley Papers, I, fo. 139.
20 PRO SP 12/13/21
21 PRO SP 12/12/51, fo. 107. 15 June 1560.
22 Dudley Papers, I, fo. 146r.

**Chapter 32**

1  LPL 3196 fo. 95; Lodge, I, pp. 312–13.
2  Haynes, *Illustrations of English History*,
   p. 305.
3  Forbes, I, p. 460.
4  Forbes, I, p. 500, cited Read, *Mr
   Secretary Cecil*, p. 177.
5  Hatfield House, Cecil Papers, vol. 152,
   fo. 177r; Haynes, p. 322.
6  Froude, VII, p. 264.
7  BL Lansdowne MS 103 fo. 5r–v.
8  Hatfield House, Cecil Papers, vol. 153,
   fo. 1r; Haynes, p. 330.
9  Haynes, p. 361.
10 Haynes, p. 360.
11 BL Cotton MS Caligula B IX fo. 135r.
12 *CSP Foreign II*, p. 385.
13 Wright, I, p. 30.
14 BL Stowe MS fo. 180v; see *CSP Foreign
   1562* App. 619. Cited Read, *Mr Secretary
   Cecil*, p. 483.
15 *Household Accounts*, p. 140.
16 *CSP Scottish I*, pp. 472–3, 25 August
   1560.

17 *CSP Spanish 1558–67*, p. 169; *CSP
   Venetian 1558–80*, p. 249; Lettenhove, II,
   pp. 442, 461, 496; *CSP Foreign 1560–61*,
   pp. 119–20, 219, 260.
18 L. Howard (ed.), *A Collection of Letters*
   (1753), pp. 210–11.
19 *Household Accounts*, p. 142
20 *Household Accounts*, p. 141
21 Dudley Papers, I, fo. 4r–v.
22 HMC Pepys I 509.
23 *Household Accounts*, pp. 128–9, 138–9:
   'Item for one paier silke hoosen bought
   at William Holbornes the xiiii day of
   Aprell lxs'; 'Item for one paier of silke
   hoose the vth daye of May bought at
   William Holbornes lxs.'
24 Dudley Papers, I, fo. 155r.

**Chapter 33**

1  Dudley Papers, IV, fo. 7r.
2  Dudley Papers, IV, fos.3–4; Jackson,
   'Amye Robsart' pp. 85–8.
3  Stubbes, *The Anatomie of Abuses*.
4  *Household Accounts*, p. 106.
5  *Household Accounts*, p. 133.
6  Jackson, 'Amye Robsart', p. 86.
7  Jackson, 'Amye Robsart', p. 87.

**Chapter 34**

1  BL Cotton MS Titus B II fo. 419r.
2  Lodge, I, 423.
3  BL Cotton MS Titus B XVIII fo. 15.
4  Froude, VII, 282.
5  PRO SP 70/17; 27 August 1560.
6  AGS, Estado 814, fo. 24; Calendared:
   *CSP Spanish, 1558–67*, pp. 174–6 [partly]
   Printed: Lettenhove, II, 529–33. I thank
   Dr Simon Adams for generously
   providing me with this accurate
   translation from the original Spanish
   manuscript at Simincas.

**Chapter 35**

1  *Household Accounts*, p. 91; Dudley Papers,
   V, fo. 285.

**Chapter 36**

1  Hunnisett, *The Medieval Coroner*, p. 13.
2  Ibid., p. 17.
3  *Records of Medieval Oxford* (1912), p. 24;
   Hunnisett, p. 19.
4  PRO E 179/74/216 mm.6.

5 BRO D/A1/103/175. I am grateful for the Archivist Alison Day for providing me with copies of wills.

6 PRO E 179/74/216 mm.5.

7 BRO Wills H 120.

8 *Household Accounts*, pp. 122, 169.

9 *Household Accounts*, pp. 40, 47.

10 *Household Accounts*, p. 143; Jackson, 'Amye Robsart', p. 89.

11 'Item, paid for mailing cord for cloth that was sent unto Oxford 1 shilling 6 pence'; 'Item, unto carriers that carried the said packs to Oxford 2 shillings'; Jackson, 'Amye Robsart', p. 89.

12 Wright, I, pp. 45–6.

13 Journal, p. 66.

**Chapter 37**

1 Haynes, p. 362.

2 Magdalene College, Cambridge, Pepys MS 2503 fo. 709r; printed in Appendix II, p. 383.

3 Pepys MS 2503 fo. 707; printed in Appendix II, p. 384.

4 Ibid.

**Chapter 38**

1 Household Accounts, p. 125.

2 Wright, I, pp. 45–6.

3 Bodleian, Dugdale MS T 2 fo. 77; reprinted in Adlard, pp. 52–5.

**Chapter 39**

1 Journal, p. 66.

2 'An Account of the Parish of Cumner, Berks', *Gentleman's Magazine* (1821), Part II, pp. 34–5, 201–5.

3 BL Additional MS 9460 fo. 78.

4 Templer, *The Staircase*, p. 5.

5 Templer, p. 4.

6 Templer, p. 138.

7 Templer, p. 140.

8 Svanstrom, *Falls on Stairs: An Epidemiological Study* (1973); Templer, p. 17.

9 J. Walter, P.E. Doris, M.A. Shaffer, 'Clinical preservation of patients with acute cervical spine injury', *Annals of Emergency Medicine* 13(7) (1984), pp. 512–15.

10 PRO SP 70/19 fo. 132r–v; Jackson, 'Amye Robsart', 89–90.

11 Dudley Papers, I, fo. 147r.

12 J.C. Cox, *The Parish Registers of England* (1910), p. 114.

13 *CSP Venetian 1558–80*, p. 69.

14 *CSP Spanish 1558–67*, pp. 56–58.

15 Aird, 'The Death of Amy Robsart', *EHR*, 71 (1956), pp. 69–79; pp. 75–6.

16 Aird, p. 76.

17 R. A. Willis, *The Spread of Tumours in the Human Body* (London, 1952), p. 232; M. Lenz and J. R. Fried, *Annals of Surgery* 93 (1931), 278.

18 For various literature on the causes and effects of hypercalcaemia, see D.M. Dent, J.L. Miller, L. Klaff, J. Barron, 'The incidence and causes of hypercalcaemia', *Postgraduate Medical Journal* (Sep 1987); 63 (743): 745–50; G.R. Mundy, T.A. Guise, 'Hypercalcemia of malignancy', *American Journal of Medicine*, Aug 1997, 103(2): 134–45; V. Grill et al. 'Parathyroid hormone-related protein …', *Journal of Clinical Endocrinology and Metabolism*, December 1991, 73(6): 1309–15; A.F. Stewart, 'Clinical practice. Hypercalcemia associated with cancer', *New England Journal of Medicine*, 27 January 2005, 352(4), 373–9.

19 Dudley Papers, IV, fo. 25.

20 *CSP Spanish 1558–67*, p. 141.

**Chapter 40**

1 Doran, *Monarchy and Matrimony*, p. 44.

2 Templer, p. 20.

3 Templer, pp. 21, 23.

4 M. Ragg, S. Hwang, B. Steinhart, 'Analysis of Serious Injuries Caused by Stairway Falls', *Emergency Medicine* 12(1) (2001), pp. 45–9.

5 Templer, p. 20.

**Chapter 41**

1 Cecil Papers, 155, fo. 47r; Haynes, I, pp. 361–2.

2 *CSP Spanish 1558–67*, p. 176; Journal, p. 66.

3 *CSP Foreign 1560–61*, p. 255.

4 BL Cotton MS Galba XI fo. 257. The letter has gone previously unnoticed.

5 *CSP Foreign 1560–61*, p. 510.

6 *CSP Spanish 1558–67*, p. 141.

7  HMC, Salisbury, I, 337.
8  Hatfield House, Cecil Papers, vol. 155, fo. 28r.

**Chapter 42**
1  PRO SP 70/22 fo. 43.
2  PRO SP 70/19 fo. 39r.
3  PRO SP 70/19 fo. 47v.
4  *CSP Foreign 1560–61*, no. 644.
5  PRO SP 70/19 fo. 132r–v; Jackson, 'Amye Robsart', 89–90.

**Chapter 43**
1  Journal, p. 67.
2  BL Cotton MS Titus B XIII fo. 28.
3  BL Additional MS 48023 fo. 353v.
4  *CSP Scottish I*, p. 501.
5  BL Cotton MS Titus B XIII fo. 26v.
6  PRO SP 63/2 fo. 82r.
7  Hatfield House, Cecil Papers, vol. 155, fo. 54r; Haynes, I, pp. 364–5; HMC Salisbury, I, p. 253.
8  *Hardwicke Papers*, pp. 121–23.
9  PRO SP 70/20, fo. 40r.
10  *CSP Foreign 1560*, p. 398.
11  *Hardwicke Papers*, I, 144.

**Chapter 44**
1  BL Cotton MS Titus B XIII fo. 28r.
2  *Household Accounts*, p. 146.
3  BL Additional MS 35830 fo. 66v–67r.
4  *Hardwicke Papers*, p. 165.

**Chapter 45**
1  J.H. Pollen (ed.), *Papal Negotiations with Mary Queen of Scots* (Scot. Hist. Soc. Xxxvii, 1901), pp. 60–1, cited Adams, p. 165n.
2  *Chronicle of Queen Jane and Mary*, p. 7.
3  PRO SP 70/20 fo. 40r.
4  *Hardwicke Papers*, p. 166.
5  Machyn, p. 245.
6  PRO SP 70/21 fo. 137v.
7  BL Cotton MS Titus B XIII fo. 26r–v.
8  PRO SP 70/21 fo. 146v.
9  *Household Accounts*, p. 160.
10  *Household Accounts*, p. 147.
11  PRO SP 70/21 fo. 146r.
12  *CSP Foreign 1560–61*, p. 475.
13  BL Harleian MS 6990/2; printed Wright, I, 58.
14  BL Cotton MS Nero B III fo. 155r.

15  *CSP Foreign 1560–61*, p. 510.
16  *Hardwicke Papers*, p.167.
17  *Hardwicke Papers*, p. 168.
18  PRO SP 70/21 fo. 117; *CSP Foreign 1560–1* p. 467.
19  *CPR 1560–63*, p. 44.
20  BL Additional MS 48023 fo. 353v.
21  Dudley Papers, I, fo. 201.
22  PRO SP 12/16/1 fo. 1r.
23  PRO SP 70/22 fo. 57r–v.
24  PRO SP 70/22 fo. 55r–v; *CSP Foreign III* p. 497. No. 881.

**Chapter 46**
1  Lettenhove, II, p. 23.
2  *CSP Spanish 1558–67*, pp. 178–9.
3  *CSP Spanish 1558–67*, p. 181.
4  *CSP Spanish 1558–67*, pp. 181–82.
5  Mary Tudor, the sister of Henry VIII, had married Charles Brandon, while the present Duchess of Suffolk had married Richard Bertie. The Duchess of Somerset, the widow of the Lord Protector Somerset, had later married Somerset's servant, Francis Newdigate.
6  *CSP Spanish 1558–67*, p. 182.
7  BL Additional MS 48023 fo. 355r.
8  *CSP Spanish 1558–67*, p. 197.
9  Doran, *Monarchy and Matrimony*, p. 48.
10  PRO SP 70/21 fos. 109r–110v; SP 70/22 fos. 88r–97v.

**Chapter 47**
1  *CSP Spanish 1558–67*, pp. 186–91.
2  Lettenhove, II, pp. 546, 548.
3  *CSP Spanish 1558–67*, p. 194.
4  *CSP Spanish 1558–67*, pp. 194–95.
5  PRO SP 12/16/49–50, 59–68; *CSP Domestic Addenda 1547–65*, p. 509.
6  *CSP Foreign 1561–2*, no. 157, 1 May 1561.
7  PRO SP 70/26 8 May 1561
8  *CSP Foreign 1561–62*, pp. 93–95, 103–105.
9  AGS E 815 fos.76–77.
10  *CSP Spanish 1558–67*, p. 200–1.
11  BL Additional MS 35830 fo. 109; *Hardwicke Papers*, II, 170.
12  BL Additional MS 35830 fo. 205; AGS E 815 fo. 105; Read, *Mr Secretary Cecil*, p. 234.
13  *CSP Foreign IV*, p. 158. No. 272.

14 *Archaelogia* XIII (1800), pp. 201–3;
   Perry, *The Word of a Prince*, p. 126.
15 Talbot Papers, p. 409.
16 CKS U1415/FO30/2 for Ambrose's
   Patent of Creation.
17 PRO SP 70/33 fo. 60r.
18 Haynes, I, 368; J.W. Buchan and H.
   Paton, *A History of Peebleshire* (3 vols,
   Glasgow, 1925–7).
19 *Hardwicke Papers*, p. 174.
20 BL Cotton Titus B XIII fo. 48v.
21 BL Cotton Titus B XIII fo. 62v.
22 BL Additional MS 35830 fo. 228r.
23 See T. Norton and T. Sackville,
   *Gorboduc: The Tragedy of Ferrex and
   Porrex* (Menston, 1968); Machyn, p.
   275. For background also *A Calendar of
   Inner Temple Records*, ed. F.A. Inderwick
   (London, 1896), I, pp. 215–20;
   Rosenberg, p. 47.
24 BL Additional MS 48023 fo. 360r.
25 *Gorboduc*, sig. B3r.
26 'tenia sus negocios en muy buen punto';
   AGS E 815 fo. 186r.
27 *CSP Spanish 1558–67*, pp. 225–6.
28 *CSP Spanish 1558–67*, p. 225.
29 *CSP Spanish 1558–67*, p. 225.
30 BL Additional MS 48023 fo. 363.
31 AGS E 815 fos.76–77.
32 BL Additional MS 48023 fo. 363.
33 Lettenhove, III, p. 11.
34 *CSP Foreign 1562*, pp. 68–9.
35 See *CSP Foreign 1562*, pp. 42, 83 and
   *CSP Spanish 1558–67*, p. 244, for details.

**Chapter 48**
1 Journal, p. 120.
2 PRO SC6/ElizI/136.
3 Hatfield House, Cecil Papers, vol. 153,
   fo. 84r.
4 Cited in Adams, *Leicester and the Court*,
   pp. 137–8.
5 Rumours before the Parliament began
   indicated that a petition would be set
   down urging the queen specifically to
   marry Dudley. AGS E 816 fos. 43, 51.
6 BL Cotton MS Titus I fos. 61–4.
7 *Household Accounts*, p. 172; Elton,
   *Parliament*, p. 358.
8 Gallys was Mayor of Windsor in 1563
   and signed the patent appointing
   Dudley High Steward of the borough

in September later that year. He was
also a tenant of Windsor Castle, of
which Dudley was Constable. In an
inventory of Dudley's possessions there
is mention of a short sword 'which was
Gallecies of Windsor'. Dudley Papers,
II, art.12; PRO SC 6/ElizI/136–47;
Dudley Papers, XIII, fo. 21r.
9 Dudley Papers, III, fo. 33.
10 BL Additional MS fos.17–20.
11 *CSP Spanish 1558–67*, p. 296.
12 Wright, I, p. 124.
13 BL Lansdowne MS 94 fo. 30r; Harleian
   MS 5176 fo. 97.
14 *CSP Scottish 1563–69*, pp. 43–4.
15 *CSP Scottish 1563–69*, pp. 56–7.
16 BL Lansdowne MS 102 fos. 107r–109r.
17 *CSP Scottish 1563–69*, p. 81.
18 BL Cotton MS Caligula B X fo. 287r.
19 *CSP Spanish 1558–67*, p. 424.
20 *CSP Scottish 1563–69*, p. 233.
21 Hatfield House, Cecil Papers, vol. 140,
   fos. 1r–2v.
22 *CSP Scottish 1563–69*, p. 124; *CSP
   Spanish 1558–67*, p. 424.
23 BL Additional MS 19401 fo. 101r.
24 BL Harleian MS 6990 fo. 68r.
25 *CSP Spanish 1558–67*, pp. 429–30.

**Chapter 49**
1 PRO SP 31/3/26 fo. 102.
2 *CSP Spanish 1558–67*, pp. 436–7.
3 *CSP Spanish 1558–67*, pp. 409–410.
4 Klarwill, p. 230.
5 *CSP Spanish 1558–67*, p. 514.
6 *CSP Spanish 1558–67* p. 531.
7 *CSP Spanish 1558–67*, p. 485.
8 *CSP Venetian 1558–80*, p. 359.
9 Jenkins, *Elizabeth and Leicester*, p. 129.
10 *CSP Spanish 1558–67*, p. 487.
11 Melville, p. 94.
12 Wright, I, pp. 206–7.
13 *CSP Spanish 1558–67*, p. 470.
14 Hatfield MS 39; Murdin, 760.
15 Collected Works, p. 132.
16 *CSP Spanish 1558–67*, p. 492.
17 BL Landsdowne MS 102 fos. 121–22.
18 *CSP Spanish 1558–67*, p. 485.
19 Waldman, p. 114.
20 Wright, I, p. 225.
21 *CSP Domestic Addenda*, XIII 8.
22 *CSP Domestic Addenda*, XIII 8.

23 SP 15/13/73; *CSP Domestic Addenda,*
   *1566–1579*, pp. 28–9.
24 Waldman, *Elizabeth and Leicester*, p. 123.

**Chapter 50**
 1 BL Lansdowne MS 102 fo.121r; Wright,
   I, 208–9.
 2 Naunton, *Fragmentia Regalia*
   (Edinburgh, 1808), pp. 208–9.
 3 *CSP Spanish 1558–67*, p. 560.
 4 PRO SP 52/10 fo. 68r.
 5 *CSP Spanish 1558–67*, p. 518.
 6 *CSP Spanish 1558–67*, pp. 511–12.
 7 PRO SP 12/36/152.
 8 PRO SP 63/18/19 fo. 44r–v.
 9 *CSP Venetian 1558–80*, p. 382.
10 *CSP Spanish 1558–67*, p. 529.
11 Chamberlin, *The Private Character of*
   *Elizabeth*, pp. 56–7.
12 BL Egerton MS 2836 fos.66–8, 72.
13 Murdin, *Collection of State Papers*, p.
   762.
14 BL Egerton MS fos. 37–71; Levine,
   *Early Elizabethan Succession Question*,
   pp. 168–9.
15 PRO SP 12/40 fo. 195.
16 Neale, *Parliaments*, p. 136.
17 *CSP Spanish 1558–67*, p. 590.
18 Disraeli, II, 184–85.
19 Commons Journal, I, 75.
20 *CSP Spanish 1558–67* pp. 591–92.
21 Hasler, *Commons*, III, pp. 60–1;
   Haynes, p. 444.
22 Murdin, p.762.
23 *CSP Spanish 1558–67*, p. 592.
24 *CSP Spanish 1558–67*, p. 595.
25 *CSP Spanish 1558–67*, p. 599.
26 BL Stowe MS 354 fos. 18–19; Neale,
   *Elizabeth I and her Parliaments 1559–*
   *1581*, p. 149.
27 CUL MS Gg III 34 fos. 208–12;
   *Collected Works*, pp. 94–98.
28 PRO SP 12/41/9 fo. 14r.
29 BL Lansdowne MS 1236 fo.42r.
30 *CSP Spanish 1558–67*, p. 614.

**Chapter 51**
 1 *CSP Spanish 1558–67*, p. 213.
 2 Hatfield House, Cecil Papers, vol. 155,
   fo. 67v.
 3 Hatfield House, Cecil Papers, vol. 155,
   fo. 68r.
 4 Hatfield House, Cecil Papers, vol. 155,
   fo. 68v.
 5 HMC Hatfield I 1151; HMC Pepys, I,
   pp. 111–12.
 6 HMC Pepys, II, p. 717.
 7 HMC Hatfield, I, p. 1136.
 8 HMC Salisbury, XIII, pp. 85–6.
 9 HMC Hatfield, I, p. 1137.
10 APC, VIII, p. 248.

**Chapter 52**
 1 Lambeth Palace Library MS 3197 fo. 79,
   printed E. Lodge, *Illustrations of British*
   *History* (2nd edn., London, 1838), II, p.
   17.
 2 Douglas's unusual Christian name
   probably came from her godmother,
   Margaret, the Countess of Lennox,
   whose maiden name had been Douglas.
 3 Read, 'Letter', p. 24.
 4 CKS U1475/L/2/4 item 3, fo. 36.
 5 Haywarde, *Les Reportes del Cases in*
   *Camera Stellata, 1593 to 1609*, p. 199.
 6 CKS U1475/L/2/3 item 13, fo. 12.
 7 Douglas testified that the marriage had
   taken place at some point between 11
   November and 25 December 1573.
 8 Dugdale, *Antiquities*, 166–67; CKS
   U1475/L/2/3.

**Chapter 53**
 1 W.B. Devereux, *Lives and Letters of the*
   *Devereux, Earls of Essex* (London, 1853),
   I, p. 12.
 2 *CSP Spanish 1558–67*, p. 431.
 3 *CSP Spanish 1558–67*, p. 511.
 4 Collinson, 'Letters of Thomas Wood',
   p. 9–10.
 5 Ibid., p. 11.
 6 Ibid., p. 15.
 7 H.E. Malden (ed.), *The Devereux*
   *Papers, 1575–1601*, Camden Society, 3rd
   series, 34 (1923), pp. 3, 11.
 8 A. Collins, *Peerage of England* (1812), IV,
   pp. 461–2.
 9 Evelyn MS 264.
10 Perry, p. 177.
11 PRO SP 12/126/10.
12 Dudley Papers, III, fo. 190r.
13 Nicolas, *Memoirs of ... Christopher*
   *Hatton*, pp. 68–70.
14 Dudley Papers, II, fo. 181r.

15  *CSP Foreign*, 24 June 1578.

**Chapter 54**

1   Doran, *Monarchy and Matrimony*, p. 171.
2   PRO SP 70/94 fos. 172–6.
3   *CSP Spanish 1568–79*, p. 14.
4   Lodge, I, p. 457.
5   Digges, *Compleat Ambassador*, pp. 226–8.
6   BL Additional MS 30156 fo. 326; Digges, *Compleat Ambassador*, pp. 220, 226–8.
7   PRO SP 83/7/73.
8   Hatfield House, Cecil Papers, vol. 148, fos.23r–v, 25r–v; HMC Hatfield 241.
9   BL Harleian MS 285 fo. 77r–78r.
10  Camden, p. 227; PRO 31/3/27; Wright, II, p. 94; Lodge, II, p. 141; HMC Salisbury, II, pp. 311, 323; *CSP Foreign 1579*, 27 March.
11  Lettenhove, *Relations Politiques*, x, p. 678.
12  *CSP Spanish 1558–67*, p. 583.
13  Labanoff, *Lettres ... de Marie Stuart*, V, p. 94.
14  *CSP Spanish 1558–67*, p. 592.
15  *CSP Spanish 1558–67*, p. 594.
16  *CSP Spanish 1580–86*, pp. 245–46.
17  HMC Salisbury II, pp. 239–45; BL Cotton MS Titus C XVIII fos. 1–21.
18  *CSP Spanish 1568–79* pp. 692–3; PRO 31/3/27 fo. 366; BN FF 15973 fos. 173–4.
19  Murdin, p. 335.
20  BL Harleian MS 6992 fo. 112r.
21  Camden, *Annals*, p. 205; see also Labanoff, *Lettres ... de Marie Stuart* V, p. 94.
22  Nicolas, *Memoirs of ... Christopher Hatton*, p. 97.
23  BL Harleian MS 6992 fo. 114r.
24  Dudley Papers, III, fo. 43–52.
25  *CSP Spanish III*, p. 2.
26  PRO SP 12/140/23.

**Chapter 55**

1   CKS U 1475/L/2/4, item 3.
2   Lettenhove, XI, pp. 304–5.
3   BL Additional MS 33594 fos. 1–3.
4   Murdin, p. 336.
5   Hatfield House, Cecil Papers, vol. 149, fo. 24.

6   26 May 1581: Huntington Library MS HA 2377.
7   Elizabeth, *Collected Works*, pp. 302–3.
8   BL Cotton MS Galba E VI fo. 244.
9   Dudley to Elizabeth, 20 September 1583; *CSP Domestic Addenda* pp. 95–6.
10  PRO SP 12/182/41.
11  *CSP Foreign Holland*, 21, ii, 94.
12  Dudley Papers, II, fo. 265.
13  'una loba' in the original Spanish report; *Coleccion de documentos*, 92.507. See also *CSP Spanish 1580–86*, p. 477.
14  HMC Bath, V, p. 44.
15  H. Nicholas, *Memoirs of ... Christopher Hatton*, pp. 381–3.
16  BL Additional MS 15891 fo. 128.
17  Chéruel, 341.

**Chapter 56**

1   BL Cotton MS Titus B VII fo. 10.
2   Peck (ed.), *Leicester's Commonwealth*, p. 125.
3   Burgoyne (ed.), *History of Queen Elizabeth, Amy Robsart and the Earl of Leicester*, p. 49.
4   Peck, p. 86.
5   Peck, pp. 82–3.
6   BL Sloane MS 1660 fos. 29v–30r.
7   Cited Horton Smith, *Dr Walter Bailey 1529–1592: Physician to Queen Elizabeth*, p. 15.

**Chapter 57**

1   Harington, *Tract on the Succession*, p. 44; *Catholic Record Society*, 21, p. 76.
2   Adlard, pp. 56–7.
3   Dudley Papers, III, fo. 209; Wilson, *Sweet Robin*, p. 268.
4   Peck (ed.), *Leicester's Commonwealth*, pp. 252–62.
5   Murdin, pp. 436–7.
6   Hicks, 'Growth of a Myth', pp. 96–7.
7   PRO SP 15/29/39.
8   Murdin, pp. 456–7.
9   PRO SP 12/151/46 fos. 103–4; BL Additional MS 15891 fo. 99.
10  'Articles wherof Oxford wold have accused Lester'; PRO SP 12/151/50 fo. 110.
11  PRO SP 12/151/46 fos. 103–4.
12  BL Cotton MS Titus C VI fos. 7–8.
13  PRO SP 12/151/44 fos. 98–99.

14 BL Cotton MS Caligula E VII fo. 174v.
15 PRO SP 15/27A/57.
16 *CSP Foreign XII*, ii, pp. 140–41.
17 *CSP Spanish 1580–86*, p. 78.
18 Oxford, 'Interrogatories to be demanded of Arundell and Howard', PRO SP 12/151/42, art. 1; Arundell denied this charge; PRO SP 12/151/43.
19 PRO SP 12/151/45.
20 PRO SP 12/151/45.
21 PRO SP 78/10/95; BL Cotton MS Galba E VI fol. 189v.
22 On Stafford, see Read, 'The Fame of Edward Stafford', *American Historical Review* 20 (1915) pp. 292–313; Read, 'The Fame of Edward Stafford', *American Historical Review* 53 (1930) pp. 560–66; Neale, 'The Fame of Edward Stafford', *English Historical Review* 44 (1929) pp. 203–19.
23 PRO SP 78/13/87.
24 PRO SP 78/15/15.
25 PRO SP 53/15/552.
26 PRO SP 78/13/86.
27 PRO SP 78/13/86.
28 PRO SP 78/13/86.
29 PRO SP 15/28/113, fos. 369–88v; fo. 375v.
30 British Library 1345.a.25, p. 14.

**Chapter 58**

1 HMC *Second Report, Appendix* (1871), p. 41.
2 BL Additional MS 48023 fo. 353r; printed in 'Journal', p. 67.
3 BL Additional MS 48023 fo. 350r; Journal, p. 54.
4 BL Additional MS 48023 fo. 355r; Journal, p. 74.
5 BL Additional MS 48023 fo. 353r; Journal, p. 67.
6 BL Additional MS 48023 fo. 368v; Journal, p. 119.
7 BL Additional MS 48023 fo. 352v; Journal, p. 65.
8 *CPR, 1559–1560* pp. 30, 422.
9 PRO LC 2/3/2.
10 CPR 1559–60, p. 380.
11 See Levine, The Early Elizabethan Succession Question 1558–1568, chapter 5.
12 Levine, pp. 72–5.

13 Hatfield House, Cecil Papers, Vol. 140 fo. 511r–v.
14 BL Additional MS 48023 fo. 353r; Journal, p. 66.
15 Jackson, Amy Robsart, p. 85.
16 Household Accounts, p. 102.
17 *Household Accounts*, p. 106.
18 Klarwill, p. 158.
19 Lettenhove, *Relations Politiques*, II., p. 187.
20 Lettenhove, Relations Politiques, I, p. 556.
21 CSP Foreign 1561–62 no. 320.
22 Dudley Papers, I, fo. 36r.
23 Warwickshire County Record Office, CR 580/349/3.
24 Adlard, *Amy Robsart*, p. 94.
25 Dudley Papers, IV, fo. 10r.
26 Wiltshire Archaeological Magazine, XVIII (1879), p. 25.
27 Household Accounts, pp. 438–39.
28 Cited, Stone, *Crisis of the Aristocracy*, p. 226.
29 Dudley Papers, I, fo. 98v.
30 Cited Jenkins, *Elizabeth and Leicester*, p. 87.
31 PRO SP 70/39 fos. 118, 119, 175–6; SP 70/40 fos. 62–88.
32 CSP Foreign 1562, p. 243.
33 CSP Spanish 1558–67, p. 516.
34 PRO SP 12/36/152.
35 CSP Foreign 1561–62, p. 424.
36 CSP Foreign 1561–62, no. 730.
37 Hatfield House, Cecil Papers Vol.155 fo. 67v.
38 Hatfield House, Cecil Papers Vol. 155 fo. 68r.
39 PRO SP 70/19 fo. 132r–v.
40 BL Additional MS 35830 fos. 66v–67r.
41 Clark, A., *Life and Times of Anthony Wood*, (1891) Vol. I, p. 260.
42 Adlard, *Amy Robsart*, p. 49.

**Chapter 59**

1 Dudley Papers, I, fo. 189.
2 Dudley Papers, I fo. 2r–v.
3 BL Additional MS 48023 fo. 353r; Journal, p. 66.
4 'Bedingfield Papers', *Norfolk Archaeology* IV, p. 184.
5 *Household Accounts*, pp. 414, 422.
6 It cannot be certain that 'John

Steaphinson Ferrar (farrier)' is the same person in question, though it provides an intriguing link.

7 Dudley Papers, IV, fo. 18.
8 Household Accounts, p. 125.
9 Household Accounts, pp. 39, 66.
10 *Household Accounts*, pp. 125–6.

**Finis**

1 BL Cotton MS Caligula D I fo. 333r.
2 *CSP Spanish IV*, p. 481.
3 HMC Bath V, p. 94.
4 BL Stowe MS 156 fo. 204v.

5 PRO SP 12/215/65.
6 A.D. Bartlett, *A historical and descriptive account of Cumnor Place, Berks*, (1850), p. 10.
7 Oxfordshire Record Office, Acc 4419/Box 5/Misc 16; printed *Oxoniensia*, XIII (1948), p. 75. I am indebted to Gary Hill for providing me with a copy of the report.

**Appendices**

1 *Leicester's Commonwealth*, p. 58.
2 *Leicester's Commonwealth*, pp. 63–4.

# ➻ Bibliography ➺

## Manuscript Sources

PUBLIC RECORD OFFICE (NATIONAL ARCHIVES, KEW)

C2: Chancery, Pleadings

C 50: Chancery, Lord Chancellor's Office

C 54: Chancery, Close Rolls

C 78: Chancery, Decree Rolls

E 101: Exchequer, King's Remembrancer, Various Accounts

E 179: Exchequer, Subsidy Rolls

E 315: Exchequer, Augmentation Office, Miscellaneous Books

E 328: Exchequer, Augmentation Office, Ancient Deeds

E 351: Exchequer, Pipe Office, Declared Accounts

KB 9: King's Bench, Ancient Indictments

LC 2: Lord Chamberlain's Department, Special Events

LC 4: Lord Chamberlain's Department, Rolls and Entry Books

LC 5: Lord Chamberlain's Department, Miscellaneous Records

LR 2: Auditors of the Land Revenue, Miscellaneous Books

PROB/11: Prerogative Court of Canterbury: Registers of Wills

SC 6: State Papers Special Collections

SP 1: State Papers Henry VIII

SP 10: State Papers Domestic Edward VI

SP 11: State Papers Domestic Mary I

SP 12: State Papers Domestic Elizabeth I

SP 15: State Papers Domestic Addenda Edward VI–James I

SP 46: State Papers Supplementary

SP 52: State Papers Scotland, Elizabeth I

SP 59: State Papers Mary Queen of Scots

SP 59: State Papers Scotland, Border Papers

SP 63: State Papers Ireland, Elizabeth I

SP 70: State Papers Foreign, General Series, Elizabeth I

SP 71: State Papers Foreign, Barbary States, Elizabeth I

SP 78: State Papers Foreign, France, Elizabeth I

31/3: Baschet's transcripts of the French ambassadors' dispatches in the Bibliotheque Nationale, Paris

ARCHIVO GENERAL DE SIMANCAS, SPAIN
Estado 812–819 Inglaterra
Estado 8340/233

BERKSHIRE RECORD OFFICE, READING
Wills D 188, G 313, H 120, H 285, J 292
D/A1/103/175

BIBLIOTHÈQUE NATIONALE DE FRANCE, PARIS
MS Français 15970

BIRMINGHAM REFERENCE LIBRARY
Hagley Hall MS 346501, 346869, 351621, 351613, 351493, 351494, 390016

BODLEIAN LIBRARY, OXFORD
Additional MS C 94
Ashmolean MS
Dugdale MS T 2
Rawlinson MS
Tanner MS

BRITISH LIBRARY, LONDON
Additional MS 15891, 19401, 30156, 32091, 33594, 35185, 35830, 35838, 48023
Cotton MS Caligula B IX, Caligula B X, Caligula D I, Caligula E VII, Galba E
    VI, Titus B I, Titus B II, Titus B VII, XIII, Titus C VI, XVIII, Vitellius C XI
Donation MS 4847
Egerton MS 2836, 33320
Harleian MS 285, 444, 4712, 5176, 6990, 6991, 6992
Hatfield MS M485/39 Vol. 150
Lansdowne MS 3, 94, 102, 103, 1236
Royal MS 17 C III
Royal MS B I
Sloane MS 1660
Stowe MS 156, 571, 856

CENTRE FOR KENTISH STUDIES
U1415/F030/2
U1475/L2/1–4

COLLEGE OF ARMS, LONDON
Arundel MS XXXV fos.18–21
M. 6 fos.56–62
Tournament Portfolio, it. 4a–f.

CORPORATION OF LONDON RECORD OFFICE
Court of Aldermen, Repertories, XIV

DURHAM UNIVERSITY LIBRARY
Bamburgh Select MS 15

HATFIELD HOUSE LIBRARY, HERTFORDSHIRE
Cecil Papers, vols. 39, 140, 148, 149, 153, 155

INNER TEMPLE LIBRARY, LONDON
Petyt MS 538

LAMBETH PALACE LIBRARY, LONDON
MS 3196, 3197

LONGLEAT HOUSE, WILTSHIRE
Dudley Papers I, II, III, IV, XIII, XIV, XV, XX
Dudley Papers, Boxes II, V
MS 3188
Thynne Papers III

MAGDALENE COLLEGE, CAMBRIDGE
Pepys MS 2503

NORFOLK RECORD OFFICE
MS MC5/29

OXFORDSHIRE RECORD OFFICE
Acc 4419/OX5/MISC 16

WARWICKSHIRE COUNTY RECORD OFFICE
CR 580/349/3

## Primary Sources

*Acts of the Privy Council* [APC], ed. J.R. Dasent (1890–1907)

Adams, S. (ed.), *Household Accounts and Disbursement Books of Robert Dudley, Earl of Leicester, 1558–1561,1584–1586*, Camden Society, 5th series, 6 (Cambridge, 1995)

Adlard, G., *Amye Robsart and the Earl of Leycester* (1870)

Ascham, Roger, *Works*, ed. J.A. Giles (London, 1864–5)

Ashmole, E., *The History and Antiquities of Berkshire*, vol. 1 (1719)

Aylmer, J., *A Harbour for Faithful and True Subjects* (1559)

Bayne, C.G., 'The Coronation of Queen Elizabeth', *English Historical Review* XII (1907)

Beale, R., 'A Treatise of the Office of a Councillor and Principal Secretary to Her Majesty' (1592) in Read, *Walsingham*, vol. 1, pp. 427–43

Bedingfield Papers, 'State Papers relating to the custody of the princess Elizabeth at Woodstock in 1554', ed. C.R. Manning, *Norfolk Archaeology*, IV (Norwich, 1855)

Birch, T., *Memoirs of the Reign of Queen Elizabeth* (1754)

J. Bruce (ed.), 'Annals of the first four years of the reign of Queen Elizabeth by Sir John Hayward', Camden Society, vol. 7 (1840)

———— *Correspondence of Matthew Parker*, Parker Society (Cambridge, 1853)

*Calendar of Letters, Despatches and State Papers relating to Negotiations between England and Spain preserved in the Archives at Simancas and elsewhere*, ed. Pascual de Gayangos et al., 1862–1954. [*CSP Spanish*]

*Calendar of Letters of State Papers relating to English affairs, preserved principally in the Archives of Simincas, Elizabeth*, ed. M.A.S. Hume et al., 1892–99 [*CSP Spanish*]

*Calendar of State Papers, Domestic Series*, ed. Robert Lemon and M.A.E. Green, 1856–72 [*CSP Domestic*]

*Calendar of State Papers, Foreign Series*, ed. Joseph Stevenson et al., 1863–1950 [*CSP Foreign*]

*Calendar of State Papers Relating to Scotland and Mary Queen of Scots*, ed. Joseph Bain et al., Edinburgh, 1898–1952 [*CSP Scottish*]

*Calendar of State Papers relating to English Affairs, preserved principally at Rome at the Vatican Archives and Library*, ed. J.M. Rigg, 1916–26 *[CSP Rome]*

*Calendar of State Papers and Manuscripts existing in the Archives and Collections of Venice*, ed. Rawdon Brown et al., 1864–98 [*CSP Venetian*]

Camden, W., *Annales: The True and Royall History of the famous Empresse Elizabeth* ... (1625)

Clapham, J., *Elizabeth of England*, eds. E.P. Read and C. Read (Oxford, 1951)

Clifford, A. (ed.), *The State Papers and Letters of Sir Ralph Sadler*, 2 vols. (Edinburgh, 1809)

*Colección de Documentos Ineditos para la Historia de Espana*, ed. M. F. Navarete et al. (Madrid, 1842–95)

Collins, A. (ed.), *Letters and Memorials of State*, 2 vols. (1746)

Collinson, P. (ed.), 'Letters of Thomas Wood, Puritan 1566–1577', *Bulletin of the Institute of Historical Research*, Special Supplement no. 5 (1960)

Cumnor Place: 'An Account of the Parish of Cumner, Berks', *Gentleman's Magazine*, 1821, Part 2, pp. 34–5, 201–5

De Maisse, A.H., *A Journal of all that was accomplished by Monsieur de Maisse, ambassador in England from King Henri IV to Queen Elizabeth, 1597*, trans. and ed. G.B. Harrison and R.A. Jones (1931)

Digges, Sir Dudley, *The Compleat Ambassador* ... (1655)

Donaldson, G. (ed.), *The Memoirs of Sir James Melville of Halhill* (1969 edn.)

*Egerton Papers*, ed. J. Payne Collier, Camden Society, 12 (1840)

Ellis, Henry (ed.), *Original Letters Illustrative of English History*, Series 1, 2 and 3 (1824–46)

Fénelon, Bertrand de Salignac, Seigneur de La Mothe, *Correspondance Diplomatique*, ed. A. Teulet, 7 vols. (Paris, 1838–40)

Feria, 'The Count of Feria's Dispatch of 14 November 1558', J. Rodriquez Salgado and S. Adams, in *Camden Miscellany*, XXVII (1984)

Forbes, P., *A Full View of the Public Transactions in the Reign of Queen Elizabeth*, vol. 1 (1740)

Fourdrinier, N., *Amy Robsart, the Wife of Lord Robert Dudley the Favourite of Queen Elizabeth I Her Life, Ancestry and the True Cause of Her Tragic Death*, Norfolk Record Office, MS MC5/29

Furnival, F.J. and W.R. Morfit, *Ballads from Manuscripts*, 2 vols. (1868–73)

Gabe, J.B., and C.A. Scham (eds.), *Thomas Chaloner's In Laudem Henrici Octavi'* (Kansas, 1979)

Gachard, M., *Correspondance de Philippe II sur les affaires des Pays-Bas* (Brussels, 1851)

Harington, J., *Nugae Antiquae*, ed. T. Park, 2 vols. (1804)

——— *A Tract on the Succession of the Crown* (1602), ed. C.R. Markham (Roxburghe Club, 1880)

Harrison, G.B., *The Letters of Queen Elizabeth* (1935)

Harrison, W., *An Historical Description of England*, 4 vols. (1908)

Hartley, T.E., *Proceedings in the Parliaments of Elizabeth I, 1558–1581* (Leicester, 1981)

Haynes, S., *Collection of State Papers . . . Left by William Cecil* (1740)

Hayward, J., *The Life and Reign of King Edward the Sixth with the Beginning of the Reign of Queen Elizabeth* (London, 1636)

——— *Annals of the First Four Years of the Reign of Queen Elizabeth* (1840)

Haywarde, J., *Les Reportes del Cases in Camera Stellata, 1593 to 1609*, ed. W.P. Baildon (London, 1894)

Hentzner, P., *A Journey into England in 1598* (Edinburgh, 1881–2)

Historical Manuscripts Commission 9, Salisbury MSS at Hatfield House, vols. 1–2 (HMC Hatfield)

Historical Manuscripts Commission 12, Rutland, vol. 5

Historical Manuscripts Commission 58, Bath MSS at Longleat House, vols. 1–5

Historical Manuscripts Commission 70, Pepys

Hoby, Sir Thomas, *The Book of the Courtier* (1561)

*Holinshed's Chronicle*, ed. H. Ellis, 6 vols. (1807–8)

Hughes, P.L. and J.F. Larkin, *Tudor Royal Proclamations*, 3 vols. (New Haven, 1964–9)

Jackson, J.E., 'Amye Robsart', *The Wiltshire Archaeological and Natural History Magazine*, 17 (1878), pp. 47–93

Jordan, W.K., *The Chronicle and Political Papers of King Edward VI* (Ithaca, NY, 1966)

*Journal of the House of Commons*, vol. 1 (1803)

*Journal of the House of Lords*, vol. 1 (1846)

Journal': 'A Journall of Matters of State happened from time to time as well within and without the realme from and before the death of King Edw. the 6th untill the yere 1562', printed in *Religion, Politics, and Society in Sixteenth-Century England*, eds. I.W. Archer, S. Adams, G.W. Bernard, Camden Society, 5th series, vol. 22 (2003), pp. 35–122

Kempe, A. (ed.), *The Loseley Manuscripts* (1836)

Kervyn de Lettenhove, J.M.B.C., *Relations politiques des Pays-Bas et de l'Angleterre, sous le règne de Philippe II*, 11 vols. (Brussels, 1882–1900)

Klarwill, Victor (ed.), *Queen Elizabeth and Some Foreigners, being a series of hitherto unpublished letters from the archives of the Hapsburg family* (London, 1928)

Le Laboureur, J., *Nouvelles Additions aux Memoires de Michel de Castelnau, Seigneur de la Mauvissiere*, 3 vols. (Brussels, 1731)

*Leicester Correspondence: Correspondence of Robert Dudley, Earl of Leicester during his Government of the Low Countries*, ed. J. Bruce, Camden Society, 27 (1844)

Leti, Gregorio, *Historia o vero vita di Elizabetta, regina d'Inghilterra* (survives only in the French edition published as *La Vie d'Elisabeth, Reine d'Angleterre, traduite d'Italien* (1692, 1696))

*Letters and Papers, Foreign and Domestic of the reign of Henry VIII, 1509–47*, eds. J. Gardiner and R.H. Brodie

Lodge, E., *Illustrations of English History, Biography and Manners ...* 2nd edn., 2 vols (1938)

MacCulloch, D. (ed.), 'The Vita Mariae Angliae Reginae of Robert Wingfield of Brantham', Camden Miscellany 28, Camden Society, 4th series, 29 (1984), pp.181–301

Malden, H.E. (ed.), *The Devereux Papers, 1575–1601* Camden Society, 3rd series, 34 (1923)

Murdin, W., *A Collection of State Papers relating to affairs in the reign of Elizabeth I* (1759)

Naunton, R., *Fragmenta Regalia* (1824)

Neale, J.E. (ed.), 'Sir Nicholas Throckmorton's Advice to Queen Elizabeth', *English Historical Review*, 65 (1950)

Nichols, J., The Progresses and Public Processions of Queen Elizabeth, 3 vols. (1823)

Nichols, J.G., *The diary of Henry Machyn, citizen and merchant tailor of London, 1550–1563*, Camden Society, 43 (1848)

——— (ed.) *Chronicle of Queen Jane and of Two Years of Queen Mary*, Camden Society, 48 (1850)

——— (ed.) *Greyfriars Chronicle*, Camden Society, 54 (1852)

——— *Literary Remains of Edward VI* (1857)

Nicolas, N.H., *Memoirs of the Life and Times of Sir Christopher Hatton* (1847)

Norton, Thomas and Thomas Sackville, *Gorboduc or Ferrex and Porrex*, ed. I.B. Cauthen Jr (1970)

Peck, D.C. (ed.), 'Another Version of the Leicester Epitaphium' *Notes and Queries*, n.s. 23 (1976) pp. 227–28

——— (ed.) '"The Letter of Estate": An Elizabethan Libel', *Notes and Queries*, n.s. 28 (February 1981), pp. 21–35

——— (ed.) *Leicester's Commonwealth: The Copy of a Letter written by a Master of Art of Cambridge (1584) and related documents* (Ohio, 1985)

Phillip, John, *The Play of Patient Grissell*, ed. R.B. McKerrow abd W.W. Greg (Malone Society, 1909)

Pollard, A.F. (ed.), *Tudor Tracts, 1532–1588*

Pollen, J.H., 'Queen Mary's Letter to the Duke of Guise January 1562', *Scottish Historical Society*, 43 (1904)

—— (ed.) *Memoirs of Robert Persons, S.J.* Catholic Record Society, 2 (1905), 4 (1907)

Read, C., 'A Letter from Robert, Earl of Leicester, to a Lady', *Huntingdon Library Quarterly* (April 1936)

Robinson, H., *The Zurich Letters*, 2 vols., Parker Society (Cambridge, 1842–5)

Rosso, G.V., *Historia delle cose occorse nel regno d'Inghilterra . . .* (1558)

Rymer, T., *Foedera* (The Hague, 1739–45)

Sidney, Philip, *Miscellaneous Prose of Sir Philip Sidney*, ed. K. Duncan-Jones and J.A. van Dorsten (Oxford, 1973)

Smith, Sir Thomas, *De Republica Anglorum*, ed. Mary Dewar (Cambridge, 1982)

Strype, J., *Ecclesiastical Memorials . . .* (Oxford, 1820–40)

Tottel, R., *The Passage of our Most Dread Sovereign Lady Queen Elizabeth through the City of London to Westminster . . .* (1960 edn)

Tytler, P.F., *England in the reigns of Edward and Mary*, 2 vols. (1839)

Vertot, R.A and C. Villaret, *Ambassades de Messieurs de Noailles en Angleterre*, 5 vols. (Leyden, 1763)

Vives, J.L., *On Education*, trans. F. Watson (1913)

Wall, A.D. (ed.), *Two Elizabethan Women: Correspondence of Joan and Maria Thynne, 1575–1611* (Devizes, 1983)

Wood, Anthony, *Athenae Oxonienses*, ed. P. Bliss, 4 vols. (Oxford, 1813–20)

Wright, T., *Queen Elizabeth and her Times*, 2 vols. (1838)

Wriothesley, Charles, *A Chronicle of England*, ed. W.D. Hamilton, Camden Society, NS 20 (London, 1877)

Yorke, P. (ed.), *Hardwicke State Papers*, 2 vols. (1778)

## Secondary Sources

Adams, S., 'The Release of Lord Darnley and the failure of the amity', in M. Lynch (ed.), *Mary Stewart: Queen in Three Kingdoms* (Oxford, 1988)

—— *Leicester and the Court: Essays on Elizabethan Politics* (Manchester, 2002)

Aird, I., 'The Death of Amy Robsart', *English Historical Review*, 71 (1956), pp. 69–79

Alford, S., *Burghley: William Cecil at the Court of Elizabeth I* (New Haven, 2008)

Archer I., Adams, S. and Bernard, G.W., 'Introduction' in *Religion, Politics, and Society in Sixteenth-Century England*, Camden Society, 5th series, 22 (2003), pp. 37–51

Axton, M., 'Robert Dudley and the Inner Temple Revels', *Historical Journal*, 13 (1970), pp. 365–78

——— *The Queen's Two Bodies* (Royal Historical Society, 1977)

Bartlett, A.D., *An Historical Descriptive Account of Cumnor Place, Berks* (Oxford, 1850)

Bernard, G.W., 'Amy Robsart' in *Power and Politics in Tudor England: Essays by G. W. Bernard* (Ashgate, 2000), pp. 161–74

Burgoyne, F.J. (ed.), *History of Queen Elizabeth, Amy Robsart and the Earl of Leicester* (1904)

Chamberlin, F., *The Private Character of Queen Elizabeth* (New York, 1922)

——— *Elizabeth and Leycester* (New York, 1939)

Cowper, J.M., *On Some Tudor Prices in Kent* (1577 Chiefly), Transactions of the Royal Historical Society (1872)

De Lisle, L., *The Sisters Who Would Be Queen* (2009)

Dewar, M., *Sir Thomas Smith: A Tudor Intellectual in Office* (1964)

Doran, S., 'The Political Career of Thomas Radcliffe, Third Earl of Sussex 1526?-1583', unpublished PhD thesis, London University (1979)

——— 'Religion and Politics at the Court of Elizabeth I: The Hapsburg marriage negotiations of 1559–67'. *English Historical Review* 104 (1989), pp. 908–26

——— 'Juno versus Diana: The treatment of Elizabeth I's marriage in plays and entertainments 1561–81'. *Historical Journal* 38 (1995), pp. 257–74

——— *Monarchy and Matrimony: The Courtships of Elizabeth I* (1996)

D'Oyley, E., 'The Death of Amy Robsart', *History Today*, 6 (1956)

Elton, G.R., *The Parliament of England, 1559–1581* (Cambridge, 1986)

Froude, J.A., *History of England from the Fall of Wolsey to the Defeat of the Spanish Armada*, vols. 6–9 (1893)

Gardiner, J., 'The Death of Amy Robsart', *English Historical Review*, 1 (1886), pp. 235–59

——— 'The Death of Amy Robsart', *English Historical Review*, 13 (1898), pp. 83–90

Gristwood, S., *Elizabeth and Leicester: Power, Passion, Politics* (2007)

Grosvenor, B. (ed.), *Lost Faces: Identity and Discovery in Tudor Royal Portraiture* (Philip Mould, 2007)

Haigh, C.A., *The Reign of Elizabeth I* (1984)

———— *Elizabeth I: Profile in power* (1988)

Hasler, P.W., *The House of Commons 1558–1603*, History of Parliament Trust (1983)

Haynes, A., *The White Bear* (1987)

Heisch, A., 'Queen Elizabeth I: Parliamentary rhetoric and the exercise of power', *Signs*, 1 (1975), pp. 31–55

Hibbert, C., *The Virgin Queen: The Personal History of Elizabeth I* (1990)

Hicks, L., 'The Growth of a Myth: Father Robert Persons, S.J., and Leicester's Commonwealth', *Studies: An Irish Quarterly*, 46 (1957), pp. 91–105

Holmes, P., 'The Authorship of 'Leicester's Commonwealth', *Journal of Ecclesiastical History*, 33 (1982), pp.424–30

Horton Smith, L.G.H., *Dr Walter Bailey 1529–1592: Physician to Queen Elizabeth* (St Albans, 1952)

Hunnisett, R.F., *The Medieval Coroner* (Cambridge, 1961)

Impey, Edward, 'The origins & development of non-conventual monastic dependencies in England and Normandy, 1000–1350', 3 vols., University of Oxford D.Phil. thesis, 1990, vol. II, pp. 44–119

Inman, Peggy, *Amy Robsart and Cumnor Place* (Cumnor History Society)

Ives, E.W., *Lady Jane Grey: A Tudor Mystery* (Oxford, 2009)

Jenkins, E., *Elizabeth the Great* (1958)

———— *Elizabeth and Leicester* (1961)

Johnson, P., *Elizabeth I: A Study in Power and Intellect* (1974)

Jones, N.L., *The Birth of the Elizabethan Age: England in the 1560s* (Oxford, 1993)

Kendall, A., *Robert Dudley, Earl of Leicester* (1980)

King, J.N., 'Queen Elizabeth I: Representations of the Virgin Queen', *Renaissance Quarterly*, 43 (1990), pp. 41–84

Levin, C., *The Heart and Stomach of a King: Elizabeth I and the Politics of Sex and Power* (Pennsylvania, 1994)

Levine, M., *The Early Elizabethan Succession Question, 1558–1568* (Stanford, 1966)

Loades, D.M., *Mary Tudor: A Life* (Oxford, 1989)

MacCaffrey, W.T., *The Shaping of the Elizabethan Regime* (1969)

———— *Queen Elizabeth and the Making of Policy 1572–1588* (Princeton, 1981)

———— *Queen Elizabeth I* (1993)

McCoy, R.C., 'From the Tower to the Tiltyard: Robert Dudley's return to glory', *Historical Journal*, 27 (1984), pp. 425–35

Neale, J.E., *Queen Elizabeth* (1934)

— *Elizabeth I and her Parliaments, 1559–1581* (1953)

Penigrew, T., *An Inquiry into . . . the death of Amy Robsart* (1859)

Perry, M., *The Word of a Prince: A life of Elizabeth I from Contemporary Documents* (Woodbridge, 1990)

Read, C., *Mr Secretary Walsingham and the Policy of Queen Elizabeth*, 3 vols. (Oxford, 1925)

———— 'The Fame of Sir Edward Stafford', *American Historical Review*, 35 (1930), pp. 560–66

———— *Mr Secretary Cecil and Queen Elizabeth* (1955)

———— *Lord Burghley and Queen Elizabeth* (1960)

Reese, M.M, *The Royal Office of Master of the Horse* (1976)

Rosenberg, E., *Leicester, Patron of Letters* (1955)

Ross, J., *Suitors to the Queen* (1985)

Rye, W., *The Murder of Amy Robsart* (1865)

Somerset, A., *Elizabeth I* (1991)

Starkey, D. et al., *The English Court from the Wars of the Roses to the Civil War* (1987)

———— *Elizabeth: Apprenticeship* (2000)

Stone, L., *The Crisis of the Aristocracy, 1558–1641* (1965)

———— *The Family, Sex and Marriage in England, 1500–1800* (1977)

Strickland, A., *Lives of the Queens of England* (1866)

Strong, R., *Portraits of Queen Elizabeth I* (Oxford, 1963)

———— *The English Renaissance Miniature* (1987)

———— *Gloriana: The Portraits of Queen Elizabeth I* (1987)

Strype, J., *The Life of the Learned Sir Thomas Smith* (Oxford, 1820)

Templer, J., *The Staircase: Studies of Hazards, Falls and Safer Design* (Massachusetts, 1992)

*Victoria History of the Counties of England*, compiled by W. Page et al. (London, 1900)

Waldman, M., *Elizabeth and Leicester* (1944)

Weir, A., Elizabeth the Queen (1998)

Williams, N., 'The Coronation of Queen Elizabeth I', *Quarterly Review*, 597 (1953)

———— *Thomas Howard, Fourth Duke of Norfolk* (1964)

——— *A Tudor Tragedy* (1989)

Williams, P., *The Later Tudors* (Oxford, 1995)

Wilson, D., *Sweet Robin: A Biography of Robert Dudley, Earl of Leicester 1533–1588* (1981)

Abingdon, Earl of, 170
Abingdon, 4, 59, 169, 171, 204, 206, 210, 213–14, 219, 368–9
Act of Uniformity, 268
Aird, Dr Ian, 227–8, 232, 357
Alba, Duke of, 122
Aldersaye, Thomas, 181
Alençon, Francis Duke of, 320–5, 328–31, 335, 345
Allen, John, 72
Angoulême, Duke of, 28
Anjou, Duke of, see Henry III, King, of France
Anne of Cleves, 110
Antwerp, 190, 326, 335, 344
Appleyard, Alice, 16
Appleyard, Anna, 15
Appleyard, Elizabeth, see Robsart, Elizabeth
Appleyard, Frances, 15–16
Appleyard, John, 15–16, 61, 95, 145, 159; and Amy Robsart's death, 204, 211, 214, 216, 299–306, 363; his rebellion and death, 306
Appleyard, Philip, 15–16
Appleyard, Roger, 15, 39, 61
Armiger, Robert, 59
Arran, James Hamilton, Earl of, 28, 158, 162, 189
Arundel, Earl of, 53, 100, 154, 164; and Amy Robsart's death, 7, 299, 303; his marriage suit, 115, 117, 136–7, 149–51; and Dudley's marital ambitions, 245–7, 255–6, 263, 269, 273–4
Arundel's tavern, 134
Arundell, Charles, 344–9, 352
Arundell, Sir Thomas, 345
Ascham, Roger, 26–7, 109, 353
Ashby-de-la-Zouche, 224
Ashley, Catherine, 29–31, 75, 78, 88, 92, 143–4, 261, 360–1
Ashley, John, 261
Ashmole, Elias, 365
Ashton in the Walls, 371
astrology, 27, 95
astronomy, 26, 28
Audley, Thomas, 19, 57
Austria, 123, 259

Aylmer, John, 24, 182

Babington, Dr, 217
Bacon, Sir Francis, 87
Bacon, Sir Nicholas, 74
Baden, Marquis of, 42
Bagnall, Sir Ralph, 133, 367
Barnet, 82
Baroncelli, Tommaso, 190
Barthewe, Francis, 370
Bartlett, Alfred, 375
Basing, 1, 196
Bath, Earl of, 35
Baylie, Elizabeth, 141
Bayly, Dr Walter, 338–41, 344, 349, 362
Baynard's Castle, 131
Beacon, Thomas, 16
Beale, Robert, 352, 354
Bedford, Earl of, 60, 63, 124, 152, 161, 189, 256, 272
Bedingfield, Edmund, 369
Bedingfield, Sir Henry, 48, 369
Belmain, Jean, 27
Benger, Thomas, 128
Berkshire, 56, 59, 148, 169
Berkshire Assizes, 230–1, 299
Bernard, George, 352
Berny (prisoner), 141
Berwick, 84, 156, 166, 177
Bircham Newton, 45
Bird, William, 181
Blackfriars, 97, 131
Blount, Sir Richard, 214
Blount, Sir Thomas, 46, 60, 82–4, 95, 130, 145, 356; and Amy Robsart's death, 6–7, 203–14, 219, 223, 225, 239, 299–303, 362–3, 367–8, 370
Blunt, Mrs, 217, 370
Board of the Green Cloth, 90
Boleyn, Anne, 28, 34, 43, 102, 110, 117, 121, 136
Boleyn, Mary, 41, 283
Book of Common Prayer, 120
Book of Ecclesiastes, 86
Book of Psalms, 70, 255
Borgarucci, Dr Julio, 310, 345

Borrowe, Thomas, 46
Borth, Francis, 140
Bosworth, battle of, 374
Botley, 172
Boulogne, siege of, 12
Bounde, William, 172
Bowes, (retainer), 203, 205–6, 363
Bowyer, Simon, 91
Briegerus, Julius, 351
Browne, Sir Anthony, 76
Bruener, Baron Caspar, 20, 94, 280; and
    marriage negotiations, 138–40, 142, 144,
    151, 153–5, 160–1, 164–6, 174; and poison
    plot, 5, 166–8, 356–7
Brussels, 165
Buckley, William, 26
Buckner, Dorothy, 173
Buckner, Thomas, 210
Bulkham, 46, 59
Buntingford, 56
Burges, Isaac, 181
Butler, Anthony, 370–1
Butler, 'Bald', 338, 352, 370–1
Butler, Mrs, 217, 370–1
Buxton, 317–18, 340

Calais, 55, 63, 75, 109, 120–1, 156, 186–8
Calvin, Jean, 86
Calvinism, 68
Camberwell, 15, 39, 145, 356
Cambridge, 14, 35
Cambridge University, 26–7
Camden, William, 2, 20, 44, 107, 118–19,
    126, 151, 278, 307, 322, 325
Carew, Sir Nicholas, 76
Carew, Sir Peter, 77
Carlisle, Bishop of, 87
Castiglione, Baldassare, 80
Castle Rising, 24
Catherine de' Medici, 122
Catherine of Aragon, 41, 47, 72, 121, 192
Catholicism, 11, 33, 41–2, 159, 176, 295; under
    Elizabeth, 68, 87–8, 120–4; and Council
    of Trent, 264–70; and queen's marriage,
    319–27, 329; and *Leicester's Commonwealth*
    conspiracy, 335, 344–9
Cave, Sir Ambrose, 147–8, 358
Cecil, Robert, 74
Cecil, Sir William, 33, 63, 88, 153, 165, 184,
    334, 348, 373–4; and Dudley's ascendancy,
    1, 3, 7, 77–8, 80, 188, 197–9, 237–42; and
    Dudley's marriage, 19–20, 39, 241; and

queen's accession, 72–5; and queen's
    marriage, 107–8, 111, 119, 158, 162, 189,
    198–200, 240–1, 272, 276–7, 287, 320–1,
    323, 325, 331; and religion, 120; and
    Scotland, 176–9, 182, 186–8, 199; and
    Amy Robsart's death, 213, 226, 234,
    237–42, 304, 357–8, 362; memorandum
    on Dudley, 241–2, 292, 337; and Dudley's
    marital ambitions, 246–9, 251–2, 256, 258,
    260–2, 268–71; and return to
    Catholicism, 266, 268–71; and Dudley's
    estrangements from queen, 283–4, 325–7;
    and succession crisis, 288–90, 294
Challoner, Sir Thomas, 108, 165
Chamberlain, Sir Thomas, 223–4, 244
Chapman, John, 181
Charing Cross, 43, 76
Charles of Austria, Archduke, 94, 123–4,
    138–40, 153–8, 160, 162, 165, 174, 240,
    280, 287–8, 295, 319–20
Charles V, Emperor, 42, 47, 123
Charles I, King, 351
Charles IX, King, of France, 287
Charterhouse, 85, 90
Chartley, 313
Chauncy, William, 82–3, 147
Cheapside, 99, 102, 185
Cheke, John, 26, 347
Chichester, Sir John, 152
Chowte, Peter, 181
Christ's Hospital, 99
Christchurch, 57, 82, 145, 147, 368
Church of England, 86–7, 120
Cicero, 27
Clapham, 91
Cleobury (impostor), 49
Clinton, Lord, 256, 320–1
Cobham, Lady, 92
Cobham, Lord, 77, 318
College of Arms, 216
College of Physicians, 340–1
Combelles (Alençon's adviser), 346
*Common Cry of Englishmen, The*, 289
Compton Verney, 147, 169, 356, 358
Cornwall, 11, 312
Cornwallis, Sir Thomas, 129
Council of Trent, 264–7, 270
Court of King's Bench, 230, 304
Court of Star Chamber, 305
Courtenay, Edward, Earl of Devon, 42–4,
    48–9, 137
Coventry, 213

Cox, Richard, 26–7

Coxford, 23

Craig, Alexander, 182

Cranmer, Thomas, 41, 48, 52

Croft, Sir James, 128

Cromwell, Thomas, 74

Cumnor (village), 59, 172–3, 210, 365–6

Cumnor Church, 171–2

Cumnor Place, 56, 59–60, 148, 169–73, 183, 192, 194–5, 217, 356; and Amy Robsart's death, 4, 6–8, 200, 204–6, 208–11, 219–22, 224–5, 227–31, 337–8, 362–6, 371, 374–5; scene of death, 219–22, 366

Cunningham, William, 28

Curson, Robert, 96


Dacre, Lady, 340

Dalton, Michael, 225

dancing, 94

Darcy, Elizabeth, Lady, 130

Darcy, Robert, 130

Darcy, Thomas, Lord, 130

Darnley, Lord Henry, 278–9

de la Quadra, Don Alvaro, 107, 180–3, 188, 260, 275; and marriage negotiations, 138, 153–60, 162–6, 174, 198–200, 240–1; and Amy Robsart's health, 146, 226–9; and Amy Robsart's death, 5, 168, 199–200, 234, 238–9, 263–4, 356–7, 362; and Cecil's retirement threats, 3–4, 198–200; and Dudley's marital ambitions, 263–6, 268–70, 272–3; his dismissal from court, 274, 282

De Noailles (French ambassador), 152

de Silva, Guzman, 281–4, 288–9, 291–3, 295, 299, 314

Dee, Dr John, 28, 95, 340

Dekesone, Edward, 367

Denchworth, 172, 210

Denmark, King of, 28, 123, 136, 162, 175

Derby, Earl of, 161, 305, 360

*Device for Alteration of Religion*, 120

Diana, goddess, 105

Dorset, Henry, Marquis of, 30

Dorset, 141

Dover, 84, 346

Dowe, Anne, 184

Doylly, Mrs, 217, 370

dresses, 192–5

Drury, Sir William, 156–7

Dublin, 315

Dudley, Ambrose, 12–13, 17, 25, 159, 314, 326; marriage, 19, 23; education, 27; imprisonment, 36–8; release from Tower, 45; and Robert's finances, 46, 59; and French campaign, 60; appearance and manner, 77, 271; and coronation, 100; created Earl of Warwick, 271–2

Dudley, Sir Andrew, 46, 57, 126

Dudley, Catherine, *see* Huntingdon, Lady Catherine, Countess of

Dudley, Edmund, 12, 126

Dudley, Elizabeth (née Whorwood), 19, 152

Dudley, Guildford, 34, 36, 43

Dudley, Henry, 12, 19, 36–8, 57, 59–60

Dudley, Jane, Duchess of Northumberland, 27, 37, 39, 45–6, 55

Dudley, John, Earl of Warwick and Duke of Northumberland, 12–14, 17–18, 115, 148, 180, 182, 271, 353; and sons' marriages, 22–4; career, 24–5; and sons' education, 26–7; and Jane Grey, 34–5, 115, 131, 255–6; imprisonment and execution, 35–7; and Order of the Garter, 126; former retainers, 128, 130; and Charles Arundell, 345

Dudley, John, of Stoke Newington, 310

Dudley, John, Viscount Lisle, 13, 25, 76, 148; marriage, 18–19, 22–3; education, 26–7; imprisonment, 36; death, 45

Dudley, Margaret (née Audley), 19, 57

Dudley, Mary, *see* Sidney, Mary

Dudley, Robert: relationship with queen, 2–3, 26, 44, 58, 77–81, 91–2, 124, 140–4, 164–5, 167, 197; appearance and manner, 2, 20, 77; and Norfolk rebellion, 12–13, 17; and Edward VI, 13, 19, 24, 26; meeting with Amy Robsart, 15–17; age, 15, 20, 55; and religion, 16, 182, 246, 264–7, 295; marriage to Amy Robsart, 18–20, 22–4, 38–9; imprisonment in Tower, 19–21, 35–40, 43–4, 129, 145, 255; oak spray symbol, 21, 38; career at court, 24–5, 55, 57, 63, 75–7; salary, 25, 77; birth, 26; education, 26–8; and Jane Grey, 35–6, 39–40, 83; childlessness, 38–9, 55, 224, 362; treason charge, 39–40, 42; and Wyatt's rebellion, 43–4; released from Tower, 45; inheritance, 45–6; finances, 46, 58–60, 180–1, 326; and French campaign, 53–4, 55, 60; household accounts, 95, 128, 133–4, 147, 180–1, 194, 216, 250, 355–6, 369–70; and coronation, 95–6, 100; and Knights of the Garter, 125–6, 146–7, 357; and family's treason, 126–7, 159, 167, 272; and petitioners and patronage, 127–30, 146–7; and gambling, 133–4, 181, 275; illnesses, 147, 340; and royal progresses, 149–50, 190, 197, 250, 271; and assassination threats, 2, 154–7, 159–60; and court factions, 159–61, 165–6, 188, 255–6, 287–8, 296; and poisoning of Amy Robsart, 166–8, 199, 356–7, 363; decline in reputation, 183–5, 241–2, 337; purchases for queen, 190; and Amy Robsart's death, 3–7, 203–15, 219, 229, 253, 299–306, 356–7, 363–4, 367, 371–2; and Amy Robsart's funeral, 216–17; and Cecil, 237–42, 357–8; and elevation to nobility, 241, 257, 259–60, 271–3, 278; return to court, 245, 247; marital ambitions, 245–79, 353; and Privy Council, 276; and Mary Queen of Scots marriage, 277–9; estrangements from queen, 283–6, 325–7; and succession crisis, 292–3, 295–6; and Douglas Sheffield, 307–12, 328, 336–7, 346–50; and Lettice Knollys, 313–18, 325–7, 336–7; and Archduke Charles marriage negotiations, 319–20; and Alençon marriage negotiations, 321–7, 329–30, 345; and his son's death, 333, 336; and *Leicester's Commonwealth*, 335–51; and his retainers, 360–3, 370–1; death, 373; his last letter, 373–4

Dudley, Robert, Baron Denbeigh, 309–12, 333

Dudley, Lord, 148, 257

Dudley Castle, 257

dukedoms, 24, 159

Dunkirk, 136

Durham House, 25, 90

Dymock, John, 58, 360–1

'dyntes', 231, 233, 365

Edney, William, 192–5, 224, 226, 357

Edward III, King, 125

Edward IV, King, 42

Edward VI, King, 28–9, 62, 72, 76, 151; and Dudley, 13, 19, 24, 26; and Somerset's protectorate, 11–12, 18; kidnap attempts, 18, 30–1; and religion, 18, 68, 86–7, 120; education, 26–7; illness and death, 33–5; and queen's coronation, 101–2; and law on retainers, 359

Egmont, Count, 42

Elizabeth I, Queen: progresses, 1, 147, 149–51, 190, 250, 271; and hunting, 1–3, 150, 196–7; and marriage, 1–2, 4, 28–9, 42–3, 48–9, 105–11, 115–24, 136–40, 143–4, 149–68, 174–5, 189–90, 198–200, 240–1, 272, 276–7, 280–2, 287–96, 319–27; relationship with Dudley, 2–3, 26, 44, 58, 77–81, 91–2, 124, 140–4, 164–5, 167, 197; London residence, 25; birth, 26; education, 27; and succession, 28, 33–4, 41–2, 63, 294; as Virgin Queen, 29, 105, 319, 372; and Sir Thomas Seymour, 29–32; and virginity, 32, 105–6, 119, 140–3, 319, 330; and her mother's death, 32, 44; and religion, 41–2, 45, 68, 86–8, 109–10, 116–17, 120–4, 294, 319–20; imprisonment in Tower, 44–5, 97; release and house arrest, 45, 48, 369; finances, 58; accession, 67–71, 82, 84–6, 105; 'body natural' and 'body politic', 71, 106; temperament, 73–4, 78; her letters, 78–80, 332; and music, 87, 94; and royal palaces, 89–90; life at court, 90–3; diet, 90–1, 151; and dancing, 94; coronation, 95–104; appearance, 98, 102; and childbearing, 105–8, 139, 321, 329, 331; and parliamentary delegation, 118–20, 125; and law on gypsies, 127; alleged sexual relations, 140–2; ill health, 151–3, 259, 275–6, 288–9, 332, 340, 369; and assassination threats, 154–7, 320, 346–7; and Mary Queen of Scots, 176–9, 187; and war with Scotland, 176–9, 186–8; unpopularity, 188–9; and Amy Robsart's death, 212, 224, 238–9, 243–4, 253–4, 260, 280, 364, 371–2; and possible marriage to Dudley, 245–79, 353; estrangements from Dudley, 283–6, 325–7; and succession crisis, 289–96; and Douglas Sheffield, 309–11, 328, 346; and Lettice Knollys, 316–18, 325–7, 336; 'sieve' portraits, 319; international isolation, 320; and Alençon, 321–31, 345–6; and new favourites, 332–3; and Walter Bayly, 339–41; and *Leicester's Commonwealth*, 342–3; and Dudley's death, 373–4

Elisabeth de Valois, 122

Elizabeth of York, Queen, 102

Elmby (servant), 145

Eltham, 197, 250

Ely Place, 13, 24

Enfield, 84

Englefield, Sir Francis, 349

Eric of Sweden, 49, 58, 142, 162–4, 174–5, 189–90, 241, 272, 360–1
Erisa, Mrs, 311–12
Esher, 311
Essex, Robert Devereux, second Earl of, 313, 332–3
Essex, Walter Devereux, first Earl of, 313–16; and *Leicester's Commonwealth* conspiracy, 337, 345–6
Essex, 11, 316, 184
Eton College, 174
Euclid, 27
Eure, William, Lord, 128
Everard, John, 125
Exeter, 11
eyesight, treatments for, 340–1

Farnham, 1, 196
Fenchurch Street, 85
fencing, 13
Ferdinand of Austria, Archduke, 123–4, 137–9
Ferdinand, Emperor, 123, 138–9, 153, 155–6, 160, 165
Feria (Spanish ambassador), 63, 68, 87–8, 142, 150, 168, 178; and marriage negotiations, 107, 109, 111, 115–16, 120–3, 136–8, 149, 157; and Dudley, 125, 129, 131–2
Ferrara, Duke of, 28
Ferrers, George, 101
Fettiplace, Ursula, 172
Flanders, 268
Fleet prison, 303–5
Fleet Street, 99, 101, 360
Flitcham, 61
Florence, Duke of, 28
*Flores Calvinistici*, 351
Flowerdew, Sir John, 16, 50, 52–3, 56, 61, 82, 194, 225
Flowerdew, William, 16
Forest, John, 83, 95
Forster, Sir Anthony, 4, 59–60, 130, 148, 169, 171–2, 194, 210, 356, 362; and Amy Robsart's death, 205, 209, 213, 231, 338, 365, 355, 370
Fowler, John, 133
Framlingham Castle, 35–6
France, 120–1, 123, 136, 149, 157, 196, 255, 328; English campaigns and loss of Calais, 53, 60, 62–3; and Scotland, 176–9, 186, 199; and Amy Robsart's death, 243–4,

249–50; and Alençon marriage negotiations, 320–7, 329
Francis I, King, of France, 28
Francis II, King, of France, 157, 176, 187, 258
Francis, Edward, 141
Frank, Hans, 95
Frankfurt, 313, 340
French language, 27
Frewen (carrier), 192, 194
Frodsham, Magdalen, 311–12

Gallys, Richard, 276
gambling, 133–4, 181
Gardiner, Stephen, 44, 101
Gargrave, Thomas, 118
*Gentleman's Magazine*, 220, 366
Germany, 326
Gilbert, William, 95
Gilpin, George, 128
Gloucester, 312
Gloucester College, Oxford, 216
Gloucestershire, 205
Goove, Edmund, 82–3, 133
*Gorboduc*, 272, 276, 354
Grafton, Richard, 118
Gravesend, 268
Great Bircham, 23, 45
Great Conduit, 99
Great Yarmouth, 24, 52
Greek, 27
Greenwich, 33, 89, 147, 160, 183, 250, 268, 302, 310, 324–5
Gresham, Sir Thomas, 174, 191
Grey, Lady Catherine, 105, 354
Grey, Frances, 34
Grey, Lady Jane, 21, 30, 48, 83, 86, 105, 115, 131, 245; and succession, 34–6, 39–41, 255–6; her execution, 40, 43–4
Grey, Lord, 152
Grice, William, 52, 194
Grindal, William, 27
Guilderstern, Nicholas, 142
Guildford, Sir Henry, 76
Guildhall, 40
Guise, Duke of, 28
Guise family, 157, 176
Gunnell, Ralph, 172
Guntor, Arthur, 246–7
Gustavus Vasa, King, of Sweden, 49, 162, 164, 174–5, 196
gypsies, 127

Haddon, Walter, 27
Hadley, 82
Hales, John, 353–4
Hales, Stephen, 353
Hales Owen, 45–6, 59–60, 82, 148
Hampton Court, 89, 152, 154, 159, 245, 250
Hapsburg dynasty, 42, 109–10, 115, 123, 131, 157, 159, 259, 295
Hardwick, Bess of, *see* Shrewsbury, Bess of Hardwick, Countess of
Harington, John, 63
Harrington, Sir John, 107, 141, 332
Harrison, William, 225
Hatfield House, 8, 33, 48–9, 58, 68, 70, 75, 82, 84–5, 93, 95, 290, 313
Hatton, Sir Christopher, 79, 141, 281, 317–18, 325, 329, 333, 340
Hawkins, Henry, 141
Hayward, Joan, 22
Helfenstein, Count George von, 123, 138, 241
Hemsby, 24
Heneage, Sir Thomas, 283, 302, 361
Henry III, King, 90
Henry VII, King, 12, 89, 102, 305, 359, 374
Henry VIII, King, 24, 115, 150, 181, 196; and succession, 11, 28, 41–2, 121, 176; last military campaign, 12–13; and religion, 16, 86, 120; and children's education, 27; and Masters of the Horse, 76; and Holbein mural, 90; and queen's coronation, 102–3; and queen's marriage, 109–10, 121, 200; and law on gypsies, 127; and dissolution of monasteries, 169; and Darnley, 278; and law on retainers, 359
Henry II, King, of France, 122, 157, 176
Henry III, King, of France (Duke of Anjou), 142, 320, 322, 329, 347
Hereford, Viscount of, 283
Herle, William, 346
Hertford, Countess of, 340
Hertford, Earl of, 134
Hertfordshire, 56–7, 82, 355
Hilliard, Nicholas, 324
Hinckley, 210
Hoby, Sir Thomas, 80
Holbein, Hans, 90, 110
Holderness, Lordship of, 180
Holinshed's Chronicle, 60, 63
Holland, Thomas, 184–5
Hollesley, 59

Holstein, Adolphus, Duke of, 136, 162, 181, 189, 240, 259
Holt, 24, 30
horses, 76–7, 135, 150, 190, 197
Horsey, Sir Edward, 310
Howard, Lord Henry, 324, 347
Howard, Lady Mary, 92
Howard, William, Baron Howard of Effingham, 308
Howard family, 16–17, 24, 324, 345–7
Howse, John, 172, 210
Howse, Richard, 210
Huggins, William, 145, 172, 194, 211, 302–3
Hugo, Victor, 7
Huicke, Dr William, 107
Hunsdon, Lord, 284
Hunsdon, 84
hunting, 1–3, 25, 150, 196–7
Huntingdon, Catherine, Countess of (née Dudley), 59, 127, 147, 284
Huntingdon, Henry Hastings, Earl of, 153, 161, 224, 229, 329
Hyde, Dudley, 57
Hyde, George, 57
Hyde, William, 50, 53, 56–8, 82, 95, 130, 133–4, 145, 172, 355–7, 363

Impey, Dr Edward, 8
infant mortality, 38
inquests, 208–9
Ireland, 197, 246, 257, 269, 287, 313–15
Isabella, Queen, of Spain, 47
Isle of Wight, 310
Italian language, 27
Italy, 191, 209

James IV, King, of Scotland, 176
James V, King, of Scotland, 176
Jennings (servant), 212
Jewel, Bishop, of Salisbury, 109
John, Duke of Finland, 163–4, 174–5, 180–2
John Frederick of Saxony, 28
Jones, Robert, 249–61, 364
Jones, Thomas, 133, 145
Jonson, Ben, 107–8
'Journall of Matters of State', 352–66, 371–2
jousting, *see* tournaments

Kene, John, 172, 210
Kenilworth, 55, 313, 325, 331
Kenninghall, 17, 159
Kett, Robert, 11, 14, 16, 18, 23–4, 35

Kew, 2, 83, 95, 134, 146, 190–1, 212–13, 237–8
Keyle, Robert, 360
Keys, Thomas, 135
Kidderminster, 46, 83
Killigrew, Sir Henry, 244, 252, 261, 371
King, John, 184
King, Robert, 172
King's Lynn, 36, 40
Kingdom of Naples, 150
Knights of the Garter, 125–6, 159, 189, 268–9, 273, 357
Knollys, Lady Catherine, 41, 88, 92, 313
Knollys, Sir Francis, 313
Knollys, Laetitia (Lettice), 283, 313–18, 325, 328, 332–4
Knyvet, Sir Thomas, 76

Laneham, Robert, 92
Langham, Edward, 145, 368
Langley, Henry, 172, 210
Languet, Hubert, 58
Latimer, Hugh, 48
Latin, 27, 87, 104
Leicester, Robert Dudley, Earl of, *see* Dudley, Robert
Leicester House, 316, 333
*Leicester's Commonwealth*, 335–52, 355–8, 362, 364–6, 370, 373
Leicestershire, 23, 43, 224
Leith, siege of, 178–9, 186
Lennox, Margaret, 278
Leti, Gregorio, 58
Lever, Thomas, 213
Lewys, Hugh, 210
Lilly (Stafford's servant), 348–9
Lincoln, 83–4, 182
Lincolnshire, 14, 82–4, 355
Little Bursted, 184
London Bridge, 131
London: and Queen Mary's accession, 35–6, 41, 62; and Wyatt's rebellion, 43; and Queen Elizabeth's accession, 71; and Queen Elizabeth's coronation, 97, 99–104; and Swedish embassy, 163
Longleat House, 8, 22
Lords of the Congregation, 177–8
Lorraine, Cardinal of, 241
love, Renaissance ideal of, 80
Lucy, Sir Thomas, 359
Lupton, Thomas, 343
Luther, Martin, 86
Lysons, Samuel, 170, 220–1, 366

Lyttleton, John, 60

Machyn, Henry, 85
Maitland, William, 275, 277
marchpane, 250
Margaret Tudor, 176
married women, 52, 55–6
Martinengo, Abbot, 266, 268
Mary of Guise (Regent of Scotland), 176–8, 187
Mary Queen of Scots (Mary Stuart), 73, 78, 105, 141, 157, 253, 258, 268; and succession, 176–9, 187; and Dudley, 246, 250–2, 277–9, 344; her marriage to Darnley, 278–9; and *Leicester's Commonwealth* conspiracy, 344, 347
Mary Tudor, 55, 76, 90, 126, 162, 263; and regency, 18; education, 27; and succession, 28, 34–5, 68, 294; and religion, 33, 41–2, 68, 294; accession, 35–6, 39, 41, 62; and Dudley brothers, 37, 45, 60; and Elizabeth, 41–2, 44–5, 48–9, 58, 63, 152, 294, 369; her marriage, 42–3, 47–8, 109, 116, 118, 276; false pregnancy, 47–8; persecutions and unpopularity, 48, 62, 68–9, 75, 86–7; French campaign and loss of Calais, 62–3; illness and death, 63, 67–71, 290; and state of England, 75; her funeral, 85–6; and Elizabeth's coronation, 101–4
Massie, Elizabeth, 141
Master of the Horse, office of, 76–7
mathematics, 26–7
Maule, Thomas, 226
Mauvissère, Michel de Castelnau, Sieur de, 142, 322, 324
Maximilian, Emperor, 123
Medici, Catherine de', 324, 330, 347
Medinaceli, Duke of, 55
Melville, Sir James, 282, 289
Melville, William, 80–1, 278
Mendoza, Don Diego de, 55
Mendoza (Spanish ambassador), 324, 326
Mildmay, Anthony, 22
Mildmay, Sir Thomas, 184
Mildmay, Sir Walter, 22
mock battles, 89–90, 93
Molyneux, master, 292
Montague, Lord, 269
Mortlake, 28
Mountjoy, Lord, 127
Mousehold Heath, 11, 16

Mulcaster, Richard, 100–1
music, 87, 94
Mutlowe, Elizabeth, 173, 217, 370

Naunton, Robert, 70, 287
navigation, 27–8
Netherlands, 321
New College, Oxford, 338–9, 341
Newenham, Sir Thomas, 182
Newmarket, 14
Newton, 23
Nonsuch Palace, 53, 150
Norfolk, Thomas Howard, Duke of, 35, 100, 115, 126, 134, 153, 281, 309; hostility to Dudley, 159–61, 166, 199, 287–8; and war with Scotland, 178, 180, 182, 186–7; and Dudley's marital ambitions, 2, 263, 269, 273–4; and Privy Council, 276; and Archduke Charles marriage negotiations, 287–8, 295; and succession crisis, 290–2; and Amy Robsart's death, 302–4, 335; and Douglas Sheffield, 311; his execution, 311, 320
Norfolk, Duchess of, 103
Norfolk, 13, 19, 159, 211; Robsart and Dudley estates, 15–16, 23–4, 45, 50, 59, 61; and Mary's accession, 34–5, 39–40
North, Lord, 85, 90, 310, 316
Northampton, Marquis of, 13–14, 243, 247, 249, 256, 274
Northumberland, Duchess of, *see* Dudley, Jane, Duchess of Northumberland
Northumberland, Duke of, *see* Dudley, John, Earl of Warwick and Duke of Northumberland
Northumberland, Earl of, 347
Norton, Thomas, 276, 354
Norwich, 11, 17–18, 40, 306
Nowell, Dr Anthony, 276

Odingsells, Elizabeth, 4, 56, 172, 206, 222, 365
Orléans, 258
Ormond, Elizabeth, Lady, 183
Ormond, Thomas, Earl of, 130
Oswald, Roger, 96
Owen, Anne, 4, 172, 206
Owen, Dr George, 4, 152, 169, 172
Owen, William, 172, 210
Oxford, Earl of, 35, 163; and *Leicester's Commonwealth* conspiracy, 345–7, 349
Oxford, 60, 169, 192, 194, 208–9; and

inquests, 184–5; Amy Robsart's funeral, 216–17; queen's visit, 338–40; Amy Robsart's tomb, 375–6
Oxfordshire, 11, 48, 355

Padua, 49
Paris, 3, 6, 162, 187; and *Leicester's Commonwealth* conspiracy, 335, 344–9
Parker, Matthew, 109
Parr, Catherine, 27, 29–30, 32, 106, 110
Parry, Thomas, 30–1, 75, 84, 154, 174, 260
Parsons, Robert, 344
Paulet, Giles, 100
Peebles, 272
Pembroke, Earl of, 53, 55, 60, 85, 131, 134, 147, 292, 303, 311; and Dudley's marital ambitions, 245, 247, 256; his death, 332
Petre, William, 188
Petworth, 347
Philip II, King, of Spain, 4, 45, 49, 55, 77, 88, 284; marriage, 42–3, 47–8, 109, 116; French campaign, 53, 62–3; and Queen Mary's death, 67–8; and marriage negotiations, 111, 115–17, 120–3, 138–9; and Dudley's marital ambitions, 263–5, 268, 270, 273, 353
Pickering, Sir William, 134, 136–7, 149, 164
Picto, Mrs, 6, 145, 148, 172, 206, 223, 356, 362
Pius IV, Pope, 157, 255, 266
players, 146–7
Pollard, Lady, 217, 370
Pope, Sir Thomas, 49
Portsmouth, 1, 33, 196
Powell (servant), 96
Poyntz, Lady Joan, 128
Poyntz, Sir Nicholas, 149
Protestant preachers, 182
Pudsey, John, 210, 230

Radcliffe, Lady, 93
Raleigh, Sir Walter, 333
Randolph, Thomas, 189–90, 197, 239, 246, 278
Reading, 231
Reformation, 11, 26, 57, 86, 120, 196
*Regans in Excelsis*, 320
Renard, Simon, 41–2
retainers, 358–61
Rich, Barnaby, 94
Rich, Lord, 184, 247, 360
Richmond, 1, 89, 190

Ridolphi Plot, 320
Robsart, Amy: age, 15, 20–1, 55; meeting
    with Dudley, 15–17; and religion, 16, 225;
    education, 17, 53; marriage, 18–20, 22–4,
    38–9; appearance, 20–1; childlessness,
    38–9, 55, 224, 362; inheritance, 45–6;
    married life, 50–6, 82–4, 169–73, 192–5;
    Norfolk accent, 53; ill health, 7, 131–2,
    146, 226–9, 338–9, 357, 362; last meeting
    with Dudley, 145–8; and poison plot,
    166–8, 199, 234, 338–9, 356–7, 363; death,
    2–7, 199–200, 206, 219–29, 299–306;
    inquest, 7–8, 208–10, 213–14, 230–4, 237,
    364–9, 371; funeral, 212, 216–19, 370–1;
    scene of death, 219–22, 366; and suicide,
    223–6, 253; and *Leicester's Commonwealth*,
    337–9, 344, 349–51, 355–7, 362, 364–6;
    and 'Journall of Matters of State', 353–66;
    her tomb, 375–6
Robsart, Arthur, 95, 214
Robsart, Elizabeth (Elizabeth Appleyard),
    15, 23, 46, 59–61
Robsart, Sir John, 14–16, 22–3, 45, 60–1
Rogers, Thomas, 344
Rome, 157
Rouen, 344
royal palaces, 89–90
royal progresses, 1, 147, 149–51, 190, 250, 271
Ruffyn, William, 210
Rullo, Donato, 150
Rutland, Earl of, 93, 126, 185

Sadler, Sir Ralph, 181, 328, 353
St Dunstan's churchyard, 99
St James's Palace, 67, 70, 89–90
St James's Park, 133
St Lawrence Pountney, 134
St Mary Axe, 137
St Paul's Cathedral, 97, 250
St Quentin, siege of, 53, 60, 62, 131
Salisbury, 312
Sandys, Edwin, Bishop of Worcester, 183–4
Savoy, Emmanuel Philibert, Duke of, 42,
    49, 115–16
Savoy, William, Duke of, 136
Sawston Hall, 34–5
Saxlingham, 24
Scotland, 156, 158, 278–9, 305; and war with
    England, 176–9, 182, 186–7, 199, 240
Scott, Elizabeth, 39
Scott, John, 15, 39, 145
Scott, Sir Walter, 7, 351, 375

Segorbe, Duke of, 42
Seymour, Anne, 18, 22
Seymour, Edward, *see* Somerset, Edward
    Seymour, Duke of
Seymour, Jane, 106, 110
Seymour, John, 12
Seymour, Sir Thomas, 29–32, 63, 73, 75, 353
Sheen, 18, 20
Sheffield, Douglas, 307–12, 314, 328, 346–50
Sheffield, Elizabeth, 310
Sheffield, Frances, 307
Sheffield, John, Lord, 13, 308, 337
Sheldon, Mr, 190
Shrewsbury, Bess of Hardwick, Countess of,
    108, 141
Shrewsbury, Earl of, 146, 271, 373
Sidney, Sir Henry, 19, 263–4, 292, 316, 343
Sidney, Lady Mary (née Dudley), 19, 92,
    153–8, 162, 264, 343
Sidney, Sir Philip, 343–4
Simier, Jean de, 141, 322, 325, 327, 346
Skelton, John, 233
Slipton, 210
Smith, Sir Richard, 210, 214, 368–71
Smith, Sir Thomas, 52, 63, 284, 287
Smithfield, 62, 69
Somerset, Edward Seymour, Duke of, 11–12,
    18, 24–5, 29, 31, 37, 134, 353–4
Somerset, Duchess of, 265
Somerset House, 25, 38–9, 90
South Denchworth, 56
Southampton, Earl of, 141
Southampton, 1, 196
Southwell, 210
Spain, 63, 121, 138, 191, 320, 323–4, 329
Spanish Armada, 373
Spene, Thomas, 172, 210
Spenser, Edmund, 319
Stafford, Sir Edward, 324, 328, 347–50
Stafford, Henry, Lord, 130
Stafford Assizes, 367
Staffordshire, 76
Stanfield, 340
Stanfield Hall, 14–17, 61
Stevenson, Edward, 210
Stevenson, John, 210, 369
Stookes, Mr, 181
Stortford, 185
Strafford, Thomas Wentworth, Earl of, 351
Strand, the, 90, 99
Stubbes, Philip, 193
Suffolk, Henry, Duke of, 43

Suffolk, Duchess of, 265
Suffolk, 11, 15, 45, 129, 145, 159, 211, 357
suicides, 225–6
Surrey, Henry Howard, Earl of, 16, 134, 136
Sussex, Countess of, 190
Sussex, Earl of, 2, 35, 111, 134, 181, 188, 197;
     hostility to Dudley, 126–7, 160, 287–8,
     296; and Dudley's marital ambitions, 246,
     257, 269, 273; and Archduke Charles
     marriage negotiations, 280–1, 287, 295,
     319–20; and Amy Robsart's death, 302–4;
     and Alençon marriage negotiations,
     323–4; and Douglas Sheffield, 328 and
     *Leicester's Commonwealth* conspiracy, 337,
     345–7; and Dudley's retainers, 361
Sussex, 347
Sutton, Lord, of Holderness, 180
Sutton, 1
Switzerland, 259
Syderstone, 15, 23, 45, 50, 52, 59–60
Syre, John, 210

Talbot, Gilbert, 307
Tamworth, John, 257, 275
Teerlinc, Lavinia, 21, 38
tennis, 134, 181, 287
Tewkesbury, 182
Thames, River, 25, 89, 93, 97, 131, 300, 330
Throcking, 56–8, 82–4, 95, 133, 145, 169, 194,
     355, 357, 363
Throckmorton, Sir Nicholas, 63, 77, 186–7,
     189, 197; and coronation ring, 70; and
     queen's marriage, 162, 241, 272; and Mary
     Queen of Scots, 176, 178–9; and Amy
     Robsart's death, 223–4, 243–4, 303, 358,
     364, 371; and Dudley's marital ambitions,
     3, 6, 247–62; and restoration of
     Catholicism, 269–70; and Dudley's
     estrangement from queen, 285; his death,
     337
Throckmorton Plot, 347
Thynne, John, 22
Tiepolo, Paulo, 124
Tothill Street, 57
Tottenham High Cross, 353
tournaments, 19–20, 25, 159–60, 183
Tower Hill, 43
Tower of London, 3, 18, 21, 31, 41, 158, 180,
     198, 325, 328; Dudley's imprisonment in,
     19–21, 35–40, 129, 145, 255; conditions in,
     19–20, 37–8; and Jane Grey, 34–5;
     menagerie, 38, 97; and Elizabeth's

imprisonment, 42, 44–5, 97; and Queen
     Elizabeth's accession, 85; and Queen
     Elizabeth's coronation, 96–7, 99–100,
     102; Surrey and Wyatt's imprisonment in,
     136; and *Leicester's Commonwealth*, 342
Traynes, Marquis of, 180
Treaty of Berwick, 178
Treaty of Cateau-Cambresis, 120, 157
Treaty of Edinburgh, 187, 199
Tresham, Dr William, 346
triumphs, 25
Trollope, Thomas, 128
Tuccia, 319
Tuckey, George, 60
Tudor dynasty, 101–2, 105–6, 176, 374
Tully, 27
Tutbury Castle, 76
Tyndall, Humphrey, 316

van Meteren, Emanuel, 55
Venturini, Borghese, 274
Verney, George, 358
Verney, Sir Richard, 130, 147–8, 169, 369;
     and Amy Robsart's death, 338, 349, 352,
     355–6, 358–9, 362–3, 366, 371
Vestal Virgins, 319
Vives, Juan Luys, 27

Waad, Armagil, 75
Waldegrave, Sir Edward, 268
Wales, 338
Walsingham, Francis, 49, 79, 318, 332, 340,
     373; and Alençon marriage negotiations,
     320–3, 328; and *Leicester's Commonwealth*,
     335, 344–5, 348, 350
Waltham, 56, 133
Wanstead House, 316, 334, 346
Ware, 56, 133
Wars of the Roses, 24
Warwick Castle, 13, 148
Warwick, Beauchamp earls of, 148
Warwick, Earl of, *see* Dudley, John, Earl of
     Warwick and Duke of Northumberland
Warwick, Richard, 360
Warwickshire, 147–8, 169, 355–6, 358
Watton, 180
Wayneman, Mrs, 217, 370
Webster, George, 250
Webster, John, 375
Westminster, 90, 95–7, 101, 104, 272
Westminster Abbey, 85, 100, 103
Westminster Hall, 103–4

Westmorland, Henry, Earl of, 115, 134, 161
White, John, 85–6
Whitehall Palace, 43, 89–90, 93, 96, 100, 116, 183, 250, 346, 354
Whorwood, William, 19
Wilkes, Thomas, 354
Williams of Thame, Lord, 59
Willoughby, Thomas, 182
Winchester, William Paulet, Marquis of, 96, 196
Winchester, 1, 196
Winchester School, 339
Windham, Edward, 360
Windsor Castle, 1, 3, 89, 93, 150, 196, 198, 275, 283; and Somerset's flight, 18, 30; Garter ceremony, 146–7; and Dudley's residence, 165–6, 169, 183, 195, 224; and news of Amy Robsart's death, 203–6, 238–9, 363
Wood, Anthony, 365
Wood, Thomas, 314
Woodstock, 48
wool, 50, 52, 180
Worcestershire, 45
Wurttemberg, Duke, 106
Wyatt, Thomas, 42–5, 134, 136–7, 152, 369
Wymondham, 14
Wytham Church, 170–1

Yaxley, Francis, 130
York, 11, 71
Yorkshire, 147, 180